D1180784

REV. KIERAN GALLACHER
ST. JOHN'S
23, SHORE STREET
PORT, GLASGOW PA14 5HD
TEL. 0475 41139

Lord Longford

To:- Kieran

From: The Camerons &
The Keoghs.

June 1994 –

Also by Peter Stanford

Believing Bishops
Hidden Hands
Catholics and Sex
Cardinal Hume and the
    Changing Face of English Catholicism

Peter Stanford

Lord Longford

A LIFE

HEINEMANN : LONDON

First published in Great Britain 1994
by William Heinemann Ltd
an imprint of Reed Consumer Books Ltd
Michelin House, 81 Fulham Road, London SW3 6RB
and Auckland, Melbourne, Singapore and Toronto

Copyright © 1994 by Peter Stanford
The author has asserted his moral rights

A CIP catalogue record for this book
is available at the British Library
ISBN 0 434 73516 7

Typeset by CentraCet Limited, Cambridge
Printed and bound in Great Britain by
Mackays of Chatham PLC

To

Anthony Gynn
who got me started

and to
Caroline Willson
who made sure I finished

Photo acknowledgements

All pictures courtesy of Elizabeth Longford except:

1) Irish Tourist Board
6) Lady Dufferin
15) Antonia Pinter
16) Hulton Deutsch Collection
17) Rachel Billington
18) The Mark Boxer Estate
19) and 21) The Catholic Herald

Contents

Acknowledgements

Lord Longford has been more than generous in the preparation of this book with his encouragement and his time – both in various bars, tea-rooms and cubby holes of the House of Lords and amid the glorious chaos of his donnish study in Sussex over a large glass of sherry. He has, infuriatingly for a biographer, discarded almost every letter he has ever received – including those written by his wife, Elizabeth. He has never kept a diary, save for one year, 1981, when a publisher commissioned him to do so. Even then he found the task an arduous one and from time to time fell back on including, with a suitably devoted and admiring credit, his wife's diary entry for the day to cover their joint activities.

While Longford's determination to continue to look to the future and what can still be achieved is one of the keys to his remarkable physical and mental vigour in his late eighties, his lack of interest in keeping a record to help those delving into his past has meant that this biography has relied on the recollections, oral and written, of those who have shared his life and worked alongside him, and on those documents that can be salvaged from their collections.

There are some who will no doubt begin their review of this book by stating that biographies of living people should not be written. I obviously do not subscribe to that school and feel that having the chance to discuss past events with Lord Longford and his contemporaries – friends and foes – has added to rather than taken away from the main conclusions of this biography. It has also been enormously enlightening to relive some of the central events of the twentieth century with men and women who were intimately involved in them.

Lord Longford's life and achievements are a subject about which everyone I speak to seems to have an opinion. Special mention, however, should go to the following who gave generously of their time and often lunch to share with me their special knowledge and insight: Bronwen Astor, the Hon. David Astor, Rachel Billington, Lord Carrington, Paul Cavadino of NACRO, Sheila Childs, John Cunningham of the *Guardian*, Maureen, Marchioness of Dufferin and Ava, Frank Field MP, Michael Foot, Lady Antonia Fraser, Lord Healey, Myra Hindley, Lord Jay, Lord Jenkins of Hillhead, Marigold Johnson, Paul Johnson, Rosie Johnston, Judith Kazantzis, The Countess of Longford, Andrew McCooey, Eric McGrath of New Bridge, Dr Roger Opie, Thomas and Valerie Pakenham, Sarah Sackville-West, Jon Snow and Auberon Waugh.

I am eternally indebted to Mary Craig who allowed me access to her own past research and to transcripts of interviews with characters in Frank Longford's life who are now beyond the reach of a tape recorder. I hope that I will be as generous to another writer should the opportunity ever arise.

Various people, too numerous to mention, have given me practical assistance and physical sustenance at different stages of the writing of this book. I cannot go without thanking my parents for use of their peaceful home when London got too much; Marjorie and Robert Crabb for similar facilities in Provence; Caroline Willson for her company and map-reading on various research trips; Lucinda Coxon, Ruth Deighton, Madeleine French, Helen Lederer, Joanna Moorhead, Cristina Odone, Shannie Ross, Kate Saunders and Rachel Ward-Lilley for listening when I needed a sounding board; my agents Imogen Parker and her successor Derek Johns and my editor Tom Weldon for their encouragement.

Introduction

> To know Frank and not to love him is to show
> there is something wrong with one's heart. To
> know him and to agree with him in all his
> extravagances would equally indicate something
> rather wrong with one's head. But that is not the
> end of the paradox
>
> *Lord Hailsham*[1]

Lord Longford is a one-off, an Irish eccentric, a maverick who combines politics with a missionary's commitment to social reform and who, in the process, has staked a claim to the moral high ground without precedent among his peers. A Cabinet minister who simultaneously befriended notorious prisoners, a pillar of Labour's front bench for twenty-two years who ran London's first centre for young, homeless, drug-abusers, a member of Hugh Gaitskell's inner circle who later campaigned against pornography, Frank Longford has attempted throughout his long life a very personal synthesis of politics and social concern.

The price of trying to reconcile the two has been his failure – despite his long front bench service, his finely tuned mind, his gifts as a speaker and his connections with the most influential figures of his generation – to make it into the first rank of politicians. His membership of the House of Lords would, in any case, have made it an uphill struggle in a party that is perennially suspicious of the privileges of birth that underpin the very existence of the Upper Chamber.

Longford has never been, paradoxically, a very political politician. Though he had designs on the Home Secretaryship, it was only as a means to an end, a forum for his reforming zeal.

From the time he joined Attlee's government, he was working to a different agenda from those around him. The constraints and compromises of Westminster and Whitehall, party and electoral politics, were dwarfed by his conviction that, faced with an unequal and unjust society, he had to make an unambiguous and active option for the poor.

He has taken this to mean not just the traditional Labour standbys of legislating for wealth redistribution and state intervention, but also a practical commitment to those so marginalised as scarcely to register on the political map, outcasts as once he was an outcast when a nervous breakdown prevented him from serving his country during the Second World War.

When he joined the Labour Party in 1936 Longford explained he was turning his back on his Conservative, aristocratic upbringing to embrace socialism because he was a Christian. Both creeds share a commitment to social equality. Four years later he became a double convert, abandoning the Anglicanism of his Anglo-Irish Ascendancy forebears for the Roman Catholicism of their tenants. Christianity and specifically Catholicism has been the motivating force in Longford's politics and in his extracurricular activities. It put conscience before his party loyalty, his heart before his head, shaping Longford's distinctive – and to his colleagues semi-detached – approach.

Such an above-party stance has been out of place in the political world of the second half of the twentieth century, belonging more to the philanthropic tradition of such figures as William Wilberforce and Lord Shaftesbury. Like them born into privilege, like them a devout Christian determined to translate faith into action, Longford has attempted, as they did, to use his political savvy to win over an initially hostile Establishment and instigate far-reaching social reform. All three men fall into the category of archetypal do-gooders, combining a principled, almost naive clear-sightedness with a shrewdness in playing their political cards to achieve their ends. Wilberforce tackled the slave trade, Shaftesbury conditions in the factories and mines, and Longford the penal system.

Where the first two succeeded, Longford has only aspired. There in no great piece of legislation to which he has put his name. Over half a century since he first visited an inmate in Oxford Jail, Britain's prisons and its justice system continue to horrify him.

He did set up in 1955 the first organisation dedicated to the welfare of ex-prisoners. The motivating force behind the still flourishing New Bridge has been taken up by a plethora of other care and rehabilitation organisations. He has awakened the conscience of Westminster to the question of penal reform. Where once he was a lone voice campaigning for change, opening the first ever debate on the subject in the House of Lords, today there is a well-organised lobby of MPs and peers with the Home Office firmly in their sights. Longford also put his name to a series of reports in the 1950s and 1960s which played a crucial role in persuading the governments of the day to introduce the parole system and upgrade the probation service.

The impression of failure, though, is hard to dispel. His cherished goals – the abolition of all sentences over ten years and an end to the treatment of prisoners and ex-prisoners as society's lepers – remain unfulfilled. He failed to convince either his Cabinet colleagues or public opinion of the need to act and has become a lone voice campaigning outside the political mainstream for change and for forgiveness of those who have broken society's laws. Having reached the pinnacle of his political career as a member of Harold Wilson's Cabinet, he realised that a seat at the top table did not bring with it more than the shadow of power. Conventional political success still left him without the means to introduce the sort of social reforms that he had dreamt of since he worked as Beveridge's right-hand man on the report that gave birth to the Welfare State. And so Longford abandoned his already uneasy place within a political system that he increasingly saw as merely constraining and concentrated on his own apostolate to prisoners, to the young homeless of London through the New Horizon Centre which he set up in 1970 and to the mentally ill.

That personal crusade, undertaken in retirement, has eclipsed Longford's previous record as a significant political player. While his former Cabinet colleagues have assumed the mantle of elder statesmen, casting a discerning eye over today's political leaders from the comfort of their firesides, Lord Longford remains, even at eighty-eight, remorselessly active, visiting prisoners, needling the Home Office from the floor of the Upper Chamber where he is, with his noble cranium and mad scientist's tonsure, among its best-known faces. Though their lordships listen with polite attention to a man who will always be a part, albeit an uncomfortable and occasionally thorny part, of the Establishment, Longford has become a figure of fun in the tabloids, one of the first in a long line of anti-heroes, set up to be mocked at every turn. His name has become a by-word for exaggerated concern and the Edwardian moral code of his childhood. He is known to a whole generation variously as Lord Porn and the Leader of the Opposition to the Permissive Society — after his much satirised pornography report of 1972 — or as Myra Hindley's friend on account of his tireless campaign to have the Moors murderess released on parole.

The two roles are contradictory. While on the one hand he is asking society to take a tolerant approach to Hindley, over pornography he was trying to legislate for intolerance. But paradoxes have been part of Longford's career from the start. He has a knack for debunking stereotypes at every turn. Hereditary peers who graduated from Eton and Oxford are not obvious recruits for the Labour Party. Neither are they usually to be found mixing with homeless drug abusers and notorious criminals. Perhaps one key to understanding the unpredictability of Longford is the strange sect into which he was born. The Anglo-Irish Ascendancy families are an odd bunch with conflicting loyalties to England and Ireland whose only common characteristic is that they refuse to typify anything. Longford is part of that tradition.

The social worker in him is accompanied by the socialite. He has, throughout his life, been drawn to larger-than-life characters, the great and the good, the glamorous. Once he had escaped his unhappy childhood, he flourished in the smart social set of the Oxford of the aesthetes and at grand country house weekends at Cliveden and Chartwell. He has brushed shoulders with a long line of Prime Ministers from Baldwin to Major and he has an uncanny ability for being there or thereabouts at crucial moments in British twentieth-century history – the anti-Chamberlain Oxford by-election of 1938, the Beveridge report, the first ever majority Labour government, the Berlin air-lift.

Faced with such a complex character as Longford, many have taken the easy option and laughed at him. He is, after all, an easy target with his benign bishop's pate, and his by now legendary eccentricity. From childhood he has lacked any concern for possessions and the proprieties of dress, turning up as Lord Privy Seal at the State Opening of Parliament without laces in his shoes. Yet he is also a showman who has played up to the Professor Brainstorm image as a way of giving himself more room for manoeuvre. His political bosses from Clement Attlee onwards were always prepared to allow Frank Longford more rope than they would other less colourful figures.

Another side of that same showmanship means that he is never camera shy. He is fair game for the satirists. His hankering for publicity can only partly be explained by his somewhat old-fashioned idea that newspapers and television have a mission to educate and that, therefore, if you put across your message clearly enough and often enough, you will change hearts and minds. As he crashes into the footlights like a character out of P. G. Wodehouse, Longford usually has a serious point that he wishes to share. Yet the image has overtaken the message, discrediting and distracting attention from the substance of what he has to say.

He shrugs off the jokes with the sort of Christian humility that he advocated in his 1969 book on the subject. Yet, having mortgaged his good name to tackle both pornography and Myra Hindley's – unjustifiable in his opinion – continuing incarceration, he finds the scorn with which both crusades are dismissed harder to take. Over pornography, subsequent events have suggested that, whatever the folly of his antics in Copenhagen's strip clubs, he may just have had a point. Though they were greeted with howls of disapproval in 1972 at the time of publication, several of the pornography report's main recommendations were taken up in the changed moral climate of the 1980s under Margaret Thatcher. The general tone of the report

– warning of the potentially corrupting influence of absolute freedom of expression on young and impressionable minds – would today find an echo in many of the concerns being expressed by politicians and public alike. If Longford failed, part of that failure was simply a question of timing, the fervent anti-smoker warning of the dangers of nicotine before the link with cancer was proved.

Whether the public will ever come round to his position on Myra Hindley and allow her to be released after almost three decades in prison remains doubtful. By linking her name with his, Longford has kept the memory of her crimes fresh. His fundamental question about why she is denied parole – because of the demands of public opinion rather than by reference to any of the criteria under which the system is supposed to operate – remains unanswered by the authorities.

To many fellow politicians and to the mandarins in the Home Office, Longford's involvement with Hindley has only convinced them that he lacks judgement. At best, they feel he is asking them to commit electoral suicide by releasing a woman who has become an icon of crime. At worst, they say that he is just a criminal's stooge. Yet such a verdict misses the point. He is not concerned with guilt or innocence. He does not want to be a Cardinal Hume figure, championing victims of miscarriages of justice. His fear is that by treating prisoners and former prisoners as the lowest of the low, locking them up and throwing away the key, society is simply storing up trouble for itself. If prisoners are not encouraged and supported on the road to rehabilitation while in jail and when released, they will merely continue committing crime.

Longford also stands accused of lacking judgement in some of the allies he has chosen in his long career. Winning the admiration and respect of Clement Attlee was a wise move that ultimately won him a seat round the Cabinet table. But linking up with Mary Whitehouse was to obscure his own New Testament message of Christian forgiveness behind her Old Testament fire and brimstone oratory. Unlike Whitehouse, Longford is not an intolerant person. He does have a Puritan code of beliefs and is not shy about calling things sinful. But he does not judge individuals and is endlessly tolerant and forgiving of whatever they have done.

His central maxim, and one that unravels some of the apparent contradictions in his crusades, has been to love the sinner and hate the sin. While modern-day Catholicism avoids talking of sin, Longford's credo belongs to an earlier and more certain age. Even when events within his own family have confronted him with the evidence that Catholic ideals do not always work out in reality, he has continued to hold to certain hard and fast rules, while at the same time attempting to square the circle by his individual concern and compassion.

The restlessness that keeps him active and fighting his corner in his late eighties means that, unlike many retired Cabinet ministers, Frank Longford has never become a back-number, as uninteresting as last year's beauty queen. The political obituary writers may ultimately judge him a failure, never quite maximising the potential that made Ernest Bevin describe him in 1945 as one of the two rising stars of the Attlee government. Longford's finest hour as a minister came in 1947 when he breathed new life and hope back into the British zone in occupied Germany in a period of food and fuel shortages and escalating international tension. Konrad Adenauer counted him among the founders of West Germany.

Even as he was winning bouquets, though, Longford's talk of Christian forgiveness of the German people stuck in the throat of the British public and his ministerial colleagues. Denis Healey sums up the politicians' verdict on Longford when he says, 'The basic thing about Frank is that he always takes things a bit far.'[2]

For a politician that is true. It is the missionary in him. As a member of the Lords, Longford has never represented a constituency, but he has appointed himself the spokesman for the marginalised, the outcasts, the prisoners and the unfashionable issues that concern them. The Upper Chamber allows him the luxury of ignoring *realpolitik*. Sitting round the Cabinet table did not and when the strain became too much he resigned.

Most politicians leave little behind, their achievements are as enduring as the impression left by a hand in a bucket of water. Longford may only have made a start on the penal system but his monuments are growing and developing. In an institutional sense there is New Bridge and New Horizon. The thousands of individual prisoners whose lives he has touched will not forget him. Some owe their freedom to him; others their second chance at finding a job, a home and happiness; others again will simply remember him as someone who was prepared to visit them when all the world shunned them.

In a personal sense too, Longford has begotten an extraordinary dynasty. Elizabeth Longford, the Zuleika Dobson of her age at Oxford, turned down proposals from Hugh Gaitskell and Maurice Bowra to marry the man whom she likened when she first saw him to a Greco-Roman god. In shorthand it was Elizabeth, as tireless a *materfamilias* as Queen Victoria about whom she has written, who converted Frank to Labour and Frank, the improbable patriarch, who converted Elizabeth to Catholicism. That symmetry has made the Longfords a national monument to marriage. Their children are as competitive as the Kennedys and as exposed as the royals in their various literary, political and diplomatic activities.

Whatever the headline writers would have us believe, Frank Longford is not a joke. His own habit of sending himself up – all the best stories about him can usually be traced back to him – should not deflect attention from what he has tried to achieve. If he has failed, fallen between the stools of politics and social work, too worldly in one sense and not worldly enough in another, then it has been a noble and entertaining failure. At eighty-eight he is an unquiet soul who is still striving to be useful. It's no use asking if Longford is barmy, Bernard Levin once wrote. The real question should be is he right?

PART ONE

The Convert

Have mercy on me, O God, in your goodness,
in your great tenderness wipe away my faults;
wash me clean of my guilt,
purify me from my sin.

For I am well aware of my faults,
I have my sin constantly in mind,
having sinned against none other than you,
having done what you regard as wrong.

You are just when you pass sentence on me,
blameless when you give judgement.
You know I was born guilty,
a sinner from the moment of conception.

The Miserere: Psalm 51

One

The second son

I was brought up to think myself Irish without
question or qualification, but the new nationalism
prefers to describe me and the like of me as Anglo-
Irish

Stephen Gwynn (1926)[1]

Ireland is shaped like a saucer. In the dip where the teacup
would stand is Tully Nally, known for generations to the locals
in the adjoining village of Castlepollard as Pakenham Hall and
the family seat of the Longfords. By a curious logic it is not in
County Longford where, under British colonial rule, various
members of the clan served as Lords Lieutenant but over the
border in neighbouring Westmeath. But then Tully Nally is a
curious and quietly eccentric place, reflecting those who have
commanded its shambolic battlements past and present.

The Irish countryside runs to castles and when it came to
building a home to match their status among the Protestant
overlords of Catholic Ireland, the wealthy Pakenhams were, like
many of their peers, slaves to fashion. When it was the vogue to
have a classical house, they employed the architect of Trinity
College, Dublin,[2] to give the hall an elegant five-bay façade.
Come the nineteenth century with its passion among the Anglo-
Irish Ascendancy families for what is rather grandly called Irish
baronial, and Tully Nally was enveloped in the mantle of a
Gothic fantasy castle.

With its portcullis and towers, this grey and damp edifice,
standing like an overblown version of Horace Walpole's Straw-
berry Hill amid green and damp countryside, used to thrill Frank

11

Longford, his elder brother Edward and his four sisters when they came over from England during the school holidays each summer and occasionally at Easter. They would roam the grounds, row on the lake, run along its endless corridors past maps of the British Empire and suits of armour tucked in every nook and cranny, and give names to the majestic stone lions that guarded the entrances to this outsized playground. 'The final touch of romance', says his sister Mary, 'was the deep ditch all around. It was dry and had iron railings in front like a London area but it was called the moat and I accepted it in the spirit in which I am sure it was meant.'[3]

Romance to one side, Tully Nally speaks volumes about the Pakenham blood that flows in Frank Longford's veins. The outward air of ostentation hides an inner plainness in keeping with the Puritanism that characterised his ancestors. As befits the inhabitants of a castle they were essentially a military clan of simple soldiers and the occasional sailor with no history of distinction in politics or the arts and little taste for luxury.

Since Tudor times the Pakenhams had been in attendance at the royal court – one helped Anne Boleyn dress for her coronation – but it was in the seventeenth century that Henry Pakenham fought with distinction for Cromwell's forces in Ireland and was given the land on which Tully Nally now stands as his reward. In best Anglo-Irish tradition he discarded the Gaelic name and styled the estate Pakenham Hall, a title that stuck until the current owner, Thomas Pakenham, Longford's son and heir, reversed the decision.[4]

In 1756 the Pakenhams' elevated standing among the new rulers of Ireland was confirmed with the granting of an Irish barony by the British crown. It was upgraded to an earldom in 1785. (The English barony of Silchester was added in 1821 by George IV as part of his coronation honours and it is on account of that hereditary title, rather than the earldom, that Frank Longford's ancestors and indeed his descendants sat and will sit in the British House of Lords, Irish titles carrying no automatic seat.)

General Sir Edward Pakenham did his duty more than adequately alongside his brother-in-law, the Duke of Wellington,[5] in the Peninsular War against Napoleon in the early years of the nineteenth century, though he was later to stumble to an unhappy defeat at New Orleans in 1815 against the Americans, a battle which cost him his life. His body, preserved in a barrel of rum, was sent back to be buried at Tully Nally. According to Thomas Pakenham, each of the thirty bedrooms that the castle boasts could be named after a defeat suffered by one of the clan on the fields of battle.

Longford's grandfather, the fourth earl, held a minor post at the War Office. His father died a hero at Gallipoli in 1915 when he was just nine. His father's cousin, Admiral Willie Pakenham, summed up the Longfords' substantial if unspectacular achievements rather neatly when he declared that 'we're a family of good second-raters'.

What impresses most about Tully Nally is its sheer size – Thomas Pakenham says that it is the largest inhabited castle in Ireland today – and the incongruity with which it rises up from the middle of the saucer that is Ireland. Elizabeth Longford, Frank's wife, remembers her initial glimpse of the castle in 1930. 'The glitter of my first visit to Pakenham Hall will never be effaced. It was the glitter of eccentricity not luxury.'[6]

Second-rate or not, the Pakenhams were not afraid to dare to be different. The social concern for which Lord Longford is today famous stretches back through the generations. Unlike many a grand Anglo-Irish country house, a great deal of Tully Nally's bulk is accounted for by staff accommodation. While their neighbours in the ruling class were nervous of having Irish employees living in for fear they would cut their masters' throats in the night, the Pakenhams in the nineteenth-century renovation of their home oversaw the building of a model kitchen, a spacious servants' hall, a laundry that was high tech by the standards of its day and staff bedrooms, all on single-sex corridors to guard against the 'disaster' of young girls being taken advantage of in service. Rather than tuck such quarters in a dark basement or high in the attics, this enlightened family built them adjoining their own apartments, with sweeping views of the grounds. (Such admirable concern for the staff is tempered, however, by the fact that Longford's grandfather had special shutters put up at the library window to guard against any disgruntled employee or ex-employee taking a pot shot at him while he read.)

While other Anglo-Irish landowners were erecting ballrooms or grand entertaining suites to impress friends, neighbours and visiting cousins over from England with their wealth, Longford's ancestors preferred to attend to an alternative set of social obligations. Part of their motivation in this was undoubtedly mercenary – the desire to get the most in financial terms out of contented employees and hence the estate. The Pakenhams when Frank Longford was a boy had substantial land holdings (subsequently broken up and sold off with the introduction of tenants' right-to-buy schemes by the Irish government in the 1930s). He grew up, however, in the declining years both of his family's fortunes and of the entire political system of which they were a part.

The leading families among Protestant Anglo-Irish were essentially a landlord class and had from Elizabethan and Cromwellian times wielded almost unfettered political power over Ireland. The height of their influence had been in the eighteenth century, the Ascendancy, when, though running Ireland as an economic, political and cultural colony of England, they had overseen day-to-day administration from their own Parliament in Dublin whose elegant squares, wide streets and public buildings of today date back to this period.

The mass of the population was, of course, Catholic and as such could neither sit in the Dublin Parliament nor vote nor bears arms nor hold office under the Crown. To the landless Catholics, the Anglo-Irish were English, a resented garrison class of horse Protestants.

In the nineteenth century, however, their power began to crumble. The rot set in with the abolition of the Dublin Parliament by the Act of Union of 1800. That pushed the Anglo-Irish into a corner from which there was ultimately no escape. They were neither one thing nor the other – too wedded to English political power to be Irish and too tied to their estates in Ireland to be English. Frank Longford was himself to highlight this dichotomy in his 1935 book on Ireland. 'In the South, from the

Union onwards, the Protestant class ranked as Loyalist to England. But most of them stayed Irish in everything but political aspiration.'[7]

Catholic emancipation in 1829 and a series of electoral reform bills meant that the majority of the voters for Ireland's seats in the House of Commons suddenly became Catholic agricultural labourers. Occasionally they would take one of the Anglo-Irish to their hearts – Charles Stewart Parnell, the leading advocate of Irish self-rule in the 1880s, being the most obvious – but in general the changes meant that the only place where landed Ascendancy families like the Pakenhams could any longer exert political influence was through their English titles in the House of Lords. The revival of the Gaelic language and culture in the later part of the nineteenth century was encouraged by the Catholic Church which became the mainstay of a new brand of nationalism that had little space for the Protestant Anglo-Irish. As the clamours for Home Rule for Ireland grew, the Anglo-Irish in the south saw their one bastion, the Lords, stripped of its power in 1911 and their cause taken over by the middle- and working-class Unionists of the north who had little interest in the Irish nation as a whole, preferring to defend their own sectarian corner.

When Frank Longford was born, the world in which his Pakenham ancestors had thrived was already effectively doomed in political terms by the growing and irresistible clamours for Home Rule. Its social traditions, though, were going strong. Diana Norman provides a less than flattering pen portrait of these in her biography of one of the most famous products of the Anglo-Irish sect, Constance Gore-Booth, later Countess Markievicz and in 1918 the first woman to be elected to the British Parliament.

> The Protestant Ascendancy was made up of English
> and Scottish invaders and settlers whose menfolk
> looked for a wife among English heiresses, daughters
> of families like their own. In the days when marriage
> was meant to advantage one's estates rather than
> one's emotional life there was no point in a legal

15

alliance with a native. And to the Victorian empire-
builders with whom the Anglo-Irish identified themselves, the indigenous Irish were just as native as the
peoples of colonial India or Africa except that they
had managed to retain the same skin colour as their
overlords.[8]

The Pakenhams conformed to Ms Norman's stereotype in several regards. Longford's father did indeed marry an English rose,
Mary Child-Villiers, daughter of the Earl of Jersey. Successive
Pakenhams had walked up the aisle in pursuit less of love than
a sizeable dowry, building up in the process the family's estates.
One profitable marriage alliance brought with it one thousand
acres around Dun Laoghaire – or Kingstown as it was then
known – when it was still a small fishing village. In 1815 when
the harbour was developed into Ireland's major port, the Earls
of Longford saw the value of their property soar.

Despite their wealth and connections, however, the Pakenhams did not belong to that section of the Ascendancy families
whose main concern was the social circuit, the extravagant
buccaneering gaylords who returned from England to their Irish
estates for a spot of shooting and a well-earned rest in the
manner of the pre-Revolution Russian aristocracy.

Going through the family records Thomas Pakenham, Longford's historian son, reports that he cannot find a single reference to his forebears doing anything as innocently social as even
going to the races. The visitors' book is equally unforthcoming.
The Pakenhams were anti-show and anti-snob, he says. 'They
wouldn't have been at all condescending. They wouldn't have
had any particular side. They never tried to be grand or talk
people down. But at the same time they would have, in the
landed gentry tradition, shrunk from anything that could be
considered showing off.'[9]

There was a strong Puritan streak in Frank Longford's ancestors. His grandfather, a wealthy man with an annual income in
the late nineteenth century that Thomas Pakenham estimates to
be in the region even then of £20,000, wrote to his wife from

overseas that he had decided against buying a Turkish carpet because it seemed expensive at £45.[10]

The one exception to the constraining Puritanism that gripped the clan's spirit – and then only in denominational terms – was Charles Reginald Pakenham, who in the first half of the nineteenth century shocked his Protestant family to the core by giving up the usual stand-by of a career in the Grenadier Guards to become a monk – and worse still a Catholic monk. Only his uncle by marriage, the Duke of Wellington, had a word of encouragement. 'Well, Charles, you have been a good soldier. Strive now to be a good monk.' And he took the Iron Duke at his word, going on to found the Passionist Order in Ireland.

It was into this unusual – eccentric would be almost too flamboyant a word – family that Francis Aungier Pakenham was born on 5 December 1905, the second son and third child of the fifth Earl of Longford and Mary Child-Villiers. Though he has throughout his adult life regarded himself as an Irishman, Longford was born at his parents' London home in Great Cumberland Place and not Tully Nally.

'We were a large family of large children,' says his sister Mary who arrived two years later. 'My mother and the doctor mutually congratulated each other when Frank weighed in at ten pounds, fourteen ounces, but I soon set up a new record with ten pounds, fifteen ounces.'[11]

Longford was born on the day that Henry Campbell-Bannerman began to form the last majority Liberal government in the wake of his landslide electoral victory. Such events would not have unduly affected the Longford parents. Neither was political, but by instinct both were Tories. They assumed that it was their party and that assumption was passed on to their children with their mother's milk. Both parents were shy and shrank from socialising. Perhaps that is what attracted them to each other for it was an unlikely match. Frank's father was thirteen years older than his mother who was considered to have married beneath her station by relatives who looked askance at the Pakenhams' Irish connections. However, others at the time spoke of a marriage built on genuine attraction rather than dynastic concerns, of a shared innocence, a naivety about the couple that made them and their burgeoning family appear self-contained and even isolated from the outside world and the social whirl.

Longford's father was an archetypal country squire, never more comfortable than when among his soldiers or shooting, hunting and overseeing his estate. He was said to be the worst-dressed man in the world, completely without interest or concern for his appearance, a trait inherited by his son. Twice wounded in the Boer War, he went on to command the Second Life Guards and at the outbreak of the First World War led a brigade of yeomanry.

Longford last saw his father when he was nine. His memories are few and mainly concern time spent with his father on holiday at Tully Nally – a link which goes some way towards explaining his subsequent and abiding emotional attachment to Ireland. They are inevitably shaped by the impact on an impressionable young boy of the fifth earl's subsequent heroic death in battle, but they conjure up a picture of a kindly, distant, almost grandfatherly figure. 'On my countless walks with him, he was patience and gentleness itself in response to my interminable questionings. "Is Bonar Law a good man? Is Lloyd George a good man? Could a British battle cruiser beat a German battleship? Could you shoot a man on that hill from here?"'[12] One suspects that this decidedly apolitical father was more at ease with the military questions than with the earlier first glimmerings of governmental interest in his second son.

'I would give ten years of my life to take part in a charge,' the fifth earl told his son just before the opening shots of the First World War. When the opportunity arose on 21 August 1915, it cost more than ten years. Brigadier-General Lord Longford, at the head of the Bucks, Berks and Dorset Yeomanry, was killed at Scimitar Hill, Gallipoli, in an operation Churchill later dismissed as 'fruitless'. Among the soldiers who survived the rout at Gallipoli was Major Clement Attlee.

Ashmead-Bartlett, in *The Uncensored Dardanelles*, gave a first-hand description of events that day at Scimitar Hill.

> It was almost impossible to see what was happening through the gathering gloom and smoke, only

relieved by bursting shells and flames. Just as darkness
settled over the scene, I distinguished a mass of men
surging once more towards the summit of this dreadful hill . . . Once again we thought that the hill had
been taken. But in reality it was impossible to hold the
crest under the withering fire of shrapnel, rifle and
machine guns. The whole position was evacuated
during the night. Not a yard of the enemy's trenches
had been taken.

One of those who fought alongside Lord Longford was later to
write to his young widow that her husband 'gave courage to all
who were near him by his example'. Quiet and self-effacing in
life, he had evidently been a giant on the field on battle. His
body was never found and it was over a year before all hope
was abandoned and the young Pakenham came up from his
prep school for a memorial service. 'The night before it my
mother, who shrank from sentiment, told me that I must never
hesitate to ask her the questions I used to ask my father,
"though", she added, "I shan't be able to answer them as he
did."'[13]
   The loss of his father when so young had a profound effect on
Longford. He has never outwardly shown any anger at the
apparent futility of the death in a battle that could not be won
(though Mary Longford retained a residual antipathy to the
government that had ordered the Gallipoli disaster and to
Winston Churchill in particular) but has concentrated more on
trying to live up to the heroism of his father's demise. As a
young man he was determined to find out more about the man
he had hardly known, seeking out his former colleagues and
hearing their stories of battlefield adventures. His friend
Maureen Dufferin recalls Longford arriving at her home slightly
the worse for wear having enjoyed a hearty, if somewhat
eccentric, breakfast with one of his father's fellow officers.
'Frank told us how this general had kept saying, "Marvellous
man, your father. He gave me a stick which I always keep by
my side." But when he called his batman and asked for the stick,
the batman replied, "What stick?" Then the general said, "If

you're a true son of your father, you'll enjoy a whisky with me." Frank scarcely drank at the time but could not say no. So they had two large whiskies for breakfast and he arrived on our doorstep very tipsy.'[14]

In the absence of his own father, Longford developed a tendency in his youth to look for surrogate fathers. Since his image of his father was that of a great military hero, he would fix on figures of the same generation of similar stature. Yet, because his recollection of his father was so sketchy and so clouded by the young Longford's impression of the romance and nobility of his death, he ended up by choosing hero figures – men like F. E. Smith, Waldorf Astor, the Tory MP and master of Cliveden, and later Clement Attlee – who were in many ways the antithesis of the unremarkable, shy, apolitical fifth earl.

But for the nine-year-old Frank Pakenham the immediate effect of his father's death was to concentrate his affections on his widowed and bereft mother. Even in less tragic circumstances, she would not have been able to respond to what she clearly saw as exaggerated demands from any of her six children. Mary Child-Villiers came from one of England's grandest aristocratic families, the earls of Jersey, but was a changeling. The flamboyance of the various homes she grew up in – Osterley Park in west London, Middleton Stoney in Oxfordshire with its collection of Van Dycks – did not engender in her any trace of the *grande dame* tradition that had blossomed among her ancestors. Frances Lady Jersey in the 1780s had replaced Mrs Fitzherbert as the future George IV's favourite. Longford's maternal great grandmother was Sir Robert Peel's daughter but was anything but conservative with her amorous charms.

More immediately his maternal grandmother who remained a figure in his life until her death at ninety in 1945 was a leading political and literary hostess who knew all the luminaries and welcomed men such as Stevenson, Kipling, Gosse, Kitchener and Chamberlain into her salon. It was again an environment where politics equalled Tory politics. The daughter of Lord Leigh of Stoneleigh, Lady Jersey's garden parties at Osterley were famous. The Pakenham children would run about around the feet of leading lights in society all teed up in their best bib and tucker. 'Occasionally,' recalls Mary, 'we were rounded up to shake hands with interesting individuals. The interesting individuals generally got the worst of it. Some Indian princes flashed their white teeth at us in embarrassed grins and were asked by Frank if they didn't know that it was very rude to laugh at people.'[15]

Such outings were very much the exception rather than the rule. Mary Longford had none of her own mother's passion for parties, politics and conversation. When her husband was alive, the couple seemed contented in each other's company. When not at Tully Nally or in London, they retreated to North Aston Hall, between Oxford and Banbury, where there was hunting aplenty. A place less like either Tully Nally or Osterley is hard to imagine. Violet, seven years her brother Frank's junior, ascribes the drabness of North Aston Hall 'to an outbreak of nineteenth-century medievalism which had turned the plain but wholesome eighteenth-century building into a mullioned and fancy-chimney-stacked imitation of an Elizabethan mansion'.[16]

Mary was more inclined to blame her parents' lack of taste.

> My parents bought it in affluent days and quickly
> fitted it out with non-committal store furniture from
> the most non-committal store in London. Unfortu-
> nately it happened that we all grew up to have
> exceptionally violent opinions about interior decora-
> tion and were not always polite enough to conceal the
> contempt in which we held the decor of our home.
> The ultimate lid was put on our dissatisfaction by
> finding all the bills and estimates, by that time nearly
> a quarter of a century old. To our post-war bed-
> sitting-room minds, they seemed as bad as the extra-
> vagances of the Bourbons.[17]

The dining room featured portraits, in the style of Joshua Reynolds, of the Longford children. Above the sideboard hung Edward, born in 1902 and after his father's death the sixth earl. Pansy, the eldest sister, born in 1904, hung next to the bay window, wearing a Kate Greenaway bridesmaid's dress. On another wall was a double portrait of Frank, born in 1905, dressed in brown velvet and holding a tall stick, and his sister Mary, two years his junior, sitting on a settee. Later two further portraits were added, by another artist, of Violet, born in 1912, and Julia, one year younger.

The change of artists – the second according to Violet rumoured to be an unmasked German spy who undertook the commission to prove his patriotism – was significant for as Mary later put it 'the family fell naturally into Us Four and The Babies', the gap of five years between Violet and Julia and their older brothers and sisters creating in effect almost two families.[18]

In an age when in any case siblings relied much more on each other and much less on their parents for entertainment than is the pattern today, the four eldest Longfords were thrown back on to each other for support as their widowed mother grew more and more remote and left them in the hands of a succession of nannies and governesses. Only for Edward, the son and heir, did she have a spark of maternal warmth and affection.

Mary Longford was a decidedly strange woman whose coldness and indifference were to leave their mark on her second son until the panacea of his marriage reversed the effects. The tragedy that overtook her own happy partnership – hearing that her husband had been 'lost' in battle, but that his body had not been recovered and therefore waiting, hoping against hope, for over a year that he might walk through the door – undoubtedly contributed to her subsequent mental state and therefore to her often unkind behaviour towards all her children. Elizabeth Longford recalls an emotional void in her future husband when she first met him. 'Frank's happiest moments seemed to be tinged with melancholy, while this state of never more than half-happiness seemed to be accepted by him without regret; rather with a kind of acquiescence.'[19]

His mother, it seems, never had any maternal instincts and simply bore children out of an exaggerated (since she had six) sense of duty. She then instilled that same idea of duty in her brood with such a force that it can still guide their actions today.

That aside, once they were born she took the minimum of interest in them that was expected of a woman of her generation and class. For much of the time they were out of sight on the nursery floor, which their mother seldom if ever visited. Although her husband had occasionally dropped in on the nannies to play with his children, Mary Longford saw them only briefly once each day before they went to bed, reading them Bible stories and teaching them to say their prayers. Again it was a matter of duty – a strict, dutiful but unimaginative Christianity.

Such an upbringing was not, of course, so very unusual for the children of the aristocracy in the Victorian and Edwardian eras. Nanny played a role that was much more akin to that which would now be shouldered by the natural mother.[20] And as a consequence parents like Mary Longford were able, like contemporary aunts or godparents, to enjoy their offspring for a carefree hour or so each day before handing back all the responsibilities to their real nurturers. The young Winston Churchill wrote pleading letters to his mother from his boarding school at Harrow asking her to come and visit. She rarely took up the invitation. Nancy Astor, more of an age with Longford's mother, was free to spearhead her crusade for equal rights for women in Parliament because she had dedicated nannies to look after her sons.

Mary Longford, however, took that distance that existed between parents and their children and made it into a gulf. In adult life Longford has become very defensive on the subject of his mother and is unforthcoming on the lingering effects of his upbringing. 'I don't know what is meant by a happy or an unhappy childhood. I was an ordinary boy, I liked sports – football and cricket – though I wasn't good at them.'[21]

Though stressing that he grew up thinking his mother perfect, he will acknowledge that she 'came of a family, a world and a generation where the distinction between the eldest and younger sons was drawn very sharply' and that he was eclipsed in her affections by his elder brother Edward.[22] An obsession with primogeniture was common among families like the Jerseys. In Mary Longford's case it was emphasised by the fact that Edward was never a healthy child.

Although not unaware of Freud and the tendency to focus on the formative years – 'a psychologist might discover ways in which this affected me subconsciously' – Longford is not willing or indeed able to analyse or recall the events of his childhood, a haziness which in itself might be judged as an attempt to forget an unhappy period in his life.[23] His son Thomas attributes this lack of memory to the fact that 'my father is very un-introspective. He doesn't remember his childhood in the same way that he doesn't want to talk about history of any kind and that he doesn't keep letters or papers. He always wants to be looking forward.'[24]

What Longford does recall can often strike the listener, if not the teller, as displaying a cruel side to his mother. He will recount, without even a hint of bitterness but sufficiently clearly many years later to show that it had a tremendous effect, how she told him when he was scarcely out of nappies that as a second son he would have to go out to work to earn his way and that unless he fell on his feet financially he would probably never be able to afford to marry or maintain a home.[25] Though that had been the lot of second sons of aristocratic families for generations, to be told so in such stark terms must have been quite a burden for an impressionable child to carry.

Longford prefers, if challenged, to concentrate on his mother's suffering, both as a young widow and later with crippling arthritis, rather than on any rejection that he felt. In an interview with the *Financial Times* in 1990 he did, however, name his mother alongside his more usual choice of being Irish as major influences on his life, adding she was 'rather cold to me'.[26] On another occasion, fifty years after his mother died, he told the authors of a book called *The Change Makers*: 'The truth is that my mother was not very cordial towards me. My elder brother she adored and always did so. I think I would have to say that I could never have satisfied my mother.'

An obvious lasting effect of his maternal upbringing has been Longford's inability to show his heart, to speak of his own feelings to anyone but his close family and a handful of friends.

As one psychotherapist friend of many years puts it: 'You know he has a heart because you can see the good works that he does. You know that he cares, but he hides his emotions behind his deeds, his heart is kept very secret.'

His sisters Pansy and Mary confirm the impression that he was starved of maternal affection as a child. But such treatment was handed out to all of them, save the son and heir Edward. In adult life Pansy told her friend Evelyn Waugh of their mother's announcement in the nursery the day her husband was reported dead. 'Children, your father has been killed in action and in future your brother, Silchester, will be addressed as "Edward".'[27]

Mary Longford, more like her husband and his ancestors than her own family, was a Puritan who never quite managed to enter into the spirit of the twentieth century, her sense of what was proper and her manners and restraint harking back to the Victorian age. Any display of emotion was frowned upon. Even on her deathbed, when her distraught daughter Mary leant forward to give her a kiss, she pushed her off saying, 'As you remember I was never very good at kissing.'[28]

Longford did, however, more than his other neglected siblings, have a knack for annoying his mother. It was as if he could not quite accept her for what she was. When, for example, he was a bright young thing at Oxford and brought friends home, she would be exasperated at the intrusion. The visitors' book at Tully Nally shows that she rarely welcomed guests to the house. If she was not a warm woman emotionally, neither did she create a warm environment in the home. Even at the most literal level, the surroundings were so cold that the children's governess used to wear her fur coat during lessons in the school room. And a natural uprightness, almost righteousness, meant that when it came to wartime rationing, the children were not allowed to indulge their taste for butter with the products of the Longford farms in Ireland. 'Most people with Irish farms had butter posted to them from Ireland where it was always abundant,' according to Mary, 'but this was actually against the law. We pointed out again and again that it was a silly law, unworthy of our notice, but she stood firm. My mother was the only person I ever heard about who made a hobby of keeping under the rations.'[29] (Such nutritional deprivation as they suffered obviously did Frank, Pansy, Mary and Violet no lasting harm since all lived to be active in their eighties.)

Denied their mother's attention, the children tried to compensate with affection from other sources. With the nursery staff, young Frank was always a hit. Thomas Pakenham recalls his Aunt Mary telling him that his father had all the love he needed as a child.

> She said his nanny thought he was wonderful and
> had eyes for no one else. The nanny was so besotted,
> Aunt Mary said, that their mother got rid of her. My
> aunt didn't seem to see the significance of this appal-
> ling thing. Here's this little third child probably with a
> bigger than average need for attention, he finds a
> nanny who thinks he's wonderful and then suddenly
> she's sacked.[30]

In his passionate desire to catch the eye of his mother, Longford struck up a special bond with the one man, except his elder brother, for whom she exhibited a degree of affection, her own younger brother Arthur Child-Villiers. Himself a second son, Arthur Villiers had made his way in the City, becoming a director of Barings Bank – merchant banking being just about on the right side of respectability for a scion of the Jerseys. But what made Villiers unusual was that he spent his money on good works – prison visiting and boys' clubs – precisely the areas that later attracted his nephew. Villiers had founded the Eton Manor Association at Hackney Wick and it was he who introduced Longford to life on the other side of the tracks when he took his sister's second son to play football with the under-privileged youths of the East End of London. It was an experience that was to echo throughout the rest of Longford's life.

It was also Villiers who encouraged him in what has become a lifelong mania for physical exercise. Eton Manor was unusual in that unlike other clubs in the same vein it was not Christian in its inspiration but athletic. Sport was all and was then, as now, a great leveller of the classes. Villiers was a keen jogger, and once on a trip on the Trans-Siberian railway he took a skipping rope and religiously got off at each station to get in a few minutes' exercise before the train pulled out.

Villiers did not lead his nephew into his mother's heart, but at least Great Aunt Caroline answered Mary Longford's fears for her second son's material well-being. A childless relative on the Pakenham side, her husband had died just days before Longford was born and she chose to make the new baby her heir and thereby the future owner of Bernhurst, a handsome house with eighty acres at Hurst Green in Sussex. Her only stipulation was that he be named after her late husband Francis and that he visit her occasionally. The latter was rarely an unpleasant task. While at Tully Nally, it was Edward who got all the attention, at Bernhurst, Longford was the star.

If relatives failed adequately to compensate the young Pakenhams for their lack of a father and their withdrawn mother, other children were only a passing distraction. Despite having innumerable Jersey cousins, Longford and his siblings grew up a rather isolated bunch. This was partly due to their mother's dislike of socialising, partly because 'Us Four' tended to be a bit of a handful, not to say a little rough, when they did come to play, and partly because they looked so odd. 'We liked the other children we saw but we did not become real buddies with them,' Mary recalled:

> Perhaps this was because we wore such out-of-date clothes. My mother had somehow not noticed that children's fashions had changed and as we grew older we became acutely aware of the eccentricity of our appearance. Our chief grievance was that summer and winter alike we had to wear brown ribbed woollen stockings and brown boots, which were a nuisance all the year round and a trial to the temper in dog-days. But worse still was the shame of them which ate into our very souls. After battling for years the Babies did finally manage to be allowed to wear shoes, but I remember Pansy, a flapper of seventeen, going out to a London tea-party on a boiling July day in brown

27

woollen stockings and brown boots and a hat kept on
by elastic under her chin. It says a lot for the polite-
ness of other children that I cannot ever remember
being actually taunted about our bizarre get-up, but
we knew quite well what they were thinking.[31]

The combined inheritance of his father's disregard for dress and
his mother's extreme parsimony bequeathed Longford early in
life a complete lack of interest in his own appearance. From
childhood onwards it would contribute to his reputation for
eccentricity – as did his disregard for possessions. When he went
away to school he chose not to be burdened down with
reminders of a difficult home life. He started looking ahead
rather than back, as his son Thomas has already described it, at
an early age.

The Longford children's eccentricity did not stop at dress.
They were a precocious bunch, fiercely competitive, old before
their years. There would, of course, be interaction in any such
large family. But these six took it to extremes. Their games were
not the more usual skipping or leap-frog favoured by their
cousins. Frank in particular was good at dreaming up complex
imitations of adult manners. One favourite was arranging books
on end along the wall and pretending to be grown-ups in a
picture gallery. He would hold up imaginary lorgnettes and say
'How ingenious' to cries of laughter from his siblings. Another
stand-by was to make lists of the names of their relatives and
give them each marks out of a hundred. 'It was against the rules
to give the same mark to any two people or to go either above
or below a hundred,' according to Mary. 'The subtlety of the
game lay in deciding if A should be minus 99 and B minus 100
or vice versa; but the thing that kept the game ever-green was
the uncertainty of Frank's vote. Without a word of warning he
would throw out all calculations by announcing a cult for one
of the old unpopulars and make them plus men, or equally
surprisingly discover that a steady favourite was really a snake
in the grass and send them hurtling below zero.'[32] A tendency
to buck the popular wisdom obviously came to Longford early.

Trips to Tully Nally gave the children the chance to show off to other passengers on the ferry to Ireland. (Their dutiful mother never missed a summer there, even when German submarines made the crossing of the Irish Sea a hazardous activity.) At the gangway those embarking were asked their nationality. 'This frivolous question seemed to call for a frivolous answer,' recalled Mary, 'and Pansy at least never failed to reply that she was the Kaiser's wife or *"Ich bin Englisch"* or with some other similar screamingly funny witticism.'[33]

A favourite object – though an unlikely preference for the future campaigner against pornography – was an engraving of a Rubens *Silenus* in Tully Nally in the best visitor's bedroom which the children considered the last word in smut. Their outdoor pursuits were so brutal that one summer Pansy tried to organise an Anti-Fighting League. If anyone attacked one of their siblings, the other three – these were still the days of 'Us Four' – would fall upon the miscreant and administer a dose of corporal punishment. Mary for one was not best pleased with Pansy's initiative. 'I liked fighting and said so. I also dimly felt that, if deeds were supplanted by words, I as the youngest would not stand much chance of making my weight felt.'[34]

The children were brought up to compete. It was natural and instinctive and it is hard to avoid concluding that their mother, who liked games and occasionally joined her children on the lawn of Tully Nally for tennis or hockey, must have been the one who encouraged this. Their father was very uncompetitive in all but the heat of battle. The Pakenhams were in general an uncompetitive lot. If the children had followed his mode, his pattern of life, they would have turned out to be very different people. But they were deprived of their father's restraining influence from an early age and their break from the traditions of that side of the family began in the nursery, hermetically sealed against the outside world, a veritable hothouse where the underlying object of the competitions was to grab their mother's attention by winning.

Though Tully Nally has a larger library than was usual in Anglo-Irish houses, the Pakenhams were not greatly cultivated people. There was no tradition in their blood of excelling in either politics or the arts and literature in contrast to the relatives on Longford's mother's side (who had a remote connection with Jane Austen) and especially his Leigh grandmother. And it was only among the go-getting Jerseys that there was any trace of the showing off so prevalent in the nursery games.

But the mixing of the different bloods was to produce quite a remarkable generation, with the six Pakenham children between them embracing worlds hithcrto foreign to carriers of that name. All six were, quite unlike their parents, exhibitionists who felt no compunction to avoid the spotlight and Frank Longford in particular, with his terrace of curls and winning smile, was a precocious performer with a ready line in conversation and charm. At another of the Osterley garden parties, while still a child, he threw a rose into a victoria full of old ladies, much to their delight.

Edward, who inherited Tully Nally and his father's title at the age of thirteen, was the least competitive of the children, partly due to his ill health. But he was no shrinking violet. He used to write plays as a child in which his siblings could take part. At school and university he proved a difficult act for his younger brother to follow, winning prizes and courting unpopularity by his ardently pro-Irish views. The two shared few interests and increasingly grew apart as adults, living on different sides of the Irish Sea. They did, however, share one Pakenham characteristic – exceptionally large skulls, very long from the tip of the nose to the back of the head. They had the two biggest heads – literally – at Eton and struggled to find hats that would fit them. (Edward Longford's widow suggested that Mary Longford's coldness towards her children may have been a result of the lingering memory of the painful births such large heads would inevitably have entailed.)

Pansy, Mary and Violet all followed up their literary exploits in the nursery by becoming authors. Books and bookishness was and remains a common characteristic, though it came to Frank Longford only late in life. Throughout much of his professional life, though surrounded by writers, he did not pay any great attention to literary pursuits. It was only when he gave up on politics that he took over as head of a publishing house. The majority of his now formidable bibliography was written in retirement. As a child he was the odd one out in the literary world of the nursery. His passion was for politics, not the arts.

In the immediate pre-First World War period when Parliament was debating Irish Home Rule, with its looming threat for the world in which the Pakenhams had prospered, the young Longford, though barely into long trousers, would follow proceedings in the papers with the concentration of an elderly clubman. The *Daily Graphic* would be sent up to the nursery and he would study it page by page. While his siblings became avid readers of literature and, in the case of Pansy, Yeats' poetry, Longford had to be bribed by his mother to turn his attention from the *Daily Graphic* to read *Tale of Two Cities* (ten shillings) and *Pickwick Papers* (fifteen).

When 'Us Four' with characteristic ingenuity decided to set up a family magazine, Edward, with his taste for the dramatic, contributed a bloody-thirsty serial called 'The Vendetta'. Pansy was official laureate with her moralising poetry while Mary was set to work transcribing everything in order to make a second copy of the magazine. Frank tried his hand at verse but with an admirable brevity and lucidity.

> On August the 4th
> Britain declared war,
> A few thought it nice
> But most a great bore.

When it came to illustrations his pictures of Parliament, with bench after bench of MPs decked out in the colours of their parties like football players, paled beside the burgeoning artistic talents of the other children.

Mary remembers that Frank was the Philistine of their bunch. His attitude to art 'was bracing and outspoken. He expressed the greatest contempt for it.'[35] Though he was later to catch up on some of the reading that he missed as a child, that early lack of interest in the arts had longer-term consequences. He has never, for example, had any appreciation of music or painting. When he appeared on *Desert Island Discs* he more or less left the

31

selection of the eight records up to others he considered to have more discernment. After a brief attempt in the early 1980s to become musical subliminally by listening to Radio 3 while he worked, he abandoned all hope of ever developing an ear for music.

If his philistinism made Longford stand out, there was certainly an element of calculation in seeking such a dubious distinction, an attempt to score over the elder brother in whose shadow he grew up. Longford, unlike his parents or his Pakenham forebears, was a showman. It was a trait that came out in his early interest in sports. Edward was never very athletic and in adult life was grossly overweight. Frank, by contrast, has always been wiry and found that his natural determination to win gave him the edge in games. Those who have played against him on a tennis court will tell that he tended to win not so much by stylish strokes or any natural co-ordination but rather by dint of an exaggerated competitive spirit. While all his siblings wanted to win at games, he was the one who would dwell on post-mortems the next day if he lost.

In their youth another issue over which the two brothers contrasted was Ireland, though in adult life they were to move closer in their views. Though never seduced by the romance of Tully Nally, Mary Longford was fiercely pro the Union and scathing about those Irish who wanted independence. Her second son sided with his mother, but the teenage sixth earl, who at Eton was a self-proclaimed Irish patriot who learnt Gaelic in his spare time, used to team up with Pansy to oppose their mother and brother. They would have bitter arguments where Mary Longford found little comfort in the support of her second son and suspected her eldest daughter of corrupting the mind of Edward.

An important element in Longford's subsequently discovered attachment to Ireland was the romantic image left by holidays in Tully Nally. Once or twice a year they would travel over from bleak and sterile North Aston Hall to a fantasy castle. The long trip by train to Holyhead, then by boat to Dun Laoghaire and onwards by train to the town of Mullingar in the very centre of Ireland, was an adventure. It set the Longfords apart from most other children they came into contact with and especially their Jersey cousins. The fourteen-mile trek by pony and trap from Mullingar to Tully Nally transported the children into another world. 'We leant out and sniffed the turf smoke of cottages and screamed a welcome to every familiar feature of the road,' Mary recalls.[36]

Yet amid that romance, and the thrill of lording it around the battlements and moat, the children grew up aware of some of the political tensions abroad. One driver who made a big impression on Mary was 'a wild-looking young Irishman – whom I considered the last word in masculine charm – wearing a new leather motor-coat – which I considered the last word in masculine dressiness. When tactlessly pressed, he owned up to being a Nationalist which meant that he was against us and all we stood for, but for the moment it didn't matter.'[37] The Anglo-Irish garrison class was, by the time of Frank Longford's childhood, beginning to feel increasingly isolated and under siege in their castles.

The children were at Tully Nally when, on 24 March 1916, the Easter Rising broke out. The Irish Republican Brotherhood, a small group of radical and romantic nationalists led by Padraic Pearse, a poet and pioneer of the Gaelic revival, rallied 800 armed supporters, seized the General Post Office in the centre of Dublin and declared a republic.[38] With a quarter of a million Irishmen fighting in the First World War under the British Crown in France, the Brotherhood's act of heroism failed to ignite the country. But the brutality of British troops in putting down the Rising and the subsequent executions of its leaders including Pearse did the rebels' work for them.

When Eamon de Valera, the one surviving commandant from the Rising, was released from an English prison in 1917 he exploited the native anger at the violence of the British reaction to galvanise Sinn Fein into a powerful and often violent force for change and for an Irish republic. In the bitter years between the end of the war and the onset of a negotiated truce between the British and Irish republican forces in 1921, the property of the Anglo-Irish, seen as standing with the British against Sinn Fein, was targeted for savage attacks of looting and burning. The arrival of British auxiliary forces – the Black and Tans – to keep the peace only added to an already brutal and lawless situation.

The uproar in Dublin that Easter week certainly registered at Tully Nally. One of their Pakenham uncles was shot in the face attempting to put down the rebellion. But the discontent that followed barely touched Castlepollard – a reflection of the absence of republican malice towards the Pakenhams. 'We were not burnt down neither were we raided.' Mary found that 'I always seemed to be having to apologise for this. "What's the shooting like round you?" people used to ask. And we had to admit that there was not much in the same shamefaced way that people in England confess that their shooting isn't good, not like Yorkshire or Norfolk.'[39]

In that brief but bloody period between the ending of the First World War and the agreement of a negotiated settlement between the British and the Irish, the worst the Longford children had to endure was when they were out one day on their bicycles and a small child stepped out and threw hay at Mary while the local people, as she puts it, 'sent up a vague anti-English hoot'.[40] On another occasion they found a green-white-and-orange Irish tricolour in the grounds and swiftly replaced it with the Union Jack.

But such patriotism in the face of the violent changes afflicting Ireland did not last into teenage years at least for Edward and Pansy. Even as youngsters they could see the injustice of British domination of Ireland. For Frank Longford it was a longer, slower conversion to the cause of an independent Ireland, prompted initially by his elder brother and later by de Valera, the revolutionary leader himself.

Longford's childhood experiences were of an Ireland at a crossroads. Like many Anglo-Irish before him, he wanted to be part of the country's future, but sensed that he did not belong. It was not his nation. Outside the battlements of Tully Nally he was aware of a veiled and sullen resentment to his kind that went deeper than the deference and the religion that separated the upper classes from their tenants.

That image of the little boy who does not quite fit in is an appropriate one for Frank Longford's childhood. While the children did not belong in Ireland, their Irish roots differentiated them from their English cousins too. They were richer and more privileged than most around them but when they went to their grandmother's family gatherings they were the poor relations.

And at a personal level, Longford knew that Tully Nally, whatever affection he felt for it, would never be his home. His mother made his non-status as a second son abundantly clear. Even among his misfit siblings he stood out as a misfit, more competitive, more exhibitionist, less interested in the arts, poetry and literature and more in politics and newspapers. There is a theory that the younger sons of aristocratic families, lacking any clear role, any vested interest in property and inherited wealth, turn out to be revolutionaries. Young Frank was certainly set to break the mould of the Pakenhams.

Two

The distracted scholar

I believe in the classless society and see education
as one of the main causes of the difference
between the classes

*Lord Longford (of his resignation from the Cabinet in
1968 over failure to put the school leaving age up to
sixteen)*[1]

In 1932 during a brief, doomed assault on the ranks of the
fourth estate Frank Pakenham was sent by Wilson Harris, his
editor at the *Spectator*, to dish the dirt on his *alma mater* Eton.
The hook was a piece in that week's *News of the World* under the
scandalous banner 'Drunkenness at Eton'. Never skilled at the
art of dissimulation, Pakenham failed miserably to convince his
former headteacher, the formidable Dr Alington, that the purpose of the proposed article was to scotch such rumours. 'If it is
your purpose, my dear Frank, to blackguard your old school,
you and I must part company.' The would-be hack retired hurt,
the allure of a scoop and a glittering career on Fleet Street
coming a poor second to loyalty to the old school tie.

For all her rationing of maternal spirit, Mary Longford was a
conventional upper-class mother when it came to her sons'
schooling. Eton had been the best start in life for her father and
brothers. And on the Pakenham side, it had long been held in
Anglo-Irish circles that to fail to send your offspring to a major
English public school was either to sink to dreary depths of
provincialism or worse – for those who preferred a Dublin
alternative – to go native.

So Edward and Frank were bound from birth for Eton. First
step, however, was a decent prep school and their mother chose

the relatively new but highly recommended Furzie Close at Barton-by-Sea in Hampshire. One of those who influenced her decision was the mother of Alec Spearman, the future Conservative MP. He was four years older than Frank and when young Pakenham arrived, aged nine, Spearman took him under his wing. As a *quid pro quo*, Frank had to help Alec unstrap his wooden leg at bedtime: a strange task for a young boy on his first night away from home, but one that evidently forged a bond between the two who remained lifelong friends in spite of subsequent political differences.

The clever, sporty, extrovert young boy of the nursery floors of Tully Nally and North Aston Hall, the darling of most adults save his mother, quickly shone at Furzie Close and went on to be head boy. His teachers and the headmaster Philip Stubbs liked him. His reports were exemplary. In classics he was 'doing more advanced work than the rest of the form'. When it came to sums and algebra he was top of the class, having the edge on Henry Whitehead, subsequently a distinguished Professor of Mathematics at Oxford. Another fellow pupil Humphrey Trevelyan – 'Bunny' when he was at Furzie Close – was later to join Longford in the Lords and as one of the select group of Knights of the Garter.

Longford spent the war years at the school and it was there that he learned of his father's death at Gallipoli. The precocious interest in the world of politics that had seen him engrossed in newspaper reports of Parliamentary debates on Ireland was maintained at Furzie Close, though occasionally he had problems getting his hands on source material. In one letter home to his mother he gave details of a recipe for potato butter the boys had been trying out and then added: 'Please could you tell me roughly what the German peace proposals are, as I only caught a hasty glimpse of them in Mr Stubbs' paper before he took it away. From what I saw it looked as if they thought they had won the war.'[2]

There was only one black spot on his academic record, an area where young Pakenham had already displayed a marked lack of ability in comparison to his siblings. His drawings, said the report, 'are remarkably unlike the object'. It added, however, foreshadowing a tenacity in the face of adversity that has been a lifetime hallmark, that 'his interest never flags'.

In sports too, Pakenham determined to take Furzie Close by storm. Although, on one occasion, he came up against an opponent who managed to dampen his enthusiasm. He reached the final of the school boxing competition: in the other corner of the ring stood Alan Griffiths, later to achieve an international reputation for saintliness as the saffron-robed Dom Bede Griffiths of the Shantivanam ashram in India, a pioneer in bringing together eastern religions and Christianity. That day, however, Griffiths was in less pacific mood and the two young pugilists slogged it out for several rounds to the delight of the crowd swollen by soldiers on leave from the local camp. When the bell rang to signal the end of the round, Pakenham retired to his corner covered in blood but he took comfort in the sight of his opponent similarly afflicted. 'It's not going too badly, is it?' he remarked. But, to his horror, his second pointed out that Griffiths was wiping off all the blood which was, in fact, Pakenham's. At that moment the referee moved over and lifted his opponent's arm in the air to indicate the victor.

Whatever his successes and disappointments at the school, there remained only one real goal in Longford's mind – to win over his mother, to make her take notice of him by his achievements there. And, as in the nursery, it proved an uphill struggle. The acute sense of rejection he felt shines through in a letter he wrote to her aged twelve. He had just sat the entrance examination for Eton and had been the youngest boy to be awarded a place. It was a time when most parents would have been showering their children with congratulations. Instead he had evidently detected a note of disappointment in his mother. 'I'm sorry I didn't do better,' he wrote to her without indicating – or indeed understanding – where there could possibly be room for improvement; and then added boisterously, 'I'm sending you a photograph which I got out of a paper of an enormous Austrian. Isn't he terrific?' Reflecting on this letter many years later, Elizabeth Longford was in no doubt about her future husband's aim. 'The motive for the photograph was clear, even if it involved a touch of sympathetic magic. For the sight of this "terrific" Austrian sent to Lady Longford by her son might suggest to her a novel association of ideas: that Frank himself was just a little bit "terrific" after all.'³

Such a cry for help from her second son is all the more poignant in the light of Mary Longford's indulgence towards his elder brother. She appears to have been wholly convinced that he was absolutely terrific. In 1920, for example, Edward's adoring mother paid to have his schoolboy verse collected and privately published under the title *A Book of Poems by L – Dedicated with kind permission to my oldest sister*.

Frank Pakenham joined his brother Edward at Eton under housemaster C. M. Wells. Both were 'Oppidans' – a less exalted though often grander cast than the 'Collegers', the seventy or so boys who had won scholarships. Mary Longford's sense of duty and her concern for her own social standing refused to allow her children to enter for a scholarship when she had ample funds to pay for them. She had no intention of playing the poor widow in need of a helping hand.

At first her second son's sainted progress at Furzie Close continued unabated at Eton. His initial reports were excellent – 'a very clever boy who can talk Latin with some fluency'. Though not blessed with a technical brain, he even came top of the class in science – but later was to ascribe this to the eccentric marking system employed by his teacher, a young John Christie, later the founder of the Glyndebourne Opera.⁴ Thereafter, however, a rapid decline is charted in Longford's reports. 'His whole life consists in a more or less elaborate pretence.' 'His written work is indescribably filthy. Considering his obvious abilities his place is discreditable.'

It was not, then, that his teachers thought him stupid, simply that he wasn't trying. For almost a decade he chose to rest on his laurels, a strange hiatus in a life otherwise marked out by a restlessness and a tremendous capacity for hard work and, when necessary, slog. It was not until the closing stages of his under-graduate days that he reverted to type, the spark being the realisation that he was likely to fall a long way short of the first he had assumed was his for the taking. 'I calculated, not quite correctly as it proved, that the moving staircase which I set foot on at twelve would bring me to the top at eighteen without any exertion of mine.'⁵

Such unshakeable confidence in his own abilities was certainly a part of this uncharacteristic, and to his tutors infuriating, period of sloth. One factor may have been that since getting good reports did not win him any additional favour in his mother's eyes, Longford calculated unhappily that academic achievement was not worth the effort. A more apparent reason was that his obsession with sports was becoming all-consuming. He still regards his crowning achievement at Eton as leading his house to victory in the final of the Eton Field Game in his last term in 1923. He claims it was his ambition from the first day he arrived there. His success was, according to those who witnessed it, a case of enthusiasm and competitiveness triumphing over a lack of natural sporting ability. Longford by this stage of his life was already suffering from short-sightedness but refused to wear his glasses. Then there were his flat feet, cured, he claims, after 'three years of walking about my bedroom with curled up toes.'⁶ The combination prevented him ever making the school team.

His academic slump was undoubtedly due partly to the proximity of his brother, Edward, already establishing a glowing reputation at Eton both as a promising classical scholar who twice won the school's Wilder Divinity Prize, and, less enviably, as a loner and an ardent Irish nationalist. These last two were inevitably linked at Eton, a bastion of the English Establishment. From his earliest years Frank had laboured to strike up a counterbalance to Edward, mainly for his mother's benefit, targeting areas to excel where his brother showed little aptitude. However, the rigorously classical curriculum at Eton gave him few chances to emerge from his elder brother's shadow.

Edward defiantly refused to court popularity and made himself an outsider in an enclosed world by openly advocating the cause of Sinn Fein, the Irish republican movement which, under the leadership of Eamon de Valera, was posing a growing threat to the nearest outpost of the British Empire in the immediate post-war years. The youthful earl added insult to injury in the eyes of his schoolfellows – many of them with fathers in the

40

British Army that was struggling to keep Ireland down – by learning Gaelic and signing himself Eamon de Longphort. They called him a communist and when he responded with 'Up the Republic', he disappeared under a mass of persecutors.

Frank Longford, naturally, rushed to his sickly brother's defence with the result that he too was stigmatised, his Irish blood eclipsing his thoroughly English Jersey connections. In later years he was to assert that 'there has never been a moment in my life when I was not proud of being an Irishman'.[7] Yet it was when faced with the consequences of Edward's pro-Sinn Fein stance that Frank realised that being Irish marked one out as different. Though he was never a sympathiser with Sinn Fein and its methods, Frank was both impressed and driven into a corner by Edward's youthful defiance. His only alternative would have been to turn his back on his brother and to disown Ireland, the memory of his father at Tully Nally and his Pakenham ancestors. And whatever rivalry he felt with his elder brother for his mother's affection, he was as loyal to him in life as he is to his memory to this day. The ties created between 'Us Four' in that hermetically sealed nursery were stronger than the taunts and threats of other boys at school or, at a later stage, those of friends. Anyone, no matter how grand, who tried to belittle or ridicule Edward's beliefs suffered the sharp end of the Pakenham tongue. Once in the mid-1930s at a smart dinner party Randolph Churchill goaded Longford, 'Your brother's a Sinn Feiner, a traitor to his country.' After trying politely but firmly to change the subject, Longford finally disarmed his tormentor by asking, 'Randolph, what did your grandfather die of?' Randolph crumpled. It was not well known in those days that Lord Randolph Churchill had died of syphilis.[8]

Family loyalty and his Irish origins meant that Frank Pakenham did not quite fit in at Eton, though, unlike Edward, he desperately wanted to be accepted, to be one of the crowd. It was the start of his curious relationship with the British Establishment, always moving amongst its members but equally always one step removed. This detachment was dramatically signalled by what has become his one lasting regret about his time at Eton: his failure to get into Pop, the group of twenty-five or so schoolboys who, in true *Lord of the Flies* English public school tradition, were elected by their fellows to rule over them, set apart by their resplendent checked trousers, coloured waistcoats, seals on their hats and other such finery.

Despite the difficulties caused by his brother's apostasy, Longford had assumed that his gusto on the sports field and seniority would be enough to get him elected as Captain of Oppidans, the non-scholars, and that he would therefore get one of the reserved places within Pop which, at that time, boasted Alec Douglas Home, the future Prime Minister, as its president. (Home's younger brother, Henry, was Longford's 'fag' at Eton.) Longford recalls – conjuring up the precocious Eton world of the early 1920s redolent of *Another Country* – the day he learnt that all his calculations had been in vain. It is a story that demonstrates a talent for telling a good tale against himself.

> It was the last Sunday of the summer 'half' of 1923. My closest friend outside our House, Ronnie Shaw Kennedy, and I were taking our Sunday afternoon stroll round Upper Club. We discussed as always the football season ahead. Then I touched on his chances of Pop. Ronnie, immensely popular among those who knew him well, had incurred the hostility of some of the faster elements by beating a prominent member of his House for smoking. Neither of us was confident that he would be elected, but I tried to be as encouraging as possible. A pause. He definitely did not take his cue or broach my own possibilities. Finally I said, a shade complacently: 'It seems rather unfair, the Captain of Oppidans getting in *ex officio*.' A further pause and then Ronnie decided that the news must be broken to me. 'Bridge is staying on another year.' 'No, no,' I began to protest, for Bridge was many months older than I; but a horrible calculation told me all too quickly that it could just about be done.

Unable to let the matter drop, but more in hope than expectation, he asked his 'close friend' Ronnie about his chances of getting elected in the ordinary way. 'Any previous pause of Ronnie's shrank beside this one. At last, very sadly, he told me: "I think you ought to know that you are the most unpopular boy in the school." '9

Though Ronnie may have been exaggerating – both he and Esmond Warner, another member of Wells House, were to remain lifelong friends of Longford – it was a severe blow that has never quite been forgotten. Its immediate effect was that Longford threw himself with renewed, though unsustained, vigour into his work, earning a half-compliment from Dr Alington on his final report. 'He is no longer such a contented dweller in Philistia.' Longford briefly dallied with the idea of staying on for an extra term to outlast Bridge and get into Pop as Captain of Oppidans but his mother, practical and as insensitive as ever to her second son's emotional needs, brusquely dismissed any such notions. He left Eton fearing that he would never be popular but with enduring confidence in his possession of an intrinsic academic worth that did not need to be fed by hours of study. He took the Oxford entrance exam as a matter of course – as his brother had before him – and, though he failed to win a scholarship, was awarded a place at New College to read history.

Outside the precincts of the school, Longford's life continued to revolve around the family and his siblings. Until he went up to Oxford he had never stayed overnight at a friend's home. Holidays were a round of trips to see relatives, jaunts down to his benefactress, Great Aunt Caroline in Sussex, and summers in Ireland. Sport remained his great solace, playing cricket with the boys from the farms at Tully Nally and the village at Bernhurst, visiting Eton Manor with his uncle, Arthur Villiers, even managing very occasionally to coax his mother out for a spot of tennis with her children. As he approached adulthood the restlessness that compels him, even in his late eighties, to keep up a gruelling schedule of activities, could make life seem very dull to him, especially when Ireland's sodden climate trapped him indoors. He told his daughter-in-law many years later of interminable holidays spent in rain-drenched County Westmeath, his only entertainment watching the drops of water trickle down the window pane.10

43

At this stage in his life, he had little notion of where he might channel his energies but remained acutely aware that he would have to find a profession, his mother's words about not being able to marry or maintain a home still ringing in his ears. It should be added, however, that his chances of spotting a bride as yet were limited in the extreme. Apart from those met at the occasional debutantes' dance, the only women he came into contact with were his sisters and female cousins. Even when he came up to Oxford, it was to a single sex world where the sight of a woman from Somerville or Lady Margaret Hall in the quad of one of the all-male colleges would cause a ripple of disapproval.

Some of those around Longford did, even at this early juncture, identify one career to which he would be well suited. In an interview – given with the benefit of hindsight before her death in 1979 – Edward Longford's widow Christine remembered the first time she met her brother-in-law, a restless but charming seventeen-year-old.

> He was described to me by Edward as somebody who was so clever he could make any argument in the family sound ridiculous. I remember him in the family. He was very good at family arguments. One could manage to get a three-cornered argument. Edward and his mother would fight, in a very friendly way, about Conservatism and what we would call communism. It was not so long after 1917. Frank would take a third point of view, whatever it might have been, and would make each side sound ridiculous. He was cut out to be a politician. Politicians always get on together because it's the job they're interested in, the common ground.[11]

Christine Longford was not the only one to spot the budding politician in her future brother-in-law. On one of his stays at Bernhurst with Great Aunt Caroline, her companion Edith Ward, who looked after her for twenty-four years and became one of the family, suggested he should study political economy at university. But his early interest in matters of state had waned and he had taken no appreciable part in Eton's politics society.

Nor did he play an active role as an undergraduate in the Oxford Union, long the early stamping ground of future performers at the Commons despatch box. This may have had something to do with an incident in 1921, before Longford arrived at Oxford, when Edward, true to form, was a lonely voice of opposition to a Union motion condemning the 'assassins' (rather than executioners) of the British Field Marshal Sir Henry Wilson, murdered by Irish nationalists in London. For his pains, a mob seized the sixth Earl of Longford on his way back from the Union building to his college, Christ Church, ducked him in Mercury, the lily pond in the centre of Tom Quad, and proceeded to destroy all the books in his rooms that contained a word of Gaelic.

Christine Longford was later to claim that the attack was due only to undergraduate high spirits and was subsequently blown out of proportion by both her brother-in-law and the papers who picked up on it at a time when Ireland was in revolt and the incident therefore newsworthy. 'It had been a very warm night and they'd all been drinking. Edward said he didn't suffer much. Frank resented all that was done to Edward, but I think he exaggerated Edward's martyrdom in Oxford.'[12]

Whatever the true significance of the incident, the rough and tumble of the Union would, in any case, have held little attraction for the younger Longford during his undergraduate days. His early passion for politics had subsided during his slothful years at Eton. Though he continued to enjoy an argument, party politics in particular was a closed book to him. He was a product of his upbringing. The Conservative Party was as natural a part of his life as the butler who would sharpen his pencils when he was busy writing. His maternal grandmother entertained Conservative statesmen in her salon and that was the limit of Longford's political horizon.

It never occurred to him to contemplate looking beyond, much less to spare a thought for the emerging Labour Party. Even on Ireland, where his views left room for argument with those otherwise of like mind, he was unwilling, as yet, to pin his colours to the mast. His fledgling republicanism was nowhere near as ardent as Edward's. He felt none of his brother's missionary zeal. In any case, in marked contrast to the Oxford Longford was to inhabit as a tutor in the late 1930s, the debates and divisions of the university city in the mid-1920s had little to do with politics and the state of the nation. This was the era of Harold Acton and the aesthetes, of Oxford bags supplanting the pagoda shoulders and tight trousers of the dandies, of the drunken excesses of the wealthy aristocrats of the Bollinger Club in Evelyn Waugh's *Decline and Fall*. This generation had its own variety of the rebellious spirit endemic to students that had in the past sparked political revolutions across Europe and would again. Their uprising was instead aimed at brushing away the *fin-de-siècle* cobwebs that they saw as still engulfing the social and intellectual world of Oxford. Hugh Gaitskell, an exact contemporary of Longford's at New College, summed up the mood of the time.

> Oxford in the middle twenties was gay, frivolous, stimulating and tremendously alive . . . it was a brief, blessed interval when the lives of the young were neither overshadowed by the consequences of the last war nor dominated by the fear of a future one. Most of us sighed with relief and settled down to the business of enjoying ourselves . . . Politics, to tell the truth, were rather at a discount. We were in revolt all right – against Victorianism, Puritanism, stuffiness of any kind, but most of us weren't sufficiently bitter – or perhaps sufficiently serious – to be angry young men . . . [in] the heavenly freedom of Oxford [revolt] took the form of an outburst of scepticism, a mistrust of dogma, a dislike of sentimentality and of over-emotional prejudices or violent crusades . . . We professed the happiness of the individual as the only acceptable social aim.[13]

Another future Labour Cabinet colleague of theirs at New College was Douglas Jay. He was a fresher when Gaitskell and

Longford were in their final year as undergraduates but he recorded the enduring apolitical atmosphere of the times.

> Though the frivolous extravagance and alleged riotous parties of the Acton epoch had worn off by 1926 and 1927, the conventional morality of the intellectuals was still violently antipathetic to politics or indeed to serious interest in anything other than philosophy, literature and the arts. We were constantly warned against 'careerism' which was regarded as the unforgivable sin.

Jay was admonished by fellow undergraduate Richard Crossman (a whole generation of Labour statesmen was formed at Oxford in this period), 'Anyone who joined the Union, or talked about politics was really falling below the minimum standard expected of an educated man.'[14]

For Longford that pursuit of individual freedom and happiness, the discarding of the old conventions and manners, offered an escape from the cold Puritanism of his home life, and especially from a mother whose ideas were trapped in pre-war notions of propriety and duty. So pained at being an outsider at Eton, he quickly found a niche for himself on the inside at Oxford, among the smart set. Attracted to the more exaggerated, glamorous personalities in the University he grew in confidence and rediscovered the talent for wit and conversation that had first flowered in the nursery.

His sometime tennis partner, the late Lord David Cecil, three years his senior, son of the Marquess of Salisbury and subsequently Professor of English Literature at Oxford, remembered Frank Pakenham for his humour.

> He was always telling stories in which he came out rather comically. He was very gay and sociable indeed. I used to have people to lunch in my rooms in Wadham and he was someone it was very good to have. He was so appreciative and quick, and when he was there the conversation flickered to and fro in a special way.[15]

Whatever Douglas Jay's recollection of the declining pull of the aesthetes when he arrived, the Oxford of the mid-1920s has taken on the halo of a golden age. John Betjeman, Poet Laureate from 1972 until his death in 1984 and another contemporary of Longford's, described it in terms of a rivalry between two camps, 'hearties' and 'aesthetes'.

> Hearties were good college men who rowed in the college boat, ate in the college hall, and drank beer and shouted. Their regulation uniform was college tie, college pullover, tweed coat and grey flannel trousers. Aesthetes, on the other hand, wore whole suits, silk ties of a single colour, and sometimes – but only for about a week or two while they were fashionable – trousers of cream or strawberry-pink flannel. They let their hair grow long, and never found out, as I never found out, where the college playing fields were or which was the college barge. Aesthetes never dined in hall, but went instead to the George restaurant on the corner of Cornmarket and George Street, where there was a band consisting of three ladies, and where punkahs, suspended from the ceiling, swayed to and fro, dispelling the smoke of Egyptian and Balkan cigarettes. Mr Ehrsam, the perfect Swiss hotelier and his wife kept order, and knew how much credit to allow us. I was an aesthete. The chief Oxford aesthete when I went up in 1925 was Harold Acton.[16]

What he did not go on to mention was that the world of the aesthetes was an all-male one and within that closed circle of English public schoolboys homoeroticism was the norm, albeit for some a passing one. Betjeman reputedly had sex with fellow undergraduate W. H. Auden for £5. Evelyn Waugh was observed by Tom Driberg, the future Labour MP, at the all-male Hypocrites' Club 'rolling on a sofa' with another man, their 'tongues licking each other's tonsils'.[17] Waugh and Betjeman both went on to marry and dismissed such homosexual romps as an aberration. Auden however married Erika, the daughter of

Thomas Mann, only to provide her with a British passport with which to escape from Nazi Germany; his marriage of convenience had no effect on his attraction to men. Driberg's promiscuous homosexuality was legendary.

Though he had many friends in the world of the aesthetes, most notably Betjeman, Longford never quite belonged. For one thing he had and retains a horror of homosexuality, founded on the strict Christian moral code instilled by his mother, and later reinforced when he embraced Catholicism. The sexual licence of some of the aesthetes would have alienated that Puritan side in him. He has always regarded sex as having a sacred purpose, hand-in-hand with marriage.

As for the aesthetes' dress code, Frank Longford has never displayed any concern for his appearance. Nor would he have had the money for an endless round of socialising at the George. His mother, who actually managed to have food left over from her rations during the war, kept him on a tight budget. More pointedly, he knew where the college sports field was. He played soccer and tennis for New College and continued his links with Eton Manor. Yet he would scarcely have merited Kipling's description of 'the flannelled fools at the wicket and the muddied oafs at the goals' that became a tag for the hearties.

Like many undergraduates of the time he was neither heartie nor aesthete, but unusually he managed to keep a foot in both camps. As Harold Acton himself remarked of that period: 'At Oxford you could lead a hundred lives and discover more friends and sympathies than elsewhere.'[18] Frank Pakenham was an occasional visitor to another of the focal points for the aesthetes, the salon of Maurice Bowra, the dean of Wadham, a First World War hero and a celebrated scholar. Today Bowra is best remembered as Oxford's Dorothy Parker, brimming with quotable one-liners, but in his time he assembled around him all the brightest stars of successive Oxford generations. As Betjeman put it, he was:

> *certain then,*
> *As now, that Maurice Bowra's company*
> *Taught me far more than all my tutors did.*

Longford sharpened up his wit in the pages of the *Oxford University Review*, an arts and satirical magazine he founded with Robert Henriques with the aesthete leanings if not the cachet of Acton's own *The Oxford Broom*. Contributors to the *Review* included Betjeman and Gaitskell and the targets of its character assassination included the 'luvvies' of the fabled OUDS, the university drama society. On setting up the *Review*, Longford wrote to many famous people asking for messages of support. Among those he approached was his fellow Anglo-Irishman George Bernard Shaw, now in his seventies and at the height of his fame with the opening of *St Joan* in 1924. He sent a terse reply. 'Anyone who fills up his first number with messages that no one wants to read will fail and will deserve to. Even young Oxford should know better than that.' With an admirable capacity to snatch victory out of the jaws of defeat, the young publisher covered the town with posters of Shaw's message in a successful campaign to promote the first issue.

From a social perspective, the high point of Longford's time at Oxford came not during evenings with Bowra or Betjeman, but rather when he was invited to become a member of the Bullingdon, the most exclusive of those dining and hunting societies that continue to thrive in the University. His admittance came through the good offices of his fellow Old Etonian Roger Chetwode (whose sister Penelope was to marry Betjeman) and went some way towards making up for his failure to get into Pop. Like the Eton elite, the Bullingdon had its own extravagant uniform and traditions, recorded and some would say exaggerated by Evelyn Waugh as the 'Bollinger'.

> For two days they had been pouring into Oxford:
> epileptic royalty from their villas of exile; uncouth
> peers from crumbling country seats; smooth young
> men of uncertain tastes from embassies and legations;
> illiterate lairds from wet granite hovels in the High-
> lands; ambitious young barristers and Conservative
> candidates torn from the London season and the
> indelicate advances of debutantes; all that was most
> sonorous of name and title was there for the beano.[19]

The high jinx of the Bullingdon/Bollinger after their drunken dinners would include smashing windows – 'the sound of English county families baying for broken glass' as Waugh memorably put it – and picking on would-be aesthetes like the young Tom Driberg who was relieved of his green Oxford bags or unpopular, socially compromised loners like the anti-hero of *Decline and Fall*, Paul Pennyfeather.

In marked contrast to such nights of excess, however, were Longford's regular trips to Eton Manor. One of those he persuaded to make the journey to the East End of London was Douglas Jay who remembers Longford cutting a 'rather elephantine' figure on the football field.

> We were playing for the Second XI, I think, and Frank asked me if I'd come and play at a boys' club in Hackney. That was the first time I had realised that he had a social conscience. Those were the days, of course, of that brand of paternal conservatism with a social conscience. I remember him about college, very vigorous, very active and I'd been told rather vaguely that he had some claim on an Irish earldom, but I wasn't sure if it was a joke or not. He was known for his extravagant jokes.[20]

Those trips down to Hackney brought the gilded youth of Oxford into contact with an altogether different reality. Eton Manor and the Bullingdon were poles apart. In the East End, already a solid block of Labour seats, save for a lone Liberal in Bethnal Green, the advent of the first socialist Prime Minister, James Ramsay MacDonald, in January 1924 gave a boost to the burgeoning trade union movement. Though Ramsay MacDonald's coalition government collapsed within the year, the growth of the Labour Party and its commitment to a welfare state would ultimately sound the death knell for the Poor Law Boards of Guardians and the sort of philanthropic Conservatism practised by men like Arthur Villiers.

In the shorter term the incoming Conservative administration of Stanley Baldwin quickly became involved in a wages dispute with the miners. Declining exports had led the employers, noted for their truculence and short-sightedness, to try to impose reduced pay and longer working days on their employees who already suffered bad and dangerous conditions. The two sides were at loggerheads when Baldwin intervened to give a government subsidy on wages until a Royal Commission reported on the problem. In effect the Prime Minister only managed to buy time. Eight months later the commission recommended that the subsidy be stopped. On 4 May 1926 the first ever General Strike began.

While Oxford with a few notable exceptions – Douglas Jay joined the Labour Party as a result of the General Strike and Hugh Gaitskell and John Betjeman both lent practical support to the protesters – slept through the nine-day confrontation, the young men whom Frank Longford and his friends came down to 'help' at Eton Manor were on the picket lines with their families. The days of the strike, according to local historian Alan Palmer, 'brought tense hours to the East End, with steel-helmeted troops ensuring the safe unloading of food supplies while loyal trade unionists watched, angrily impotent, from outside the dock gates'.[21] The General Strike was only one of many disputes in the area around Hackney Wick in this period. There were stoppages on the buses, on the trams, in the docks, at Covent Garden fruit market. Many of them were started unofficially as part of a struggle for the recognition of larger unions, principally the Transport and General Workers under Longford's future boss, Ernest Bevin.

The pressures on the young undergraduate to give some thought to his philanthropic Conservatism were mounting. After a couple of terms of reading history, Longford decided it was not the subject for him and obtained permission from his tutors to change course to the new and as yet not quite established school of Modern Greats – known today as PPE: politics, philosophy and economics. When he took his finals in 1927 he had fewer than 200 predecessors. 'I originally chose the school', he recalled, 'for the rather degraded reason that, unless I went in for something like Oriental Languages, it was the one chance offered me for making up for nine or ten years of relative slackness and starting level with my contemporaries.'²² There was also the attraction that it broke with the classicism that had characterised his Eton education and which his brother had claimed for his own.

When he went to see Lionel Robbins, the economics tutor, about some additional reading over the long vacation to catch up on what he had missed, Longford hardly made a good impression. Confronted with an endless list of weighty tomes, he smiled brightly and said, 'They sound rather dull.' Robbins asked him if he disliked dull books and when Longford, the flippant Old Etonian, said that he did, his tutor retorted: 'I should have thought that they would rather have appealed to you.'²³

The sting in the tail obviously had its effect for under Robbins and Harold Salvesen Longford was challenged to rediscover his early capacity for study. His tutorial partner – and in his final year his flatmate at 2 Isis Street near Folly Bridge – was Hugh Gaitskell, then known to his friends as Sam. 'I think that Harold Salvesen always preferred the mind of Hugh to mine. Again and again he advised me to model my literary style on Hugh's which possessed a charm and lucidity I sadly lacked.'²⁴ Thereby began a friendly rivalry that was to endure until Gaitskell's death in 1963, with one in the Lords, one in the Commons, and Longford habitually, in Labour Party terms at least, lagging a few paces behind, less glamorous, less able to manipulate situations to his advantage, and ultimately slower to rise to Cabinet office.

Despite their political differences during these undergraduate days – Gaitskell had already become involved in Labour Party politics – the two had much in common. Both had lost their fathers at an identical stage, Gaitskell's dying from a disease contracted when working for the Indian Civil Service in Burma. Both were second sons who had gone through school, Gaitskell at Winchester, in the shadow of elder brothers who won all the academic prizes. Both had been poor relations in their extended families. Both liked sports. Gaitskell, however, preferred individual games – tennis, golf – to the team sports Longford enjoyed. Gaitskell's mother was an unconventional and high-spirited woman with a sense of humour. When her husband was a prominent official in Rangoon she had once slipped away from her own dinner party to switch various street signs. She passed on to her son a warmth and exuberance that Longford could not quite match. Though both found their feet in the social world of Oxford and rekindled academic interest that had been eclipsed during their schooldays, Gaitskell's time at New College saw his political values crystalise as he took the decisive step away from the values of his upper-middle-class background and into the Labour Party. Longford began to question his instinctive Conservatism but fought shy of such a radical change.

Gaitskell's growing convictions took hold in his studies. He chose as his special subject the history of the Labour Movement, while Longford concentrated on the less emotionally charged area of economic theory. The constant comparison with Gaitskell in their tutorials, however, managed to break the spell of Longford's unshakeable academic complacency and goad him into action.

> One evening in my second year Harold Salvesen was so rough with me that I could not help asking him finally: 'I suppose you do feel that I can get a First if I really work, which I admit I am not doing at present?' He refused to commit himself and that night a sort of anger took possession of me which spurred me on and did not finally exhaust itself until eighteen months later when, for good or ill, I had done with schools and my fate was settled.[25]

As he buried himself in books, Longford developed a passion for economic theory which was to stay with him in his immediate post-Oxford years. This was the pre-Keynesian era when many Conservatives were none the less beginning to question the prevailing economic wisdom of *laissez-faire* and free trade.[26] There was a growing school of thought that a return to protectionism was needed. In keeping with his own philanthropic background, Longford opposed such a retreat into tariff barriers and held up unfettered private enterprise as the best way to improve the lot of the working classes. It was the sight, in the wake of the Wall Street Crash of 1929, of all his sacred cows failing to arrest the slide into depression and deprivation that was to accelerate his progress towards the Labour Party and socialism.

Along with Gaitskell, who combined support of Labour with evenings with Bowra and the aesthetes, Longford struck up a close friendship at New College with Evan Durbin. The three of them formed a sort of triumvirate. Durbin was the first out-and-out socialist the earl's son had met. The child of a Non-Conformist minister, he had come from humble beginnings to win a scholarship to Oxford. In later years he used to describe his first sightings of Frank Pakenham in the Junior Common Room, full of the 'arrogance and stupidity of the privileged classes'. The two of them got into a political argument which ended with Durbin saying: 'Man, have you ever been hungry?' (In retrospect Longford is sure that Durbin himself rather exaggerated the exigencies of his childhood.)

After that encounter, they were often to be found debating the relative merits of their political positions on the staircase of New Buildings where they both had rooms. 'He forced me', Longford was later to admit, 'to build up a kind of intellectual defence of Conservatism, to rationalise what I really believed in. From that time on I was never oblivious or ignorant of the Labour case in broad outline.'[27]

If Evan Durbin began to make Frank Longford question his own instinctive political credo, Hugh Gaitskell was, in those undergraduate days, to change the course of his life. According to his biographer Philip Williams, 'Gaitskell spent much more time with girls than most undergraduates did.'[28] His natural and easy charm made him something of a lady killer in the chaste and segregated atmosphere of those times. In his final year Gaitskell's cousin Audrey Townsend came up to Lady Margaret Hall. Through her Gaitskell got to know her fellow 'undergraduette' Elizabeth Harman, the daughter of a well-to-do Harley Street ophthalmic surgeon and a relative on her mother's side of the Chamberlain clan. He introduced her into the almost exclusively male world of the Bowra salon where she scored quite a hit. (Both Gaitskell and Bowra were to propose to her.)

55

And, in the social whirl that followed his finals, he invited her to the Magdalen and New College summer balls and unwittingly introduced Frank Longford to his future wife.

Elizabeth takes up the story at the first of these two grand events.

> About midnight, on my way back from the cloakroom to the dance floor, I was astonished to see a large sleeping figure draped over a garden chair in the middle of a wide canvas corridor. As I approached the figure on tiptoe I saw that it was wearing a 'Bullingdon' uniform, the last word in social glamour: yellow waistcoat and navy blue tailcoat with white facings and brass buttons. The face was of monumental beauty, as if some Greco-Roman statue – the Sleeping Student maybe – had been dressed up in modern clothes by some group of jokers. I stood for a moment admiring but puzzled. 'What sort of girl', I asked myself, 'could have allowed such a magnificent partner to spend the best part of the night alone and asleep.'[29]

The sleeping beauty was Gaitskell's friend, Frank Pakenham, who had been abandoned by his partner for the evening Alice Buchan, daughter of John Buchan the novelist.

Elizabeth continues:

> After a good day's sleep myself, I awoke refreshed for the New College Ball on the following evening, 28 June 1927. For the first and only time I wore my most poetic dance frock of lavender taffeta printed with bunches of little flowers floating in four petal-shaped panels, with a chiffon underskirt and knickers to match. Next morning I found that I had been literally (but not metaphorically) deflowered: one of the petals had floated away or been torn off. Though today it has faded to a twilight grey like my hair, I have kept it because of what happened that night; and I have never worn it again because of the missing petal.

Some time after midnight Hugh took me along to the room in Garden Quad that Ken McKinnon, a third-year Australian scholar, had hired for the occasion. At that time 'Provvy', as Jeremy Bentham used to call Providence, began to show her hand. There, extended on Ken's sofa, lay my vision of the night before, again deeply and serenely asleep. This time I did not hesitate. A performance of the Sleeping Beauty act was clearly called for in reverse. Bending over his mop of classical brown curls I kissed him on the forehead. His brown (as I now saw they were) eyes opened wide. 'I'd like to kiss you but I can't . . .'

And Frank Longford slumped back, fast asleep. But in that moment Elizabeth Harman had made an impression. A few days after the ball, he heard that he had got one of the two best firsts for his year. His anxiety that his illegible handwriting might have let him down proved groundless. For once he had gone one better than his rival Gaitskell who had to endure a long viva before scraping his first.

Mary Longford, travelling up to London by train with her friend Mrs Barry, scanned the results in *The Times*. With characteristic under-expectation, she started with the seconds, worked her way down through the thirds and fourths and then concluded resignedly to her companion, 'Frank must have failed altogether.' Mrs Barry took the copy of *The Times* and began reading from the top. Almost at once she pointed to Frank Pakenham among the firsts.

He celebrated with a dinner for a few close friends at the Café Royal in London, followed by an outing to the theatre. And among those he invited was Elizabeth Harman.

Three

The party-goer

> . . . Masked parties, Savage parties, Victorian
> parties, Greek parties, Wild West parties, Russian
> parties, Circus parties, parties where one had to
> dress as somebody else, almost naked parties in St
> John's Wood, parties in flats and studios and
> hotels and night clubs, in windmills and swimming
> baths, tea-parties at school where one ate muffins
> and meringues and tinned crab, parties at Oxford
> where one drank brown sherry and smoked
> Turkish cigarettes, dull dances in London and
> comic dances in Scotland and disgusting dances in
> Paris – all that succession and repetition of massed
> humanity . . . Those vile bodies . . .
>
> *Evelyn Waugh* Vile Bodies[1]

Elizabeth Harman's awakening of her future husband like
George IV arousing the spirit of Brighton in Rex Whistler's
allegorical painting failed in the short-term at least to spark their
romance. After the celebratory dinner at the Café Royal in the
summer of 1927, the couple scarcely saw each other for three
years. She continued her studies at Oxford while for Longford it
was time to face up to those career choices that his mother had
been signposting for her second son from the cradle.

His passion for economics was undiminished by the fact that
it was the only paper in his finals where he had failed to get a
straight alpha. However, in the end he opted for the law,
deciding, he now recalls, that it was more likely to help him pay
his way.[2] He had planned to study in London but at the last
moment changed his mind and stayed on for his second degree
in Oxford. In his 1953 book, *Born to Believe*, he suggests that this
volte face was a result of his encounter with Elizabeth.

> I fear I never gave my mother or anyone else the real
> reason for the change and perhaps I hardly admitted it
> to myself. But as with the lesser things in my life, a
> good start having been made, I failed to follow my
> inspiration; indeed I seemed to lose awareness of it,
> while in fact retaining it below the level of
> consciousness.

That passage was written with the glow of hindsight when the Longfords were already nearing their silver wedding anniversary and had eight children. It is hard to credit that for the three years from 1927, firstly in the tight-knit community of Oxford and then in a social world where they had friends in common, even someone so emotionally repressed as Longford carried the seeds of this blossoming romance in his heart without once acting upon them. And if his explanation is accepted, he certainly did not let this buried desire for Elizabeth cramp his style. For these were three years of endless partying with the 'bright young people', whose antics were recorded by Evelyn Waugh in *Vile Bodies*, of friendships with the rich and famous and of the occasional romantic frisson.

Longford had many more obvious reasons for staying on in Oxford to study law. His success in finals had convinced the Warden of New College, H. A. L. Fisher, that he had an academic high-flyer on his hands. After years of living in the shadow of his scholarly elder brother, Longford was now being tempted with the prospect of a fellowship at All Souls. (When he finally took the examination in the autumn of 1929, however, he was ill-prepared and failed to gain admittance to the academic inner sanctum of the university, performing with distinction only in his economics papers.)

Oxford too was a place where – after the isolation of his childhood and the sense of being a misfit at Eton – he had grown to feel comfortable, accepted, even admired. However, whereas in undergraduate days he had been catholic in his choice of friends, from Michaelmas Term 1927 onwards his social orbit became rather more exclusive. The end of his Modern Greats degree at New College had seen the departure of the two friends who had been challenging Longford to reconsider his political opinions. Hugh Gaitskell went first to the heart of the Nottinghamshire coalfield for a year to teach in an adult education centre before taking up a post at University College, London, where Evan Durbin was also on the staff. In 1930 Durbin moved on to the London School of Economics and both became active in Labour circles, with Durbin standing in the 1931 election in the unwinnable seat of East Grinstead in Sussex.

Deprived of such radical influences, Longford's political pilgrimage away from his inbred Conservatism temporarily lost what momentum it had picked up. Indeed politics took a poor second place to a social life which revolved almost exclusively around the university's smart set where Conservatism was taken as read. He struck up enduring friendships with two glamorous freshmen, Basil Dufferin, grandson of the Viceroy of India and the Marquis of Dufferin and Ava, and Freddy Furneaux, later Earl of Birkenhead.

His glittering first, his Bullingdon connections and his growing reputation as a wit had made Longford quite a star on the Oxford stage and drew in freshers like Dufferin and Furneaux (who was to take over the editorship of the *Oxford University Review*). These two had a worldly élan and ready access to influential circles. To Longford – scarred by his early experience of being ostracised – they were immediately attractive.

Basil Dufferin was also Anglo-Irish, his family seat being at Clandeboye in Co. Down, a house every bit as eccentric in its own Victorian way as Tully Nally. Dufferin's daughter, Lady Caroline Blackwood, painted a thinly veiled portrait of Clandeboye in her novel *Great Granny Webster* evoking the damp-infested library, the idiosyncratic plumbing – 'it was considered a luxury if anyone managed to get a peat-brown trickle of a bath' – and the leaking roof which necessitated a constant juggling act with buckets and jugs when it rained.[3]

The 1920s and 1930s were the golden age of the house party when the aristocracy would organise weekends and sojourns of hunting, eating, drinking and conversation at their country estates for friends and colleagues. Longford was a regular visitor to Clandeboye, along with other Oxford friends of Dufferin like

John Betjeman who in a letter of September 1928 recalled trying – unsuccessfully – to learn the Charleston in its parquet-floored salon.[4]

Betjeman wrote of the Byronesque Dufferin as 'the dark, heavy-lidded companion' in his poem 'Brackenbury Scholar of Balliol'. Elizabeth Longford, who got to know Basil Dufferin well in the 1930s when he was a rising young minister in Conservative governments, describes him as 'brilliantly clever, extremely handsome and very athletic', all three qualities acting as a magnet to her future husband.[5] Longford developed early in life a taste for glamorous, remarkable and attractive people, combining it increasingly with an attachment to those at the other end of the social scale, the needy, the oppressed, the unloved and the marginalised. He has never paid much notice to mediocrity.

From university days until his death at the end of the Second World War in Burma, Dufferin and his wife Maureen, a member of the Guinness clan whom he married in 1930, remained close friends of the Longfords, part of the grand social world in which they moved in the London of the 1930s. Maureen Dufferin recalls the young Frank Pakenham above all for his humour.

> He wasn't madly good looking. And I don't remember
> him as especially eccentric at that point. He never had
> the right clothes and was always borrowing black-tie
> and jacket. But it was his wit and his stories. He and
> my husband were both very funny and very clever.[6]

More immediately significant in this interlude in Frank Longford's life, however, was Freddy Furneaux, son and heir to the Earl of Birkenhead, who as F. E. Smith had risen from middle-class origins on Merseyside to be Lord Chancellor and one of the most formidable characters in the Conservative Party.

> Freddy and his family soon came to occupy a place
> apart in my eyes. Through them and their expanding
> circle I was initiated into Conservative politics at their
> most romantic: at the point, that is, where they made

contact with the more intellectual side of London society.[7]

There was already a family connection between the Longfords and the Smiths. F. E. had served in the Oxfordshire Yeomanry under Longford's father, while Lady Birkenhead's father had been rector at Heyford, a few miles from the Jerseys' home at Middleton Stoney where he was a regular visitor. North Aston Hall which remained Mary Longford's home until 1929 was only eight miles from Charlton, F. E. Smith's beloved country seat.

However, the contrast between Frank Longford's English home and the atmosphere which greeted him when he went to Charlton with Furneaux could not have been greater, the one solemn, enclosed, hostile to visitors, eternally in mourning, the other dynamic, bursting with life and well-connected callers, 'an adult culture' as Frank Longford now describes it.[8]

> I easily recall my nervousness as I approached the house for my first visit, on an April evening in 1928. Margaret Birkenhead gave me that wonderful sparkling welcome of hers. 'You know my daughters,' she said, pointing to a sofa where Eleanor, already grown up, and Pam, a child of fourteen, sat with their backs to me. Both subsequently melted towards me. But that evening neither Eleanor nor Pam was interested in the stranger. Eleanor, without turning her head, stretched her hand and arm over the back of the sofa and Pam, after a furtive glance sideways, copied her elder sister precisely. Totally non-plussed, I grasped Eleanor's hand in one of mine and Pam's in the other and stood there gaping while Margaret Birkenhead burst into laughter.[9]

Longford's embarrassment was saved – temporarily it turned out – by the arrival of the man of the house. F. E. Smith had made his name as an eloquent barrister, entering the Commons in time to play an outspoken part in the opposition to Lloyd

George's 'People's Budget' and in the 1909–11 crisis that surrounded House of Lords attempts to block it. Smith had become one of the most persuasive advocates of the Ulster Protestants in the pre-war Home Rule Crisis, and in 1916 successfully and flamboyantly led the prosecution of Roger Casement who was convicted of planning a republican rising in Ireland with German help and hanged. From 1919 to 1922 he sat on the Woolsack and returned for a second spell in the Cabinet from 1924 to 1928 as Secretary of State for India.

George Dangerfield, admittedly a partisan observer, summed up in *The Strange Death of Liberal England* the reputation F. E. enjoyed at the time Longford first met him on that April evening.

> Many people loved him, most distrusted him, some
> despised him, and he despised almost everybody. In
> his later career as Earl of Birkenhead he served him-
> self more faithfully than God or his country . . . he
> was without question the most fascinating creature of
> his times.

Birkenhead rescued the young Frank Pakenham from his daughters that evening by suggesting they went for a ride. The visitor failed to reveal that his exploits on a horse had been limited to playing on ponies on the farm at Tully Nally and duly disgraced himself by losing control of his steed, in the process frightening his host's horse.

> We jogged back in silence. When we reached the
> house Lord Birkenhead turned to me. 'We have sur-
> vived,' he said, 'though you will not, I feel sure, claim
> an undue share of the credit for that achievement. We
> have preserved our skins, if not our dignity. In reciting
> these events to the ladies it would be unwise and,
> indeed, injudicious to depress their spirits and our
> own prestige with too slavish an adherence to the
> literal facts as they may have appeared at the moment
> of their occurrence.' He shot me the rich, warm,

illuminating smile of partnership that I came to know
so well, and went in to pitch some tremendous yarn
in which he and I won infinite glory and saved each
other's lives.[10]

Out of that economy with the truth and shared delight in
spinning a tale grew an unlikely friendship, the estate agent's
son with a chip on his shoulder and the minor aristocrat, the
adopted son of Ulster Unionism and the romantic Irish nationalist, the waning star of Conservatism and the future Labour
Cabinet minister.

It was not politics that each admired in the other. It was the
same combination that drew Frank Longford to Basil Dufferin –
a common passion for sport and a brilliant, showy cleverness. A
weekend at Charlton revolved around physical exertion with F.
E. at the centre of events – golf before lunch, tennis all afternoon
– and throughout the proceedings conversation where the
mental gymnastics were as impressive as anything seen on the
playing field. Frank Longford was able to sparkle, matching his
host's enthusiasms and his humour. One of Longford's favourite
examples of the Birkenhead wit – and one that he quotes to this
day with a smile of admiration – concerns a clash that took place
in the House of Lords with F. E. on the Woolsack facing the
scorn of his old Unionist ally Sir Edward (now Lord) Carson
following his part in the 1921 treaty which set up the Irish Free
State.

I've never looked this up but I like it the way F. E.
told it. Carson rose and asked, pointing at Birkenhead,
'What are we to think of a man who uses men as a
ladder to climb to fame and then casts them away
from beneath him. Such a man I proscribe from
friendship forever.' Birkenhead sat impassive for a
while. But then he rose to speak and said that Carson's speech 'would have sounded mature on the lips
of a hysterical schoolgirl'. Some mutual friend then
decided to reconcile them and sat them side by side at
dinner. They were getting on well when F. E. turned

to Carson and said, 'Ned, there was just one thing you
said that was hurtful – that I used you as a ladder to
climb to fame and then cast you away from beneath
me.' 'Well, F. E., what was wrong with that?' asked
Carson. And he replied, 'It was so damned true.'[11]

Birkenhead's independent views and outspokenness increasingly led to him being shunned by former colleagues in his last
years – he died in 1930 at the age of fifty-eight. Plagued by
financial worries that threatened to force the sale of Charlton,
he preferred the company and adulation of his children's friends.

'He was a tremendously amusing, funny, glamorous man,'
Longford says now. 'You don't get that sort of outsized character
any more. It was the listening to him that I enjoyed, not so
much his views. And even if he had been trying to influence me
he didn't succeed because soon afterwards I went Labour.'[12]
Birkenhead's physical vigour, his refusal to play the great
statesman with his son's young friends, was in marked contrast
to others of similar stature that Longford met during this period.

Among the other guests at one of Lady Desborough's house
parties (immortalised in Max Beerbohm's *Seven Men*) which
Longford attended while at Oxford was Winston Churchill.

He was out of government, the great man in exile,
and would hold forth on politics over lunch while we
all sat and listened. F. E. wasn't like that. He was out
and about with us. They used to say he taught young
men to drink. We certainly drank a lot but we weren't
drunk all the time.[13]

Birkenhead, the most unlikely in the growing list of hero figures,
substitute fathers, to whom Frank Longford was drawn as a
young man, had little in common with Longford's own reserved,
taciturn, apolitical father.

It is easy to label Longford's friendship with Birkenhead as
essentially social, two witty men enjoying each other's company.
From a party political point of view Longford's time at Charlton
was a minor blip in a slow but inexorable drift from student

days onwards, from Conservative to Labour, from privilege to an overriding concern for the underdog.

But such a perception pigeon-holes both Birkenhead and Longford. While the basic paradox in their friendship cannot be ignored, the long-term political significance in this father–son relationship lay in Birkenhead's willingness to be independent, to go against his party on a point of principle even if it cost him friends and influence. Birkenhead was, in Longford's own description, a romantic Conservative, detached in his thinking, casting a critical eye – and tongue – over the Establishment from its outskirts, a radical who never really wanted to precipitate a revolution, a man with the common touch, able to sympathise with the position of those less fortunate than himself without ever contemplating giving up any of his hard-won privileges to make for a more equal society.

This style of Conservatism, close to but more thoughtful than the philanthropy of his uncle, Arthur Villiers, was a staging post for Longford in the late 1920s and early 1930s on his political journey. And that very quality of being above party that Birkenhead often displayed in his politics – so much more common in Victorian and Edwardian times in men like Joseph Chamberlain and Winston Churchill than now – was one which Frank Longford inherited in his own political career. As a member of both Attlee's and Wilson's governments, he showed himself willing on more than one occasion to put principle before party.

It was a tendency that was encouraged by Lord Waldorf Astor, another of the elder statesmen who took a shine to the youthful Longford in this period. Their friendship had its origins – like so much else in Longford's life at this time – in the Bullingdon. Unperturbed by his equestrian failure on his first visit to Charlton, he and his friend from Eton days, Roger Chetwode, were among the organisers of a Bullingdon point-to-point in the spring of 1928. After a good deal of practising in secret, Longford turned up on the day in his pale mauve jockey's outfit riding a trusty but plodding horse called Bosun. The event was quite a social gathering and guest riders who had been invited to take part included Bill Astor, heir to Cliveden and son of Lord Astor and his formidable wife Nancy.

Siegfried Sassoon captured the atmosphere of the privileged at play in his poem 'What the Captain said at the Point-to-Point'.

> *I've had a good bump round; my little horse*
> *Refused the brook first time,*
> *Then jumped it prime;*
> *And ran out at the double,*
> *But of course*
> *There's always trouble at a double*

Longford did not have to wait to get to the double to get into trouble. Bosun threw him off at the first fence. But his competitive urges, fine-tuned since those days in the Tully Nally nursery, soon had him back in the saddle and chasing the field. Disaster struck at the final fence of the first round.

'I only remember hitting it very hard, breast high it seemed; then oblivion. I awoke to find myself lying on the ground with the horse plucking idly at the fence.' Longford again remounted but, severely concussed and a little confused, set off in the wrong direction and came face-to-face with Bill Astor. 'He was coming at me full tilt and gesticulating, as well he might, like a madman. "That's the way," he shouted, pointing over my shoulder. "That's the way," I retorted, pointing over his and we zigzagged this way and that while he strove to save his victory from what seemed to him my crazy antics. Finally he gave us the slip and I was led away by the spectators.'[14]

Bill Astor had, before this confrontation on the course, invited Longford to dine with his family that evening at Cliveden, Barry's classical palazzo on the Thames at Taplow. His father, owner of the *Observer* and *The Times*, wanted to meet some of the brightest young men of that generation at Oxford. Concussion rendered Longford unable to string a sentence together, much less produce the sort of sparkling repartee for which he was well-known in the university's smart set. Lord Astor plied him with endless questions on every political topic of the day and received only a melancholy series of grunts in return. (Bill Astor much later told his wife Bronwen that Longford's taciturn performance that evening had placed a question mark in his father's mind over his eldest son's judgement and may have cost him the editorship of the *Observer*.)[15]

Despite such an inauspicious start, however, Lord Astor spotted something of interest in his guest and afterwards Longford was to be a regular visitor at Cliveden where his burgeoning reputation for eccentricity only served to inflate his reputation. There was always a stud missing in his collar, a tear in his clothing, the wrong laces in his shoes, or an ill-matched combination of garments held up by a safety pin.

Bill Astor, a contemporary, and his brother David, seven years younger than Longford, became lifelong friends. To David Astor, who was to take over the editorship of the *Observer*, Longford became 'a funny sort of godfather. I was just leaving school and was a very idealistic youth. He encouraged me.'[16]

Although both the Astors and the Birkenheads were new aristocracy in the sense that their titles were recently acquired, the Astors, with their roots in North America, had a longer pedigree in terms of wealth. Cliveden tended to look down on Charlton, while at Charlton the strict teetotal temperance of Cliveden – a result of the Astors' Christian Scientist beliefs – was a subject of mirth. In retrospect Longford is doubtful that anyone else was a habitué of both these rival establishments.[17]

There were, however, common features between the two heads of household that explain their attraction to Longford. Waldorf Astor had been a Conservative MP alongside F. E. Smith from 1910 until he inherited his father's title in 1919 and reluctantly had to stand down from the Commons. (Indeed he tried unsuccessfully to introduce legislation to allow peers to sit in the Commons in a precursor to Longford's own attempts in the 1960s to exchange his seat in the hereditary chamber for one in the elected.)

Waldorf Astor was the antithesis of Smith in his understatement and in his progressive views. While the future Earl of Birkenhead turned his rhetoric on Lloyd George's attempts to introduce the first vestiges of a welfare state in the 'People's

Budget', Astor went against his Conservative colleagues and voted for the measure. Both Astor and Birkenhead had independence of mind and the courage to put their conscience before their party, qualities which had a profound influence on Longford's political development. Longford was later to describe Waldorf Astor as 'a progressive Conservative' adding 'but I find it hard to think of him in terms of party politics for which I do not think he ever had much appetite'.[18]

'Frank and my father were very alike in some ways,' says David Astor, 'in their dedication, their sense of service, their courage in standing up for what they believed to be right in the face of any opposition. I think to some extent Frank modelled himself on my father.'[19]

When Waldorf Astor had to give up his Plymouth Sutton seat in 1919 the new Conservative candidate was Nancy, his wife. Her victory led to her becoming, on 2 December 1919, the first woman to take her seat in the House of Commons. The daughter of a Virginia planter, she was, like Birkenhead, a larger-than-life character with independent views and no qualms about expressing them in colourful language. In the male bastion of the Commons she found 'all the ingenuous shyness of boys at their first dance'.[20] Her debating style so needled Aneurin Bevan that he once remarked while she was speaking: 'It really is intolerable when this old gas-bag gets up and gabbles away.'[21]

At Cliveden, less than an hour from London, Nancy Astor and her husband gathered around them people they found interesting. It would never be just a straightforward 'political' weekend though the leading statesmen of the day were often on the guest list. The Astors were semi-detached from the Conservative Party, outsiders in their North American roots. Neither harboured ambitions for high office. Their guests tended to be judged not on their political credentials but on whether or not they had something to say – a trait designed to appeal to Longford. Thus a typical house party would include the occasional world leader or royalty. Gandhi sat turning his wheel in the drawing room while the future Edward VIII popped in for a round of golf. There would be writers like George Bernard Shaw, whom Longford once heard recite *The Applecart* to the other assembled guests 'nearly falling off his chair with amusement over his own jokes', and Hilaire Belloc.[22] Making up the numbers would be members of the far-flung Astor clan and their friends and various 'lost causes' that Nancy's Christian Scientist missionary spirit prompted her to take in.

Longford was one of her favourite guests, falling into the category of 'extended family'.[23] In the discussions and debates that would often go on into the night at Cliveden among the guests, David Astor recalls that Longford was never in awe of the company or frightened to challenge even the most eminent man or woman if he disagreed with them. 'He and my mother were devoted to each other,' according to Astor. 'He loved that courageous outspoken part of her and she regarded him as a very close relative.'[24] Longford went on to campaign for Lady Astor in Plymouth during the 1929 general election.

By the time of the poll, for all his powerful friends, Longford was at a loose end, his academic career in tatters. His law studies had come to a rather abrupt end after the incident at the point-to-point. A doctor diagnosed a severe case of concussion and recommended prolonged rest and categorically ruled out the prospect of taking the law exam that was looming at the end of the Trinity term in 1928.

He recuperated at his mother's home at North Aston over that summer, spending a good deal of time with the Birkenheads and popping down to Cliveden and London for parties and dinners with Oxford friends. He had no clear idea of what he wanted to do. The prospect of spending another year waiting to resit the law examination did not appeal to him. His Jersey grandmother and his friends in Conservative circles floated the idea of finding him a safe Tory seat. But Longford remained indecisive. He had by now rediscovered his early interest in politics, thanks to spending time in the company of many of the leading political figures of the day. Yet those same people had made him pause to think, sowing enough doubts in his mind to cause him to question whether he could represent the Conservative Party with a clear conscience.

Standing at a crossroads, he was, for the one time in his life, bitten by the travel bug — and even then in a fairly half-hearted fashion. He decided that he needed to learn German so set off for Austria but failed to discover either the joys of being in foreign parts or any hidden talent as a linguist. The sole achievement of this brief sojourn in the autumn of 1928 was getting through three rounds of the Lower Austria Tennis Championships. (Travel has never held any great appeal for him. When challenged on his lack of wanderlust, he replies, 'When people travel they don't always do a lot except just look at things and I'm not keen on just looking at things.'[25] On one occasion he admitted: 'I have never understood the philosophy of taking a holiday.')[26]

Spring of the next year found him following Arthur Villiers into the City and briefly dallying with a career as a stockbroker, a suitable profession for a gentleman and one where Longford hoped that his background in economics might be put to good use. His timing was appalling. Within a few months of him joining Buckmaster and Moore, Wall Street collapsed taking the world markets with it. As well as closing off a career avenue, it cost Longford a large chunk of what capital he had. Inspired by his new job, he had bought shares in Radio Corporation at 109 only to see them slide to just 5.

His one hope of turning this interlude in the City to good effect evaporated when he sought out the rising star of economists, Maynard Keynes, and asked if he could go and work with him at Cambridge. 'I am afraid', said Keynes, 'that I cannot see inside your head. I simply can't tell whether you could be any good to us.'[27] And he turned him down flat.

By October of 1929, Longford's career had once more ground to a halt. He had failed the All Souls exam, dropped his plans to be a lawyer and had a fairly disastrous brush with the City. The country was in little better condition. Labour had been returned as a minority government in the spring of 1929 promising peace, full employment and slum clearances – 'a wonderful, almost miraculous victory', Hugh Gaitskell later recalled.[28] But the stock market crash and ensuing depression threw the government into chaos. At the start of 1930 there were 1.5 million unemployed. By December that figure had almost doubled to 2.5 million. Ramsay MacDonald's attempts to deal with the crisis

71

split his party and in 1931 he and two senior Labour colleagues joined with Conservatives and Liberals to form a National Government with the express intention of saving the pound. He promptly abandoned the gold standard, cut unemployment benefit and went to the country.

The Labour Party saw MacDonald as a traitor to the working class, a tool in the hands of the bankers, and campaigned against him. In the election of 1931 Labour was reduced to a rump of fifty MPs and condemned to opposition until after the Second World War.

The stock market crash and ensuing depression cast its shadow even over the carefree, glamorous world of Oxford. As Elizabeth Longford later wrote:

> The ivory tower of aestheticism could not stand up to
> the buffets of the economic blizzard which began to
> blow in 1929. As my older contemporaries left and the
> younger generation came up, politics began to oust
> poetry. If I had had to take a refresher course to
> qualify for elite male society, it would have been on
> Karl Marx not Oscar Wilde.[29]

For Frank Longford there was no hiding place from the events that were changing the world. Seeing what social costs the slump brought in its wake, he could no longer feel entirely easy with a life of house parties, treading water until he found a Tory seat. On his trips to Hackney Wick, he saw the poverty and unemployment caused by the financial crisis at first hand. His experiences at the Eton Manor Boys Club made him susceptible to a quite unusual offer of work that came in the autumn of 1929. Sandy Lindsay, the Master of Balliol, suggested that he become a lecturer in the Workers' Educational Association in Stoke-on-Trent. From an office in Oxford, run by Stuart Cartwright, young graduates were sent out to spread their learning among those who had not enjoyed their educational privileges but who wanted to tackle such subjects as economics and politics. Gaitskell and Durbin had both joined fellow Oxford socialists as WEA lecturers but it was rare for someone with

Longford's Conservative background to sign up. There was an echo of Durbin's undergraduate challenge 'Have you ever been hungry?' in Longford's decision to take up the post. Still considering a political career and the qualifications necessary to be successful, Longford 'wanted to live under working-class conditions and I was beginning, both psychologically and financially, to desire some modest remuneration for my labours.'[30] The WEA was for many a two-way process, the academic learning of its lecturers exchanged for the worldly wisdom of their pupils.

The influence of Lindsay was significant. He was another of Longford's heroes, but unlike Birkenhead or the Astors he was a committed socialist, the product, he said, of his Christian beliefs. It was a phrase Longford himself was later to employ. Lindsay had been one of Longford's examiners in Modern Greats and had spotted a young man searching for something to believe in. The 'learn-while-you-teach' ethos of the WEA certainly gave his former student something to think about.

In Stoke-on-Trent Longford lectured in economics and politics in the evening and supplemented this by teaching during the day, first in a primary and then a secondary school. He lodged with a local railway foreman and his family in Longdon. Two-up, two-down was a far cry from weekends at Cliveden with its forty-six bedrooms and uniformed domestic staff. As Elizabeth Longford was later to put it: 'Frank was used to extremes of grandeur or informality.'[31] For the first time Longford lived among those at the other end of the social spectrum. On his trips to Hackney Wick it had always been a case of the young aristocrat breezing in from Oxford to play football, having a chat with the chaps and then leaving. Maureen Dufferin, who in the early 1930s used take meals to poor families living in the St Pancras area, recalls the sometimes awkward juxtaposition of such sallies with the social round of cocktail parties and week-ends away with friends.[32]

Longford's time at Hackney Wick may have provided an example of what he was to experience in Stoke-on-Trent but the former paled in significance to the latter. To his pupils, Longford was just another lecturer who thought he knew it all because he had been to Oxford. They, trade unionists and socialists to a man despite the supposedly apolitical status of the WEA, set out at once to relieve him of his pretensions. Ultimately it was their judgement that mattered for, at the end of the year, the class had to say whether or not their lecturer was worth his pay and should be kept on. Longford, contrary to what one might think, recalls finding the lively debate an enjoyable experience. 'I was young and when you're young you don't mind a challenge. You're not set in your ways.'[33] He was not so at ease though that he mentioned his courtesy title – the Honorable Frank Pakenham. It was kept a closely guarded secret.

Despite seeing at first hand the poverty and deprivation brought by the slump and facing the onslaught of his students, Longford, buttressed by occasional weekend breaks with his Conservative friends, still clung to the notion that some sort of synthesis could be made between Toryism and an articulate working class demanding equality, a twentieth-century variation on Disraeli's 'one nation' ideals. But it was a tenuous hope and rested, in Longford's mind, on finding a moral basis for Conservatism. How could he justify a system where his landlords in Longton laboured all the hours God sent for very little while the people he mixed with at weekend parties had every material comfort through inheritance? He found this dichotomy increasingly difficult to stomach. His heart was attracted to the socialist cause. But in his head, dominated as it was then by economics, he could not have faith in the Labour programme of state control and nationalisation to bring prosperity.

From the day Gaitskell and Durbin had first challenged him to justify his inbred Conservatism, he had been struggling. His time living and working in Stoke was another stage in a drift leftwards as 1929 turned into 1930. Indeed he might have completed his journey to Labour much sooner had he not been snatched away from the Potteries by an invitation to join the newly formed Conservative Research Department under Neville Chamberlain.

Based in central London at Old Queen Street, overlooking St James's Park, the Research Department, which was ultimately to grow into Conservative Central Office, was set up to attempt to promote some new economic thinking in a Tory Party that had seen many of its cherished icons destroyed by the 1929 crash. It was a pioneering venture, very much Chamberlain's, without a great deal of support in the rest of the party. When Chamberlain went to the Treasury as part of the Conservative-dominated coalition that took power after the 1931 election, the Research Department was eclipsed.

But for a brief spell in 1930 and 1931 its small team of researchers was buzzing with ideas. Henry Brooke, a future Home Secretary under Harold Macmillan, worked alongside Longford. Both had served as WEA lecturers and both were wrestling with the problem of reconciling Conservatism and its dogmas with the conditions they had witnessed in working-class areas.

Speaking in a House of Lords debate in February 1993, Longford recalled a leader in *The Times* that won particular applause among his colleagues in the Research Department. It characterised the sort of economic wisdom to which Longford subscribed at that time and which held him back from socialism. While he believed in the equality of humankind, his economic training led him to conclude that it was, in practical terms, a Utopian dream. Socialism's economic programme could never achieve the goal that it had set itself. 'The article said that unfortunately wealth is like heat. It is only when it is unequally distributed that it performs what the physicists call work; in other words that is the doctrine of inequality of wealth as against equality of wealth.'[34]

He spent most of his time at the Research Department on Chamberlain's pet scheme – the question of introducing protectionist tariffs on imported goods to bring an end to the depression. It had been the failure of his plans to end free trade that had broken the political career of Neville Chamberlain's father Joseph and the work done at Old Queen Street was the basis for legislation introduced when the director became Chancellor of the Exchequer.

The tariff question to one side, however, Longford was continually frustrated at how little impact such input from the

Research Department had on party policy. The Tory grandees seemed to see Chamberlain's team as little better than administrative assistants. During the 1931 general election, for example, Longford was assigned the mundane task of monitoring Liberal party publications.

However, by the time of that poll events in his personal life had moved at such a pace that the election had to take second place to thoughts of Elizabeth Harman. Longford's social success at Charlton, Cliveden, Clandeboye and the other grand houses where he became a feature on the guest list had launched him into a world of beautiful, aristocratic women. It was from this group that Longford was expected to find a wife. The Birkenhead girls, Eleanor and Pamela Smith, and their friends Zita and 'Baby' Jungmann, were at the epicentre of the bright young people set. Eleanor, a budding romantic novelist, and Baby in particular were shining stars, the latter counting Evelyn Waugh, Lord David Cecil and Longford among her admirers.

In the three-year gap between his first romantic encounter with Elizabeth and their meeting again, Longford stepped out with Baby Jungmann. They had met at the Birkenheads in the spring of 1928. Her father was a Dutch artist whom her mother had left, later marrying one of the Guinness clan. Baby's lack of social credentials did not seem to stop her being much in demand along with Eleanor Smith by some of London's grandest hostesses. Unusually for society belles of the time, Baby had a social conscience and used to join Maureen Dufferin in delivering meals to the needy around St Pancras several days a week.

Longford remembered later that he had thought they would marry though he never even kissed her. Baby was a strict Catholic and was devoted to her difficult mother – known to some of the bright young people as 'Gloomy' and a dab hand at scaring off or intimidating potential suitors, of whom Baby was never short. At the same time as she was enthralling Frank Longford, she was – like the oft-engaged Nina Blount in Waugh's *Vile Bodies* – also fighting off a whole host of other suitors with ambitions to accompany her up the aisle. (She was eventually to marry a Canadian during the war.)

However in June 1930, when Longford was paying a visit to

old friends in Oxford, he had a dream about the girl – quite unlike these society belles – who had kissed him as he slept at New College Ball. The next day he sought her out in her lodgings in Chadlington Road in North Oxford where she was preparing for finals. Elizabeth opened the door and was greeted by Frank Pakenham.

> My first impression was repeated, of an extraordinary pink and white complexion combined with classical curls, Greco-Roman features and a far from classically tailored suit of untidy clothes. A taxi was ticking over at the garden gate. He must have kept it ticking there for at least 20 minutes, a habit I was soon to discover could be extended to last if necessary for an hour.[35]

They agreed to meet the following week. Anxious to make up for lost time, Longford asked his future wife to come and stay at Tully Nally – or Pakenham Hall as it was called then – in August. And never one to do things by halves, he also suggested that she might like to join him before then as one of the tutors at a WEA summer school in Oxford. Faced with this onslaught on her diary, Elizabeth felt 'an overpowering but inexplicable conviction that something unalterable had been mapped for the future'.[36]

Since their first meeting back in the summer of 1927, Elizabeth Harman's social and intellectual success had been on a scale to match Longford's while her looks were every bit as admired as Baby Jungmann's. *Isis*, the university magazine, chose her as one of the first undergraduettes to be honoured as an 'Isis Idol'. Its eulogy described her as 'artistic, beautiful, cultured, decorative, enigmatic, fashionable, even headstrong. If in full womanhood she fulfils the wide promise of her brilliant maidenhood then she will take her place in the honoured band of female worthies.' Elizabeth Harman came of family where women were not used to confining their attention to keeping house, looking attractive and having children (though she was to excel at all three). Her mother had been one of the first women to train as a doctor and her grandmother had been one of the first of her sex to go on to higher education. Quite unlike Longford's sisters whose education had been confined to a succession of governesses or the society belles whose principal concern was marrying well, Elizabeth Harman stood outside her future husband's orbit.

During the first three or four decades of their existence, the women's colleges of Oxford were a blue-stocking world, full of earnest young women reading English or Modern Languages and scarcely disturbing the male bastion of the University. The girls who attended Commem. balls were just as likely to have travelled up from London as they were to have come from Lady Margaret Hall or St Hilda's. As her mother and grandmother had done before her, Elizabeth Harman was a pioneer in breaking down barriers but managed it with such wit and charm that she was a welcome invader in a male world. Her tutors and her friends in the Bowra circle had assumed she would get a first. When she just missed one, she was comforted by receiving over forty-eight letters of condolence.

Though her degree had been in classics (she abandoned the more traditionally female English after a year), Longford decided that his new recruit should teach economics at the WEA summer school. Over a lunch with Evan Durbin, by now a tutor at the London School of Economics, Longford tried to cram her with enough information to enable her to get by. In the end Elizabeth spent the week with a North Staffordshire school-teacher, trying to unravel Rousseau's *Social Contract* and its implications for the Potteries.

The WEA gave Elizabeth a new perspective. Though her family background was political – her mother's uncle was Joseph Chamberlain – she had shown little interest in such matters when at Oxford. Betjeman's silver age of the aesthetes had become rather tarnished by the time Elizabeth Harman took her finals in the summer of 1930 but her university circle remained largely self-consciously literary, introspective and slow to come to terms with economic forces that were shaking the world outside. Attending the WEA summer school at Balliol College were out-of-work coal miners from North Staffordshire, men and women passionately seeking the education she had taken for granted, but at the same time politically conscious and often sardonic. She did not approach the WEA with any of the political baggage of her future husband. She knew little of economics and therefore shared few of his reservations about social parity on that front. She was quick to realise that she could not remain indifferent to what she saw and heard. Education seemed the key to emancipating the working classes and achieving social equality. So she decided to become a full-time WEA tutor but first was persuaded by Evan Durbin to get some economic qualifications herself by attending the LSE.

Before that, however, there was the trip to Ireland. Mary Longford had no patience at all with her second son's attempts to bring friends home to North Aston Hall. Where they found him amusing and entertaining, she was merely irritated. Fortunately for Frank Longford, however, his brother Edward was more accommodating with Tully Nally. Edward Longford had come into his inheritance in 1923 and he and his wife Christine, whom he met while an undergraduate at Oxford, set about putting their stamp on the family seat. They went for an Oriental feel, painting the entrance hall flaming red and littering the rooms with Japanese and Chinese vases.

The rest of their fortune they sank into the theatre. That summer of 1930 Edward Longford had just become chairman of the Gate in Dublin, where various of his translations of Greek classics and his own works like *Yahoo*, based on the life of Dean Swift, were performed. The Gate became an obsession with the childless couple over the next thirty years and a financial burden that ate away at the Longford fortune.

To Elizabeth Harman, however, her hosts were captivating.

> The uncontested king and queen of this fairyland
> were Edward and Christine Longford, though Edward
> was more like a gigantic Tweedledum than Oberon,
> while Christine's clever face and curious constricted
> gestures could have been found at any donnish high
> table rather than on Titania's throne.[37]

79

Edward had already fallen prey to a gargantuan appetite which saw him balloon to thirty stone and accelerated his death.

Other guests included Frank Longford's friend from undergraduate days, John Betjeman, and Evelyn Waugh whom he had got to know well through the author's friendship with his oldest sister Pansy. Several of the Pakenham sisters were also there. Pansy had caused something of a stir by marrying the divorced artist Henry Lamb two years earlier. Violet was eighteen and Julia still a schoolgirl.

Betjeman arrived before the other guests. His hosts were not quite sure who or what to expect. With a disregard for detail that used to drive his mother mad, Frank Longford had sent a note warning of Betjeman's plans but his handwriting, erratic and illegible, had defeated Edward and Christine.

Even when he arrived, Frank Longford left his guests in the capable hands of his brother while he hurried off to the Cavan Tennis Tournament for his daily dose of 'ekker' (as he used to call exercise). When they were not exploring Tully Nally and its grounds, Edward would try and share his love of Ireland by piling his visitors into his car and taking them on a tour of local Celtic ruins. An alternative was to play republican songs on the gramophone – or better still to sing them. Edward's fervent belief in Ireland's nationhood had not been dimmed by years.

However, there was no sharp political edge to discussions. The atmosphere was decidedly relaxed. 'I have seen at Pakenham what I have seen nowhere else,' Waugh later wrote, 'an entirely sober host literally rolling about the carpet with merriment.'[38]

The guests hit it off well. Betjeman and Waugh were to return several times to stay with Edward and Christine Longford. Betjeman shared Edward's High Church Anglicanism – the pair would indulge in bouts of hymn-singing after dinner – while he described his wife, on the publication of her novel *Making Conversation* in 1931, as 'the funniest woman I ever knew'.

Elizabeth Harman was a hit with everybody – except Evelyn Waugh who told mutual friends for years to come that Frank Longford had married beneath himself. He used to annoy Elizabeth by always greeting her with 'How's hockey?' as if she was a hearty schoolgirl.

In that summer of 1930 Waugh's first marriage to Pansy's friend Evelyn Gardiner had broken up and he was in a dark mood throughout the holiday. Occasionally it lifted to reveal his mischievous side as on the last night when after dinner, as the guests trooped upstairs to bed, he seized Elizabeth's arm. 'Go after Frank,' he whispered. 'Go up with him. Follow him. Go on.' Taking his advice, Elizabeth sprinted up the staircase and joined her future husband in his bedroom.

> There was a double bed but I didn't get into it, just sat
> on the edge, while we conducted an ardent but chaste
> and anxious conversation about ourselves far into the
> night. I can remember only one of the nice things he
> said: 'Why doesn't your face fall to pieces at night like
> other people's?'[39]

Frank Longford was smitten and the romance of Tully Nally had worked its spell on Elizabeth. On their return to London – he at the Conservative Research Department and she at the LSE – they saw each other a great deal. While economics did not prove nearly so interesting as Elizabeth had hoped (she abandoned her course after a year), the couple were travelling up to the Potteries each week on WEA work. Longford had continued to give economics lectures and his new belle was to teach literature. They managed to schedule their classes at the same time so they could catch the last train back to London together.

Longford soon found that his protégé was fast being swept past him in political development. He had introduced Elizabeth to the WEA but it was she, previously unconcerned about politics, who took her experiences in Stoke to heart and head. While he was able to feel the attraction of socialism when confronted with the poverty of working-class life in the depression-ridden 1930s but could not convince himself as an economist that Labour would actually make conditions any better, Elizabeth's reaction was an emotional and instant one. Encouraged by her old friend Hugh Gaitskell, now a rising star in the Labour Party and soon to be adopted as a parliamentary candidate at Chatham, and inspired by her pupils, she visited their workplaces, went down a mine, accompanied a district nurse on her rounds. It was the most natural thing for her to do to begin attending the local Labour Party meetings. For a while there was talk of her standing in the 1931 election for the local constituency of Stone.

If their reactions to Stoke were beginning to drive a wedge between the couple, the late-night train journey back to London allowed them some time on their own to put such worries to one side. While neither had any great experience of physical intimacy with the opposite sex, it was Longford whose inhibition began to make Elizabeth doubt his professions of love. Although sex before marriage was still something that well-brought-up young women would not even contemplate, Longford's emotional repression was such that he found it very hard even to kiss the woman he said he loved. It took Elizabeth a good few weeks to melt away his shyness.

> Our usual routine was to pass the time waiting for the train in the lounge of the North Stafford Hotel after the station waiting room had closed for the night. On 21 November the night outside seemed as cold as Ilkley Moor 'baht' at'. But we were snugly inside the North Staffs lounge, sitting on one of the velour settees clasped in each other's arms. Suddenly the hotel manager arrived to put out the lights. 'Here you can't do that there, not in my hotel you can't.' Driven out on to the windy platform like Adam and Eve, but conscious of a glow rather than a guilt, we were still warm enough when the train came in to continue our conversation. Frank showed himself 'capable of endearments', contrary to his own analysis, and at 2.15 a.m. proposed that we should get married.[40]

Elizabeth accepted and soon afterwards Longford went to her father's consulting rooms in Harley Street to ask for her hand. All did not go according to plan but through no fault of the prospective bride's father. Longford was struck down by indecision.

Elizabeth was at first puzzled, suggesting he seek medical treatment, and then began to despair. Slowly her future husband managed to unburden himself to her and out came all the anxieties and unhappinesses that he had stored up from boyhood – that he was unlovable, unworthy of affection, that as a second son he would not be able to support her or any children. Subconsciously he had made a decision – like many younger sons of aristocratic families at that time – that if he did marry it would have to be when he was older and had carved out a career in the City or politics and with it an income for himself. His ancestor Katharine Pakenham had turned down the proposal of the future Duke of Wellington on the grounds that he was a poor second son of an Anglo-Irish aristocratic family (their castle was at Trim, close to Tully Nally). It was only when he had proved himself in India and earned the rank of major-general that she consented to marry him.

If Longford had subconsciously intended to put off marriage until he had established himself (or at least until Great Aunt Caroline died and he became the master of Bernhurst), then Elizabeth had thrown such plans into chaos. Temporarily he was paralysed emotionally. On 5 December 1930, the occasion of his twenty-fifth birthday and a couple of weeks after the débâcle at Harley Street, he wrote to her of his fears and confusion. He ended his letter: 'What a way to write. As though a false step would be fatal and a step in any direction likely to be a false one.' By Christmas things were not much better. On the card he attached to her present – a pearl bar brooch – he wrote: 'Elizabeth from Frank. Love, kisses and tears.'[41]

Already, however, the pattern of their relationship was being established. It was Elizabeth who was the strong one, who patiently sat out this crisis, postponed the wedding, quelled his fears, unravelled his tangled emotions. Her love was enough, she convinced him, to make up for all that he felt he had been denied in the past.

After Christmas they paid a return visit to Tully Nally – again with Betjeman – and this seemed to raise Longford's spirits. Between them the couple began to deal with the barriers to their marriage. From a practical point of view both had a private income of around £300 each year. Longford earned £500 with the Conservatives and another £100 with the WEA. Elizabeth was getting £85 from the same source. They decided that £1000 would see them through if they were careful.

Time too allowed Longford to cast off his fears of commitment, of being unworthy. Elizabeth's love healed the wounds that past deprivation had left. The one obstacle left between them lay in their political differences. Elizabeth's growing commitment to Stoke and the community in which she was spending more and more time sparked off a lively debate between them over economic policy, currently top of Longford's agenda at the Conservative Research Department. 'Frank and I did not see eye to eye on the causes of the slump,' recalls Elizabeth. 'Their word was "over-production", ours in Stoke was "under-consumption". That put the difference in a nutshell. But it did not get us any nearer to solving the country's problems or our own problem either.'[42]

While Elizabeth was being courted as possible Labour candidate in the 1931 election for Stoke, Longford was still considering whether he should yield to pressure from friends and family and stand for the Tories, despite his dwindling faith in their policies. His continued attendance at the parties of the grand and good strained Elizabeth's patience. 'I learned to speak their language – "pith" for everything good and nice, "path" for everything nasty.'[43]

Such terms did not figure in the political arguments they conducted by letter from positions that were as far apart geographically – London and Stoke – as they were politically. The gap between Elizabeth's faith in democracy and equality of all and Longford's agonised and dwindling trust in the sort of paternal philanthropy characterised by his uncle Arthur Villiers came through in his defence of the principle of rulers and ruled.

> You seem to me [he wrote] not to realise the import-
> ance of rule in life. I look upon it as a fortunate
> accident that men living in society require co-ordina-
> tion . . . correction and guidance. The accident is for-
> tunate in that it gives the opportunity for rulers to

arise. If all men were perfect, it would be very difficult
for the 'men born to be kings', even minor kings, to
serve a useful purpose and their special talents to be
lost to the world.[44]

When the logic of Elizabeth's arguments touched a nerve, he
would lapse into a rather romantic notion about how the couple
would divide their life into separate but complimentary spheres.
In exchange for a free hand in literature and painting, Elizabeth
would give up her political notions:

> What you don't realise is that I know a great deal
> about politics. My views may be terribly dull and even
> inconsistent, but if one treated English politics in its
> widest aspects as a technical subject, I have the wide
> knowledge that one would expect of an experienced,
> if stupid, technician.[45]

This mixture of self-deprecation and pulling rank did not cut
much ice with a woman who had deliberately turned her back
on 'female' subjects while at Oxford. Neither was invoking a
spirit of pragmatism much of an answer to the strong emotions
prompted by the privations suffered by the people of Stoke.

On 8 March a truce was temporarily called. Longford went
down with bronchial pneumonia and pleurisy. In his youth,
despite an obsession with physical fitness, he was prone to
nervous exhaustion. His mother – true to form – refused to let
him convalesce at her new home, Peverel Court, near Ayles-
bury, so instead Elizabeth rushed to his bedside to read and mop
his brow until 20 March when Mary Longford finally relented
and took him in.

Longford's slow recovery took the steam out of their political
differences and left a little space for romance. In June they went
to Oxford to attend the Balliol Commem. Ball and, in that same
world where first they had caught sight of each other, they
announced their engagement. And, in an attempt to reproduce
those original circumstances as accurately as possible, by midnight Longford was dead to the world. Feeling that she could

not abandon her fiancé on such a night, Elizabeth found them an empty bed in one of the students' rooms where they both fell asleep at once, virtue intact. Nancy Astor's quip to Longford on hearing of the engagement, 'It's only her body you want', was as yet wide of the mark.

The wedding date was set for 27 October but it had to be put off for a week because it clashed with the 1931 general election. Longford took leave of absence from his job to campaign for Lady Astor in Plymouth. Elizabeth spoke in King's Norton in Birmingham alongside Hugh Gaitskell in support of the Labour candidate, Dick Mitchison, husband of her friend the novelist Naomi Mitchison. He was defeated – as were all but fifty Labour candidates.

But such disappointments were put behind them the following week. The wedding on 3 November was a grand affair. Elizabeth wore cream satin with a wreath of orange blossom and was attended by twelve bridesmaids. Longford had chosen Freddy Birkenhead (who had succeeded to the title on his father's death the previous year) as his best man. The church was St Margaret's, Westminster, next door to Westminster Abbey – scene earlier that year of Basil Dufferin's marriage to Maureen Guinness. Displaying that eccentric charm that was fast becoming a part of his character, Longford arrived at the Abbey by mistake. He was a little despondent to find that there were no guests. Birkenhead tried to console him. 'People don't go to weddings nowadays.' Finally they realised their mistake.

After a reception at the Grosvenor, the newly-weds set off for their honeymoon in the land that always inspired Longford to romance, Ireland.

Four

The Irish socialist

We are souls in hell; who hear no gradual music
Advancing on the air, on wave-lengths walking.
We are lost in life; who listen for hope and hear but
The tyrant and the politician talking

Out of the nothingness of night they tell
Our need of guns, our servitude to strife.
O heaven of music, absolve us from this hell
Unto unmechanised mastery over life

Siegfried Sassoon 'A Prayer from 1936'

According to Quentin Bell the thirties was a decade of 'mounting despair . . . unable to shake the complacency of a torpid nation, we saw the champions of war, tyranny and racial persecution winning . . . it was bloody to be alive and to be young was very hell'.[1]

As economic recession fast became depression and unemployment soared, the mainstream political parties struggled to come up with a response. Their inability to provide answers gave rise to radical alternatives with ready solutions to grip the popular imagination. Most notorious was Oswald Mosley, a Labour Cabinet minister in the 1929 government, who set up his New Party of black-shirted fascists in 1931 and stormed up and down the country preaching an anti-semitic, anti-establishment gospel that dwelt on the shining example of Hitler's Germany.

By the time of his marriage to Elizabeth in 1931, Longford's faith in the Conservatism that had hitherto been second nature to him had been shattered. The onset of mass unemployment and industrial and financial collapse had a profound personal impact on him through his observations at Hackney Wick boys' club and with the WEA in Stoke. The radical ideas that Hugh

Gaitskell and Evan Durbin had sown in Longford at Oxford were further developed by his contact with the independent spirit of F. E. Smith and the Astors. Yet finding it increasingly difficult to make a moral case for Conservatism in regard of its social policies, Longford remained attached to that favourite Research Department economic notion of wealth as heat, working efficiently only when it is unevenly distributed.

In the immediate aftermath of their wedding, Longford continued to work – albeit with ebbing enthusiasm and growing doubts – at the Conservative Research Department. Its already tenuous status within the party had been further reduced by the departure of its founder Neville Chamberlain to become Chancellor of the Exchequer after the 1931 Conservative election victory. It was on account of the increased burden of work that came with this new post that Chamberlain, Elizabeth's first cousin, declined his invitation to the Longfords' wedding. His wife attended and their daughter, Dorothy, was one of the bridesmaids but the future Prime Minister stayed rooted behind his desk and added insult to injury by insisting that the staff of the Research Department skip the wedding reception and return to work after the church service. Longford graciously accepted his apologies but Elizabeth subsequently suggested that Cousin Neville had heard the rumour that 'young Pakenham' was flirting with socialism and therefore 'thought it best not to embroil himself too deeply with a man of such curious fancies'.[2] Longford had made public his doubts about Conservatism in discussions with friends and fellow guests at various parties and news of his restlessness, given his background, his social connections and his current employment, had clearly travelled fast.

Longford struggled on in the leaderless Research Department until the spring of 1932 when he resigned. It was to be the end of his formal attachment to Conservatism. Those last few months did, however, give him a breathing space to adjust to married life.

The honeymoon had got off to a rough start. The Irish Sea did not afford a placid welcome to the newly-weds and the couple's journey over to the west coast of Ireland had to be broken at an empty and cold Tully Nally. 'Nor was sex the elixir and panacea it was to become,' Elizabeth recalled, 'despite the fact that Dr Helena Wright – a world famous gynaecologist who lived well into her nineties – had prepared both Frank and me for our first experience.'[3] Things began to look up, however, when they finally arrived in Connemara where they stayed at the Renvyle Hotel, run by the Irish wit Oliver St John Gogarty, the model for Buck Mulligan in James Joyce's *Ulysses*.[4] The trip was rounded off by a few days with Longford's decidedly eccentric uncle, Lord Dunsany, who dabbled in writing, painting and modelling at his castle in County Meath.[5]

Back in England, the newly-weds made their home in the village of Stone in Buckinghamshire, in an outsized cottage that was a gift from Longford's mother. Originally two workers' cottages, it had been knocked into one but still retained both its original staircases and was, for that reason, christened Stairways. It was part of the Peverel estate to which Mary Longford had moved after leaving North Aston Hall in 1929. Physical proximity managed to effect something of a reconciliation between mother and son in the short time before Mary Longford's premature death in 1933. She got on well with Elizabeth, giving her advice on the cottage garden and even breaking into a smile when her daughter-in-law announced that she planned to plant 'Cotton Easters'. Longford, sure of Elizabeth's love after labouring for so long and so unsuccessfully to win his mother's affection, was now able to relax more in her company. No longer was he so anxious to win her endorsement, to catch her eye. He grew to admire her quiet courage in battling with the crippling arthritis that was to precipitate her demise. Mary Longford, often unable to take more than a few steps at a time, used to keep an eye on her estate by circling it in her Baby Austin. When she died, he wept. He had loved her.

During the week, when they were in London, the couple rented a one-room flat on the Embankment but it was at Stairways, at weekends, that they would welcome their friends and repay past hospitality. The style was modest in comparison to Cliveden, Clandeboye and Charlton – though they did employ a married couple to cook, clean and drive the car since neither Longford nor his wife then possessed a licence. There was a constant procession of guests who squeezed into Stairways four at a time. One of the first was Lady Birkenhead who described the cottage as 'very comfortable'. Others were less flattering. Arthur Villiers, Longford's philanthropic uncle, compared it to a battered HQ behind the lines in war-torn Flanders. Among other names in the visitors' book were Esmond Warner, an old Eton colleague who shared Longford's passion for sport and helped him discover the local golf clubs; John Betjeman, for whom the newly-weds undertook some ultimately successful match-making with Penelope Chetwode, sister of Roger who had got Longford into the Bullingdon; Naomi Mitchison, the novelist; Evan Durbin and Hugh Gaitskell. Longford's two youngest sisters were also regular visitors. Violet in particular struck up a friendship with Elizabeth and the two were close in those early years of the Longford marriage. In 1934 Violet married Longford's Eton contemporary the novelist Anthony Powell – they had been introduced by Elizabeth. Violet herself wrote two volumes of autobiography – *Five Out of Six* and *Within the Family Circle* – and a life of her maternal grandmother Lady Jersey, among other books.

Neither his own humble abode nor marriage to a self-avowed and unrepentant socialist appeared to diminish Frank Longford's élan as a weekend guest at the various great houses where he had earned a reputation as a rising Conservative political star, though occasionally some people made little asides. When Elizabeth was photographed outside Buckingham Palace, complying with her mother-in-law's wishes to present herself at court after marriage, the cutting was captioned by Arthur Villiers 'socialette at play'.

At Hatfield, home of the Tory grandees Lord and Lady Salisbury, parents of Lord David Cecil, Stanley Baldwin, three times Prime Minister and the most influential politician of the period, requested Longford's company on a Sunday afternoon constitutional. It was tantamount to a summons but once striding across the great park the young man could not think of any pearls of wisdom with which to impress Baldwin. He fell back on talking about the Workers Educational Association and the poverty he had seen in the Potteries, hardly a subject designed to impress and win preferment. (Longford was later to wonder whether the initiative for the walk came from Baldwin or from Lady Salisbury, anxious to find her young guest a place within the Conservative Party.)

Despite the imminent arrival of their first child, the summer of 1932 found Frank Longford once again drifting without any particular career direction. He dabbled briefly in journalism, but showed little of the talent that was later in the decade to make his sister Mary – by then married to Meysey Clive – a star turn in Beaverbrook's *Evening Standard*. Longford was taken on as a stand-in for Peter Fleming as literary editor at the *Spectator*, then as now known for its pro-Conservative sympathies. Fleming, who had his eye on the editorship and therefore saw Longford as a potential long-term custodian of the books pages, went off on a holiday to the Amazon. He had, however, made little allowance in his calculations for Longford's lack of interest in books, which had first become apparent when his mother had to bribe him as a child to read various classics. And the incumbent editor, Wilson Harris, had other ideas for their new recruit, including the ill-fated assignment at Eton.

As a result by the time Fleming returned from his voyage of discovery, Longford had moved on to pastures fresh at the *Daily Mail* as a leader writer. Again his Conservative pedigree appealed to his new employers. Yet he was soon to find himself a fish out of water. This son of Ireland was greeted on his first day by H. W. Wilson who had been the paper's sole leader writer for a good many years and whose tactlessness can perhaps be explained by the fact that he would have viewed the interloper with some suspicion. 'I am glad to have you to help us. You will find our policy easy enough to understand. I regard the Germans as the cruellest people in the world, except the Chinese – and of course the Irish.'[6]

Such prejudices were not, Longford was soon to discover when he attempted to dispel them, open to debate. But it was not only ideological clashes that blighted his journalistic career. His illegible handwriting and his inability to type did not help much. And Wilson set him to writing the 'leaderettes' at the bottom of the main editorials, the bit of froth that came as an afterthought to the paper's principal daily statement of opinion. Many of Longford's contributions landed on the spike. The man who had inherited his father's disregard for clothes and personal appearance did, however, become something of an expert on fashion. 'The hobble is here again,' began his eulogy to the vogue for tight-fitting narrow skirts. Another leaderette, starting with the arresting thought 'Woman this year is to be very demure, very modest and very plain Jane', caught the eye of the *Mail*'s proprietor, Esmond Harmsworth, who invited the Longfords to stay with him for the weekend as a reward.

Antonia was born on 27 August 1932, ten months after the Longfords' wedding. The father – uncommonly for the time – was present at the bedside throughout a long labour which was not helped by the fact that London was in the midst of a heatwave. (It was not an experience he particularly enjoyed: 'I didn't want to see any more babies born after that. I was always in the house when the others were born – except for Michael when I had to be away – but I didn't watch them being born.')[7]

Longford's sister Mary was the first visitor to the nursery and temporarily named the baby Gandhi – she was suffering from a mild dose of jaundice. In the end the couple decided on Antonia after Willa Cather's novel, *My Antonia*. Maureen Dufferin and Lady Birkenhead, F. E.'s widow, were among her godparents.

Longford did not instantly take to fatherhood. A decade later when his third daughter Rachel was born, he wrote to Elizabeth – he was away in London at the time – to announce a new-found interest in babies. He ascribed this change of heart to a variety of reasons. 'Partly perhaps because I am fundamentally much more interested in children of all ages than I was – no doubt through having studied and loved ours. When Antonia was a baby, I was hardly interested in children at all, but that is quite changed now.'[8] The truth of that admission can be judged by the occasion when Longford went to collect Antonia, then aged fifteen months, from a children's party at the Dufferins. Catching sight of a little mass of curls and frills among the other guests, he turned to Maureen Dufferin and remarked, 'That's a jolly little child.' 'Yes, it's your daughter,' the hostess replied.[9]

Longford would be the first to admit that he found fatherhood a difficult role. 'I would say that I was an alpha beta/beta alpha father. I would play games with the children and unlike many fathers I came home most nights – except when I was in London during the war.' But, like many of his generation, he tended to leave the task of child-rearing to his wife. He still finds the idea of a man pushing a pram ludicrous and never had anything to do with nappy-changing and the like. 'I wasn't trusted to do that.'[10]

Fatherhood did, however, increase the burden on him to 'settle down' as the family's main breadwinner. The careful financial calculations made at the time of their marriage had not allowed much for bringing up children and it was only a matter of months after Antonia's birth that Elizabeth found herself pregnant again, though 'found' is too passive a word in Elizabeth's case. Despite her husband's slow adaptation to the role of father and the couple's financial limitations, Elizabeth enjoyed having children enormously. Within months of one birth, she would experience what she has called 'the baby-itch'. Even the rigours of childbirth did not put her off and in the 1940s she was to sacrifice a hugely promising political career to continue expanding her family.

The anti-Irish sentiments Longford had met at the *Daily Mail* coincided with a growing political interest in his homeland. Previously his ties with Ireland had been romantic and emotional. However, events in Dublin began to concentrate his mind on more practical questions. After the rebellion and civil disorder that followed the First World War and British mishandling of the aftermath of the Easter Rising, a peace treaty had been agreed between Lloyd George and the Irish leaders Arthur Griffith and Michael Collins in 1921, partitioning off the north east corner of Ulster which remained part of the United Kingdom and giving the rest of Ireland semi-independent dominion status under the Imperial crown. The Irish Free State was to run its own affairs but was still bound to the British in matters of defence and foreign policy.

The treaty split Ireland. The pro faction – led by Griffith and Collins – and the anti forces – headed by the charismatic figure of Eamon de Valera – fought out a bloody civil war. The majority of the population was in favour of the treaty, for all its shortcomings, and the pro forces triumphed with William Cosgrave ruling the Free State for a decade (Collins had been murdered in the civil war and Griffith died in 1922 a broken man). In February 1932, however, de Valera, the sole survivor of the leaders of the 1916 rising and the leading opponent of the treaty, defeated Cosgrave at the polls and ushered in a period of renewed Irish republicanism and consequent tension between Dublin and the Imperial capital.

Longford was attracted by the character of de Valera, the single-minded patriot whom he saw as being prepared to put principles before party. It was another case of hero-worship, another larger-than-life man of independent spirit in the mould of F. E. Smith winning Longford's unquestioning admiration. Again de Valera was an unlikely choice, both because of the extremes of his views and the contrast between his character and that of Longford. As Thomas Pakenham puts it:

> De Valera was a puritan – more puritanical even than
> my father. He was also a violent Irish nationalist –
> more fanatical than my father. In fact many of de
> Valera's qualities were the very reverse of what was
> considered Irish. He wasn't good company. He didn't
> like conversation. He didn't like discussing things with
> people. He was a very alien figure to my father who
> had always loved discussing things. He loves talking.[11]

This hero-worship – which was to endure throughout de Valera's long life until his death in 1975 – was all the more unlikely because the Irish leader was almost universally condemned in Britain in the early 1930s as the man who had precipitated a civil war and betrayed Collins, Griffith, the 1921 agreement and all hopes of peace and co-existence.

Showing an early attraction for those society vilifies that was later to be much more prevalent, Longford managed, through friends in Dublin, to arrange to meet de Valera in the spring of 1932. 'I fell an instant victim to his charm and the more I studied it, as I began to do with real earnestness, to his case.'[12]

Not long after this meeting, Longford was roped in as a speaker at Chatham House on Ireland – after the invited guest dropped out at the last minute. John Betjeman was later to paint an idealised picture of the scene. 'Obviously this was no practised or accomplished speaker, but as he went on the strange, hurried young man began to make an impression.'[13] The truth was somewhat harsher. Longford wore his pro-Ireland sympathies on his sleeve to the annoyance of many of the audience who were backing the British government in its tough stance against de Valera. 'You can tell the Irish farmer doesn't know which side his bread is buttered,' one heckler in the audience called out.

Frank Pakenham was developing a reputation for his iconoclastic views on Ireland among his friends in the British Establishment. Hitherto they had been aware that he had a family home in Ireland but beyond that had not taken such roots very seriously. And, despite the occasional flourish at Eton and Oxford, Longford could scarcely claim to have made much play of being Irish. He had left that to his brother and indeed when he discovered early in life, principally through the example of Edward, that Tully Nally and his Anglo-Irish blood set him apart from others in the English aristocratic circles in which he mixed, he had down-played them.

Yet after 1932 all that was different. Ireland, hitherto rather a remote ideal for Longford, the place that he associated with his dead father and his noble ancestors, began to figure large in his life, though he freely admits that the initial attraction was neither practical nor academic.

> Irish nationalism had begun to stir me emotionally, but it was all on an imaginative, almost poetic plane. Yeats' poems and autobiographies jostled for pride of place with Roger Casement's speech from the dock. 'Loyalty is a sentiment not a law. It rests on love not restraint.' It was all a far cry from my future career in British politics.[14]

Yet a crucial step in Longford's career was made in Ireland.

Given that he had a wife and child to support – with another baby on the way – following up a romantic attachment to Irish nationalism may not seem, with hindsight, to have been the most practical course for Longford. But he had not shown any great inclination towards standard career choices thus far in his life. He had been something of a dilettante, dabbling in different areas.

However, fortune intervened in the spring of 1932 to give him a helping hand and quell his restlessness. He was snatched away from writing about fashion on the *Daily Mail* by the offer of a part-time lectureship at the London School of Economics – teaching alongside Evan Durbin and under the directorship of Sir William Beveridge. It was the first step on the ladder of academia. In the autumn he was appointed to a lectureship in politics at Christ Church, his brother's old college and scene of his famous ducking.

The academic world, which was to occupy Longford sporadically until the mid-1950s, gave him the impetus and the time to pursue his growing interest in Ireland. Chance again played a part when, staying with friends in Ireland, he was presented with a unique set of papers dealing with the 1921 treaty. He and Elizabeth were guests at the home of Robert Barton at Glendalough House, close to one of Ireland's best-known Christian shrines in the wilds of the Wicklow Mountains. Barton, like Longford, was a product of the Ascendancy with an Irish father and English mother. He had served under Collins and Griffith in the Irish delegation at the London peace conference in 1921. Until the last moment he had been torn between Collins' pragmatic acceptance that the terms Lloyd George had put on the table were the best on offer and de Valera's insistence, back in Dublin, that Ireland had to achieve a greater measure of independence than the halfway house of dominion status under the British Crown. Barton had in fact signed the treaty but later repudiated his action and sided with de Valera.

Barton was the first cousin of another Anglo-Irish member of the Collins delegation, Erskine Childers, author of *The Riddle of the Sands*. Childers had opposed the treaty all along and had been seized at Glendalough House in 1922 and hauled off on a trumped up charge of possessing an illegal firearm to face a Free

State firing squad. (Ironically the gun had been given to him by Michael Collins.) Childers' American widow, Mollie, continued to live with the Bartons.

Barton took to Longford, recognising in the young man's background elements of his own upbringing. As Anglo-Irish men Barton and Longford had a foot in both camps regarding the 1921 negotiations. Through his pro-treaty brother, Longford had ready access to the leading lights among the Free Staters, notably Desmond Fitzgerald, father of the 1980s Taoiseach, Garret Fitzgerald. Yet he had also developed a profound admiration for de Valera.

Barton was equally impressed by Longford's connections with many of the principal players on the Imperial side in the 1921 negotiations. Austen Chamberlain, a relation of Elizabeth's, and F. E. Smith had worked alongside Lloyd George. On the stairwell at Charlton hung a portrait of Collins whom Birkenhead had grown to admire. Winston Churchill, whom Longford was to visit at Chartwell in the mid-1930s, was also on the British team.

And so Barton entrusted to a young man with no track record as a writer or a historian and, in truth, fairly flimsy credentials as an Irish patriot, his papers from 1921 covering that crucial period of negotiation between 11 October and 6 December when the fateful deal was signed. 'I have been exceptionally fortunate in my material,' Longford acknowledged, with a heavy dose of understatement, in the preface to the 1935 edition. Barton was confident that Longford would write a book that was fair to both sides in the negotiations and to both factions on the Irish side – in so far as that was possible about an event that continues to mark the division between Ireland's two political parties to this day.

Barton was not to be disappointed. *Peace by Ordeal*, published in 1935, was widely acclaimed and remains the standard – in fact the only – book on that crucial turning-point in Anglo-Irish relations, a towering achievement for one so young and inexperienced as a writer. It has been reprinted four times, most recently in 1992, and has never been surpassed. Those looking for some of the historical and political roots of the current troubles in the north of Ireland will find them cogently outlined in *Peace by Ordeal*.

The historical background as to how part of Ulster came to be detached from the rest of Ireland is told in impartial detail from the dawn of the Home Rule movement through to the implementation of the 1921 treaty. The hope – indeed the assumption by some of the participants in the negotiations – that setting up separate Parliaments in Belfast and Dublin under the Imperial Crown would enable Ireland to remain in effect as one played an important part in the background to the treaty.

Longford shows how in the heat of the moment, with the threat of civil war throughout Ireland, the concessions made to the Ulster Protestants were seen as a way of ensuring peace. In retrospect, they paved the way for the current guerrilla war in the north. Writing in 1935, Longford himself in the text of *Peace by Ordeal* seems confident of an eventual coming together of the whole of Ireland. Reflecting on the experience of northern Protestants since the 1921 treaty Longford – then a southern Protestant – praises the Dublin government for 'the justice it has provided for minorities' and expresses his hope, while acknowledging the bitterness felt in the north, that de Valera's policy of non-coercion of the Orangemen might one day heal the divide.

By studying the background to the treaty, Longford became an Irish republican, convinced that the island should be one independent country, that that was in fact the ultimate aim of the participants. It is a stance that he has maintained in all his many subsequent dealings with Ireland and one which continues to make him an unpopular figure among northern Loyalists.

Peace by Ordeal was undoubtedly Longford's most successful and most acclaimed book. At the time of publication it added great weight to his academic reputation. Michael Foot, who was a student at Wadham in the mid-1930s and President of the Oxford Union, today recalls that it was when he read *Peace by Ordeal* that he became aware of Frank Pakenham as one of the leading lights among the university teaching staff.[15]

Foot also credits Longford with challenging the widespread

British prejudice against de Valera. 'Frank and his book certainly influenced my opinion on de Valera. He stopped me adopting the unthinking anti attitude that was then prevalent.'[16] If *Peace by Ordeal* was criticised by reviewers in British papers, it was because of its pro de Valera stance at a time when he was still regarded as a bogey-man. But that was precisely Longford's aim in writing the book, to begin to redress what he saw as an imbalance.

After Barton gave him the source material, it was through the Birkenhead family that Longford found a publisher. Lady Eleanor Smith, a bestselling romantic novelist, introduced him to Peter Davies, who was convinced by the children and widow of F. E. Smith that an untried author would do justice to such an important and recent subject. Later Davies was to hand over the book to Jonathan Cape.

Barton's notes provided Longford with a complete record of the negotiations from the Irish side, supplemented by his own conversations with de Valera. Regarding background on the British position, his past friendship with Lord Birkenhead was augmented by assistance from both Austen Chamberlain, his relative by marriage, and Lloyd George.

Chamberlain would not show Longford his papers but did read to him extracts from those covering the crucial points in the negotiations. His reluctance to permit full access was prompted in part at least by the fact that Longford never tried to hide his own feelings for de Valera, though stressing at the same time his intention of being fair to all sides. When the book was finally published Chamberlain, while giving it general praise, took special exception to a passage in which Longford doubts the imperative behind the crucial incident that forced the Irish delegation to sign the treaty. Lloyd George issued the Irish with an ultimatum on 6 December 1921: sign by a certain time or risk a war. The time limit was set by Lloyd George so that he could dispatch a messenger to Belfast to inform the Ulster Protestant leader, Lord Craigavon, of the outcome of negotiations. Longford suggests in the text that the Prime Minister might have telephoned Craigavon 'but it would have been worse diplomacy and worse fun'. Chamberlain took great offence at the word 'fun'. 'You damn us with a word,' he told the young author. 'I can assure you, my dear boy, there was no question of fun in our minds that night.'[17]

Chamberlain was willing, at least, to discuss the events of December 1921. Through Lady Lavery, a friend of Collins, Longford gained an introduction to Lloyd George. He travelled down with Lady Lavery – whose face was later to grace Irish banknotes – to Churt, Lloyd George's country retreat. According to Longford's own account of the visit, he took a line of questioning that was little changed in its naive approach from that which he had used on his own father years before during walks at Tully Nally. 'Was Arthur Griffith a great man?' Lloyd George replied, 'pretty big'. 'And Michael Collins?' 'Quite considerable.' The interview crawled along for a few minutes before Lloyd George seized a large bell and began ringing it. His dogs were let into the room, along with various family members and friends. Tea was served and the Irish treaty was never mentioned again.[18]

If Austen Chamberlain was disappointed with *Peace by Ordeal* when it was published so were several on the Irish side. They were dismayed that Longford had not been tougher on de Valera and in particular probed why it was that Dev had not gone to the peace talks himself but had left Collins and Griffith to carry the burden. Longford in the text accepts at face value de Valera's explanation that as President of Ireland he needed to stay above the fray. 'The strategy was understandable enough. As long as de Valera was in reserve the Irish delegates could avoid being rushed into any hasty decisions.'

Those who saw de Valera's refusal to endorse the treaty as a betrayal of Collins and Griffith, however, found such an explanation less than convincing. Desmond Fitzgerald, Edward Longford's friend and a pro-treaty man, criticised *Peace by Ordeal* on this account as did Mrs Llewelyn Davies, another intimate of Collins who had helped Frank Longford in his research.

In a new introduction to the 1992 edition, the Irish historian Tim Pat Coogan, Collins' biographer, attacked Longford's homage to de Valera. The president, according to Coogan, brooked no rivals to his throne and avoided going to London in

1921 not because he was prepared to trust his colleagues and sometime rivals for power, but rather because he wanted to 'distance himself from the harsh realities of a debate which he knew was bound to involve compromise'. He thus 'managed to wriggle out of entering the lion's den'.

The de Valera question notwithstanding the consensus on both sides of the Irish Sea was that Frank Longford had achieved a commendable intellectual and political balancing act. His divided loyalties between Ireland and Britain had allowed him to see the conflict from both sides. In a characteristic passage he writes of the bloody civil unrest that led up to the 1921 peace talks:

> The British showed scant respect for the rules of the
> Hague Convention. They carried hostages on lorries,
> they terrorised the civil population, they destroyed the
> property of civilians when no military necessity dic-
> tated. But on the other hand the Irish forces seldom
> wore uniform or distinctive badges, and they could
> hardly expect much encouragement from an appeal to
> any generally recognised code. Each side in fact made
> its own precedents and used all methods judged
> essential for victory, in so far as seemed expedient in
> view of world opinion and in so far as its own
> humanity permitted.

Again in dealing with characters for whom he personally had the greatest of admiration, he does not fail to see them from the other side. His hero, Lord Birkenhead, is described through Irish eyes.

> Carson's galloper in 1914,[19] he had more recently
> been foremost in the public reiteration that the [Irish]
> rebels must be crushed by force. The South thought of
> him as a materialist, with what political altruism he
> possessed used up in fierce allegiance to the British
> Crown; full of contempt for what was small, and
> callousness towards what was suffering; as one likely

101

to pay scant attention to the plea for special treatment of what he probably regarded as a disloyal and treacherous sect.

With the publication of *Peace by Ordeal* in 1935 Frank Longford's academic star was in the ascendant. The previous year he had been appointed to a studentship at Christ Church. He would now be a full-time tutor in politics at £1000 a year, double his previous wage. In choosing Longford, Christ Church turned down the philosopher Freddie Ayer. The new don took his place alongside Patrick Gordon Walker in teaching politics, the Christ Church authorities no doubt calculating that Longford's Conservatism would counterbalance Gordon Walker's outspoken support of Labour. (In Oxford at this period, pro-Labour views could still be a disadvantage in seeking academic preferment. Evan Durbin had been passed over for a fellowship because of his political sympathies.)

If the publication of *Peace by Ordeal* brought academic benefits to Longford, it also served to distance him further from the Conservative Party.

> I decided I had to leave the Carlton Club because *Peace by Ordeal* was pro-de Valera. I told the chairman of the club while he was having port with some other members. I perched nervously on the edge of the armchair and told him about the book, said that I thought it might cause trouble and said I would leave the club. He told me not to be so silly, that if everyone who had written a book resigned, there would be no members.[20]

Longford was temporarily deflected but he returned to the subject several months later when Elizabeth stood as the Labour candidate in the November 1935 general election at Cheltenham. 'Even then the club secretary took me to one side and said that if I was ever in trouble overseas . . . He obviously thought I would have to leave the country.'[21] After bidding the secretary goodbye, Longford had also to take leave of the Carlton's barbers where he had been a regular customer. He laid in a substantial stock of hair oil, but was advised not to buy too much. 'You'll be bald in three years whatever you do.'

Eventually *Peace by Ordeal* completed Longford's break with Conservatism. With the same political naivety that had prompted him to dream in the Research Department of a new alliance between Conservatism and the militant working class he had encountered in Stoke, Longford had hoped that his book would change the open hostility shown towards the Irish government and de Valera in particular by the Tory-dominated Ramsay MacDonald government and Baldwin's administration that superseded it in 1935. 'It was not that the whole subject was brushed aside or that I personally was told to go away and play. My reports aroused, as far as I could judge, a good deal of interest for in those days in England first-hand contact with Mr de Valera was rare.' What surprised Longford was the prejudice that obliterated principle in Conservative circles in dealing with the Irish government.

> I had always assumed till then that whatever the theoretical arguments either way, the best Conserva-tives would approach a particular problem of states-manship without distorting prejudice; that they would meet argument with argument; that whether I agreed with them or not they would always be able to convince me that they were acting on a plausible principle.[22]

Longford believed wholeheartedly that in his battles with the British Conservatives in the 1930s de Valera was acting out of deeply-held principles, that he was, as he wrote in the introduc-tion to the 1992 edition of *Peace by Ordeal*, 'a great Christian man'. When he came to power de Valera moved quickly to reduce the role of the British Governor-General in Dublin, to drop the oath of allegiance to the Crown from the constitution and to cancel land annuity payments, the mortgages to the British treasury paid by Irish farmers so that they could become owners of the land they worked.

Longford had a good deal of sympathy with de Valera's stance. By contrast he saw the reaction of Baldwin and his ministers in imposing economic sanctions on Ireland as that of a group of bigots, riding roughshod over Ireland because it was weaker, abandoning any principle in order to extract revenge for the events of 1921, the first crack in the image of the Empire over which the sun would never set.

> I began to ponder for the first time over the deeper
> meanings of international principles and values.
> Hitherto I had taken for granted basic assumptions
> and techniques of British foreign and imperial policy.
> But now they were to come under a new scrutiny and
> be subjected to more rigorous criteria.[23]

Though Ireland destroyed any residual faith Frank Longford had in the Conservative Party, he was still holding back from casting his lot in with Labour. Over Ireland he and Elizabeth had found a common cause. As Elizabeth was to write later: 'Ireland was the only political problem – or rather, political answer – on which I accepted without question the judgement of Frank's head and heart. At the same time, it was a minority cause and perceptibly drew him nearer to my way of thinking on English politics.'[24] For in siding with the Irish against the British, Longford was not only turning his back on the traditions of his Ascendancy ancestors, he was also taking the part of the underdogs, the powerless. Longford had indeed shown such sympathies in private practical endeavours such as going to Hackney Wick, to Stoke, but until now he had never spoken out so publicly in defence of them.

His friend David Astor sees Longford's Irish nationalism as significant in his change of political allegiances. 'You could see Frank's life as a long search to be on the side of the people. That's why he became a socialist. He wanted to be with the people.'[25]

When Elizabeth accepted the nomination to stand for Labour in the no-hope Conservative seat of Cheltenham, her husband gave her enthusiastic, if qualified, backing. He spoke for her once on a public platform – stressing, unsurprisingly, his personal esteem for her, praising her attachment to the League of Nations (at that time the cornerstone of Labour foreign policy as a block on Hitler's ambitions and as an alternative to the need to rearm) and then, to the confusion of the audience, referring to his own Conservatism. Elizabeth managed to increase the Labour vote notwithstanding and cut the Conservative majority of Sir Walter Preston in a town known then for its retired colonels. Her worst moment during convassing came when she was introduced, wearing her red rosette, to a group of Catholic nuns. Noting the candidate's surname, they launched into a eulogy of Blessed Mary Pakenham, the male founder of the Passionist Order in Ireland who, as was the Catholic tradition, had taken on the name of the Virgin. Sadly Elizabeth had not been made aware of this ancestor or his sex and parried the nuns' praises by expressing her own view that Blessed Mary was a fine woman.

Longford spent the election in a non-party political capacity as agent to Alan Herbert who stood as an Independent in one of the Oxford University seats. Herbert was persuaded by Longford to run against the Conservatives on a ticket of defending academic freedom. Herbert was an impressive, articulate candidate in comparison to his Tory rival, the bumbling Hertford don C. M. Cruttwell – much despised by Evelyn Waugh who introduced a villainous character with the same name into his novels. Longford's campaign organisation was widely hailed – a new-found talent and one that was to come in useful in future appointments, notably alongside Sir William Beveridge in the 1940s.

While his siding with Herbert against the Tories can be seen in the light of Longford's broader switch from right to left, a decidedly personal factor should not be overlooked. His Christ Church colleague and friend from days at Charlton, Professor Lindemann, had been passed over – unjustly Longford felt – for the Conservative nomination in favour of Cruttwell. Furthermore Herbert's views – notably his tireless work towards easing the restrictions on divorce – found no great favour with his agent.

In fact his years in Oxford at Christ Church saw Longford keeping up many of his Conservative associations. In the spring of 1933 the Oxford Union held its famous 'King and Country' debate. When, in the wake of the national outcry at the refusal of the cream of the generation to take up arms, Randolph Churchill, then an undergraduate at Oxford, tried to get the motion overturned, Longford, who had struck up a friendship with Winston Churchill's son, was at his side. The anti-war stance of Labour under its pacifist leader George Lansbury was another aspect of party policy that Longford could not stomach. He was conscious both of the growing threat posed by the European fascists and of the military tradition of the Pakenhams.

Randolph Churchill addressed the Union, with Longford in support. They were heckled, booed, shouted down and showered with stink bombs. There was something in Churchill's manner, Longford later concluded, reflecting on the incident, that provoked strangers. On that particular evening, so provoked did the crowd become that Longford and Churchill had to make a hasty exit, mission unaccomplished, to cries of 'To the Cherwell with both of them'. For a moment it looked as if Longford was going to suffer a post-Union meeting ducking as once his brother had, but an icy stare from Churchill managed to disarm his accusers. The students restrained themselves from attacking one of their dons.

Churchill was soon afterwards to offer Longford the post of secretary to the India Defence Committee, a group which he chaired with Lord Lloyd whose purpose was to defeat the India reforms proposed by the Baldwin government. The committee suspected that the reforms were aimed at paving the way for eventual Indian independence. If Randolph Churchill was officially at the head of this group, it was his father Winston who was the leading light. Longford went to one of the meetings of the committee, with Winston Churchill in attendance. It was not a crusade Longford had any interest in (indeed in its keep-the-Empire-together-at-any-cost message, it ran counter to all his views on Ireland) and he politely but firmly declined.

Even if he had wanted to take up the job offer, it would have been difficult for him to do so without earning the enmity of his mother. Mary Longford, shortly before her death, on hearing that her son had even considered such a post, told him: 'You would never have been able to look me in the face if you had accepted a position under Winston Churchill.' She held Churchill responsible for her husband's death at Gallipoli and by association for all her own sufferings thereafter. Churchill, as First Lord of the Admiralty and then Chancellor of the Duchy of Lancaster in the wartime cabinets of first Asquith and then Lloyd George, was credited with ordering the assault on Gallipoli. He added insult to injury in Mary Longford's eyes when he wrote of the ill-fated campaign in his book *World Crisis*: 'On that battlefield of fog and flame fell Brigadier General The Earl of Longford . . . and other Paladins.'

When Longford was appointed to the full-time fellowship at Christ Church in 1934, he and Elizabeth decided to move their burgeoning family to Oxford. Thomas had been born on 14 August 1933, thirteen days before Antonia was a year old and just in time for Mary Longford to see the future eighth earl christened in Hartwell Church. Edward and Christine Longford were by the time of his mother's death despairing of producing an heir. Elizabeth says she 'always felt that she [Mary Longford] wished and wished that Thomas was Edward's son and not Frank's'.[26]

The new family home was at Singletree in Rose Hill, east of the city centre between the village of Iffley and the industrial suburb of Cowley. Designed by an Oxford chemist to match the grand architectural style of the university's academic buildings, it abounded with carved oak mantels, parquet floors and even an odd bow window in the drawing room. Within months of the Longfords' arrival, its countryside views were marred by the building of the Florence Park Estate nearby, not that the couple, with their social consciences, could complain.

Oxford was the closest Longford came in the first half of his life to finding a place where he belonged. His student days had been a time when he laid many of the anxieties of his childhood to rest, found his feet academically and socially. It was a city where his eccentricities in dress and manner went almost

107

unnoticed and where his wit and ready capacity for conversation were admired. It had also been the city where he met Elizabeth. As a tutor he was respected by colleagues and regarded with affection by his students. Among those whom he taught was Philip Toynbee, the writer and a life-long friend. In an interview before his death Toynbee talked about Longford the tutor. 'He was popular with undergraduates, slightly laughed at, but I think he was good at his job. We used to call him Polkinghorn. No sexual application, just a kind of joke name, old Frankie Polkinghorn. Because he was clumsy and odd-looking, though actually he was quite dextrous with his tongue. He was perfectly capable of looking after himself if attacked.'[27]

Longford never played the distant, detached tutor with his undergraduates. He was always happy to sit down with them over a tumbler of sherry – an enduring predilection – and talk about anything but work. Throughout his life he has retained a knack for drawing out young people, listening to their views and never dismissing them with the mock gravitas of an elder statesman. According to Toynbee, it was not only politics that interested Longford. 'He was always asking about my girlfriends. He was fascinated by my goings-on.'[28] Perhaps it was a hankering after his bachelor days. For however much Elizabeth shouldered the burden of the day-to-day care of their children (combining motherhood with her commitments to the WEA and adult education), there were inevitably moments of domestic crisis at Singletree. At Easter 1936 Antonia developed a pain in her right leg and could not walk. She was staying in Torpoint with her nanny and Thomas while the Longfords visited Elizabeth's parents. A local doctor mentioned the word polio. Longford took his daughter back to Oxford by train, carrying her wrapped in a blanket in his arms. When the local doctor came to examine her, Antonia was mysteriously restored to health. She ran across the room to greet the doctor.

Sport remained Longford's great pastime and in Toynbee he found a willing tennis partner. Again there was a mixture of respect and ridicule between tutor and student. Toynbee recalled that Longford 'played in a ludicrously clumsy way' but usually won.[29]

Restored to the academic world of Oxford, the Longfords were an instant success. Elizabeth's old friend Maurice Bowra featured large in their social circuit. Longford was very influenced, Philip Toynbee later suggested, by Bowra and the rather malicious style of wit then popular at Oxford where cruel stories were told about anyone and everyone.

> There was an old don at Christ Church who died and
> Bowra said to Frank, and I happened to be there,
> 'Well, what's the reaction at the House [Christ
> Church] to the death?' And Frank said, 'Oh, immense
> relief.' It was a typical Bowra remark, but not a typical
> Frank remark. But Frank was under his thumb. He
> was even a bit sycophantic to Maurice Bowra.[30]

Through Elizabeth, who had become an active member of the Oxford Labour Party, holding fêtes for the Cowley branch in the garden at Singletree, Longford also moved increasingly in socialist circles. Patrick Gordon Walker, the Labour candidate for Oxford, a Christ Church colleague and later a short-lived Foreign Secretary in the Wilson Cabinet, became a great friend, as did Dick Crossman, then a don at New College, a Labour councillor and another future member of the Wilson team.

The Oxford City Labour Party in the 1930s was the incubator for a future generation of Labour Cabinet ministers of the 1960s. As a branch it had a radical, questioning environment with a heavy over-representation of dons and a corresponding lack of the union figures who are usually the backbone of many a local Labour Party. In this homogeneous atmosphere, Oxford's academic socialists moved to the left wing of a national party that was deeply divided in its reaction to Ramsay MacDonald's defection to the Conservatives in 1931 and over the rising threat of fascism on the continent.

After the general election catastrophe of 1931 and faced with a perilous economic situation, most of Labour's parliamentary leadership shifted dramatically to the left under the pacifist

George Lansbury. The fall of the minority Labour government in 1931 was blamed on MacDonald's treachery but also on the economic pressures applied by the banks and the 'capitalists'. The whole parliamentary system was questioned and class struggle became the rhetoric of the day. There was talk of Labour taking 'emergency powers' to run the country on behalf of the 'workers' against the 'capitalists'. Hugh Gaitskell was later to refer to this period as 'the only time I have ever questioned the practicability of democratic socialism'.[31]

By 1934, however, under pressure from moderate trade union leaders like Ernest Bevin, Labour began to pull back from the brink and the revolutionary talk was dropped. The Oxford Party lacked any such restraining union influence and it grew dissatisfied with the more moderate guidance offered by Transport House.

Slower to be toned down at a national level was the party's emotionally rooted commitment to pacifism. In the iconography of the Labour Party, war was seen as a matter of worker fighting worker on behalf of the capitalists and imperialists. Pacifism was therefore the logical response, an international workers' solidarity against such exploitation. On the reformist wing of Labour, men like Hugh Dalton sought to temper their party's instinctive opposition to the growing cries for rearmament against Hitler with a more positive commitment to meet the threat through collective security under the banner of a League of Nations. The left wing saw the League as a capitalists' organisation, the tool, as Sir Stafford Cripps another of the prominent pacifists in the leadership put it, of the haves against the have-nots, the 'International Burglars' Union'.

The disagreement came to a head in October 1935 at the Labour Party conference which coincided with Mussolini's invasion of Abyssinia. The left opposed a motion calling for concerted League of Nations action and sanctions. Lansbury, the leader of the Parliamentary Labour Party, made a highly emotional speech emphasising his own Christian pacifism and calling for the motion to be rejected. Those who lived by the sword, he warned, died by the sword. But he was defeated in the vote after a decisive intervention by Ernest Bevin, and replaced by Clement Attlee who was in favour of collective security under the auspices of an anti-fascist (not pro-capitalist as the left claimed in its rhetoric) League of Nations.

Though the 1935 conference saw more moderate voices taking charge of the Labour Party, defeat in the general election several months later meant that the left, led by Sir Stafford Cripps, felt justified in continuing to rock the boat, exploiting the widespread dissatisfaction within the party at being out of power for so long.

The Oxford City branch reflected these divisions in the wider Labour movement. But in the academic hothouse, practical considerations were debated alongside Marxist theory which was the fashionable response of many to every problem. Longford, whose own particular interest in economics had encompassed a detailed examination of Marx, was not convinced by his thinking.

> In his 'Labour Theory of Value' and his 'Surplus Value' I still found a stimulating though inadequate effort to provide an economic justification for his sense of moral indignation; and I had a similar opinion of the other main feature of his economics – his claim that capitalism inevitably breaks down owing to its inherent tendency to produce more than it can consume.[32]

Though he felt increasingly drawn to the Labour Party on moral and ethical grounds, and found Cripps an attractive figure as he battled for his ideals against the more pragmatic party leadership, Longford was put off by the Marxist bent of the local party which exacerbated his own long-standing doubts as to any economic basis for socialism. All his training and the instincts that he had developed at Conservative Central Office had taught him that inequality was inevitable, that there was no quick fix. Longford was convinced of the socialist case for a redistribution of wealth. His work among the poor had shattered any residual attachment to capitalism and he felt no great attachment to his own worldly goods. But he was far from sure that such sacrifices would have any practical effect. When radical voices in the Labour Party pointed to the economic example of Soviet Russia, he was troubled by the few facts and figures that they could quote in their eulogies.

Perhaps if he had lived somewhere other than Oxford, he might have found the local party more amenable, less strident, less idealistic. In effect Labour's economic programme at a national level was not so radical as his conversations with Oxford socialists might have suggested. The 1935 manifesto did promise measures such as bank nationalisation, but nowhere was there a hint of trying to bring a Soviet-style, centrally controlled economy to Britain. Longford hovered on the brink of the Labour Party, sure in his heart but his academic scruples not wholly satisfied. It took a bump on the head to sort things out.

Oswald Mosley had made great capital out of Britain's economic distress in the first half of the 1930s, contrasting it unfavourably with what was happening in Germany and Italy under fascist rule. A handsome, mustachioed figure, clad all in black and surrounded by henchmen in similar attire, Mosley was a polished speaker with a provocative line in argument. Booking the Carfax Assembly Rooms in central Oxford on 14 May 1936 was a typical gesture. His aim was to goad the academic Establishment and the university's socialists in particular. They responded as he had expected and packed out the hall. The Longfords were there as were most of their circle – Crossman, Toynbee, Gordon Walker. But Mosley also had a wider pull. There was a large contingent of bus drivers, staunch Labour members and implacable opponents of Mosley who came to give him a rough ride. They lined up alongside their academic comrades. On the other side were what Longford called 'the bourgeois Conservatives of north Oxford' who were attracted by Mosley's recipe for success.[33]

In this tense atmosphere someone stood up and shouted 'Red Front' and gave the clenched fist salute. Mosley responded at once to this act of provocation. 'The next man who shouts "Red Front" goes out.' Several others defied the speaker but he made a show of ignoring them, at the same time beckoning his

Blackshirts, complete with their rubber truncheons, up the aisles. And then up stood the somewhat incongruous figure of Basil Murray, Philip Toynbee's uncle, who had been chatting with Longford outside the hall, and repeated the 'blasphemy'. Mosley's massed supporters pounced on Murray and within minutes the room was one big scuffle. The busmen took the lead in responding to the fascists' aggression. Heavy buckled belts met with steel chairs. Longford, who had been sitting in the row behind Murray, dived into the fray. 'I can remember struggling with a little team of fascists, all much shorter than I, but each one, I expect, at least as good as I was in the rough and tumble.'[34] Despite his boxing training, they soon had Longford on the floor and were kicking him in the kidneys with their jack-boots. He was saved by a timely intervention from the police. Philip Toynbee, blood streaming down his face, greeted his tutor as a fellow revolutionary.

Elizabeth, who had been separated from her husband in the mêlée, returned home to find him already in bed, with a doctor in attendance. He diagnosed concussion, two black eyes and minor injuries to the kidneys and ordered complete rest.

Never a man to stay still for very long, Longford's frustration at being laid up only added to his anger at what he had witnessed. When the police announced they were to prosecute Basil Murray, Longford's disgust was total. Several weeks later when the local magistrates fined Murray £2, Longford rose to his feet in the public gallery and shouted, 'I'd like to tell those buggers on the bench what I think of them.' The chair of the bench had been the wife of one of the professors at Christ Church. Having narrowly escaped disciplinary action by the university authorities for this breach of etiquette Longford did not let the matter drop and obtained an interview with the Home Secretary to lodge his protest. Sir John Simon, a friend of Basil Murray's parents, listened politely but declined to take any further action.

Any residual faith Longford had in the Establishment evaporated when he failed to get the authorities to take what had happened seriously. Their unwillingness to face up to Mosley seemed to him almost worse than what had taken place in the

Carfax Assembly Rooms. Official indifference was to Longford a moral abdication, a tacit approval of Mosley's methods. In a highly emotional state and still nursing his injuries, Longford saw the issue crystallise into terms of childlike simplicity. His previous doubts and equivocations over economic policy disappeared. His careful academic weighing of Labour's claims seemed suddenly like fiddling while Rome burnt.

> In that room I could see only two sides. The solid
> citizens of north Oxford and the busmen. And there
> was only one side for me. My life at Oxford at that
> time had been one of entering into the lives of the
> working classes. I was enthusiastic about the spirit I
> found in Cowley on our doorstep.[35]

These words, spoken almost sixty years after the event, still summon up the heady mixture of emotion, anger and frustration that the Mosley meeting aroused in Longford. He felt himself at a crossroads. He could stay in his academic ivory tower, comparing and contrasting the different political parties. Or he could act, get his hands dirty in the struggle for principles he felt were at stake in the aftermath of the Mosley rally. If the Establishment was content to sit back and do nothing, he was convinced he had to fight.

There is a naivety in such a pattern of behaviour, but it was characteristic of Longford in this period. There is also sincerity and optimism in his conviction. Two more events hastened his decision to join Labour. In 1936 the Spanish Civil War broke out. It was a seminal event for many in his generation. Again Longford did not dwell on the nuances of the situation. His interests at the time were very parochial. However, he took sides – against Franco and the fascists and for the democratically elected socialist government of Spain.

To compound his sins Franco was taking help from Hitler and Mussolini. The British Conservative government refused to intervene – another moral abdication. The Longfords were involved in raising funds for the International Brigade which

114

went to fight for democracy in Spain. Their friend Basil Murray joined up and was to die in the struggle against Franco.

Owing to her prominence in Labour politics in Oxford and the good show she had put up in Cheltenham, in August 1936 Elizabeth was invited to take over from her friend Naomi Mitchison's husband as candidate for the eminently winnable Birmingham seat of King's Norton. Longford was right behind her decision to accept the challenge of winning the seat, in the Chamberlain heartland, from the incumbent Conservative, Ronald Cartland, brother of the bestselling romantic novelist.

The couple were becoming increasingly united in their political thoughts and deeds. In September, they travelled to Berlin for a conference on peace and democracy with European academics. They were initially reluctant to go to Hitler's Germany, Longford maintaining his dislike of overseas travel, but the trip was to prove the final push into the arms of Labour. Though little that was dramatic happened when they were in Germany – the gathering was one of academics, with any anti-Hitler talk secondary – on their return Longford joined the Cowley and Iffley Labour Party.

Longford was at this moment at the height of his academic powers, widely admired for his book *Peace by Ordeal* and regarded by his colleagues as a clever man able to grasp and convey to students the intricacies of political thought and debate. Yet in his response to his encounter with Oswald Mosley, to official indifference in its aftermath and to a whole range of important events in Europe, he acted in a linear fashion, rejecting intellectual subtleties in favour of a passionate determination and almost childlike faith in one view of the situation. His heart was ruling his head for the first time. Where before – even over his marriage to Elizabeth – he had been a mass of equivocation, paralysed as he attempted to think through every possible scenario, wanting to be convinced on every point, it was as if the Mosley meeting made him cast such caution to the wind. Extraordinary times, Longford concluded, called for extraordinary measures. Had it been any other decade – one less polarised, less steeped in human misery – perhaps he would have continued sitting on the fence. His previous long deferment of making decisions would certainly suggest that such was his instinct.

Legend has it that the concussion he sustained after that evening in the Carfax Assembly Rooms knocked away any residual Conservative economic theory still lurking in his thoughts. Like every legend it contains an element of truth but is largely caricature. Longford has related this story with a chuckle in many a newspaper interview since and it has become the hallmark of his ability to make fun of himself. At a stroke one of the most serious and agonising decisions of his life is transmogrified into a witty anecdote.

In a letter written in the late 1980s to his erstwhile Cabinet colleague Roy Jenkins, where he apologised for ridiculing him in a House of Lords speech, Longford pinpointed his knee-jerk reaction to being presented with an audience: 'All my life I have suffered from a fatal desire to amuse which I have never been able to resist.'[36] His best jokes have been stories about himself. Indeed his lifelong friend David Astor is convinced that 'all the best stories about Frank have been told by him first'.[37] For a budding politician, a man who behind the mask of humour wants to be taken seriously, such a capacity for self-mockery can be a handicap. As Longford once remarked to his former student and friend Philip Toynbee; 'It's dangerous to tell stories against oneself because people always remember the stories but forget who told them in the first place.'[38]

Five

The radical don

> In the great debates on sanctions and rearmament
> which divided the Labour movement in the mid-
> 1930s, there were two logical positions: Lansbury's
> and Bevin's. According to Lansbury, war was
> wrong and therefore sanctions and rearmament
> must be wrong. According to Bevin, sanctions and
> rearmament were necessary as the only way to
> stop fascism before it was too late[1]
>
> *David Marquand* The Progressive Dilemma

With his decision to join the Labour Party, Longford embarked on one of the most frenetic periods of his life. In addition to his teaching duties, the usual round of sporting and social activities and the demands of a growing family, he was at the troubled heart of a particularly volatile local branch party whose divisions reflected those of a national movement unable to agree a common response to the rise of fascism.

Part of Longford's frenzy was the ardour of the new convert, anxious to prove his credentials as a socialist. Part was a conscious effort to bury his past academic doubts about socialism in an orgy of activity, hoping the practical would vanquish the cerebral. But part too was engendered by his own reaction to the historic events of the time. In March 1936 Hitler marched into the demilitarised zone of the Rhineland; in March 1938 he seized Austria; the following year it was Czechoslovakia. The growing Nazi menace and the Spanish Civil War combined to define political positions across a whole generation.

In a period of uncertainty and fear, Longford was anxious to act but was unsure quite what to do. With a wife and family he could scarcely join up with fellow socialists in the International Brigades in Spain. He had to make do with collecting signatures on petitions and donations for the republican cause in Spain. As a recent recruit to the Labour Party he could not command any great respect in its decision-making process. His scope was geographically and politically limited to Oxford but within that narrow, parochial orbit he eagerly seized every chance to work for peace in Europe. His motivation was clear but in the heat of the moment he occasionally acted with what he later came to regard as a lack of discernment.

In the autumn of 1937 Longford's increasing involvement in local Labour politics led to his election as councillor for his home ward of Cowley and Iffley. He scored the largest majority ever for a Labour candidate in the city, a sign of the industrial transformation that had overtaken Oxford in the 1930s. In the 1931 general election, Labour did not even bother to field a candidate. Yet the growth of Cowley, alongside the Morris car factory where most of its inhabitants worked, was changing the local political map.

As a councillor Longford tackled his duties with extreme, almost fanatical diligence. It was indeed the only time in his life when he represented a constituency and he thoroughly enjoyed the experience. Meetings with the City Engineer over waste-collection on the Bullingdon Housing Estate or the level of pavements in Fernhill Road, visiting Oxford City Prison on behalf of his constituents, lobbying alongside the pension movement crowded his diary between tutorials, tennis matches with Philip Toynbee and formal hall with his fellow dons in Christ Church. Longford felt unqualified enthusiasm for Labour's social policy and from the start he focused on these issues with a social worker's determination to better the lot of the underdogs.

But Longford took it a step further. In the first flush of conversion – naively he would now concede – he yearned for the removal of all obstacles that he saw as separating him from his constituents. He wanted none of the deference of Eton Manor or aristocratic titles. When in 1938 he inherited a sizeable sum of money, he had to spend it as soon as possible for the good of the cause. One venture he paid for, in the wake of Hitler's aggression towards Czechoslovakia and Chamberlain's capitulation at Munich, was the digging of trenches by local unemployed men around the Florence Park Estate that bordered Singletree. The prospect of a German invasion of Oxford was somewhat remote. Longford's eccentric act was born of his anxiety about Britain's ill-preparedness for the onset of war and of his burning desire to redistribute his own wealth. He was putting his own house in order in the light of his socialist beliefs. Unemployment was bad so he would pay for people not to be unemployed.

It was, Elizabeth Longford says with her habitual knack for putting the best possible gloss on her husband's actions, a 'whimsical' gesture on his part.

> But he does get these ideas. Though he agreed entirely with Labour on the view of the League of Nations and collective security as the best way to prevent a war, he did feel that there was a danger that our theoretical belief had to be shown to be working and that until it could be then people should make efforts towards defence. Never forget that he was the son of an army officer and that he always had an interest in defence. And it only lasted for three days. Even though he knew a great many Cowley workers, he had no idea of what it would cost to pay the wages. It was a thunderbolt for him. He would soon have been bankrupt.[2]

This desire to become one of the people, to share their burdens, highlights one of the contradictions that has dogged Longford's life in the Labour Party. By the standards of his constituents, he was and remains well-off. He has suffered no physical depriva-tions. He has never been short of food or a roof over his head or a well-connected friend to find him work. His mother may not have shown any affection towards him, but his childhood was insulated from economic hardship.

Such privilege weighed heavily on his conscience, set him apart. Yet he could not easily dispose of his worldly goods. He simply had to learn to live with the contradiction so ably described in the book *Hons and Rebels* by Elizabeth's friend, the aristocratic Jessica Mitford, who turned her back on her upbringing and embraced communism.

The gap between Longford and those whose causes he took up was brought home to him when he invited one of the prisoners he had been visiting at Oxford Jail to come to Singletree to celebrate his release. He generously laid on a bottle of Liebfraumilch with tall glasses with long pale green stems. The visitor and his family were no doubt grateful for the intention but, as Elizabeth noticed, 'did not know what to make of this finicky liquor'.[3]

In this wish to cast off the trappings of privilege and become one of the people, Longford stood in marked contrast to other socialist dons on the council – men like Dick Crossman who represented Headington from 1935. They preferred academic discussions at the Labour Club about the nature of democracy, the merits of Marx, the future of socialism and the Oxford Party's running battle with Transport House.

Longford wanted both – the practical and the theoretical, local and national, to be a social worker and a politician. In the Oxford whirlpool of these extraordinary times, the dichotomy could be resolved in a way that would later prove impossible when Longford took on national responsibilities. As the spokesman for Cowley and Iffley, Longford would career around Oxford in pursuit of his constituents' grievances on his children's bicycles, knees stuck out at curious angles, hair all of a tangle and scruffy tennis shoes under the formal attire he had worn to hall at Christ Church. As secretary of the city's branch party, he was also to be found chairing meetings for distinguished visiting speakers with international concerns to articulate.

Oxford proved an irresistible draw to the great and the good of the Labour movement, a stage on which the confusions and contradictions that beset the national party were played out before an audience of socialist academics and ardent activists. The left-wing local party, however, became a running wound in the side of the moderate leadership and of Transport House. With the pacifist Lansbury's defeat at the 1935 Labour conference – which Longford attended with Elizabeth, she a candidate but he still not a member of the party – Clement Attlee was elected leader with strong backing from the trade union movement and Ernest Bevin in particular.

Under Attlee's guidance, Labour came back from the brink of questioning the whole system of parliamentary democracy and abandoned for ever talk of a socialist government taking 'emergency powers' to defeat the 'capitalists' who were credited with bringing down Labour in 1931. In place of talk of the class struggle came a commitment to social justice through wealth redistribution and social democracy.

It was over foreign policy, looming so large on the national psyche with events in Europe, that Labour fought most of its internal battles. The question of how to respond to Hitler came to represent a wider ideological divide in the party. The moderate Attlee and his supporters, in a fashion later adopted by Neil Kinnock, set about convincing the electorate that, after a period of radicalism, Labour was once again a creditable government-in-waiting. Attlee thereby distanced himself from the left of the Party, their doubts about the workings of the democratic system in the wake of the events of 1931 and their vocal support for the Soviet Union.

While Attlee's strategy might have ultimately united the party in more peaceful times, the second half of the thirties saw Europe, and Britain with it, lurching towards conflict. Many in the rank and file like Longford became increasingly alarmed at the fascist menace. Yet Attlee in his studied moderation appeared unable or unwilling to deflect Chamberlain from an appeasement policy that was failing to hold back Hitler's territorial aggrandisement.

Attlee's alternative to appeasement was to contain the fascist threat through collective security, under the banner of the League of Nations. Yet, to the left and its champion Sir Stafford Cripps, the League was a compromised organisation, an 'International Burglars' Union' as he tagged it at the time of the Abyssinia crisis in 1935.

The only people the Labour left could envisage standing up to Hitler in continental Europe were the Communists. Cripps' constant demand therefore was that Attlee endorse an alliance between Labour and the Communists to reverse the policy of appeasement.

The question of an alliance against Hitler arose on a broader scale between Britain and the Soviet Union. It became a key issue dividing the Labour left from the party leadership. To Cripps and his supporters it was a means for the workers of Europe to unite against the fascists. To Attlee it was a potential vote-loser, hinting at a Labour return to the revolutionary rhetoric of the early 1930s. Also, Attlee saw that the British Communists were trying to infiltrate the Labour movement. While the continental Communists enjoyed substantial support from the working classes, in Britain they were but a small sect and Labour, a much larger church than its socialist counterparts in Europe, did not need Communist back-up in its claim to represent the British workers.

The Oxford party could not, however, see the need for keeping its distance from the local Communists. Overtly and covertly, it was pervaded by a small but powerful Communist group. Some of the subversives kept their real loyalty hidden and, posing as left-wing socialists, managed to gain influence and pull strings behind the scenes. Others were less discreet. When Longford stood for Cowley and Iffley in 1937, he was joined on the Labour ticket by a man he later described as a 'crypto-com'.[4] With its sizeable contingent of Communists, the Oxford party rejected the line taken by Attlee and embraced with enthusiasm the notion of a grand alliance of the left across Europe to counter the threat of Hitler. Cripps, a nephew of Beatrice Webb, enjoyed great popularity in Oxford and was a hero to the Longfords. They voted for him as leader and were frustrated by Bevin's use of the trade union vote to maintain Attlee in position.[5]

In a divided movement, the Oxford party was opposed to its national leaders. When Labour General-Secretary George Shepherd came to try and explain Transport House's reservations about alliances with Communists, he was barracked and nicknamed 'the Pope'. As secretary of a branch party that was on the left, Longford developed a reputation as a radical. Though he decisively rejected Philip Toynbee's invitation – made in Dublin where they were observing the 1937 Irish general election – to join the Communist Party, he was convinced of the need to work with the far left against Hitler. He backed the wisdom of a Popular Front of the left and even considered leaving the party in 1939 when Cripps was expelled for his efforts on behalf of such an alliance. (Cripps convinced him of the futility of the gesture.)

In his preoccupation with events on the continent, Longford was unaware of the extent to which the Communists had infiltrated the local branch party. Rather like Militant's activities in 1980s Liverpool, the true picture did not become clear to many of those at the centre of events until much later. Longford was, however, warned of what was going on by some of those around him, but he preferred to ignore their advice. His Christ Church colleague, Patrick Gordon Walker, the official Labour candidate for Oxford, recognised the extent to which Communists were exploiting a genuine desire for peace to attempt to take over the local group. In his diary, Gordon Walker describes a meeting of the Left Book Club with Longford in the chair. 'It is an obvious Communist Party thing – with their usual semi-deceit etc.'[6]

Elizabeth Longford feels that too much can be made of the Communist influence on the Oxford party.

> There certainly wasn't any conscious working for the Communists. If they turned up supporting the same cause as we were, we would work with them. The same with the Liberals. I know you could say that the Communists infiltrated in the sense of working with the Labour Party, but they didn't infiltrate in a really deep, profound and obvious way. In one sense they were infiltrated the other way round. They took the Labour line. Nobody ever looks at it that way. It was both ways round. You can't have infiltration without both sides being influenced.'[7]

In June 1938, however, Labour's national agent reported unfavourably on efforts by the Oxford party to establish an *ad hoc* Popular Front against Hitler with local Communists and Liberals in the form of the Oxford Co-ordinating Committee for Peace and Democracy. Transport House gave the constituency party fourteen days to leave the umbrella organisation on pain of disaffiliation. Longford and his colleagues agreed to this ultimatum grudgingly, noting 'the discouraging effect on workers in the party' of the national line.

Events in the Oxford party came to a head in the autumn of 1938. Neville Chamberlain returned from Munich on 30 September 1938, clutching his infamous piece of paper and promising peace in our time. In the Commons Attlee attacked the Prime Minister for betraying Czechoslovakia, and for giving in to Hitler. But the radical elements in the Labour Party wanted more than fine words. Cripps renewed his appeal for a Popular Front, and even extended an invitation to the anti-Chamberlain Tories, led by Winston Churchill and Anthony Eden, to join.

The malcontents, determined to give Chamberlain a bloody nose, turned their attention to a by-election that was pending in Oxford. In August 1938 Captain Bourne, the local Conservative MP, had died. The parliamentary constituency did not yet include the Cowley housing estates where Longford was local councillor and it seemed unlikely that Labour alone could mount much of a challenge to Bourne's successor, Quintin Hogg, then a young Fellow at All Souls, later Lord Hailsham, and a friend and admirer of Elizabeth's from student days.

On 13 September, even before Chamberlain's peace mission, the Liberal candidate, Ivor Davies, had offered to stand down on condition that the Labour candidate, Patrick Gordon Walker, did likewise and that a non-party, anti-Conservative candidate was put up instead. It was an offer that instantly struck a chord with those in the Labour camp who dreamt of a Popular Front. With Chamberlain's return from Munich and the distribution of 84,700 gas masks to the civilian population in Oxford, it seemed to many to be irresistible.

Gordon Walker was as left-wing in the late 1930s as many of his Oxford colleagues. (Later when in the Wilson Cabinet he was described by Ian Mikado as 'as far right as you can get in the Labour Party without toppling over the edge'.)[8] He had stood in 1935 on a left-wing programme of bank nationalisation and wealth redistribution and was just as affected by the political idealism of the time as Longford.

However, unlike his fellow Christ Church tutor, he was also acutely aware of the Communist infiltration of the local party and was therefore implacably opposed from the start to any Popular Front candidate in the by-election. Longford was not so sure and found himself in an agonising position. Gordon Walker was a close friend and in several respects a political soul-mate. Yet Longford was convinced that Chamberlain needed to change course, that peace was still possible but that appeasement was leading Britain into a potentially disastrous war. Davies' offer seemed too good an opportunity to turn down.

For the first time since he had joined Labour, he put principle over party and gave enthusiastic backing to the idea of an 'Independent Progressive' candidate. Using the term Popular Front was judged as too provocative. Crossman was also behind the scheme and the two young dons hit on A. D. 'Sandy' Lindsay, a former Vice-Chancellor of the university and Master of Balliol, the man who had first involved Longford in the WEA, as their compromise candidate. The scenes in the Commons after Chamberlain's return confirmed them in their determination to mount an effective challenge to the Prime Minister.

Longford, egged on by those in the local branch, became the prime mover in the campaign to replace Gordon Walker with Lindsay. Only later did he reflect ruefully that 'the coup was engineered by the Oxford Communists with the rest of us more or less starry-eyed dupes'.[9]

Gordon Walker, with no stars in his eyes, refused to give in gracefully and fought his corner, initially with the backing of Transport House. However, Munich affected the national leadership as much as it did the local party. Attlee and his colleagues despaired of convincing Chamberlain to stand up to Hitler. The clamour that Labour should be seen to be acting was growing daily. After a lot of behind-the-scenes lobbying Transport House was convinced that the circumstances in Oxford in the aftermath of Munich were so exceptional that the decision should be left to the local party. It was in effect an abdication of responsibility, though Lindsay's long record of vehement anti-Communism was no doubt a strong and reassuring factor in Transport House's decision to abandon Gordon Walker.

With Labour won over, the Liberals now began to waver. They were suspicious of Lindsay. As a long-standing member of the Labour Party, they protested, he could hardly be counted as independent. They had also already spent some £300 on their campaign and wanted reimbursing before they would sign up to the joint ticket. It was to be a one-off protest. Longford, who had come into an inheritance, dug into his own pocket to deal with this obstacle and at the same time convinced them of Lindsay's *bona fide* by promising that he would not seek re-election. (Hailsham was later to claim that this was Longford's great mistake in the by-election campaign. By saying that Lindsay would hold the seat only until the next election – expected in 1940 at the latest – the Popular Front was, Hailsham kept repeating in his speeches and propaganda, putting up a lame duck candidate. He even rather mischievously suggested subsequently that Longford had engineered the whole matter for his own benefit at the next general election. 'Was it, as I rather uncharitably was inclined to suspect at the time, a clever ruse by Frank Pakenham himself, hoping once he had got rid of Gordon Walker, to have the revision of the seat himself?')[10]

Once the Liberals were mollified through Longford's patient diplomacy, Labour met on 17 October and voted forty-eight to twelve in favour of backing Lindsay. 'I am not standing down,' Gordon Walker retorted. 'The local Labour Party is withdrawing the Labour candidate.' He took little part in the subsequent campaign and would never entirely forgive Longford. Their friendship cooled considerably and though they were later to sit in Cabinet together, they remained distant. 'It represents the political step which I would most prefer to have back if I could have my time again,' Longford later remarked.[11]

But for the moment he was caught up in the fever of the campaign and put personal considerations to one side. The Oxford by-election marked the debut of the opinion poll, not to mention one of the first outings of the Mass Observation data-collecting initiative started by anthropologist Tom Harrison.

With so much attention focused on one result, the campaign took on a broader national significance. It became a mini-referendum on Chamberlain. It was, in truth, very much a university affair with the *Picture Post* reporting that 'an interesting feature of the by-election was the intense interest taken by undergraduates, who had no votes, and the comparative apathy of the townsmen, who had.' The academic community divided over the candidates with different groups of dons compiling pro or anti manifestos in first the *Oxford Mail* and then *The Times*.[12]

Lindsay was a huge disappointment to his backers. Though he was a commanding figure in the university world, to the voters he lacked any great appeal. He was, Elizabeth later wrote, 'both too amateurish and too lofty to face a political orator like Quintin Hogg. The press was non-plussed by Lindsay's unconventional conferences, conducted in the college kitchen with Lindsay sitting on the kitchen table nonchalantly swinging his long legs.'[13]

He was also increasingly unhappy at some of the tactics being employed on his behalf. The slogan 'A vote for Hogg is a vote for Hitler' particularly angered him. Yet he carried with him the hopes of a disparate group of anti-appeasement zealots. Harold Macmillan, the future Prime Minister and an opponent of Chamberlain's policy, spoke for him, reportedly giving Lindsay Churchill's blessing. Those in the Labour party who hoped to ginger up their leadership into reconsidering a Popular Front staked all on a Lindsay victory. Attlee and his colleagues watched with interest.

In the end Lindsay could not fulfil the expectations that had been placed on his candidature. The count on 27 October showed that he had increased by 6 per cent Gordon Walker's share of the vote in 1935 but he was still just under 3500 behind Hogg who instantly proclaimed, 'It is not my victory but Mr Chamberlain's.'[14]

The significance of the Oxford by-election in national terms is hard to assess. It certainly focused attention on events in Europe and Britain's state of unpreparedness to fight. For Chamberlain it was a short-lived triumph. At Bridgewater three weeks later in another by-election in a Tory seat, a Liberal candidate running with Labour backing as an Independent Progressive defeated the Conservative challenger.

When the constituency came to select its candidate for what was assumed would be the 1940 general election, Gordon Walker had already put himself out of the running by attacking the backers of the Independent Progressive candidate in the aftermath of polling day. In a valedictory interview with the *Oxford Mail* he described Lindsay's excursion into politics as

> initiated in middle-class and university circles. There has been no shortage of money in a most lavish campaign. The progress of this Democratic Front to a large extent reflected the views of people who are rich enough to afford the luxury of ignoring everything except foreign policy.

Though the description could have applied to any of Lindsay's backers, Longford felt that its criticism was directed against him personally. If this was the case, Gordon Walker had hit Longford's Achilles heel: his fervent desire to be a people's politician embracing popular concerns, not a patrician embracing those of an academic and privileged elite.

On 2 December 1938, Frank Pakenham was adopted as the official Labour candidate for Oxford. Quintin Hogg no doubt smiled knowingly when he heard the news, given his speculation as to Longford's motives in promoting Lindsay as a Popular Front candidate. It is tempting to give credence to the suggestion that Longford skilfully manoeuvred Gordon Walker out of the way to win the seat for himself. It would have been a deft political coup.

But Longford was not at the time a planner and has never subsequently shown any great talent for political intrigue. He was however zealously concerned about developments in Europe and, with the wishful thinking born of intense worry, Longford sincerely believed a Popular Front candidate might win the seat and in the process sound the death knell for appeasement. And even if the thought of getting the Oxford nomination for himself might have been lurking somewhere in the back of his mind, he would also have been aware that, without the voters of the working-class estates of Cowley and Headington (at that time lumped together with rural Oxfordshire seats), he stood no chance. That revision was not to come about until the late 1940s.

More tellingly, Longford had already accepted the candidature for eminently winnable West Birmingham and had been enthusiastically nurturing the seat for months. The pull of Oxford, which had become as close to a home town as he had ever known, proved too great. Longford threw over the Birmingham seat.

For a moment, however, it seemed as if Transport House might block him in Oxford in an act of revenge for his apostasy over the by-election, but that threat soon evaporated after a good-hearted interview at Labour headquarters.

'I was ecstatic,' Elizabeth recalls. 'Already I saw myself entering Westminster along with Frank, architects of the New Jerusalem. I took it for granted that Oxford was more "winnable" than Birmingham. All the more need to nurse King's Norton as effectively as Frank would nurse Oxford.'[15] It was an inspiring dream, typical of the idealism that they felt at the time – husband and wife entering the Commons together to start building a new society. History had other plans and by the time of the 1945 general election their circumstances were much changed.

However, with their dual candidature, well-placed friends and academic credentials, the Longfords were fast acquiring a reputation on a national Labour stage. Elizabeth continued to commute between Oxford and her constituency in Birmingham. In the spring of 1939 she rented a house in King's Norton for overnight stays and even removed Antonia and Thomas from their smart prep school in Oxford and enrolled them in the local primary school for a week. They survived with flying colours. Longford wrote to his wife, full of the ardour and naivety that characterised his politics at the time, 'I am so glad that they enjoy the school – a good omen for their great working-class-leadership careers.'[16]

For the time being Elizabeth's dedication to politics and

motherhood went hand-in-hand. She had by now learnt to drive – Longford has never quite managed to achieve the degree of co-ordination necessary – and would travel between home and King's Norton with the children sleeping peacefully on the back seat of the car. And she was still intent on expanding her brood. In an interview with the *Daily Express* many years later, she admitted, 'I really got mad about families. Every time the baby became a toddler I wanted to have another one. It's absolutely addictive.'[17]

Longford played only a supporting role in the upbringing of his young children. In his crowded diary of politics, teaching and sport, something had to give and often it was family. However, as Antonia and Thomas grew older, started walking and talking, asking questions, his interest in them increased. 'Frank is a middle and later life expert in the sense that he doesn't remember his own childhood,' says Elizabeth.

> That affected his relations with young children. He
> just wasn't a playing-horses-on-the-floor sort of
> person. He's tremendously cerebral. The moment the
> children reached a point where they could argue with
> him or discuss or be taken to rugger matches, then he
> was extremely interested in them and very popular
> with them.[18]

Both Antonia and Thomas were precocious in their intellectual development, a facet their mother puts down to their father's donnish desire to

> stir up their minds. If they raised topics in the middle
> of a meal, he would get up and look up the book and
> find the answer if he couldn't remember it. The most
> important thing at that moment was to answer the
> question. I don't think that he really lost anything
> through his lack of romping.[19]

At a routine check-up in 1936 with her gynaecologist, Dr Helena Wright, Elizabeth was persuaded to take part in a research programme. Dr Wright was convinced that the sex of a baby could be determined by the fact that male sperm preferred an alkaline solution in the uterus while female sperm preferred an acid one. Elizabeth wanted another boy and, following the steps advocated by Dr Wright, had her wish fulfilled. Patrick was born on 17 April 1937. His arrival was precipitous, and the doctor didn't arrive in time. Instead their live-in nurse had to deliver the baby, assisted, not altogether ably, by Longford. Elizabeth was more concerned that he might injure himself opening the sterilised drum containing bandages, gauze and other essentials than she was with her own pain.

Mother, father and second son came through the ordeal unscathed. The last months of Elizabeth's pregnancy had been overshadowed, however, by a scare over Thomas's health. He fell ill over Christmas of 1936 and had to forgo the pleasure of the festive season with his Lamb cousins. When there was no improvement, he was taken to hospital for tests and was diagnosed as having polio. There followed four anxious months in hospital and even when he was allowed to return home he had to wear a splint on his left arm and a steel and leather collar to support his neck.

For his parents – especially Elizabeth who took care of all domestic arrangements – striking a balance between political ambitions and family was a difficult task. Longford's selection as candidate for Oxford at least meant that they were not both in a state of perpetual transit between home and Birmingham. And since Oxford was a relatively small city, his teaching schedule allowed him time to drop in at Singletree at all hours of the day.

Until 1938 the Longfords' lifestyle had been comfortable if not lavish. (Quite how different it was from that of ordinary working-class families was revealed to the couple when the two young sons of Elizabeth's King's Norton agent came to stay at Singletree and quickly revealed that the size of the house and the novel food made them homesick not happy.) When they were not hosting local branch meetings or fêtes, they were welcoming old friends and fellow socialists to their home – Douglas Jay, Hugh Gaitskell, Evan Durbin.

Through such contacts they participated in the wider debates in the Labour Party concerning the sort of society that would be built in the New Jerusalem. Jay and Durbin were working to evolve a sound socialist economic policy with sympathisers in the City at regular meetings of the XYZ Club, founded in 1932. Longford occasionally attended but did not play any great part in the deliberations of this influential group. Gaitskell, from his academic base at University College, London, was moving among the left-leaning Bloomsbury set, though he was more drawn to the political and economic circle that gathered around Francis Meynell than to Virginia Woolf's artistic set.

The passion of the Longfords' socialism in these years did not inhibit old friendships with those on the other side of the political divide. There was the same contrast between Cowley and Cliveden as there had been between Stoke and Clandeboye. Despite Longford's evident and fervent desire to share the lives and concerns of the people he represented, he did not martyr himself to his convictions. 'Socialist principles did not require one to diminish the quality of life by giving up one's friends,' Elizabeth wrote.[20] Though the couple never made any attempt to hide their beliefs, their friends noted a certain schizophrenia in Longford. In political terms he may have become a committed socialist, but in many of his social attitudes he had not changed at all. 'At heart he has always remained very conservative,' says Maureen Dufferin. 'I remember when my daughter Perdita was coming out. Frank was her godfather and wrote to her saying that he hoped the young men at the coming-out dances still wore gloves.'[21]

Cliveden, in particular, was hostile to Longford's anti-Chamberlain sentiments. Waldorf and Nancy Astor were decidedly pro appeasement and their papers, *The Times* and the *Observer*, followed that line. Much has been written about the influence of the 'Cliveden Set' on Chamberlain. The phrase was coined by Claud Cockburn in *This Week* in 1937 but no real lobby has ever been proved conclusively to have existed, as Longford's presence at Cliveden in this period would suggest. Nancy Astor was later to quip, 'I am supposed to have more power than had Queen Elizabeth, Marie-Antoinette and Cleopatra combined.'[22]

Rather more conducive to Longford's growing enthusiasm for

a Popular Front that would unite left and right in opposition to appeasement were his visits to Chartwell, home of Winston Churchill. Randolph Churchill, having forgiven Longford for turning down the post on the Indian Defence Committee, invited him down to lunch with his father in the autumn of 1935. Conversation inevitably turned to Germany. 'If the Germans are already as strong as you say, what could we do if they landed here?' Longford asked. Churchill, helped no doubt by the copious quantities of alcohol that had been consumed over lunch, replied:

> That should not prove an insoluble conundrum. We are here five able-bodied men. The armoury at our disposal is not perhaps very modern but none of us would be without a weapon. We should sally forth. I should venture to assume the responsibilities of command. If the worst came to the worst, we should sell our lives dearly. Whatever the outcome we should, I feel confident, render a good account of ourselves.[23]

Such fighting talk inspired Longford (and may even have given him the notion of the Florence Park trenches) as it was later to inspire the nation, but he never imagined that Churchill, whom he regarded at this juncture as something of a relic from the past, would ever hold high office again. The friendship between the two men developed. Elizabeth's parents had a house in Kent, just four miles from Chartwell, and, with their children safely in the hands of their grandparents, the young socialists would visit the brooding reactionary in exile. They would occasionally be joined by Professor Lindemann, an old friend of Longford's from Charlton days and the man whose failure to be selected as Conservative candidate in 1935 had led to him organising Herbert's campaign. Lindemann, later Lord Cherwell, was Churchill's scientific adviser, a post he held through the war.

Spending time with friends of differing political opinions did open Longford up to the risk of compromise in the eyes of his electors. Never more so than when the Longfords visited his old

Furzie Close classmate Alec Spearman, now a Tory MP, at his Essex home. Among other guests was Unity Mitford, sister of Jessica and one of the sextet of famous daughters of Lord Redesdale. She was so mesmerised by her friendship with Adolf Hitler that she had become a Nazi and was later to take her own life when she found her country at war with Germany. On the Sunday evening Unity Mitford was heading back to her parents' home and offered Longford, who had an early meeting on the Monday morning, a lift to Oxford *en route*. Longford had cheerfully accepted before he noticed that her car was flying the swastika. Not wanting to appear rude, he hit on a pragmatic and face-saving compromise. As they approached Oxford, he was dropped on the outskirts and managed to disappear down a side-street before the Labour councillor for Cowley was spotted.[24]

In the spring of 1938, Longford's financial circumstances changed quite dramatically when his Uncle Bingo – his father's unmarried brother – died leaving everything to his nephew. Longford, whose socialist principles in theory left little space for inherited wealth, became the rather guilty owner of a furnished house just off Park Lane and a collection of his grandmother's jewellery. Uncle Bingo's decision to omit Edward Longford from the will was thought to be due either to a distaste for his ardent Irish republicanism – a crime infinitely worse, evidently, than joining the Labour Party – or to unhappiness at the way the sixth earl was selling off the family silver to fund the Gate Theatre. Elizabeth prefers the version that attributes Uncle Bingo's unexpected generosity to his entrancement at watching baby Patrick playing one day on the lawn at Great Aunt Caroline's house in Sussex.[25]

Just a couple of months after Bingo's death, Caroline Lady Pakenham passed on, at the age of ninety-six. Bernhurst, her house at Hurst Green and the ample grounds that surrounded it, went, as had been arranged at his birth, to her godson Frank Longford. At last he had the home his mother had always told him was a prerequisite of marriage.

This Georgian house, its Regency additions giving it the look of an elegant rectory, had a five-acre garden with a view of the valley beyond, where the field patterns were little changed from the time of Henry II, Elizabeth was later to discover.[26] It was large enough to accommodate the Longfords' growing family and after the Second World War it became a much loved family home, a weekend retreat from the political world and in their retirement a peaceful haven in which they could write and entertain grandchildren. But in the rush of events leading up to the outbreak of war, there was no time for the family to become significantly attached to Bernhurst before it was requisitioned for use by the Canadians.

The acquisition of such wealth (Bernhurst also had a seventy-five-acre estate) was a burden and to some extent an embarrassment for Longford: the contradiction between his lifestyle and his creed was once again highlighted. But it would enable him to look forward to life as an MP without the attendant worries about providing for his family – at that time the post carried only minimal financial reward. The best way for Longford to ease his conscience would be to spend his fortune on promoting the cause. Some of the money went on bailing out the Liberals in the Oxford by-election. Another slice of wealth was redistributed among the workers who dug the trenches around the Florence Park Estate. But by far the largest amount went to buy the *Town Crier*, a small and unassuming Labour Party newspaper published in Birmingham.

In a keynote leading article, Longford set the radical tone for his paper. It is an uncharacteristically graphic, almost crude, piece of writing whose passion can be understood only in the light of his anxiety to prove his credentials to his new-found party.

> I learnt at first hand the snobbery and corruption that are the lifeblood of the Conversative machine. My stomach turned and reaching for a basin I said 'good-bye to all that' . . . I know the whole dirty business from the inside – I shall never hesitate to use that knowledge for the benefit of the working class.

The new proprietor replaced the incumbent editor, Herbert Green, with his old friend Philip Toynbee, a member of the

Communist Party, and drafted in his sister, Pansy, as women's page editor. Dick Crossman wrote a column on international affairs and Auden a review. Toynbee took to his task with relish, replacing Green's parish pump approach with the ambition to exceed by far the current circulation of 2600 and take the nation by storm. After Eden's resignation as Foreign Secretary in February 1938, the *Town Crier* boldly demanded, 'Chamberlain must go. The *Crier* will make Birmingham too hot to hold him.' (Chamberlain represented the Edgbaston division of Birmingham from 1929.)

Another of Great Aunt Caroline's legacies, her grey Standard car, came in useful in the hands of George Tyler who became both circulation manager for the *Town Crier* and, briefly, Longford's election agent in West Birmingham. The new team at the paper and its proprietor saw it as in the vanguard of a Labour sweep of Birmingham seats. Protest meetings were organised for *Crier* readers to lambast the government. They were moderately well attended. But circulation plummeted.

As a financial venture the *Town Crier* was about as successful as Longford's sally into the world of stocks and shares in 1929. However, it did salve his conscience, but with his nomination as Labour candidate for Oxford in 1939, be became less willing to shoulder the heavy losses for the good of Labour in Birmingham. He reluctantly sold the *Town Crier* at a huge loss. The new proprietor replaced Toynbee with Green and the paper returned to worthy but dull accounts of local meetings.

When he had joined Labour in 1936 Longford had announced, 'I am socialist because I am a Christian.' Though the two creeds were later to be intimately linked in his work, the claim was at this stage fairly loose, simply referring to their common principle of fundamental equality for all. The principle of universal equality remains the rock on which Longford's membership of the Labour Party is built. But Christianity was not yet a central force in Longford's life.

As a child he had been brought up to say his night and morning prayers and, when in Tully Nally, to take his place along the Pakenham pew in the Church of Ireland in the neighbouring village of Castlepollard. At North Aston Hall, spiritual solace had been closer at hand. There was an Anglican chapel attached to the Longfords' Oxfordshire home.

Furzie Close and Eton reinforced this dutiful Christianity, inseparable from public service in Longford's mind. His uncle, Arthur Villiers, for example, claimed a Christian basis for his work in Eton Manor. The moral code which taught that the wealthy should be made aware of the less fortunate and make personal efforts to redress the imbalance was synonymous in political and social terms with Christianity. But despite such a grounding – or indeed because of it – Longford more or less neglected church attendance when he encountered the freedom and attractions of student life at New College.

However in 1925, while still an undergraduate, Longford underwent an operation on his knee for the removal of cartilage. The period of convalescence and forced inactivity which followed made Longford very restless and led in turn to one of the bouts of depression which were to dog his early years. It was during this period that he first began to examine his Christian beliefs more closely. He experienced, he recalls, a burning desire for faith, for something to believe in.[27] Quite what prompted this moment of doubt is hard to ascertain. It may have been youthful idealism or perhaps he was coming to terms with the uncertainties of adult life after his protected childhood.

He remembers one summer day in 1925 practising his serve on the tennis court at North Aston Hall and contemplating life without the hope of an after-life. '"Suppose that there is no such person as God? Suppose there is no one and nothing there at all?" I was overwhelmed; I was temporarily shattered.'[28] He prayed for faith but to no avail. He therefore abandoned his childhood dislike of books and began what has become a lifelong addiction, reading works about Christianity like Lowes Dickinson's *Meaning of Good*. But he also sought out the other position – principally by ploughing through Darwin's *On the Origin of Species*.

From that moment on Longford embarked on a search for a deeper meaning to life. He continued to read, though in a desultory fashion. He defiantly called himself a Christian in fashionable circles where his claim would provoke a good deal of debate and not a little ridicule. But then he had always enjoyed being the odd one out, the iconoclast at weekend house parties.

However, he made little attempt to pursue his interest further – by discussing it with priests or theologians for example, or even by attending church regularly. When he married Elizabeth in 1931, he found little encouragement for his desire to investigate Christianity. Her upbringing had been a strictly Protestant one – 'simple in content and serious in tone. No frills like cribs at Christmas'.[24] Though she had married in a church, had her children baptised and subscribed to a strong ethical code, she had little time for organised religion and a particular dislike of the dogma of Roman Catholicism.

Longford's marriage hastened his conversion to socialism and part of the attraction of the Labour Party was the moral basis for its policies of social justice and wealth redistribution. For a while socialism was enough to satisfy his craving for belief, and thoughts of Christianity retreated in his mind. The role of the Church in the Spanish Civil War, siding with the right-wing forces and the army against the republicans, horrified Longford. And the very circles in which he was moving were strongly anti-Christian. Freddie Ayer, who had been elected to a Christ Church Fellowship the year after Longford, had no time at all for Christianity and the pair of them would have long arguments in the Senior Common Room with Longford usually coming off worse, Philip Toynbee later recalled.[30] The Oxford academic Establishment at the time was disbelieving, though individual dons were practising Christians.

Even in this discouraging atmosphere, however, Longford could not bring himself to bury his doubts. His activism on behalf of the Labour Party did not provide the ready answers to life's big questions that he had hoped for. When he encountered suffering and deprivation and compared it to his own relative good fortune, he could find no coherent explanation in his political creed. He was passionate in his socialism, happy in his work, fortunate in his family life. But there remained what Sartre would later call 'a God-shaped hole'. There was almost an element of guilt in Longford's search.

> The very possession of all these advantages gave me
> the sense of all the holes being stopped. I had nothing
> to fear, but equally nothing to hope for so long as all
> that mattered most at the centre was missing or
> confused or deliberately repressed.[31]

Longford's conversion, during his research for *Peace by Ordeal*, to Irish republicanism was an important factor which both drew him towards the Catholic Church and at the same time pushed him away. It was Catholicism that had given backbone to the Gaelic revival of the late nineteenth century in Ireland which had in turn fed into political discontent and the growth of nationalist claims. The Catholic Church epitomised the differences between Ireland and England and was one reason why the Protestant Anglo-Irish like Longford were out of place in their own land. Eamon de Valera, with whom Longford struck up a close friendship in the 1930s, was an ardent Catholic with great faith in the Church's capacity to effect the smooth and just running of society, so much faith in fact that he enshrined a 'special place' for Catholicism in the 1937 constitution that he drew up for Ireland.

Yet while ideologically Catholicism would complement Longford's Irish nationalism, it was also rather incongruous with the peculiar circumstances of his own childhood there. 'My father once told me' says Antonia Fraser

> when we were staying at Tully Nally with my brother
> and we all were going to Mass that as a child he had
> been brought up to think of the Catholic Church as
> the 'dirty church' – exactly those words. When he
> became a Catholic, it was all done in England. But
> then when he had to go to the Castlepollard Catholic
> church, it was a real problem for him. Not a problem
> that he allowed to surmount him but psychologically
> in his childhood they had been a true Ascendancy
> family – the servants were Catholics and the gentry
> were Protestants.[32]

In theory, as a socialist, Longford wanted to break free of such divisions and go to church with the servants, to be a true Irishman. Yet in practice, when he was staying at Tully Nally, it was not so easy. Another inhibitor was the fact that, whatever De Valera's enthusiasm, the Catholic Church in Ireland had little in its policies to recommend it to a liberal-minded Oxford-based socialist.

It was the decisive influence of Father Martin D'Arcy that turned Longford's conflicting emotions and his sporadic religious search into something much more purposeful. The Jesuit Master of Campion Hall in Oxford was a well-known figure in university circles. Patrick O'Donovan, the *Observer* journalist and a Christ Church undergraduate in the late 1930s, described D'Arcy as 'the epitome of all that was brilliant or dangerous within the Roman Church, of all that was sensitive or guileful among the Jesuits'.[33] Such a combination of glamour and cleverness inevitably appealed to Longford. Elizabeth first met D'Arcy when she was an undergraduate. They both attended a lunch party at Balliol. First impressions were clouded by the anti-Catholicism of her Unitarian upbringing.

> His elegant figure, dark wavy hair, aristocratic features
> and air of subtle sophistication immediately made me
> think of Mephistopheles – a character who in any case
> I tended to equate with all but the untidiest priests.
> But when, at the end of lunch, Father D'Arcy politely
> offered me my coat back to front so that I could not
> get into the sleeves, I realised I had got him wrong.[34]

In 1931 D'Arcy published a book *The Nature of Belief* which Longford enjoyed and the two met occasionally. D'Arcy was friendly with Evelyn Waugh whom he had converted to Catholicism in 1930. The character of Father Rothschild in Waugh's *Vile Bodies* was reportedly based on Father D'Arcy. Campion Hall, only a stone's throw from Christ Church, was a collection of students' lodgings when D'Arcy took charge. When he left it had been transformed into a handsome building by Sir Edward Lutyens.

In addition to his Christian reading at the time, Longford had been taking another look at Marx and trying to sort out some kind of synthesis between the Marxist view of class struggle and Jesus Christ's words in the Sermon on the Mount, 'Blessed are the poor'. It was a difficult task – as subsequent generations of liberation theologians will testify – and Longford was making little progress when he recalls bumping into Father D'Arcy. 'I had just chaired a meeting for a visiting speaker, the general-secretary of the Communist Party, at the Town Hall and I was walking back to my room in Tom Quad when I ran into Father D'Arcy. I felt like St Peter seeing Christ.'[35]

Longford outlined his confusion to the Jesuit and was invited to visit him in Campion Hall. It was only a short walk but the decision to go ranks as one of the most significant moments in Longford's life.

> I rang the bell, asked to see the Master and fortu-
> nately found him at home. Within half an hour he
> knew all, and no doubt more than all, that I thought
> worth telling him about myself.[36]

Their relationship quickly developed. Longford would visit Campion Hall whenever his already overcrowded schedule allowed. Father D'Arcy would suggest books – starting with St Augustine's *Confessions* – that he should read to move him forward in his search for faith. On Sundays Longford would attend Mass at the Greyfriars' Franciscan Church on Iffley Road near Singletree.

He held back from embarking on formal instruction as a prelude to joining up. There was the problem of Rome's stance in the Spanish Civil War but Longford managed, with Father D'Arcy's encouragement, to separate the political acts of particular leaders from questions of faith and morals. The main obstacle remained the intellectual way in which Longford insisted on evaluating Catholicism. Just as he had taken socialism to his heart long before he was convinced in his head, he knew quite soon that he wanted to be a Catholic, but he could not make such a leap of faith unless he could convince himself of the truth of the fundamental tenets of Catholicism. The rigid adherence to the Church's rules demanded of all Catholics also proved a stumbling block. To be bound to a set of regulations handed down from on high went against Longford's democratic beliefs.

Though it had been his personal admiration of Father D'Arcy and his own ardent Irish republicanism that led Longford initially to seek out Catholic counsel, he did also consider the claims of his own Anglicanism. But that same academic rigour that made him scrutinise each and every claim of the Church also led him to reject the Church of England's historical base. Discussing in 1953 the difference between the Church of his birth and Catholicism he wrote:

> Either you base yourself, it seems to me, on the idea
> of the one Church founded by Our Lord with a
> guarantee of endurance and continuance from His day
> to ours. That leads you, or at least it has led me, to
> Rome. Or you can discover the Holy Ghost wherever
> two or three are gathered together which validates the
> Church of England.[37]

At Greyfriars Longford grew attached to the Catholic ritual, its mixture of certainty and humility and its ability to draw together the high and the low as equal before God – an achievement that had eluded him in his political activities in Cowley. Accepting that Christian ethics – particularly those concerning society – were compatible with his socialist principles was no great problem. But Longford had to justify any conversion in absolute terms. With Father D'Arcy's help, he began to ask the fundamental questions – does God exist? Was Jesus divine?

Much of his reading centred on the resurrection. If the tomb could be proved to be empty, if the change in the behaviour of the disciples after they claimed to see the risen Lord could be accepted, then the divinity of Christ, for Longford, followed.

> After a few months [of study with Father D'Arcy] I
> knew in outline the main arguments for and against
> the existence of God. But I soon saw that some of the
> deepest philosophical problems centring round God's

existence – I mention only the problem of suffering –
were not going to decide the issue one way or the
other for me. If I could believe in the Son of the
Gospels, I could believe in the Father described
there.[38]

The challenge then for Longford was to take the gospel accounts
at face value. Once he had achieved that, all else would follow
naturally. As he pondered over this, there remained one further
obstacle to Longford's conversion. His wife had not the least
idea why he had been visiting Father D'Arcy nor of what he
was contemplating. He knew that she would be horrified both
at his betrayal and at his choice.

Six

The outcast

Frank, full of ambitions to serve in any capacity,
civil or military, greatly dismayed by the obscenity
of conversations among private soldiers and full of
resentment that he was obliged to attend Church
of England ceremonies

Evelyn Waugh's Diary: *October 1939*[1]

In early 1939 Winston Churchill paid a visit to the Oxford
Union, the scene six years earlier of the landmark rejection of
the 'King and Country' motion and of his son's subsequent
ignominious failure to have it overturned. It was symbolic of the
changing mood both in the university and the country at large
that Churchill's fighting talk about facing up to the fascist threat
was loudly applauded by an audience which reflected all shades
of political opinion. In place of the divisions and differences that
had left Britain impotent in the face of Hitler and Mussolini for
much of the decade, a consensus was emerging. Longford was
there to see Churchill responding to his ovation by saying, 'I
have not changed but you have trained on.'

Hitler's naked aggression towards Czechoslovakia in March of
1939 made a mockery of the Munich settlement and hopes for
'peace in our time'. Mussolini's invasion of Albania the following
month destroyed Chamberlain's hopes of detaching Italy from
its alliance with Germany and opened up the prospect of further
territorial aggrandisement by the Axis powers in the Balkans.
Chamberlain's blithe statement a week before the German
takeover of Czechoslovakia that 'Europe was settling down to a
period of tranquillity' made him look increasingly foolish and
out of touch. Pressed by public opinion, the Labour opposition

and his own backbenchers, on 31 March Chamberlain guaranteed Poland's independence and integrity against Germany, in effect marking the end of appeasement. War loomed ever larger.

Even in the face of such military expansionism, some on the left of the Labour Party continued to cling to the hope that peace could be maintained through an alliance with the Soviet Union. But such a dream was effectively dashed when in August 1939 the Communists sided with the fascists in the Molotov-Ribbentrop pact. Those like Gaitskell who had long warned that Popular Front ideas were not the ready answer they seemed were not surprised. But for those who had put their trust in a defensive agreement with the Soviets to contain Hitler it was a heavy blow.

After Mussolini's invasion of Albania, however, Longford had moved away from the left and its conviction that a Popular Front could halt Hitler. He had begun to doubt that such an alliance would be enough and became more and more convinced that war was inevitable. If it came to a fight, he would have no truck with those on the pacifist wing. He was willing to defend king and country.

The divisions in the Labour Party between the left and the national leadership over how to avoid war started to seem irrelevant. The real question was what role to play in the preparations for the fight. When, as a response to the Italians' takeover of King Zog's realm, Chamberlain introduced conscription – six months for men of twenty – Attlee and his team voted against. Part of their reasoning was that the Tories were breaking a guarantee given only weeks before not to opt for conscription. There were also fears among the union leaders that the measure was a prelude to industrial conscription, forcing workers to labour in the armament factories.

Attlee said in effect that his party had no objection to men volunteering and saw it as a better way to build a strong and motivated defence force. Hugh Dalton reinforced the point in a document he presented to the party conference in Southport in the summer, adding a plea that the hierarchical structure of the military be reviewed in line with democratic principles.

Critics of the Labour stance said that the party was paying lip service to fighting the Nazi menace without giving the government practical support. But Longford, who had attended the Southport conference, swung behind his party leaders and was attracted to the loophole that the Attlee–Dalton line offered to those who wanted to prepare for war in a practical way by volunteering. So while he was attending protest meetings in Oxford's Co-op Hall on behalf of Labour, alongside such youthful Communists as Denis Healey,[2] then an undergraduate at Balliol, to condemn the policy of conscription, he had also volunteered for service. Proud of his physical fitness (he reached the semi-finals of the *Oxford Mail* tennis championships in 1939 and ran regularly around Christ Church Meadow clocking up a five minute mile), and drawn to the romantic figure of his father falling at the head of his troops on Scimitar Hill, he could not remain idle. The desire to act, to prove he was willing to defend his country, that had partly inspired the Florence Park trenches, led him to break ranks with many in the Labour Party and enlist with the local territorials.

He was disappointed at the time that so few of the young lionhearts in the Labour movement joined him. Certainly among his progressively minded intellectual friends, he noticed a marked reluctance to act which he was fond of contrasting with the public-spirited rallying to the flag of what he called 'the more dissolute type of West End club man'.[3] His dual allegiances were exposed – to an aristocratic heritage which stressed from an early age that a young man's place in times of national trial was at the Front on the one hand, and on the other to a Labour movement reluctant to get entangled in a capitalists' war as some of the more radical left supporters then regarded it.

Yet for all the Pakenhams' long history of service on the field of battle, Longford had little, beyond his physical fitness, to offer the territorials. Already in his mid-thirties and suffering the first twinges of rheumatism and lumbago, he had not even been a member of the 'Corps' at Eton. Indeed his house had taken 'playing soldiers' with a healthy dose of humorous scepticism. 'There was a terrible occasion when our Company turned out on the great day of Inspection in false horn-rimmed spectacles and when called upon to number rapped out very smartly one, two, three, four, five, six, seven, eight, nine, ten, knave, queen, king.'⁴ Edward Longford refused to join the Corps on the grounds of his Irish nationalism. For Frank Longford it was a less principled stance. To join would have meant rifle practice. Rifle practice would have meant wearing his glasses and his vanity intervened.

However, such youthful omissions were more than redressed when, in the tense months of 1938 and 1939, Europe was shaken by crisis after crisis over Hitler's aggression and Mussolini's expansionism. Longford's response to these events was as instant as it was sporadic. One outrage sent him off to the barrack square at Cowley where he cut a rather lonely figure as he was put through his paces by a genial Regimental Sergeant Major. Another saw him doing early morning manoeuvres in Port Meadow with the university OTC's cavalry section. Hitler was to be rebuffed by Oxford dons and undergraduates on horseback. At the time of Munich, as well as digging trenches, he took the first steps towards enlisting, but his enthusiasm ebbed as the crisis passed.

However, in the wake of the Albania episode and the growing realisation that war was imminent, Longford made what he describes as 'an emotional dash'⁵ to volunteer for service in the newly formed Fifth (Territorial) Battalion of the Oxford and Bucks Light Infantry. As a good socialist and mindful of Dalton's demand in Southport that the forces be democratised, he preferred to be a private and not an officer.

Enlisting was not much more than a gesture and did not greatly disturb his teaching and political duties. There was drill once a week, the occasional spot of target practice at Bicester, and then a fortnight's camp in August. But as a gesture it carried great resonance in the city. Here was the progressively minded, some would say Communist-influenced, donnish Labour parliamentary candidate for Oxford joining the humble ranks of the territorials to do his patriotic best. To critics it was an election ruse to restore the credibility of a party which overall seemed to be at best equivocal about fighting. For others it only enhanced Longford's reputation for eccentricity as they watched him marching up the High Street at the rear of the column. 'He was a very weird soldier because he was so uncoordinated,' says Denis Healey.[6]

Other left-wing activists took a very dim view indeed of what they saw as his *de facto* – if not *de jure* – desertion of the party line but the *Oxford Mail* loved it and ran a big picture of 'Private Pack' offering one of the lads a light for his cigarette. 'Have a fag, mate' was the caption. Longford has never smoked but it was considered a suitable gesture of male solidarity.

Private Pack found male bonding a little strained when he attended summer camp in 1939. Since none of his fellow Oxford socialists had joined the ranks, he was deprived of like-minded company. The ritual of preparing his uniform for parade was more than he could manage. He ended up by paying a kindly sergeant ten-bob-a-go to do it for him. Notwithstanding his attachment to a more equal society where all class barriers were removed, sleeping twelve to a tent was quite beyond him, while the four-letter words that peppered his colleagues' prose left him speechless. He had picked up enough of this badinage, Elizabeth recalls, to shock the local vicar when they played tennis several weeks later.[7]

The deference demanded of the ranks offended both his socialist principles and his aristocratic upbringing. Some of the more staunchly Conservative members of the officer corps regarded having the local Labour candidate in the ranks as a chance to teach him a lesson. Longford did not enjoy the endless round of saluting men who made little attempt to disguise their aim of needling him. His dream of military heroism was already turning sour. Antonia Fraser recalls going with her mother to visit her father at the summer camp. They found him very depressed. 'It was a ghastly experience, a canvas camp with the stink of latrines and Dadda looking ludicrous in his uniform – like a noble lion.'[8]

A brief respite at Bernhurst was all he managed after a thoroughly disheartening two weeks at camp. It did little to lift the cloud of depression that was descending on him. When the family returned to Oxford at the end of August, he was recalled to his unit with the outbreak of war now predicted any day. Elizabeth took the children to stay with friends at Water Eaton

Manor to the north of the city. It was there that she heard on the wireless Chamberlain's announcement of war on the morning of 3 September. Longford was listening at camp near Banbury.

The phoney war was a time of contrasting fortunes for the Longfords. (They had handed Singletree over to the council, complete with furniture and fittings, for the use of evacuees.) Elizabeth and the children, living in the countryside, found it was almost a rural idyll. For Longford himself, however, it was abject misery. With the official declaration of hostilities he was persuaded to drop his objections to the officer caste and was elevated from the ranks to Second Lieutenant. At least it meant that any open hostility to him by officers could be side-stepped. His appointed task at the battalion's base at Banbury was welfare work, his lack of skill with military hardware having already been noted. This detail included giving French lessons both to officers and NCOs: the defence of France was envisaged as one of the first tasks of the British troops. Longford's WEA training also came in handy when he was called on to give the privates history lectures. 'When I asked them,' he wrote to Elizabeth, "Hands up those who knew that Austria-Hungary existed before the Great War?" – one hand went up. "What is neutrality?" – half knew.'[9]

The image of his father at Gallipoli, in the heart of the battle dying for his country, seemed light years away. Longford's mental state deteriorated. The phoney war was a trying time for the entire nation and Longford's gloom reflected the strain, inactivity exacerbating his disillusion with the army and the future. His vision of a Labour victory at the 1940 general election and a seat in the Commons next to his wife, building a New Jerusalem, faded like a mirage.

The cloud lifted briefly in October when he was approached by the Ministry of Information. His reputation as the author of *Peace by Ordeal* and as a friend of the Irish leader de Valera had preceded him. The British government was keen to secure Irish involvement in the war against Hitler and the use of Ireland's ports for the Royal Navy. The fear was that Ireland – which had determined on a neutral position – would be exploited by the

Germans as a back-door route to attack Britain and British shipping. The Germans were thought to be no great respecters of neutrality and confirmed these suspicions by their occupation of neutral Norway in May 1940. Wanting to persuade de Valera to change his mind, the government turned to the one man who had stood up for the Irish leader.

Longford felt uneasy in the role. He was in effect, as he later remarked, a 'double agent', ostensibly anxious to promote the British war effort, a parliamentary candidate for an English seat and a member of the British army.[10] Yet he was also an Irish republican, an admirer of de Valera and strongly sympathised with his old friend's determination to keep Ireland out of the war. Longford approached his task in two minds and thus with little hope of success – though he was thankful at least to escape camp routine for a while.

His career as a diplomat lasted only a week. He arranged a meeting with de Valera but could not think how to persuade him. 'Dev seemed terribly tired,' he wrote to Elizabeth. 'It was heroic of him to see me at eight o'clock – but when I repeated Winston Churchill's rude remarks about Ireland's part in the war, he perked up.'[11] He abandoned his mission.

Back in Banbury any interest in national and international politics was quickly dispelled by the daily drudgery. There was talk that the battalion would be part of a British Expeditionary Force to the continent but beyond such a glimmer of what Longford took to be future glory there was only his reading to keep him occupied. He found living in a community impossible. Visits to Hackney Wick and occasional stays in Stoke had not prepared him for the grim reality of a life where all the privileges and privacy he took for granted were replaced by a strict and unbending hierarchy of ranks. He sought solitude in a hut on the base and tried to teach himself to admire the qualities that were valued in the army. He swotted up on his military strategy books – anxious in some small way to make good his own deficiencies with his kit and in arms drill. 'And like every other intellectual of my acquaintance I returned to *War and Peace* and said how like the past was the present, and Napoleon's role to Hitler's.'[12]

All of which left little time for the spiritual reading prescribed by Father D'Arcy. War found Longford in a similar prevaricative state about the Catholic Church as he had been about the Labour Party a few years earlier. His old friend Evelyn Waugh was later to attribute this equivocation to Father D'Arcy. 'He likes to keep his converts hovering on the edge of the Church,' Waugh told Longford.[13] But the block was Longford's, not Father D'Arcy's. Emotionally won over, he could not quite accept all the Church's claims on an intellectual level. The don in him had been holding him back. But now he found himself not in the secluded environment of Tom Quad but as part of a battalion of soldiers preparing for combat. Just as the Mosley meeting had instantaneously dissolved the intellectual obstacles to his political conversion, so the possibility of front-line service precipitated his religious conversion.

In November Longford received a letter at Banbury from Waugh asking him to act as godfather to his son Auberon. Waugh had heard, erroneously, that Longford had finally come over to Rome. Writing back to disabuse him, Longford revealed that he was very close to the Church but not quite in the fold. (Though that did not stop him going on to be godfather, a role in which he has served, according to his charge, with distinction, save for one occasion when he sent the teenage Auberon a Neville Shute novel as a Christmas present, only to be rebuked by his father over its snares for an impressionable mind.)[14]

Evelyn Waugh responded to Longford's letter by advising him to cast aside his doubts and his reading and take the plunge. 'There is nothing to stop you asking for immediate reception. Discussion can become a pure luxury. This is no time for a soldier to delay.'[15] The battalion, he pointed out, was expected to be sent overseas and there might never be another chance.

Longford likens the effect of reading this letter to St Augustine hearing a voice in the garden telling him to pick up the Bible. On absorbing a couple of verses, Augustine wrote: 'No further would I read; nor needed I; for instantly at the end of this sentence by a light as it were of serenity infused into my heart, all the darkness of doubt vanished away.'

Inspired by Waugh's straight talking, Longford went to seek

151

out his spiritual mentor. Father D'Arcy, however, was away in America (reportedly as an agent of the British government sent to win over the Catholic community there to the war effort, though this was never confirmed). So he turned instead to Father Wulfstan, the Guardian of Greyfriars in Iffley where he had been attending Mass for some eighteen months. He asked for formal instruction with a view to joining the Church and, given the imminence of his battalion's departure for the field of battle, was rushed through the various stages. He would get leave to visit Father Wulfstan and was taken through the clauses of the *Penny Catechism* beginning with 'Do you believe in God?' It was a very different approach from the intellectual subtleties of Father D'Arcy but one well suited to Longford's mood. When he finally embraced socialism he did so in an atmosphere of emotion and practicality rather than one of tortuous reason and logic. It was the same with Catholicism. Under stress, believing himself to be facing death, he buried his intellectual doubts and took to heart a black and white Catholicism that left little room for debate of fundamental doctrines.

In January news came through that his battalion was being sent to the Isle of Wight. He obtained a night's leave and spent it with the community at Greyfriars. That evening he was received into the Church and took communion for the first time at Mass the next morning. Though he made the step at a time when his morale was very low, Longford has never questioned the wisdom of what he did in those hours at Greyfriars. The doubts that remained in his mind at that point have been overtaken by the years and by subsequent experiences. Academic conversations in those immediate pre-war days about St Thomas and his four proofs of the existence of God have been replaced by an instinctive, profound and unshakeable faith.

Though Waugh played a part in Longford's final leap of faith, the two belonged to different Catholic Churches. Both shared a fierce loyalty to Church doctrine but Waugh moved in circles peopled with glamorous converts and the scions of Catholic recusant families of old. He recorded such a world in *Brideshead Revisited*[16] (a book which Longford considers depressing in its depiction of English Catholicism).[17] Waugh's Catholicism had a social aspect. Longford's was more socialist. The ethics of his politics dovetailed with his Christian belief. In his conversion lay a desire to belong with the people: at one level as a son of Ireland in his membership of their national Church; at another as an equal before God with fellow parishioners at Greyfriars.

The joy of reception into the Church that Sunday in January was rapidly overtaken by the prospect of telling Elizabeth what he had done. His searching for a Christian belief had been undertaken alone. It was the first significant decision during their marriage that they had not shared. While the two of them had, at differing paces, been convinced of the worth of socialism, Longford's conviction that socialist ideas of the equal worth of human beings led to a Christian belief that we are all children of the one God was not shared by his wife. Her upbringing had left her with a residual antipathy to organised religion in general and the dogma of Roman Catholicism in particular.

Elizabeth knew he had been going to Mass, seeing Father D'Arcy, but she was not prepared for the news he brought her that Sunday. 'I knew it was going on but we would perform parts. I never once said, "Don't go to mass this morning. Let's have a morning off", or anything like that. But we didn't discuss it.'[18]

When he came to her after the events at Greyfriars, Elizabeth was angry and betrayed. It was the worst crisis of their marriage. 'We didn't have a bloody row or anything of that sort. Frank said it was better this way, a *fait accompli*. If I had known I would have felt obliged to do everything I could to stop him. This way there was nothing I could do except leave him and I wasn't going to do that.'[19] In retrospect, she concedes that his tactic may well have been the right one, but that did not stop her feeling wounded at the time.

She felt, she recalls, as if a barrier had been erected between them, a barrier of priests. Part of her phobia about Catholics had centred on the influence of clerics over their flocks. 'A black beetle has got on my tram,' she once wrote as a student to her parents when she spotted a Catholic priest. There were also more recent grounds for her dislike. Spurred on by Dr Helena Wright, her gynaecologist, Elizabeth supported the wider availability of contraception, and had spoken up for the cause in an Oxford Union debate. Such views were tantamount to heresy in the Catholic Church of the 1930s. It was only in the 1950s that the Pope accepted that women might legitimately space the births of their children. Artificial contraception remains banned.

She worried about the children too. Would they be expected to convert to Catholicism and where would that leave her? And would Catholicism be a handicap to Longford's career? Nancy Astor, for one, was horrified by his conversion. Though her anti-Catholicism had a fanatical edge on account of her Christian Scientist beliefs, it was not uncommon among the ruling classes. (David Astor says that his mother's disagreement with Longford over his change of faith did not come between them for long. 'Soon he was teasing her about it. They were both at a Buckingham Palace garden party once when Frank spotted a cardinal. He rushed over to kiss his ring like a good Catholic should. My mother thought he was doing it just to annoy her.')[20]

In the 1930s and 1940s the Catholic Church in England had yet to emerge from internal exile. Its hierarchy had been restored less than 100 years previously after the persecutions of the post-Reformation period. Civil rights had only been conceded to Catholics the previous century and in the folklore of the Church memories of past injustices remained fresh. It stood, for the most part, semi-detached from national life, acutely aware it was different, outside the establishment of which Frank Longford had hitherto been an – albeit eccentric – part. This was the era of the 'fortress' Church, as Cardinal Basil Hume was later to call it, when Catholics huddled together in their schools and parishes and avoided contact with a wider world. Their allegiance to the Pope – a foreign power – and their prayers for the conversion of England – 'Mary's dowry' – made the Catholic community an object of suspicion for many in the governing classes. Catholic MPs were still rare (though Elizabeth had faced the formidable D. W. J. O'Donovan in the Union debate on contraception) and it was thought that Catholicism could be a severe handicap for a young man with aspirations to sit in the Cabinet.

Elizabeth's sense of betrayal and of suppressed anger took a long time to subside. Antonia remembers an incident one Sunday morning in the summer of 1940 when their father arrived back from Mass.

> My mother said, 'Beat the Orange drum children. Go on, beat the Orange drum!' So I said, 'What do you mean?' I'd imagined this orange drum. And she said 'Oh well daddy's been to church, beat the Orange drum'. Then I think she got quite embarrassed. But it was significant, a very hostile kind of behaviour from my mother who unqualifiedly adores my father.[21]

On the surface, however, Elizabeth's anger could not last for long. For Longford was off to camp on the Isle of Wight and his letters were full of woe. If he had expected conversion and Catholicism to ease the ordeal of being in the army, he was quickly disillusioned. Though he had been out of the familiar, comforting and stimulating Oxford world during the five months he had spent at Banbury, he had been within striking distance, able to pop back to talk to old acquaintances, engage in debate and discussion, see his family.

But all ties with kindred spirits were broken when the Oxford and Bucks arrived on the south coast. Longford did not make himself popular with his fellow officers who regarded this don in their midst as a 'know-all subaltern' for asking for Labour's *Daily Herald* to be ordered for the mess as an alternative to the *Daily Telegraph* and *Times*. There was no longer time for educational and welfare activities. At Banbury his inability to make his bed to the regulation formula or to keep in step when on marches had been put down to a likeable eccentricity. Lieutenant Pakenham, the socialist aristocrat, had been treated like a battalion mascot. However, with front-line service imminent, such indulgence evaporated as the Oxford and Bucks was put through its paces.

Longford's health had been poor since the summer camp of the previous year. He had suffered a series of colds and 'flus which had coincided with his depression and frustration at the inactivity of the phoney war and the philistinism of those around him. Despite his outward physical fitness, he has been prone throughout his life to mild attacks of nervous exhaustion. (Evelyn Waugh records in his diary for July 1947 that Longford was suffering from fainting fits.)[22] Usually these could be dealt with by a couple of days of taking it easy, watched over by Elizabeth. But on a wintry Isle of Wight with war looming there could be no such respite.

He tried to summon up the enthusiasm to join in with drilling and assault courses in arctic conditions. But, despite his pride in keeping fit, he was so depressed that he could not find the necessary spark. Far from giving him a new lease of life as he had fervently hoped it would, faith had only added to his troubles by involving him in an unhappy situation at home with his angry wife. When he crept away to the chapel to pray for strength and endurance, he found little solace. In such a low state of mind, Longford succumbed, after crawling through a wet field on exercises, to a bout of gastric 'flu.

Less than a week after he had left for the Isle of Wight on 11 January, news came through to Elizabeth that her husband was in hospital in London. His physical and mental wretchedness did not stop him trying to return to camp several weeks later to do his patriotic duty as generations of Pakenhams had before him, but by March he was back in hospital with a second attack of 'flu. Army life, even in the relatively gentle atmosphere of a training camp, did not suit him. Regimentation and order broke his spirit. The gap between his romantic ideals and the reality of battalion life was insufferable. Boredom, inactivity and a sense of powerlessness did the rest. Though it was his body that was letting him down, Longford was suffering a mental breakdown. Physical fitness has always been one of Longford's obsessive interests. Had he been in the right frame of mind then his body would not have failed him.

Two months later, during his second stay in hospital in London, he received what he described to Elizabeth in a letter as a 'congenial' note from the adjutant in his battalion, 'saying that a Board would be arranged when he applied for it – no hurry suggested'.[23] The Board would probably decide Longford should be invalided out on health grounds. The battalion had clearly decided he was not an asset to the army.

On the one hand Longford fervently wanted to be invalided out as a means of escaping the mental torture he had endured. Yet on the other he felt humiliated by failure to serve his country and countrymen in their hour of need. His confused reaction became apparent when he was released from hospital in April and spent some time on leave with Elizabeth and the children at Bernhurst. While he would admit to Elizabeth that the Board might be a blessing in disguise, that he indeed might not be suited to army life and could better help the war effort with his mind rather than his body, with Thomas and Antonia he would plan and eventually carry out a mock assault on the house from the woods beyond. Bernhurst was after all a Pakenham house and it was his signal failure to live up to the Pakenham ideal that Longford found the most painful part of the impending Board.

During his convalescence, he had been visited by many friends among them Evan Durbin, Douglas Jay, his former student and future government colleague, Christopher Mayhew, who was in the British Expeditionary Force in France, and Douglas Woodruff, the editor of the Catholic weekly *The Tablet*. Woodruff had known Longford slightly through his Christ Church links and had been told of his conversion and breakdown.

Visitors could not distract Longford from an overwhelming sense of impotence as Britain finally shook off the lethargy of the phoney war and Churchill took over as Prime Minister. The declaration of war had been followed by the partitioning of Poland between the Germans and Russians. Chamberlain tried to salvage his reputation by including erstwhile opponents of his failed appeasement policies in his War Cabinet. Churchill returned as First Lord of the Admiralty and Eden as Dominions Secretary. Labour supported wholeheartedly the war effort and hence the government, though it did not prevent Attlee from pointing up some of the shortcomings in Chamberlain's actions. Why, he asked in March 1940, after six months of war were there still 1.4 million unemployed when pits, ships and ports were lying idle?

Chamberlain's final downfall came in May. Norway, though officially neutral, had been invaded by Hitler in April. The British troops sent out there were ill-equipped and were forced to evacuate on 2 May.

In May, just as the Oxford and Bucks was preparing to depart for the Low Countries, Second Lieutenant Francis Pakenham was gazetted as having resigned his commission owing to ill-health. He had not applied for release – that would have been to compound what was already almost unbearable – but neither did he protest against the decision which was approved by two medical boards. His battalion went on to serve with honour in France but at the cost of many casualties.

Though not unexpected the Board's verdict devastated Longford. For him it was absolute failure. The scar it left has never healed. He has always sought ways to make good that failure. When he joined Attlee's government in 1945 he begged for some role with the army and the Prime Minister duly obliged.

If such efforts did not permit Longford to close that unhappy chapter in his life, he was ultimately to turn the residual trauma to good effect. 'I think now', he says,

> that my war record was more glorious than if I hadn't
> tried at all. I try now to take a philosophical view, that
> it was good for me to fail. I was so privileged – a don,
> an Honourable, at Christ Church. I had a wonderful
> marriage, children. Everything was going so well. In a
> practical way I was humiliated. Not to be in uniform
> when my whole background revolved around
> whether you had had a good or bad war was a
> humiliation. Yet to have failed and to be aware of it –
> for better or worse – means that you can share with
> people. When I meet people society despises, I know
> what it is like to be humiliated.[24]

It was an experience, Elizabeth says, that gave her husband greater understanding of others who had been brought, perhaps not before an army board, but before a magistrates' court and sent, not back to civilian life, but to prison.[25]

And in time, as with most of the significant events in his life, Longford managed to turn his army débâcle into a joke against himself. He wrote an article in *Horizon*, a magazine founded by Cyril Connolly and Stephen Spender, about the pain of being of an age to serve your country when it is at war, but not being able to take the pace. He signed the piece 'Neuro' but made little attempt to hide his identity as the author. Indeed he often used to sign letters to his old friend David Astor with the same epithet. 'He just made a joke of himself. He's an amazingly honest person like that.'[26]

Longford was not alone among his contemporaries in finding the rigours of military life too much. John Betjeman failed his medical board and was sent to Ireland as press attaché in the Dublin embassy. Others, more clear-sighted than Longford and not weighed down by a Pakenham upbringing, saw at once that they could best serve their country with their brains and intellects rather than their brawn. Longford never stopped to think about such an alternative and paid the price for such impulsiveness. He rushed to join the territorials; he rushed to join the ranks; and despite his complete antipathy for military life he fixed his gaze on front-line service.

Though he was later to express regret at not having seen active service, Hugh Gaitskell was recruited before the war broke out, as that rare commodity, a German-speaking economist, into the Ministry of Economic Warfare where he worked under Dalton. Douglas Jay went into the Ministry of Supply moving later to the Board of Trade where he worked alongside Evan Durbin. While Longford was agonising over not being in the field, his circle was laying foundations for future careers in government. Because of his military interlude, in effect, he lost his chance.

The April trip to Bernhurst was to be the last the Longfords made for the duration of the war. Four days after their return to Water Eaton Manor on 6 May, Hitler launched his attack on the Benelux countries. As his forces swept away all opposition they rolled into France, pushing the British Expeditionary Force back to Dunkirk. Because of the invasion scare, families living near the south coast – Bernhurst is just thirteen miles from Hastings

– were given the choice to evacuate. Longford had been offered his old job back at Christ Church so the furniture was put in storage and the house was taken over by the government.

Back in Oxford, the Longfords began slowly to rebuild their lives. Water Eaton Manor had been only a temporary refuge and Elizabeth decided that she had better find a home for her family. The task was all the more urgent since she was pregnant. The house she chose – 8, Chadlington Road in north Oxford – was next door to her student digs, the place where Longford had visited her back in 1930 after his dream to invite her to Ireland. The only drawback was the neighbourhood. It was staunchly Conservative, not the place for the city's Labour candidate as his colleagues in the party pointed out when they joked about his home in the 'White Highlands'. Judith was born on 14 August 1940, during the Battle of Britain.

Back at Christ Church, Longford could almost have missed the fact that there was a war going on. There were still students to teach and the only privation the dons had to suffer was a three-course lunch instead of four. A. J. P. Taylor described Oxford as 'a haven of peace' during the war years. Such cushioning only made Longford feel worse about his military failure. Salvation was at hand though, in a scheme Churchill launched in the summer of 1940.

By June of 1940 Britain was 'standing alone' after the invasion of France. To defend the island fortress, Churchill backed a plan to raise Local Defence Volunteers but changed the name to the Home Guard. It was a godsend to Longford. He was able to displace some of his guilt about not being in France by setting up the South Company of the Oxford City Battalion with his friend Maurice Bowra, the Warden of Wadham and a veteran of the Great War, as his number two. It was, he was later to claim, the keenest company in Britain, eclipsing even that of Warmington-on-Sea.

Its activities were not, however, without a touch of *Dad's Army* about them. Longford's war wound was inflicted when one of the privates in the battalion accidentally discharged his gun into the pavement of the Abingdon Road. The bullets ricocheted into the feet of three officers standing nearby. Longford suffered most and was rushed to hospital where an incompetent doctor managed to sew his wounded foot and his sock together. It began to suppurate and only the speedy intervention of another more skilled medic managed to drain the poison and save the foot. Longford kept the splinters of bullet as a war memorial to show his grandchildren.

On another occasion, Elizabeth woke in the middle of the night to the sound of the church bells ringing. This was the signal for a German invasion. When she tried to rouse her husband, a notoriously heavy sleeper as she had discovered the first time she met him, he merely turned over and did not wake. Luckily for him it was a false alarm.

Oxford escaped the German bombardment. When other historic towns like Bath were targeted, the people of Oxford held their breath. When the bombers did not come a rumour began to circulate that Hitler wanted Oxford as the capital of the Nazi colony of Britain and was therefore keeping it intact. One malicious tongue even suggested that Longford's old adversary from the 1935 election, Cruttwell, was to be the Germans' cultural attaché. But if Oxford escaped, the war was never very far away from some other towns. Elizabeth used to lie awake at night listening to the distant drone of the planes passing overhead, aiming for Birmingham and the factories of her King's Norton constituency where they were to drop their bombs. And almost daily news would arrive of another friend lost in action. Ronald Cartland, her Conservative opponent in King's Norton, was killed with the British Expeditionary Force while Aidan Crawley, a fighter pilot and good friend of the couple, was shot down and incarcerated in Germany. Oxford felt just a little bit too comfortable.

Soon after his Board Longford went with Philip Toynbee to see a film, *The Four Feathers*. Starring Ralph Richardson and John Clements, it was about a man from a family with military traditions who is accused of cowardice and then subsequently redeems himself through acts of great courage in the Sudan. As they left the cinema Longford told his old student how much he wished he could act out that story. The circumstances were to be very different, but the chance was at hand.

PART TWO

The Cabinet Minister

Happy those who hunger and thirst for what is right;
they shall be satisfied.
Happy the merciful;
they shall have mercy shown them.

Matthew 5:1–12

Seven

The post-war planner

It is the first time that anyone has set out to
embody the whole spirit of the Christian ethic in
an Act of Parliament

*William Temple, Archbishop of Canterbury, on
Beveridge's Report*

Longford's conversion to Catholicism was to have a profound
impact on his politics. Catholicism did not eclipse his passion for
Labour but it certainly replaced it as the central influence in his
life with socialism playing a supporting, interlocking but increasingly secondary role as the years went by. He never lost faith in
his chosen career of politics, nor has he ever contemplated
leaving the Labour Party, but, in contrast to his enthusiasms of
the late 1930s, he grew to see politics as a means to an end, that
end being to put Christian values into practice on a personal,
party, national and, briefly, international level. While his reading in preparation for reception into the Church had been
principally theological, surrounding the nature of the Resurrection and the existence of God, once in the fold he began to
range more widely. Catholic social teaching caught his eye. It
was his studies in this area that led him to shift his allegiances
within the Labour movement from the leftist radicalism of the
late 1930s to a more mainstream position by 1945. He had thus
prepared the ground for his advancement as a government
minister under Attlee and a member of Harold Wilson's Cabinet.

The post-war years saw the development of avowedly Catholic parties in West Germany and Italy. Under Konrad Adenauer
and De Gaspari the Christian Democrats occupied the centre-

right political ground, building up mass movements that united the pulpit and the political platform to counter what they regarded as the atheistic, Marxist-inspired socialism of the Labour movement. Separate Catholic unions were established to run against their secular counterparts. Yet these Catholic parties were not out-and-out conservatives in the British sense. There was also a commitment in their programmes to limited social reform and to state involvement. The landmark papal encyclical *Rerum Novarum* (1891) had at the end of the nineteenth century set Catholicism's face against unbridled capitalism and its social concern had been reiterated in *Quadragesimo Anno* (1931).

In the forties and fifties the continental Catholic parties (and indeed the Vatican, which worked closely with De Gaspari and, to a lesser extent, with Adenauer) regarded socialism as anticlerical and intent on dismantling the Church's influence, especially in schools. To them Longford's claim to be a Catholic socialist would have been untenable. (The *rapprochement* between socialism and Catholicism on the continent did not come until the more open era of the reforming and modernising Second Vatican Council of the mid-1960s.)

Yet in Britain, Longford was not so unusual. Although his own constituency party in Oxford held a meeting in the summer of 1940 to discuss their candidate's conversion to Catholicism, their response was a tolerant one. The Labour Party had no denominational bias and believed everyone had a right to any religious faith or apostasy. A few dissident voices highlighted the less than democratic nature of the Catholic Church, but they were brushed aside by the constituency party chairman, a Unitarian minister. Frank Pakenham was confirmed as Parliamentary candidate.

English Catholics, making up around ten per cent of the population, were in this period mostly of Irish descent and the vast majority were urban, working-class Labour voters. (It was only with the post-war influx of European émigré Catholics that the picture began to change significantly.) The English hierarchy had none of its continental cousins' ambitions to set up separate parties or unions nor did it share their suspicion of socialism.

They contented themselves with Catholic caucus groups within the broader union movement, aimed at influencing but not undermining. Under first Cardinal Hinsley (1935–43) and then Cardinal Griffin (1943–56) Catholics were encouraged to venture out of their parishes and get involved in politics of whatever party they felt best represented Christian ideals (so long as it wasn't with the Communists). Men like Frank Longford and his Catholic colleague in Attlee's government, Richard Stokes, were held up as role models of a new more integrated, more assertive Catholicism.

The great political challenge for the English Catholic Church in these years was to integrate its separate school system into the national state education network for five- to fifteen-year-olds set up by R. A. Butler in 1944. Here the Catholic leaders were fighting both the Labour and Conservative parties of the wartime coalition to get the best deal possible in terms of state funding and autonomy. There was no conflict over schools between socialists and clerics in England as there had been in Europe. Longford's measured stance in backing his Church's right to educate its young attracted little opposition from the mainstream of his party.

Through his reading of the Catholic social encyclicals, which trod a careful line between right and left in politics, Longford came to realise how seeking the goal of equality, so central to his conversion to socialism, could potentially involve diminishing liberty, how the state, even out of well-intentioned anxiety to improve the lot of the majority, could in the process trample their freedom.

> I realised that it was not enough to insist on the preservation of formal democratic rights; freedom of speech and religion and democratic elections. One must ask oneself additionally at every turn whether the extra equality being achieved by a deleterious increase in the role of the State was justified so that the good was outweighed by evil. More fundamentally, I came to realise that it was not enough to preach a Society based on the equal worth of all of us

> in the sight of God. Such a creed could cover a
> complete disregard of the dignity and self-respect of
> the individual by treating each of us as equally
> valueless.[1]

Any admiration Longford may have developed for the Soviet system in his pre-war anxiety to forge an effective alliance against Hitler disappeared as he applied the restraining influence of Catholic social teaching to his socialism. 'My shallow revolutionary emotions, a by-product of near-Marxism operating on a somewhat excitable temperament, had lost all intellectual validity.'[2]

The Catholic Church's social teaching is often called its 'best-kept secret' and to many in Labour circles Longford's enthusiasm for it would have run counter to their own woeful impression of a Church which had sided against socialism in the Spanish Civil War, which was building anti-socialist parties in post-war Europe, which was thoroughly undemocratic in its organisation and whose teaching on sexual morality deprived women of the chance to limit the size of their families. Women in the Labour Party like Elizabeth Longford and Naomi Mitchison would attack the Church for its stance against contraception. 'But in Frank's defence,' Elizabeth says,

> he has never been interested in medical matters and
> those kind of things. Over our own family he realised
> perfectly well that those arguments affected me more
> than him and he never tried to impose a 'Catholic'
> solution. And for him Catholicism has always been
> more about personal relationships – love your neigh-
> bour. It's age-old that side of Catholicism. After all
> Jesus wasn't able to tell us anything about the safe
> period but He did tell us to love our neighbour.[3]

Such a view of Catholicism could justifiably be described as *à la carte*. Yet it was a typical Longford way of approaching a broad issue. Where he was enthusiastic, he would be engaged at full throttle. No doubt mindful of the Catholic adage for dissenters 'if you don't like the rules, don't join the club', he would accept less favoured edicts, but was half-hearted in their defence. Thus he would give general backing to papal teaching on contentious issues – and still does when pressed in public – yet avoid being drawn into lengthy discussion. He would shirk from questioning the Pope's wisdom even when he knew it was not right. (It is a habit he has never lost. He was once the only voice to offer his unconditional support to the policies of John Paul II in a roomful of liberal Catholics attacking the Church's teaching on sex.) He became Catholic in an age when dissent was not fashionable. Even in 1953 Elizabeth, having by then joined the Church, felt obliged to attempt – unsuccessfully she now concedes – to formulate a defence of the Roman line on birth control in a book of essays she edited called *Catholic Approaches*.[4]

In the early forties, as the implications of his heat-of-the-moment conversion dawned on him, Longford began to retreat from the near-extremist views he had espoused in the thirties and shift towards a more pragmatic political position.

His move towards the middle ground of the Labour Party was in marked contrast to his wife's leanings to the left. Her King's Norton constituency party was expelled by the national leadership in 1941 for arguing that, despite the restrictions placed on it by membership of a wartime coalition, Labour should be working harder to promote its distinctive programme in preparation for peacetime.

Longford's re-evaluation of his own position within Labour was hastened considerably when, out of the blue, he received an invitation to act as Personal Assistant to Sir William Beveridge. The appointment would contribute enormously to his political reputation. He took over from another young Oxford don, Harold Wilson. His task was to work with Beveridge on two reports commissioned by the wartime coalition government. The first was essentially technical, ordered by Ernest Bevin as Minister of Labour, on 'The Use of Skilled Man-Power in the Services'. The second, commissioned by Arthur Greenwood, the Lord Privy Seal, was destined to become one of the landmarks in British twentieth-century history, on 'Social Insurance and Allied Services'.

169

Longford had known Beveridge slightly when the latter was Director of the London School of Economics and he had been a part-time lecturer there in the early 1930s. Beveridge had then moved on to become Master of University College, Oxford, where he would have been aware both of Longford's academic reputation and of his political activities. Janet Mair, Beveridge's companion and later his wife, had struck up a friendship with Longford and before his marriage he had been a visitor at the couple's country retreat, Green Street, near Avebury.[5]

On the outbreak of war, Beveridge had placed his formidable skills at the disposal of the government. Throughout the autumn of 1940 he had chaired a secret committee into the allocation of manpower in relation to munitions and other industrial production. After that he had been seconded to the Ministry of Labour under Ernest Bevin. However, Beveridge, despite his distinguished academic and public service record, was not a man for team-work, and his colleagues found him lofty, austere and solitary. Several of the Ministry officials complained to Bevin, himself notorious for his single-mindedness, and it was decided in May 1941 that Beveridge had to be shuffled to one side and set to work on the two reports. When told the news he is reported to have broken down and wept.

However, whatever his disappointment at not being at the heart of the war effort, he took to his appointed task with gusto and within six months had delivered his report on skilled men in the services. Among its recommendations was the establishment of the Army Corps, later to become the Royal Electrical and Mechanical Engineers.

The report on social security initially filled him with less enthusiasm. He saw planning for the post-war society as a distraction when Britain was facing a Nazi invasion. However, Janet Mair convinced him that it was a heaven-sent opportunity to bring together in a single comprehensive scheme different aspects of work on social security that he had been undertaking for nearly forty years. In the pre-First World War years he had worked with Churchill to set up Labour Exchanges and unemployment insurance and then in 1924, when Churchill became

Chancellor, he had again called on Beveridge to assist him in implementing his promise of old-age pensions.

Beveridge's break-neck pace of working suited Longford well. He would spend the week in London with his new master, returning to Oxford at the weekends. It very soon became apparent that the advisory committee which was to assist Beveridge in drawing up his report was more of a hindrance than a help and it was quietly abandoned. Beveridge, with Longford at his side, would not tolerate any restraints on his field of inquiry and set about assembling the evidence over twelve months that was to lead to his landmark report.

Politically a Liberal – he briefly held Berwick-on-Tweed for the party in 1944–5 – he and his Labour assistant were united in wanting to create a more equal society. For Longford it was a point of principle. For Beveridge it was a practical dilemma to harness society's wealth in order to eliminate the extremes of poverty. He did not believe, as Longford did, that an imposed redistribution, taking money from the rich to give to the poor, was the answer. Rather he aimed at allowing individuals to provide for themselves. They would set aside earnings when in work to provide for the times when they were out of work (during illness, unemployment or in old age). The pool made from their contributions would be supplemented by funds from state taxation and employers' profits.

Longford's role in the production of the Beveridge Report was essentially that of organiser. He would set up the various meetings, travelling around the country with his master as he examined various aspects of employment policy, health and education provision. 'I was like a man's wife,' he says.

> I was there the whole time, rather like one of those
> personal assistants that important men have today –
> the Sarah Hogg to Beveridge's John Major. Because of
> the war, Beveridge had hardly any staff at all. I would
> travel with him as he assembled the material. I think
> he saw my economic training as an advantage
> because, although he had got a double first at Oxford

– in maths and classics – and had been master of the
LSE, he wasn't an economist.[6]

Several of Longford's friends feel that he has, modestly and out
of loyalty to Beveridge, played down his own role in the writing
of the report. David Astor, who was in close contact with
Longford at this time, describes his friend's role as more akin to
that of co-author.[7] Beveridge certainly grew to depend on his
young assistant. Longford is emphatic that the main body of the
text was all Beveridge's own work, a product of his long
experience in the social services. 'He would dictate the report
[though for more difficult passages Beveridge, once a leader
writer on the *Morning Post*, liked to write out his draft in long-
hand] and occasionally pause and ask me what I thought.'[8]

Longford will concede that his social connections proved
useful to Beveridge in opening doors as they conducted the
research. He will even admit that Beveridge was difficult and
often grumpy to work for. One day, feeling that his ceaseless
labours were not receiving quite the recognition that they might,
Longford wrote to his wife at home in Oxford: 'No acolyte ever
worshipped as Beveridge does at the altar of his own work.'[9]

Janet Mair, later Lady Beveridge, perhaps gives the most
credible picture of Longford's role – more than a glorified PA but
short of a full collaborator – in her husband's office in Buckingham Gate during this period of frenetic activity.

> He threw himself into the work, becoming absorbed
> in the task of the administration of the continuous
> interviews, consultations and deliberations. He kept at
> bay the press and the photographers without giving
> offence, and he coped with a stream of correspon-
> dence, both relevant and irrelevant. He looked after
> William and the interests of the Report with com-
> pletely impersonal devotion.[10]

The two became less employer and employee, more mentor and
protégé, with Longford taking Antonia and Thomas for tea with
Beveridge at his house in Oxford. On a professional level,

Longford learnt an invaluable skill from Beveridge: how to commit one's deeply held beliefs to paper in a report with clarity, precision and persuasiveness. Longford favoured such methods in his own later campaigns.

As he grew used to Beveridge's unusual ways of working, Longford came to admire him more and more, finally elevating him to hero status. He shared the independence of mind, the fixed gaze and the touch of vanity that Longford had found so attractive and glamorous in men like Birkenhead and de Valera. Beveridge was one of a rare and now, in our less paternalistic times, almost extinct breed – the public-spirited pro-consuls, spreading their wisdom in a grave and magisterial way through independent, non-political reports and quangos. Beveridge even revealed a dry sense of humour, evident in this interview with an employer over industrial insurance that Longford recounted in a letter to Elizabeth:

> *Beveridge*: There's no real reason, is there, for dis-
> tinguishing between the man who is run over by a
> lorry inside the works and the man who is run down
> outside?
> *Employer*: No reason – from the point of view of the
> man – no.
> *Beveridge*: Well, we're hardly concerned with the point
> of view of the lorry, are we – um – um. (No laughter
> for once from the chairman's sycophantic
> associates.)[12]

The Beveridge Report was published on 1 December 1942, the greatest civilian event of the war years. Longford had learnt from his master's thoroughness and when asked to organise the publicity for the launch took to the task with the same sort of enthusiasm he had shown fleetingly at the 1935 general election. A report that promised to 'abolish want' did not need a great deal of pushing to make the front pages. But the keen sense of anticipation on the eve of publication, the subsequent interest it generated, its impact on the public imagination and its decisive role in the 1945 general election result were extraordinary.

Having abandoned his committee, Beveridge decided to sign the report himself. He identified five evil giants. 'To get the New Britain of all our desires,' he said at the time of publication, 'we must deal not only with Want but . . . with Disease (that is the purpose of the National Health Service), with Ignorance (dealing with that means more and better schools), with Squalor (curing that means better planning of towns and countryside and more and better houses), with Idleness, that is to say unemployment.'[13] He showed in detail how with the help of the state this could be achieved. In the case of want it was to be a double process of redistribution: by social insurance between times of earning and times of unemployment, sickness and retirement; and by children's allowances between times of large and small family responsibilities. Planning was an essential tenet of his programme.

> Nothing worth having can be had for nothing; every
> good thing has its price. Maintenance of employment
> – prevention of mass idleness after the war – is a good
> thing worth any price, except war or surrender of
> essential liberties. It can be had without that surren-
> der, but not without giving up something; chiefly we
> must give up our darling vice of not looking ahead as
> a nation.[14]

It was an inspiring message which found a ready echo among British troops as something worth fighting for beyond sheer survival. Its appearance coincided with the culmination of a series of victories – El Alamein, Stalingrad and Guadalcanal. It was, as Beveridge realised when he took responsibility by signing the report, a challenge to the politicians. It struck an immediate chord in a nation that sensed the tide of war was beginning to turn and which saw in Beveridge's vision a peacetime El Dorado where the deprivation of the 1930s would be banished for ever. The newspapers, guided by Longford who on the eve of publication dined with Lord Rothermere, owner of his erstwhile employer the *Daily Mail*, took up the report with enthusiasm. 'Freedom from want' was the headline on *The Times'* leader.

'Beveridge tells how to banish want' trumpeted the *Daily Mirror*. The *Manchester Guardian* heralded a 'big and fine thing'. On the morning after publication Longford went to his local newsagent only to find all the papers had been sold. 'You don't think I've got any papers left this morning,' the assistant told him. 'It's that Sir William Beveridge. He's going to abolish want.'[15]

Beveridge became a household name overnight. Not everyone was as enthusiastic in their praise as the newspaper editors. To Longford's acute personal distress, some sections of the Catholic Church, including his mentor Father D'Arcy, gave a less than enthusiastic greeting to a report that Longford saw as putting Christian principles into practice. 'There is a certain kind of very devout and gifted Catholic to whom not only socialism but what may be called the whole progressive movement of social reform is singularly repugnant,' Longford concluded sadly afterwards.[16] Such a viewpoint was completely at odds with his own synthesis of Catholic social teaching and socialist doctrines, but he detected in some clerics and lay Catholics – like his friend Douglas Woodruff, editor of *The Tablet* – an instinctive dislike of any expansion of state activity and a corresponding scepticism in 'man-made schemes' for bettering the lot of humankind. At his local Catholic church on the Sunday after publication, Longford sat with barely disguised anger as the priest attacked Beveridge in his sermon from the pulpit. Elizabeth, who had accompanied him on this occasion, was confirmed in her dislike of the 'black beetles'.

Changing such negative opinions became a personal crusade for Longford in the aftermath of publication. In addition to responding to the flood of invitations to go and explain the report to groups of servicemen, workers, students and whoever wanted to hear (Beveridge delegated these mundane tasks to his assistant, preferring himself to travel to America to greet supporters of his work), Longford also got involved in debates with Catholic opponents of the plan. On one occasion he attended a meeting of the Sword of the Spirit movement – founded by Barbara (later Baroness) Ward and Christopher Dawson during the darkest days of the war as an expression of Catholic patriotism – to face Douglas Woodruff. His opponent said that he feared that an element of state compulsion would result from the implementation of Beveridge. If everyone was going to be looked after from the cradle to the grave, they would have to do the work the state set for them. Woodruff quoted Hilaire Belloc on the 'servile state' to prove his case that Beveridge was dangerous.[17] Longford successfully countered such arguments, emphasising his belief that all men were equal before God and that the plan was a way of redressing some of the worst excesses of the 1930s. He won the day. On another occasion he was due to face Woodruff before an audience of troops at Windsor but failed to turn up, his new-found organisational skills momentarily giving way to his more habitual vagueness about times and places, leaving the *Tablet* editor to be shouted down by his audience.

If the reaction from certain quarters of the Church upset Longford he was deeply dismayed by the attitude of the government to the report, in particular that of his Labour colleagues in the wartime cabinet. As the finishing touches were being put to the report, Whitehall began to hear disturbing rumours about the nature, extent and detail of Beveridge's plan. What had been intended as a sop to keep a distinguished public servant quietly occupied looked like turning into a major political event.

Initially, the Minister of Information Brendan Bracken seemed inclined to play down the publication fearing the 'socialism' of the report. When it became clear that Longford's work in preparing the press would make that impossible, Bracken decided to chair the launch conference himself. He pledged abundant goodwill to the plan but was not specific. Beveridge became the name on everyone's lips – eclipsing briefly that of Churchill – and 635,000 copies of the report were sold. A telegram from Buckingham Palace commanded Beveridge's presence the week after publication. Lloyd George travelled up from his country retreat to congratulate the author.

But the government remained ominously quiet. A fortnight after the report's publication the Archbishop of Canterbury married Beveridge and Janet Mair, with Longford organising both the event and the publicity. Churchill sent his own four volume *Marlborough: His Life and Times* and inscribed it to

Beveridge adding, 'May he bring the magic of averages to the rescue of millions.'[18] Yet he made no attempt to meet Beveridge.

It was not until the following February that the government found time to debate the report in the Commons and then under the guise of a bland, non-specific motion of welcome. When it became clear that there was no official intention of taking any steps towards implementing Beveridge, a group of dissident Labour MPs, including Manny Shinwell, put down a motion deploring the lack of action. Though the front bench felt unable to back it out of loyalty to the coalition government, 121 mainly Labour members did, the largest Commons revolt in the war years.

Longford was disappointed by Churchill's negative reaction. In view of his earlier political record in introducing insurance measures, Churchill's disdain for Beveridge puzzled his young admirer. He came to see that Churchill was fighting shy of the 'socialism' of the report and did not want to be the Prime Minister to introduce such measures. But Longford never quite forgave Churchill's personal dismissal of Beveridge. His failure even to mention the report in his triumphal *War Memoirs* was 'tepid and crabbed' and the government's refusal to employ Beveridge further for the remaining period of the war 'deplorable'.[19]

The Labour Party's equivocation caused him deeper personal distress. Here was a plan that set out the longed-for economic means for putting cherished beliefs into practice, a way of reconciling the emotional pull of socialism with a hard-headed scheme to bring greater equality. Here, Longford was sure, was a potential vote-winner, a blueprint for a post-war Labour government.

Attlee, as he made clear in an interview just before the report came out, saw social security and state planning not as an alternative to socialism but as part of it. Yet he was torn by his desire for Labour to be seen as wholly loyal to the coalition. Given Churchill's implacable opposition to the plan, Attlee did not want to divide the government over it. He was in any case under fierce pressure from Ernest Bevin who said he would resign if Labour went into the lobby against the government. In the end Attlee managed to force Churchill into the compromise motion which the government placed before the Commons, welcoming the plan. While many of his own back-benchers rejected this and voted with Shinwell for the rebel amendment – ninety-seven for, with only Attlee and twenty-two colleagues against – Labour managed to emerge from the episode in the public's mind as pro-Beveridge while the leadership had not betrayed the coalition government.

Longford, however, was not prepared to let the matter drop. He was convinced that Sir William Beveridge would be a great asset to the Labour Party. He therefore worked out a scheme with Arthur Jenkins, father of Roy and Parliamentary Private Secretary to Attlee. The two young men would get their bosses together over dinner in the hope that Attlee would convince Beveridge to sign up for Labour. The dinner took place at the Oxford and Cambridge Club but the desired alliance did not materialise. 'Beveridge', Longford recalls,

> unwisely laid down the law on many matters involved
> in the running of the war, with which Attlee, Deputy
> Prime Minister, was too closely concerned to discuss
> them. He lapsed into almost total silence. Finally, after
> dinner, he disappeared into the depths of an armchair
> and fell asleep. By the time he woke, Beveridge had
> followed his example, leaving Arthur Jenkins and
> myself to chatter away as best we could. Soon after,
> the party broke up. Our masters walked along Pall
> Mall together, Arthur and I following at a respectful
> distance. Arthur turned to me and said 'I think it went
> pretty well, don't you?' Feeling that it could hardly
> have gone worse, I made no comment.[20]

Soon afterwards Beveridge told Longford he was joining the Liberals, the only party which had been united and enthusiastic in backing his plan.

Longford's lifelong habit of thinking that bringing two people together over a dinner table will help them to bury their differences came an even more spectacular cropper when he decided to introduce Beveridge to Evelyn Waugh, one of the vocal Catholic critics of the plan. Beveridge, already afflicted with vanity and currently riding a wave of national adulation, found Waugh somewhat off-hand. 'Tell me, Sir William,' said Waugh, 'how do you get your main pleasure in life?'

'I get it', Beveridge replied, 'by trying to leave the world a little better place than I found it.'

'And I get mine', Waugh retorted, 'in trying to spread alarm and despondency, and I expect I get a great deal more than you do.' Afterwards Beveridge kept shaking his head and asking Longford, 'That fellow Waugh, he was a crackpot, wasn't he?'[21]

The incident not only revealed Longford's naivety, it also symbolises a divide in his attitudes that was to deepen further in these years. He rather admired Waugh's waspish humour, just as he had delighted in the bitchy world of Maurice Bowra and thirties Oxford. It appealed to the sense of humour that still fuels his jokes against himself, making him a witty raconteur and an entertaining after-dinner speaker. But his social Catholic conscience, intent on improving the world, admired Beveridge's high-mindedness and was outraged at Waugh's behaviour. As his Catholicism came more and more to shape his politics and his outlook on life, the latter attitude came to dominate. 'Frank was a master of the witty phrase,' says David Astor. 'He still can be in private when he is relaxed and among friends. But he developed away from it. He saw it increasingly as an unkind, un-Christian thing to do, to dismiss people with a joke.'[22]

Even though the government was not going to give him any more work, Beveridge determined to continue his task of shaping post-war Britain. During his research, he had become convinced of the need to investigate the whole question of full employment, fearing that with peace would come a return to the dole queues of the 1930s. Admirers provided the finance for this new venture and Longford was again at Beveridge's side. They began work in the spring of 1943 and were almost at once made aware of the government's hostility when an order issued from the Chancellor of the Exchequer's office banned all communication between Whitehall and the new Beveridge enquiry.

Friends and colleagues from a lifetime of public service were prevented from talking to Beveridge about full employment.

Faced by such an obstacle the new report never quite built up the momentum of its predecessor. Beveridge himself became distracted by Liberal party politics (he was elected to the House of Commons as a Liberal for Berwick-on-Tweed in October 1944) and by the continuing struggle to get his earlier work taken seriously by the government.

On the advice of David Astor, Longford employed Fritz Schumacher, a German exile and economist (who later wrote *Small is Beautiful*) to work alongside Beveridge. Another recruit was Barbara (later Baroness) Wootton whom Longford had first met when he applied to work with the WEA. Wootton had been less than impressed that his application was sent on Carlton Club notepaper.

Longford's own involvement with Beveridge's work was then scaled down and in 1944 he returned to academic life at Christ Church, to his constituency and to his family in north Oxford. (Living in London had been hazardous. He began by staying in a hotel whose address, Heartowest, Leicester Square, did not ring any alarm bells in his head but which he soon discovered after a couple of noisy nights there was in fact a brothel. He then moved to a room in Charlotte Street which narrowly missed being bombed.)

His work with Beveridge did something towards restoring Longford's shattered confidence. It was a task to which he felt deeply committed, leading him to reject more conventional avenues to repair the damage done by his military débâcle – like Randolph Churchill's invitation to became a wartime military spokesman in Cairo.

Though at first it must have seemed a long way removed from front-line action, the Beveridge report and the acclaim it subsequently received – save in government and church circles – reflected well on Longford and enhanced his political reputation. He had been fortunate in landing a job where his academic skills had been put to good populist effect. And to his credit he had stuck at the task and recognised its potential. If Beveridge himself could not be wooed into Labour then at least the party could point to having his number two among its Parliamentary candidates.

Yet, for all the kudos that it brought him, Beveridge was never more than second best in Longford's eyes, a distraction from the real business of war, the arena where he had tried but failed to make his mark. In later years he could quite justifiably have sidestepped awkward questions about his military service during the war by reference to his role in a landmark report that changed British society, but he never sought such shelter. When asked, 'Did you have a good war?' he would inevitably recount the tale of the camp on the Isle of Wight, gastric 'flu and being invalided out. He felt his own failure too deeply to indulge in such an economy with the truth. Indeed when faced with some of the Tory opponents of Beveridge's plans he often found himself in those closing months of the war holding back from winning the political points. Many of them had distinguished military records. His achievement alongside Beveridge, he felt, paled into insignificance. 'As I watched so many Conservative contemporaries – though not of course only Conservatives – making the sacrifice that I had proved incapable of making, the impulse to denounce or expose half the country or even its leaders faded and finally died.'[23] While Longford could still have a political argument and come out shining, that sharp and abrasive edge necessary for party knock-abouts eluded him. His wartime experiences certainly played their part in undermining his confidence, but those who saw him perform on public platforms – as opposed to over dinner tables – in his pre-war zealot days report that even then he was not a great orator.

Back in Oxford in 1944 there were family decisions to be made – like which school to send the children to. Given Elizabeth's dislike of Catholicism, he made no attempt to stake a claim for Catholic education. There was a choice between state and private education. Chadlington Road was a stone's throw from the Dragon School, *alma mater* of Longford's contemporaries Hugh Gaitskell and John Betjeman. It enjoyed an unparalleled academic reputation in the town but was just the sort of bastion of educational privilege that was anathema to the left of the Labour Party. Longford justified the decision to send

Antonia, Thomas, Patrick and later Judith there on the age-old grounds that there was no point depriving them of a good education to prove that he was dedicated to improving the standards in the state system. This, of course, stood in direct contradiction to his belief in the redistribution of wealth. 'In the case of material things a levelling would be certain to contain some element of levelling down for certain people,' he was later to write.

> I myself incidentally would lose by it. But in the case
> of education you cannot level down without destroy-
> ing what might never, or not for years, be replaced –
> the spirit of a noble institution. This conclusion did
> not make me less a leveller in education, but it made
> me hostile to any educational reforms that did not
> consist in preserving the highest levels and extending
> them widely and rapidly.[25]

Judith was only one when Elizabeth got her 'baby-itch' again. In May 1942, Rachel arrived, a little too quickly for the doctor and the midwife and was therefore delivered by the district nurse. By the summer of 1943 Michael was on the way and Elizabeth's constituency party in King's Norton were growing restive about the ever-expanding Pakenham clan and the drain such a large family would place on their candidate. Longford missed Michael's birth in November 1943 – the only time he was away for such an event – because of work with Beveridge in the north of England. Solly Zuckerman, the scientist and later adviser to the Wilson government, recalled visiting the Paken- hams at Chadlington Road soon afterwards to be greeted by a distracted Longford at the door, surrounded by children, saying, 'Come in quickly or they'll fall out.'

The crowded house resounded, Antonia now recalls, with her father's students – mostly older men, the younger generation having abandoned their studies in favour of front-line service. And Longford maintained his interest in prisoners, later to become such a feature of his public work but at this point one

1 The Gothic castle of Tully Nally, the Longford family seat in Co Westmeath, described by Elizabeth on her first visit as glittering in its eccentricity.

2 Frank with his Great Aunt Caroline at Bernhurst. As a second son, Frank could expect no inheritance, but his childless great aunt made him her heir and left him her country home in Sussex.

3 'Us Four': (*from left*) Pansy, four and a half, Frank, three, Edward, six, and Mary, one and a half. Their nursery was a hothouse of precocious competitiveness, their games a contest to win the attention and affection of their distant mother.

4 A studio portrait of Frank, aged nine, taken around the time that he heard his father had been killed at Gallipoli.

5 At the opening of Hurst
Green Village Hall in 1927.
The tradition of
philanthrophy was well-
established in the Pakenham
family. Frank is seated second
from the left next to his Great
Aunt Caroline.

6 Bright young
things: Frank (*seated*)
with, from the left,
Evelyn Waugh, Fred
Warnes and Maureen,
Marchioness of
Dufferin and Ava.

7 Frank and Elizabeth's
wedding, in 1931, at St
Margaret's, Westminster. The
groom turned up at the
adjacent Westminster Abbey
which was empty. 'People
don't go to weddings these
days,' his best man consoled
him before they realised their
mistake.

8 Frank in front of
Stairways in
Buckinghamshire
where he and
Elizabeth moved after
their wedding.

9 Edward Longford
raising funds for his
beloved Gate Theatre
on the streets of
Dublin. He became
chairman in 1930 and
exhausted the family
fortune through his
support of the theatre.

10 Still a keen jogger in his 80s, Frank as a lecturer in the 1930s at Christ Church, Oxford, leads the field around Christ Church Meadows.

11 'Private Pack' in the Oxford and Bucks Light Infantry in 1939. 'He was a very weird soldier because he was so uncoordinated,' Denis Healey said of Longford.

12 In a refugee bunker in
Hanover in June 1947 as
Minister for Germany. Never
a party politician Longford
embarrassed his colleagues in
government by telling
journalists that conditions in
the British Zone in Germany
were appalling.

13 In Paris in 1948 as
Minister of Civil Aviation
getting into a tangle with a
map. Longford surprised his
colleagues – who could not
see beyond his donnish,
dishevelled appearance – by
his inspired stewardship of an
essentially technical ministry.

among many concerns. Antonia can picture one particular newly released prisoner who was invited to tea.

> I remember having arson explained to me because
> this person had committed arson. I was amazed
> because it seemed like such a strange thing to do. And
> I remember thinking that it was very odd that, since
> this person had done it, my father should invite them
> home for tea. I thought perhaps I hadn't quite got the
> point of the crime.[26]

In January 1944, after much agonising, Elizabeth resigned as Labour candidate in King's Norton. Although the local party had given her their backing, despite doubts as to her capacity to combine the roles of mother and MP, Elizabeth herself had begun to worry about the practicalities of the undertaking. Henceforth the couple's political ambitions were to sit on Longford's shoulders.

Eight

The Lord-in-Waiting

Ever since I spotted Lord Pakenham, when a
minister, striding out of a Victoria Street shop with
a newly-bought collar, unwrapped, in his hand, I
have suspected that he was different from the
general run of politicians

John Redfern in the Daily Express[1]

The 1945 general election took place on 5 July, two months
after the German surrender. The conflict in the Far East continued until August when the dropping of atom bombs on
Hiroshima and Nagasaki hastened the Japanese capitulation. By
that time Clement Attlee had been Prime Minister of Great
Britain and Northern Ireland for over a month, in command of
the first-ever Labour majority in the House of Commons.

After his successful conduct of the war, Winston Churchill,
and indeed many in the Labour Party, had expected a Conservative 'khaki victory'. But, as polling day drew closer, Attlee and
his colleagues grew more optimistic. The Conservatives' failure
to offer any sort of vision of a post-war Britain to an electorate
anxious to make a fresh start contrasted sharply with Labour's
commitment to wide-scale nationalisation and its promise, a
crucial factor in the landslide victory, to introduce a Beveridge-
style welfare state. Churchill's virulent attacks on Labour –
'Socialism is inseparably woven with totalitarianism and the
abject worship of the state' he commented in a radio broadcast
on 4 June – were widely regarded as having backfired, emphasising less Attlee's shortcomings than the difference between
Churchill the wartime patriot and Churchill the Conservative
politician of the 1930s, a decade of mass unemployment and
economic hardship.

One of the Conservatives frustrated by his party's reliance on Churchill's past record was Quintin Hogg, defending the Oxford City seat he had won at the 1938 by-election against Antony Norman for the Liberals and Frank Pakenham for Labour. A member of the progressively minded Tory Reform Committee and a rising star on what would now be called the wet wing of the Conservative Party, Hogg's credentials were not so different from Longford's. Both were somewhat donnish in appearance and academic in background, unafraid to speak of Christian values and morality at the hustings. (Though a friend of Father D'Arcy's, Hogg was a convinced Anglican.) While Longford could score points by rightly pointing to his key role alongside Beveridge, any kudos he gained in the eyes of the electorate from his wartime service was undermined by a combination of Hogg's (and indeed Norman's) distinguished military exploits and Beveridge's endorsement of Norman. When Hogg shrugged off his war wound Longford could only reflect on his own inglorious failure to make it to the front line. Beveridge's message of support for his Liberal opponent was a bitter pill to swallow.

Hogg's friendship with the Longfords further complicated the campaign. When he called at Chadlington Road on the eve of the hustings, everyone managed to be very civil about the election battle ahead except for young Paddy, who refused out of loyalty to his father to get an extra tea cup for Mr Hogg. In the middle of the campaign, Elizabeth's father died, so party politics were put to one side for a moment when Hogg called again to offer his condolences.

Longford fought a mediocre campaign. His instinct for publicity, seen to effect with the pre-war 'Private Pack' newspaper pictures and later in organising the press coverage for Beveridge, did not always serve him well. Riding through the city in a pony and trap with Elizabeth, Judith, Rachel and Michael allowed him to counter any Churchillian rhetoric about totalitarianism and present himself instead as both a family man and a likeable eccentric – in case the Oxford electors had not already realised. However, his attempts to suggest that Hogg was less than dedicated to his constituency misfired badly. The Conservative candidate was on the selection committee of the St George's division of Westminster and a letter to the *Oxford Mail* during the campaign, signed by a little-known trade unionist, indicated that Hogg had unsuccessfully sought the nomination there instead of in Oxford. When Hogg threatened to sue the editor for libel, Longford telephoned and admitted that he was behind the letter.[2] Hogg made great play of this on the platform and the gloves were off. In the ensuing fight, Hogg proved the more effective.

As ever Evelyn Waugh was on hand to mock Longford's efforts and rub salt into his wounds (in the spirit of friendship, Longford maintains to this day). Returning with him by train from a memorial service in London for Basil Dufferin who had been killed in action in Burma, Waugh suggested that Longford should stand 'as an eccentric foreign nobleman who had beaten the record for demobilisation'.[3] Later the same month, on the eve of the Oxford poll, Waugh ended a letter to John Betjeman, 'Vote for Pakenham, the old booby!'[4]

In pinpointing the reasons for his victory in 1945, Hogg writes in his autobiography: 'Frank crudely overreached himself and early on in the campaign practised some sharp tactics which rebounded badly on his own head.'[5] He might have added that Longford was not a particularly effective speaker from the platform, especially since his new-found Catholicism inhibited his previous penchant for personal invective. He could not bring to the hustings the wit that still serves him so well at dinner parties and even occasionally on the floor of the House of Lords. In the pre-television era such a failing was more of a handicap to a budding politician, especially in a marginal seat, than it would be today.

Hogg omits to mention the key factor in the election result: the exclusion of the working-class districts of Cowley and Headington.

Longford managed to reduce Hogg's 1938 majority to just under 3000 – an achievement given that seven years earlier he had been facing a single opponent. Until the last minute Longford continued to hope for victory. The announcement of the election result was delayed until 25 July to allow the servicemen's votes, cast in the overseas theatres of war, to be counted. When news began to leak out that these had been overwhelmingly in favour of Labour, Hogg seemed vulnerable. Antonia Fraser recalls arriving back in Oxford from her boarding school on the day the winner was to be revealed.

> I had my trunk and I got a taxi – a habit not encour-
> aged in the Pakenham household. I made the taxi go
> round by the Town Hall so I could see my father being
> elected. But he came second and I burst into floods of
> tears and got a very unsympathetic welcome at home
> for having wasted money on a taxi.[6]

It was a cruel blow to Longford, particularly since Hogg – a contemporary, blue-blooded old Etonian – symbolised the safe Tory world that he had abandoned by joining the Labour Party. If he had not followed his conscience, he could have been a left-wing Tory like Hogg. To exacerbate his disappointment, news was flooding in of friends and colleagues elected around the country in the Labour landslide. Evan Durbin, Hugh Gaitskell, Christopher Mayhew, Patrick Gordon Walker, Richard Crossman would all be playing their part in building the New Jerusalem. Depressed and not a little envious, Longford repaired to the Trout, a favourite pub on the outskirts of Oxford, for a solitary post-mortem. His spirits were not helped by the news that Labour had won West Birmingham, the seat he had abandoned in favour of Oxford. King's Norton too had returned a Labour candidate.

Longford's political career was in tatters. Having turned his back on a comfortable life in the Conservative Party, he was now relegated to the margins of Labour. The best he could hope for was to settle back into the enclosed academic world of Oxford and wait for the next by-election. Whatever reputation he had achieved in the Labour Party would now be eclipsed as a new generation of eager young men, held back by the Second World War, entered Parliament and rose through the ranks. In this moment of despair and envy, his ambition got the better of his Christianity.

Succour, however, was at hand. When he returned to Chadlington Road for what he had assumed would be a funereal tea, he found Evan and Majorie Durbin, fresh from the victory platform in Edmonton. Since those early encounters at New College, Durbin had developed a profound admiration and loyal friendship for Longford. With Gaitskell they formed a trio with a united vision. Durbin was determined to get Longford into Parliament somehow to see their dream into reality.

For the first time they discussed the option for Longford of the House of Lords. Edward and Christine Longford were by now clearly not going to produce an heir. At thirty stone and in poor health, Edward could not reasonably be expected to outlast his younger brother. So one day Longford would become the seventh earl and hence a member of the House of Lords. Why not accelerate the process, Durbin suggested. Labour was perilously short of supporters in the Upper House – especially of those who were young and vigorous enough to see a lengthy and controversial programme of legislation through an overwhelmingly Conservative chamber. Lord Addison, who had led the Labour peers during the war years, estimated that he had a total of sixteen supporters at his disposal in a House of 831 voting members. Only eight of these supporters were up to active and regular service. Attlee would have to create some peers. Why should not Longford be one of them? It would only be anticipating the day when he would inherit a title from his brother.

By lunchtime the next day Attlee had been asked by George VI to form the next government. At the heart of his Cabinet was a group of five: Foreign Secretary Ernest Bevin; Herbert Morrison as Lord President with overall responsibility for the programme of nationalisation; Sir Stafford Cripps, newly restored to the Labour fold at the Board of Trade after his apostasy of 1939; Chancellor Hugh Dalton and Attlee himself. Durbin, with his economic background and track record at the XYZ Club, was appointed as Dalton's Parliamentary Private Secretary and at once set about singing Frank Pakenham's praises.

By the weekend, Durbin had arranged a meeting between the Longfords – significantly they were presented as a couple – and

Dalton who was staying with friends at Burford near Oxford. On the surface there was no pressing reason why Dalton should help Longford. In the run-up to the Second World War, Dalton had been a hated figure among left-wingers in the Labour Party because of his opposition to talk of a Popular Front. The Oxford party would have had little time for him, nor he for it. At the height of his enthusiasm for left-wing ideas and Stafford Cripps in the late 1930s, Longford had written an article in the *Spectator* criticising the personal credo in Dalton's book *Practical Socialism* as 'very tender towards the susceptibilities of capitalists'.

However, Longford, as Durbin no doubt pointed out, was now a reformed character politically, his Catholicism and his work with Beveridge having banished any previous tendencies to extremism and class rhetoric. As an academic, an economist and a man with intimate knowledge of Beveridge's plans for a post-war welfare state, he would be an asset to the incoming Labour administration. Dalton enjoyed a reputation for encouraging rising young stars in the party, 'the class of '45', men like Durbin and Gaitskell. George Brown was later to note that Dalton had a particular liking for 'university socialites'.[7] Later as Chancellor he had a private list of young politicians who were to be given automatic access to him whenever he was not in a meeting or conference. Longford was on it.

Dalton was sufficiently impressed after the encounter at Burford to find time that evening to write notes to several of the leading members of the government commending Longford to their notice. A few days later a call came through to Chadlington Road asking Longford to come to London to meet the Lord Privy Seal, Arthur Greenwood, a stalwart of the 1929 Labour government and the man who commissioned the Beveridge enquiry. Attlee had decided to have several non-departmental ministers in his Cabinet to oversee major areas of legislation. Morrison was to be one and Greenwood another, with responsibility for social services and the implementation of Beveridge. Greenwood wanted Longford as his personal assistant. He accepted the post without hesitation.

During the brief period that he spent in Greenwood's office, Longford grew fond of his boss. He spoke for him in his

Wakefield constituency and was eager to get down to work. But Greenwood's most influential days in the Labour Party had passed. He had something of a reputation as a drinker, though Longford reported to Elizabeth that he saw no sign of any empty bottles hidden in his desk. However, Greenwood did, he noted, often speak 'through a haze of distant benevolence'.[8] On one occasion, Longford mentioned his friendship with Evan Durbin. 'Oh yes,' said Greenwood, 'I know him well. Such a nice chap. Awful pity that his health is bad. His heart, you know . . .' Longford suggested that perhaps Greenwood was thinking of Hugh Gaitskell. 'Oh, I know him too,' he went on. 'He's another nice chap. His heart's bad also. Funny thing, all the Dalton boys have got bad hearts.'[9]

Before Longford had the chance to get frustrated with Greenwood's ways, he was summoned to 10 Downing Street for an interview with the Prime Minister. The two had met in 1938 when Attlee had visited Oxford in the immediate aftermath of Eden's resignation from Chamberlain's government in frustration at the appeasement policy. Attlee, not usually a particularly effective public speaker, had risen to the occasion and demanded before a packed meeting chaired by Longford that Chamberlain too should go. Such were the passions abroad at that time that Attlee was given a standing ovation and carried shoulder-high down the High Street.

In the wake of his own defeat at Oxford in 1945, Longford had written to Attlee congratulating the new Prime Minister on the scale of Labour's victory. The letter, though it could hardly be described as a deft piece of political intrigue, was clearly more than a courtesy. Longford was blatantly and rather obviously fishing. Wheels were turning behind the scenes. Longford's conversations with Durbin and Dalton had reached the Prime Minister, who was being assisted by another old New College colleague Douglas Jay. Attlee replied to Longford's letter, congratulating him on a fight well fought in Oxford. The very fact that he had found time to answer was significant. Several weeks later came the call to Downing Street. Attlee explained Labour's predicament in the House of Lords to Longford and asked him, in view of the likelihood that he would one day inherit his brother's earldom, if he would consider accepting a peerage at once. Longford accepted enthusiastically. Attlee then asked if Longford would agree to become a Lord-in-Waiting, so that he could speak for the government in the House of Lords. It would be the most junior of ministerial ranks. Again Longford accepted with delight. In the space of a couple of weeks he had gone from nowhere to a government post.

While the question of being a Lord-in-Waiting was a new one, the possibility of taking a peerage had been mooted following his discussions with Durbin and Dalton. He therefore had his reply ready for the Prime Minister. Though he was able to answer Attlee without hesitation, the decision to enter the House of Lords had been arrived at only after much thought and discussion with Elizabeth. It was one of the crucial decisions that was to shape his political life, a fact of which they were all too aware in 1945. While he was prepared to compromise, accept a way to get into Parliament and abandon his ambitions to enter the Commons, Elizabeth initially was implacably opposed. His pragmatism clashed with her principle. She had fought the 1935 general election on a pledge to abolish the Lords and regarded it as superfluous. The Commons was where the real action took place. Unless her husband took his place there, he would never wield influence or hold high office. The best he could hope for as a peer, she predicted accurately, was to be Leader of the House of Lords in a Labour Cabinet. Though the Tories were more flexible about giving senior positions to peers, Labour would be much less likely to hand over a major department of state to someone in the Upper House.

'It was the House of Commons that to me meant reality and romance,' Elizabeth wrote later.

> I had lectured endlessly on the grand old men who
> had operated there and the even grander women who
> had tried to breach its walls but failed. In a sense I too
> had failed because I was a woman and I wanted
> Frank, my *alter ego*, to succeed. Unprepossessing
> though I found the central lobby of the House of
> Commons, decked out as it was with huge marble

tailcoats and togas swathing the limbs of Victorian
patriarchs, it still gave me a lift of excitement to think
that a Gladstone, an O'Connell, a Keir Hardie had
trodden these tessellated floors. The House of Lords I
had never set eyes on, merely demanding its abolition
in my Cheltenham campaign.[10]

Evan Durbin countered Elizabeth's arguments. Because Edward
had not produced an heir, Longford would end up in the House
of Lords anyway. Hence any career he might have in the
Commons would be blighted. (The possibility of setting peerages
aside, as suggested by Waldorf Astor back in the 1910s, was at
that time out of the question.) And as a Roman Catholic, Durbin
offered, Longford had already saddled himself with a handicap
when it came to high office. This was an age when the names of
the few Roman Catholic members of the House of Lords were
still italicised in *Vacher's Parliamentary Companion*.

The couple came to a decision about the future during a walk
around the Dragon School cricket field. Longford was well aware
of the shortcomings of the Lords. One of his standard essays for
his politics undergraduates was to discuss the role of second
chambers. Yet in the end he and Elizabeth decided that Longford
should accept. It was his only chance to be part of a social
revolution about which they had talked, planned and dreamt
for years. To sit back as a Christ Church don and see it all
happen without having even the small influence that a place in
the Lords might offer would be too much. To be in Oxford when
the political world revolved around Westminster would be
intolerable. To wait five years until the next election, or to pin
his hopes on a fortuitous by-election, would be an unendurable
ordeal for such a restless figure as Longford.

The decision was not made without a tinge of regret. Despite
his failure on the hustings, he had been a successful local
councillor, and had enjoyed the work of representing a constituency. That avenue would now be forever barred. If he wanted
to represent any one group in the Lords in future it would have
to be as a self-appointed spokesman. (He made sure he would

never forget his former constituents by taking as his title Baron Pakenham of Cowley.)

In retrospect, Elizabeth acknowledges that they made the right decision. Defeat at Oxford and Durbin's intervention were a happy accident. The Lords was better suited to her husband's increasingly independent line in Christian socialism. There may be an element of *post hoc* rationalisation in this. Perhaps membership of the Lords accelerated his departure from the official party line, already under way when he embraced Catholicism. The less polarised, pragmatic atmosphere of the Lords, where there is a genuine fraternity between members on different sides of the House, allowed him to take up some of the causes for which he was later to gain notoriety.

'I wouldn't have survived in the Commons,' Longford now says. 'To be a top politician you've got to be an egotist, not just to get there but to stay there. Leaders have to show toughness. Look at the ridicule that was heaped on Margaret Thatcher. No one would make those sorts of allegations in the House of Lords.'[11]

In the light of the treatment he has received since becoming a member, his statement may sound surprising but most of the insults have been directed at him from outside the chamber of the Lords. There at least a rigorous, indeed often stifling, courtesy is maintained at all times. Longford claims that he enjoys the gentlemanly quality of the House of Lords debates but his sharp wit would doubtlessly have made him a formidable opponent in the Commons. While he was not a public platform orator, in the claustrophobic cut and thrust environment of the Commons, his laconic and sardonic performance would have found an audience. As with Waugh and Beveridge, he was suppressing his acerbic wit in favour of a more constructive attitude towards his fellow beings. The House of Lords was particularly conducive to the latter outlook.

Elizabeth has practical reasons for not regretting her husband's decision.

> There's the physical thing. Late nights are not Frank's thing at all and never have been [as she remembers

from their first encounter]. If he'd sat in the Commons he wouldn't have remained as wonderfully
healthy for so long. He's extremely dutiful and he
would have stayed on for those late night votes and
fallen off his seat fast asleep.[12]

In the short term, like a booster injection, membership of the
House of Lords artificially accelerated Longford's career. While
his great rival Hugh Gaitskell had to wait before getting a
government job, Longford was up on his feet defending the
government's record within minutes of being introduced into
the Lords. It was only later when he aspired to more senior
posts in government that he began to feel the disadvantages of
being in the Upper House. Never one to plan, he had taken the
immediate benefit without sufficiently weighing what it might
ultimately cost him.

Before he could take his place on the front bench in 1945,
Longford had to be presented as a Lord-in-Waiting to the King.
His title was technically a court appointment, though his role
would be a political one.

I had always foolishly assumed that Royalty would
begin with something very ordinary and non-commit-
tal. Instead, he gazed at me quietly but penetratingly,
and after a pause said suddenly, 'Why did you . . . join
them?' For a moment I could not for the life of me
think what he meant. I was in any case suitably
nervous. Could he mean the Catholic Church? No –
hardly. It must be the Labour Party – and I realised
later it was. It would have been a difficult enough
question to answer in any circumstances. I am apt to
give the short answer: 'Because I believe that each
one of us is of equal and infinite importance in the
sight of God.' But that seemed to me, standing there
in Buckingham Palace in front of my sovereign, to be
liable to smack of impertinence. I stammered out
some rather involved account of my political
experiences.[13]

George VI made sympathetic noises, Longford said, when later recounting the incident.[14] Evelyn Waugh casts doubts on such a claim, recording in his diary for February 1946 that Longford was complaining that 'the King never sees him. He has only seen him once since he has been in office and is not asked to the UNO parties.'[15]

On 16 October 1945 Baron Pakenham of Cowley took his place in the Lords, with Elizabeth and Antonia sitting watching him from the gallery. At thirty-nine he was the youngest peer to be awarded a title – rather than inherit it – since Beaverbrook in 1916. 'All I can remember is that my father seemed at least forty years younger than anyone else there,' says Antonia.[16] 'The House was then much more Conservative than it is now,' says Longford. 'But it was a friendly place. I wasn't nervous because I was so full of Labour convictions, solemnly and deliberately speaking for the government like the Pope, honoured in that extreme and rather juvenile fashion.'[17]

That early ardour was noted over lunch in a London restaurant by Patrick O'Donovan, a fellow Catholic and an *Observer* journalist who got to know Longford well in this period. 'I was with him during rationing at the Gay Hussar. Someone offered him food over and above the ration and he got terribly angry. He thought it immoral.'[18]

Any teething problems in the Lords were soon soothed away under the watchful gaze of the Labour Leader in the Upper Chamber, Lord Addison, a scientist who had been in Lloyd George's 1920 Cabinet. During Longford's maiden speech in a debate extending wartime controls over certain basic supplies, he received a kick in the back of the calf from Addison. 'Take your hands out of your pockets,' he rebuked his junior colleague. On another occasion a similarly deft blow was followed by the advice, 'Sit down now. You've got the House with you. You'll lose them if you go on any longer.'[19]

Longford's other mentor was the Lord Chancellor, Lord Jowitt.

> He once told me that the secret of advocacy is to find
> out the worst thing that your opponent can say about

195

your case and then say it yourself in your own way. I
may be slightly, but not much, caricaturing when I
recall his method of introducing a Bill unwelcome to
the Conservatives. 'My Lords, I hate this bill. I don't
suppose that there is anyone in this House who dis-
likes it as much as I do. But, My Lords, have we any
alternative?'[20]

Under such tutelage, Longford quickly established a reputation
as an effective debater. His early *faux pas* were few and far
between. His disregard for detail strengthened his eccentric
reputation. Once, when confronted with an unusually full
government front bench, he took a seat in an adjoining row.
Only when he noticed most of the chamber staring at him did
he realise that he had sat in the place reserved for the Archbishop of Canterbury.

Longford wrote to Elizabeth back in Oxford about his excitement at being part of the government, albeit in a minor role.
Even with six children, she felt underemployed (Antonia was
now away at boarding school and Thomas had taken his
entrance exam to Eton) and out of the mainstream.

She was appointed to the local Rent Tribunal, an innovation
of the Labour government aimed at protecting tenants against
their landlords. She would give the occasional lecture on
'Women's place in the New Britain'. But such events paled into
insignificance next to her husband's accounts of evenings in
London spent discussing theology, politics, the relative merits of
the Soviet and capitalist systems with Dick Crossman and Philip
Toynbee. Elizabeth would join Longford for ceremonial events
– as a Lord-in-Waiting he was expected to attend various court
functions like the visit of Queen Juliana of the Netherlands –
but family life became a continual shuttle backwards and
forwards from London to Oxford.

In July 1947, pregnant with their seventh child, she decided
to uproot and move to the capital. She found a neo-Georgian,
Lutyens-style house with an annexe, large garden and tennis
court – an invaluable asset in the eyes of her husband – in
Linnell Drive in Hampstead Garden Suburb. It had a view of the

Heath and was thus part of the Hampstead 'colony', a generic term to describe the cluster of homes of young Labour hopefuls – the Jays, the Gaitskells, the Durbins, the Wilsons and now the Pakenhams – in that area of north-west London.

The house had cost £14,000, a considerable sum by the standards of the day. The Longfords had lost their other London property – inherited from Uncle Bingo – during the war when structural decay had forced them to sell it at a knock-down price. But with Longford's government salary, the couple's small private incomes and an inheritance from Elizabeth's father, they managed to live comfortably and pay for their children to attend private schools.

The death of Nathaniel Bishop Harman in the middle of the 1945 general election campaign hit the couple hard. In retirement he had found more time for his daughter and son-in-law. Writing to Elizabeth from London when he was working alongside Beveridge, Longford recounted having breakfast with her father.

> He was *charming* . . . I saw at once how popular a man
> he is likely to be when he is laying himself out to be
> pleasant. He was sweet about you and thought
> Thomas 'very thoughtful' . . . He is now 'my favourite
> man'.[21]

The loss of her father coincided with Elizabeth's growing interest in religion. Though her initial reaction to her husband's conversion had been an angry anti-clericalism, it had not seriously damaged their relationship. Having seen what an important part Catholicism came to play in his life and his politics, she had been forced to reconsider and had slowly mellowed. The loss of her father, with his strict Unitarian views, removed a major psychological obstacle to her joining her husband in the Catholic Church.

It had been the tragically early death of her brother Roger in 1941, caused by a brain tumour, and her despair at his unfulfilled promise that first directed her to thoughts of an after-life. That in turn led to sporadic reading of Longford's religious books – what she had hitherto described as a 'Chamber of Horrors' and relegated to the bottom shelf of a bookcase in the hallway. Some of the more traditional and dogmatic tomes confirmed all her worst prejudices. But others, notably the liberally minded French Catholic scholar Jacques Maritain, came as a pleasant surprise and spurred her on to read the New Testament. When Paddy fell ill with mastoid problems and his fate hung briefly in the balance, Elizabeth found herself turning to prayer.

All the Longford children had been christened in the Anglican Church – Judith, Rachel and Michael at a time when their father was Catholic and their mother agnostic. At the start of 1944 Elizabeth took Thomas and Antonia, thus far brought up without any great emphasis on religion, to the High Anglican Church of St Paul's in south Oxford for preparation for their first communion. She accompanied them to church each Sunday and by the autumn of that year was under instruction and was received as an Anglican before Christmas.

The Church of England was a halfway house. While Longford had never pushed her, the couple both realised that they were drawing closer on the one issue that had divided them. They talked of prayer and discussed theology, Anglo-Catholic dogma not being so very far removed from the papal line. Elizabeth baulked at some cherished Catholic notions – the Virgin Mary remained a problem for her until many years later.

Each Sunday as the Longford family set off to church, she felt a great emotional wrench as her husband turned one way to go to the Catholic Church and she and the children the other to go to St Paul's. Paddy would occasionally insist on accompanying his father. When she discussed her pain at this division in the family with Dr Kirk, the Bishop of Oxford, he agreed that it was unnatural. It was Elizabeth who had to make the compromise. When she decided to join the Catholic Church, Dr Kirk wrote to her, 'I rejoice that you are both to walk along the same path even though it's not the same as mine.'[22]

After instruction from Father Gervase Mathew, she was received on Easter Sunday 1946. Longford was overjoyed at being a 'household of faith'. The fact that his wife had 'come over to Rome' served only to reinforce his own conviction and to increase his eagerness to persuade others to join up, often in spite of their insistence that they were not interested in religion. Friends recount his repeated, half-humorous, half-serious references in conversations to 'coming over'. Father D'Arcy was regularly introduced to those who Longford, with missionary zeal, felt were ripe for conversion. No doubt reasoning that if someone as antipathetic to religion as his wife could be convinced, Longford became a crusader for converts, typically taking the Christian call to spread the good news in very literal terms.

Catherine was born in February 1946 and was the first of the Longford children to be baptised a Catholic. Her siblings were to follow her, the younger ones as a matter of course. Antonia and Thomas were deemed old enough to make up their own minds. Antonia did not need to stop to think. She had always wanted to be a Catholic, she recalls.[23] She transferred to St Mary's Ascot, a convent boarding school run by the Institute of the Blessed Virgin Mary. Thomas was less wholehearted about conversion though he was to benefit from an Ampleforth education he was later to reject Catholicism.

He recalls the events surrounding his mother's conversion as causing a great physical dislocation in his life but without altering anything fundamental at home.

> It was all very sudden. We moved rapidly from nothing – high agnostic – to Anglicanism. Then we were suddenly told that we were no longer Anglo-Catholics, that we were moving on again. Like Mother Courage our chariot was moving on, and we were becoming Catholics. Antonia asked me if I thought we were ratting. The change meant that we were snatched away from one school and sent to another. As newcomers my parents felt they must be extra conscientious and send us to Catholic schools. But it didn't change the essential character of the family or our relationship with our parents. We didn't suddenly

> have family prayers. We'd had them before. It didn't
> change anything.[24]

Change was afoot in Longford's political career. In the autumn
of 1946, the Prime Minister reshuffled his government and
summoned his Lord-in-Waiting to Downing Street. He offered
Longford the post of Parliamentary Secretary at the Ministry of
National Insurance, calculating that given his Beveridge background, he would leap at the chance. The legislation executing
the main ideas of the report he had worked on was pending and
the job would give him ample opportunity to shine.

Confronted with such pressing reasons, Longford said yes. But
as he walked back along Whitehall, his doubts grew. It was not
so much that he did not want to work on national insurance.
Rather that there was something else he wanted to do much
more. He returned to Downing Street and with what he now
admits was extraordinary effrontery and arrogance begged a
surprised Attlee to be appointed Under-Secretary of State for
War. The memory of his failure as a soldier was still very fresh.
When he had been invalided out of the army, Leslie Hore-
Belisha, a former Secretary of State for War, had written to him
saying that 'if you can't do something in the army, perhaps one
day you'll do something for the army'. In the autumn of 1946
Longford saw his chance. Attlee, doubtless slightly taken aback,
did not say yes or no at once, but having given the matter some
consideration came back and granted Longford's wish.

The Prime Minister cannot have had many junior ministers
making such an unusual request, especially at a time when he
had a surplus of talented young Labour MPs, held up by the
war, eager for ministerial promotion. His indulgence towards
Longford can be explained partly by his own habit, akin to that
of Dalton, of encouraging the younger members of his party.
But it also seems that he had a particular soft spot for Longford
and envisaged a glittering career ahead for him.

Longford later came to rank Attlee alongside de Valera at the
top of the list of the men he most admired (though Longford's
public defence of de Valera had almost dissuaded Attlee from
offering him a peerage in 1945, considering that a man with

such opinions must have poor judgement). The fact that Long-ford's ministerial career prospered under Attlee's patronage contributed to his admiration, but it was more than simple self-seeking. It was another case of the hero-worship to which Longford was prone as a young man. Indeed Attlee was perhaps the last name to join the list of older men to whom Longford had been drawn since he had lost his own father. Attlee was also the most unlikely. A man less like the flamboyant F. E. Smith or the ruthless de Valera it is hard to imagine.

Attlee had risen to the leadership of the Labour Party by an accident of history. He was one of the few Labour MPs to survive the 1931 general election. In 1935, following Lansbury's defeat at party conference, he had been the compromise candidate for the leadership and since then had survived various attempts to unseat him, some of them supported in pre-war years by the pro-Cripps Longford. Even after he had delivered victory in the 1945 general election, Attlee had to fight off a challenge by Morrison. Had Morrison succeeded, Longford's career would have been very different. Indeed he may not even have had a political career at all. At a wartime dinner party which he attended with Longford, Morrison gestured at him and said to the hostess: 'Here I am from the lower classes joining the upper classes. He is a member of the upper classes who has joined the lower classes. That always causes trouble.' When pressed on what sort of trouble he meant, Morrison retorted: 'Because he gets keener on the party than the party is on itself.'[25]

Attlee by contrast had none of Morrison's suspicions. He came from a well-to-do family, had fought at Gallipoli alongside Longford's father and had shared some of his junior minister's own agonies over reconciling a privileged background with a belief in socialism. Like Longford he had worked among the underprivileged in the East End of London. Furthermore, he was not one of those – like Morrison – who were wary of intellectuals in the party.

Alhough perhaps not in an obvious way, Attlee did share some characteristics with men like F. E. Smith. He was brave – in the face of the constant sniping, both from within the ranks of his own party and in the field of battle. He had been decorated in the First World War. He could be, if not sparklingly witty, then at least laconic. Longford is fond of quoting his remark to Harold Laski – 'a period of silence on your part will be advantageous' – and his interview with Richard Crossman, whose family he knew but for whom he had little time. Crossman spent half an hour outlining his perceptions of the situation in Palestine, a matter of great concern to the Labour government in the late 1940s. When he paused to draw breath, Attlee cut him dead with, 'And how's your mother?'[26]

Attlee was a practical, pragmatic socialist, a position to which Longford had been evolving during the war years. A genuine friendship grew up between the two of them. On one occasion after he had retired, Attlee and his wife Vi took the Longfords out to dinner. They went to a restaurant in Sloane Square that none of them knew well.

> We had a delightful meal together, but afterwards
> there was a further moment of embarrassment. He
> took me aside and asked if I wouldn't mind paying the
> bill; he would give me his cheque for the amount.
> 'Afraid they wouldn't know me here.' He had been
> Prime Minister . . . but had no more sense of his own
> importance than if he had been some young Parlia-
> mentary candidate.[27]

Longford, who was one of the few senior Labour figures who continued to visit Attlee right up to his death, has long liked to point to a Christian side in Attlee that gave him moral authority. 'Clement Attlee was an ethical giant, soaked in Christianity,' Longford says. 'It was an old-fashioned public school type of Christianity, a tremendous sense of obligation towards the underprivileged.'[28] Yet Longford overlooks Attlee's own denial of Christianity. Questioned by his biographer, Kenneth Harris, he replied, 'I'm one of those people incapable of religious experience. Believe in the ethics of Christianity. Can't believe the mumbo jumbo.'[29]

Newly installed at the War Office, Longford served under Fred Bellenger the Secretary of State and the Financial Secretary,

John Freeman, a fellow protégé of Dalton, later a journalist and noted television interviewer and British Ambassador in Washington. One of the Under-Secretary of State's tasks was liaison with the senior generals. Part of Longford thrilled at the prospect of meeting with those like his father who had led their men in battle. Yet another side of him shrank from the encounter because of his own military failure. He decided the best policy was honesty and never made a secret of his own war record. It was almost as if he wanted the generals to absolve him from his sin of omission. Above all, it was Field Marshal Lord Montgomery who performed the act. He would dine with Longford and talk with him about politics as an equal. When the minister had to attend an army staff college, 'Monty' was at his side for support.

Among Longford's continuing duties in the Lords was to speak about British policy in occupied Germany. He had long been an admirer of the Jewish publisher and founder of the Left Book Club, Victor Gollancz. During the war years, Gollancz had played a leading role in awakening the British public to the full horror of Nazism and the concentration camps. In the immediate aftermath of the conflict, Gollancz was one of an influential group of voices criticising British policy in occupied Germany and what he saw as the unnecessary suffering and privations of the German people. Longford stood up on 6 November 1946 to defend the government's policy uneasily in the face of such attacks. He had not set foot in the country since the end of hostilities but post-war Germany was, he conceded, 'a tragic mess', adding, 'a mess of her [Germany's] own making. God forgive me if to say that is to speak unfairly of a people who are suffering as they are suffering now.'

Mentioning God's name did not disguise the fundamental lack of Christianity in a policy designed to wreak revenge on the German people, Gollancz wrote in the *News Chronicle* several days later. Longford's speech had been 'a model of feebleness and futility', Gollancz charged. 'Have these Christian statesmen of ours the slightest idea of what is going on in Germany? Apparently not, for if they had they would not make the idiotic statements that cause such consternation.'[30] In the city of

Düsseldorf, in the British occupied zone, Gollancz reported, people were living on between 400 and 1000 calories per day. 'Four hundred – and I have been in many homes where this has been the daily ration – is half the Belsen rate.' Gollancz's message was not a universally popular one. Many British people felt that the Germans must be punished. At a time of rationing at home, they were not prepared to feel sorry for the vanquished Germans. Forgiveness was out of the question.

However, Longford was stung by Gollancz's criticisms. His own reading had convinced him that forgiveness was one of the central Christian virtues. He felt that as a Christian he was being challenged to forgive the German people. He set to work at once in gathering exact details of what was happening in the British zone of occupied Germany. When he discovered that there was substance in Gollancz's charge that Britain was allowing the Germans to starve, he wrote to Clement Attlee expressing his own difficulty in defending the government position unless steps were taken to improve the situation. The Prime Minister, if he had not already realised, saw that he had a tender conscience on his hands. He summoned his young minister and listened with interest to his plea. But little changed over the severe winter of 1946–7. As well as shortages of food, there was little fuel for heating and an acute lack of housing.

In February Longford was on his feet again, defending the government's policy of keeping German prisoners of war in this country so that they could do reparation work before being sent home. The policy came under fierce attack from Bishop Bell of Chichester, often a lonely voice during the war years in questioning government conduct of the campaign and its insistence on Germany's unconditional surrender. The argument Longford had to put forward was that by doing agricultural labours in this country, German PoWs were contributing to the common task of feeding both Britain and their own country. He was far from convinced by his own words and made his unhappiness known in government circles.

In March he travelled to Austria, where he had tried to learn German in 1930, and saw at first hand people who were desperate, starving and without adequate shelter. His troubled conscience led him, on his return, to bring up the matter repeatedly with more senior colleagues. In April, he was called to Downing Street. Attlee offered him the chance to do something about a policy which he clearly had little faith in. Longford was appointed Chancellor of the Duchy of Lancaster, responsible to the Foreign Office, a post outside the Cabinet but with responsibility for the British zones of both Germany and Austria. It was to be both his finest hour in government and a period of intense frustration as he grappled with international problems that were quite beyond his control.

Nine

The minister for Germany

Two things only are certain. If he fails he will confess to failure. And if he is impeded he will resign

Observer *profile of Longford on his appointment to Germany*

Once the Allies had decided upon a policy of forcing the Nazis to surrender unconditionally, it was inevitable that after defeating Hitler's armies the whole of Germany must be occupied. In June 1945 the Allied Control Council in Berlin, made up of Britain, America, Russia and France, took on responsibility for running Germany in the absence of a national government. Joint decisions were to be put into effect in each occupying power's zone. The British oversaw the north and west of Germany, the industrial heartland. Berlin, the capital of the Third Reich, was split between the occupying powers despite sitting in the middle of the Russian zone.

From the start joint action proved impossible. While all four Allies agreed that National Socialism had to be eliminated and the German war machine permanently disabled, little else was decided. There was talk from some – notably the US Secretary to the Treasury Henry Morgenthau – that Germany's industrial base should be smashed, its economic power thereby removed and the country turned over to pasture. Others wanted to see the Third Reich split up into three separate states so as to cripple the German nation for ever. Another viewpoint suggested that the Allies should continue to run Germany for up to fifty years.

It was over reparations that the wartime Allies fell apart. After the unhappy experience of 1919 when attempts to get financial compensation out of a defeated Germany had proved counter-productive, they agreed in principle to take reparations in kind, dismantling German industry and shipping plant and machinery back home at the same time as seizing a percentage of remaining manufacturing output. German prisoners-of-war were to be used for ten years to work on reconstruction. The Russians, and to a lesser extent the French, were keener than their Allies on the idea of reparations. Unlike Britain and America, they had suffered Nazi occupation. Their determination to get their revenge on Germany, and not just in their own zone, was one of the causes of the destitution that Victor Gollancz had detailed and which greeted Longford when he arrived in the British zone. The produce of the Industrial Ruhr in the British zone was a special target for Moscow and Paris.

Ever the enthusiast for a new challenge, Longford arranged for news of his appointment to be delayed for a couple of weeks to give him time to brush up on what little German he had already grasped in between tennis matches on his pre-war trip to Austria. His chosen method was to study the New Testament for half an hour each morning – a devotion he had taken up on becoming a Catholic – in German. This link between his Christianity and his work in Germany was to have symbolic resonance in subsequent events.

With his usual sharp eye for the value of publicity, when his new job was revealed to the press he let it be known also that he was enrolling his two eldest children, Thomas and Antonia, in German classes. 'It was the most eccentric, horrifying idea at the time,' says Antonia. 'People were so anti-German that they talked of killing dachshunds in the street. When I told Mutter Hilda at St Mary's Ascot that I wanted to learn German, she cried and said, "I never thought I would teach that language again."'[1]

Longford's rushed preparations were interrupted by a bout of gastric 'flu. The family had not yet moved into their Hampstead home, so he received a stream of visitors at his sick bed at the Athenaeum. Never one to bear grudges, Longford made sure that Victor Gollancz was among those who briefed him. Gollancz's book *Darkest Germany* had done much to alert British public opinion to the food, fuel and housing shortages that were afflicting a demoralised German people in the severe winter of 1946–7. At a memorial service in 1967, Longford paid tribute to Gollancz and the influence he had exerted on a newly appointed minister.

> Victor Gollancz did more than any other single man
> after the last war to awaken the British conscience
> with regard to the suffering of the German people,
> especially of the inhabitants of the British zone of
> occupation. [He] attained an ardour of prophetic fire
> unequalled among the British public in my lifetime.

As Gollancz's biographer Ruth Dudley Edwards comments of those meetings in April 1947: 'Pakenham had a tender conscience and such people were vulnerable to Victor.'[2]

Gollancz and others of like mind had set up the Save Europe Now campaign, aimed at changing Allied policy towards Germany and rescuing its people from starvation. The challenge that Gollancz set Longford was tailor-made to inspire him. Bearing in mind the minister's own views and experience of the British rule in Ireland, how could the occupation policy in Germany be carried out without stifling the natural feelings and just demands of its inhabitants? Were the Germans not, like the Irish before the 1921 treaty, prisoners and the British minister, by dint of superior force, the prison governor? Gollancz counselled Longford to aim in this potential battleground for a principle of partnership. To many of his officials' and colleagues' alarm, Longford veered more towards taking the side of the prisoner.

He set off at once for Berlin where he was to meet the Foreign Secretary, Ernest Bevin, for a briefing about government policy in Germany. Bevin had been to Moscow trying to persuade the Russians, with little success, to co-operate in reaching joint decisions over Germany on the Control Council. As the Russians extracted their pound of flesh, in the process leaving Germany bankrupt and starving, it fell to the British and Americans to send in emergency supplies to feed the Germans. While Bevin had not yet entirely despaired of an agreement being reached – that possibility was finally extinguished at a Foreign Ministers' meeting in London in November – the American delegate General Marshall left Moscow convinced that the Russians were stalling in the hope that the ensuing chaos would hasten the spread of Communism across Europe. Back in America, Marshall began drawing up his plan to save western Europe from the Soviet menace.

With Bevin reflecting on this international *impasse* on his journey from Moscow to Berlin, Longford had already arrived and caused quite a stir. When his official plane landed at Berlin's Gatow Airport, he was exceedingly fired up for the challenge ahead.

> My sole preoccupation was to set foot on German soil and to 'get on with the job'. When the plane came to a standstill, there seemed to my heated fancy to be some delay in pushing forward the steps. Without premeditation or reflection I performed what the *Daily Mail* described as 'the Pakenham leap' – quite a number of feet to the ground. At the moment of my leap, however, the steps arrived at a good round pace and collided somewhat violently with my face. My glasses were knocked off, a small cut opened in my forehead, and taken all round it was a somewhat unusual arrival for a British minister in an occupied territory.[3]

Quite what the assembled dignitaries made of the spectacle is not recorded. A more eccentric, less statesman-like gesture is hard to imagine. The press loved it. Conscious or not at the moment he abandoned protocol, Longford made sure he made the front pages the next day. The bump on his head had almost as dramatic an effect as that sustained at the Mosley meeting. Having prepared no speech, and without consulting with his boss, Ernest Bevin, or indeed any senior British official in

Germany, Longford proceeded, with blood trickling down his face, to outline British policy to the assembled crowd.

> I come to Germany in a spirit of goodwill. I am a believer in Christianity, both as regards justice and mercy. In this job I shall attempt to apply Christian principles, not forgetting the past but with my eyes mainly on the future. I am particularly interested in the youth of Germany.

As a personal credo, it was an accurate picture of his own beliefs and highly individual approach to politics. As a statement of government policy, it was ill-considered. In a tense international situation, Bevin had no intention of letting Britain be seen as siding with the Germans.

The destitution and hopelessness that greeted Longford when he toured the British zone only confirmed his determination to speak up for the Germans. 'The only policy is one of friendliness,' he told his officials as he toured the occupied lands. It was one thing to read the statistics – living standards had dropped by 74 per cent since 1932, the slump year paving Hitler's way to power. It was another to see them at first hand. In his pre-war wrestling with the relative claims of conservatism and socialism and indeed in his work with Beveridge, Longford the don had operated at an intellectul and cerebral level, weighing up arguments and theories. In Germany as a politician he was greeted by hundreds of individual stories of tragedy. It was as if the people of the British zone became his constituents and he took them to his heart with the same dedication that he had shown to the people of Cowley. Yet he was in a curiously ambiguous position, both their representative and, as a British minister, their oppressor.

At times his emotional response, working up from personal observations towards general principles, exposed Longford to the charge of lack of political judgement. It certainly reduced his effectiveness in directing the British Cabinet and was ultimately to render him a figurehead. At one meeting with German students at Göttingen, he listened to their tales of woe and promised them immediate action. When he instructed his officials to act upon those promises, they had to explain that it was much more complicated and that with the best will in the world they couldn't hope for much progress. That 'tender conscience' in Germany in 1947, as in so many later instances, was to make him a maverick among politicians, instantly attractive to his 'constituents' and a thorn in the side of bureaucracy.

One of the first cities that the new minister visited was Düsseldorf. He was met by local German politicians, including the Christian Democrat leader and future Chancellor Konrad Adenauer, and led round the ruins of the bombed-out centre. They stopped off at a school where the children recited poems to Longford. Moved by what he saw, he told them, in what he admits were the first words that came to his lips: 'Never believe that the whole world is against you. Never believe that England is against you. There is much goodwill towards Germany in England. I have seven children of my own. When you grow up I hope that you will come to England and meet my own and other English children.' The children then sang his favourite prayer, Psalm 51, the Miserere, with its message of forgiveness.

Such heartfelt words were neither an accurate portrait of official policy or of British public opinion – unconvinced of the need to send food to their recent enemies at a time when basic foodstuffs were rationed at home and certainly not in the mood for forgiveness. Longford remembers that after his impromptu speech to the children, his civil servants grew noticeably irritated. This was not how they expected their minister to behave. They considered he had gone native. But he was not to be put off. He was on a mission. He told his friend Douglas Woodruff that when he arrived in Germany, he had a feeling of *déjà vu*. It was like the Dublin of his childhood, a people suffering under British rule. He identified the downtrodden Germans with the Irish.[4] Where his involvement had been too late to ensure that the British, in the wake of the First World War, showed a measure of justice to the Irish, he believed that in Germany's case, he had a chance to avoid repeating past errors.

His job intensified into a crusade where his Christianity and his socialism worked hand in hand. In the ensuing year he was to travel to Germany twenty-six times in all, an average of one trip every two weeks.

> Tearing up and down on foot, in official cars under military convoy, in the omnipresent aeroplane; plunging down mines; exploring the innermost recesses of internment camps; plodding through endless ruins to discover the precise number of calories consumed by pitiable families, I seemed unable to rest and unable to tire.[5]

Perhaps from tiredness, perhaps through his eminently quotable remarks, perhaps from his Christian conviction to speak the truth, Longford was becoming outspoken enough to make Whitehall blush. In a conversation with journalists, which he believed was off the record, he described conditions in the British zone as 'appalling', adding, 'I pray for the Germans night and morning.' Longford's description was of course accurate, but rising politicians with sensitive missions were supposed to be diplomatic with the truth. The next day, Longford flew back to London to be greeted with banner headlines: 'Conditions in British zone appalling. Pakenham prays for Germans.'

At times his Christian intentions were severely tried. When he once visited a prison, he met a group of former concentration camp guards. He later told David Astor how at that moment he realised he was looking into the faces of perpetrators of great evil. Attempting to convey the Christian message of mercy and forgiveness had been an almost insurmountable task.[6]

At other times, his Catholicism caused embarrassment to his officials. When Longford paid a courtesy call on Cardinal Frings of Cologne, his slavish devotion to Catholic ritual triumphed over any sense of his own importance as the representative of the occupying power. 'When I saw him,' one of Longford's officials said later, 'a Minister of the Crown, going down on his knee and kissing that man's ring, I wished that the earth could have opened and swallowed me.'[7]

Behind the flurry of activity and gestures of goodwill and forgiveness, though, did Longford achieve a great deal in

Germany? On the ground he was responsible for 26,000 civil servants (one of whom would have been the late Robert Maxwell). Though those in the ranks dealing each day with destitute Germans were sympathetic to Longford's approach, the more senior officials were alarmed at the independent line that their new chief was taking and did their best to frustrate some of his best intentions. While the Military Governor of the British zone Sholto Douglas was anxious to relinquish his post and placed few obstacles in Longford's path, the Chief of State General Brian Robertson had little respect for the minister's unorthodox attitudes and was prone to turn to Ernest Bevin for support, especially on financial matters where the junior minister's freedom of manoeuvre was limited. Longford did, however, find an invaluable ally in the American Military Governor, General Lucius Clay, who shared his growing concern about the short-sightedness of the reparations policy. A destitute Germany would be either an eternal burden on the West or a magnet to Communist subversion.

However, the real block to Longford's effectiveness was the Foreign Secretary, Ernest Bevin, who had an instinctive antipathy for the Germans that accurately reflected the contemporary prejudice of many British people. When Longford tried to persuade the Foreign Secretary to echo some of his words of encouragement as a gesture to the German people, Bevin retorted 'I'm not going to get sentimental over them. I'll leave that to you.' Bevin believed that the Germans only respected strength and that by offering them compassion Longford was merely appearing weak and earning their contempt. On another occasion, pressed as to his attitude to Germans, he told General Robertson, 'I 'ates them.'

It was not only personal prejudice that stopped Bevin backing his enthusiastic colleague in his crusade. While Longford had only his German constituents to consider, Bevin was playing a delicate balancing game between Washington and Moscow over the composition of the post-war world political map. Germany was the immediate matter under discussion but Bevin had always to consider a wider picture. While he and Longford shared a conviction that co-operation with the Soviets would ultimately be impossible, Bevin was reluctant to give up on his attempts to play Moscow off against Washington and so keep Britain's independent foreign policy.

Britain controlled four German regions – North-Rhine West-phalia, with a population as large as the Netherlands and encompassing both the industrial complex of the Ruhr and its agricultural hinterland, Lower Saxony, Schleswig-Holstein and Hamburg. Longford's most immediate problem was the shortage of food. The lack of co-operation between the Allies in their zones, plus the handing over of a large chunk of eastern Germany to Poland, meant that whole swathes of the traditional agricultural areas were cut off from the British zone. Compounding the crisis, the western regions saw the influx of an estimated nine million refugees from the east, a combination of those fearful of falling under Soviet rule and ethnic Germans, such as those expelled from the Sudetenland in 1945. The scant food supplies in the British zone were being hoarded by farmers, unwilling to sell their produce in exchange for a German currency that was worthless, thanks to the Russians' inflationary habit of printing marks in the east to pay their soldiers.

When Longford arrived in Germany the people of the US and UK zones were being kept alive on a subsistence diet of 1.5 million tons of food imports grudgingly paid for by British and American taxpayers, as, with German industry in tatters, there was no other money to cover the cost. All the coal the German miners – starving and disheartened – were producing was shipped to France as reparations. In the meantime the Germans had no fuel to heat their homes or run the trains.

Longford soon came to realise that the Germans would never be able to support themselves until they had a stronger currency and until reparations stopped bleeding their industry. It was principally over the question of dismantling German factories that he took his stand against his own government, though he did play a supporting role in pressing for and planning currency reform. The British government, pushed by the Russians and French in particular over reparations, had agreed reluctantly to a list of industrial complexes that were to be dismantled. Bevin and the Americans were unwilling as yet to break ranks with the Russians. Germany could be kept down, and peace therefore assured, they calculated, only with Soviet co-operation.

Longford and his officials were for once united in having little stomach for the task, but their complaints cut little ice at the Foreign Office. Longford did not carry sufficient weight in government circles to get the policy blocked. He could only chip away at the edges, ensuring that dismantling in the British zone was carried out on a smaller scale than elsewhere. Despite his efforts, 1636 factories disappeared in the British and American zones alone and Germany's merchant marine was seized as part of reparations.

Longford became more and more convinced that British policy was fundamentally flawed not only in its inhuman treatment of the Germans, but in its geo-political ambitions. By concentrating on the recent past and the need to hold down Germany, Bevin was underestimating, in Longford's opinion, the real enemy to freedom and peace, the Soviet Union. Leaving Germany destitute as a punishment for its wartime crimes may have satisfied a widespread desire for revenge, but was simply allowing Russia and its supporters to gain more and more influence. The Foreign Secretary was not blind to Soviet schemes and his principal private secretary, Frank Roberts, later wrote that as early as the autumn of 1946 Bevin had grown disillusioned with attempts to work with the Soviets and was leaning more heavily on the Americans.[8] Yet Bevin did not share a suspicion and dislike of the Soviets that Longford had been developing in the war years and which, with his posting to Germany, became a lifelong antipathy.

From the entry of the Soviets into the war on the Allied side in 1941, Longford had been wary of their true motives. He was much influenced by his friend Michael de la Bedoyere, editor of the *Catholic Herald*, who acknowledged the *realpolitik* behind the alliance with the Russians, but held that the Soviets could never be friends of the West. In a leader published in 1941 (which so infuriated Churchill that he considered serving a closure notice on the *Catholic Herald* under wartime regulations) de la Bedoyere wrote: 'We do protest as strongly as we can against any treaty with a power whose avowed policy remains the spread of godless Marxism by inciting world revolution.' Newly converted to Catholicism and switching his allegiances within the Labour movement from the Communist-infiltrated left wing to a more centrist Christian Socialist position, Longford endorsed de la Bedoyere's warning and carried his suspicion of the Soviets to his post in Germany. The support the Catholic editor gave to the Save Europe Now movement only increased Longford's respect for his opinion.

In the eastern zone of Germany occupied by the Russians, Communists were given special preference in local elections and moderate Social Democrats were browbeaten into alliance with them. Longford was convinced that the Soviet gaze was spreading across the whole of Germany. He tried to make Bevin and his Cabinet colleagues see that the West could not suppress the Russians and the Germans simultaneously. If they wanted a bulwark against the menace of Soviet-style Communism consuming the continent, they needed a strong, united Germany. By punishing the Germans and keeping them on the poverty-line, they were only pushing them into the arms of the Soviets.

As Longford grew more frustrated, Bevin reacted to each new outburst from his junior colleague – whom he insisted on calling Pake-en-ham – with mounting irritation. Despite the vast gulf between them in terms of upbringing – Bevin was illegitimate and grew up in great poverty in the West Country – and over policy, Longford maintained a loyalty in public to the Foreign Secretary. Evelyn Waugh describes Longford at one of their meetings as 'in a daze of hero-worship of Mr Ernest Bevin'.[9]

Bevin, for his part, viewed Longford with a mixture of respect and amusement. During the meeting of the foreign ministers of the four occupying powers in December 1947, which signalled the progressive breakdown of co-operation in policy towards their respective zones, Longford accompanied Bevin to a dinner at the Russian Embassy. Molotov, the Soviet foreign Minister, leant over and asked, 'Are you a Marxist, Lord Pakenham?'

'No,' he replied. 'I have studied Karl Marx a good deal, but I am anything but a Marxist.'

'I could hardly expect to find a good Marxist in the House of Lords,' the ambassador retorted.

'That's just where you're wrong,' Bevin interrupted. 'The

House of Lords are the only people in England who've got time to read Karl Marx.'[10]

Such friendly banter could not however disguise the fact that Longford was failing to convince Bevin of the need to halt reparations at once. Neither was the Cabinet moved by his protestations. Longford was faced with an obvious choice. Resign over a strategy he found short-sighted or remain and try to ameliorate its worst excesses from within. He decided to consult his confessor, Father D'Arcy, for guidance but found that the Jesuit had a much clearer view than his pupil of the demarcation between matters political and matters spiritual. Spiritual advisers could not give guidance on resignation from the government. Longford learnt not to ask again.

Despite realising the brief storm of publicity his resignation would cause, and the pressure it would place on the British government, he calculated that he would do more for the Germans in practical terms by fighting from inside Whitehall.

It was not an entirely altruistic decision. When he spoke to Evan Durbin of resignation, his old friend pointed out that while the party was tolerant of dissidents and eccentrics within its ranks, resignation from a Labour government was regarded as an unforgivable step. You could battle and criticise from within, but to resign was to injure not just the party but the whole cause, the movement, in a public way. Longford's political career would be at an end. The example of Ramsay MacDonald and Jimmy Thomas, who had abandoned Labour in 1931 and been ostracised by the movement thereafter for their act of betrayal, was still fresh in people's minds. Harold Wilson's return from the grave of his 1951 resignation was yet to come.

Longford tried to rally support from within the Labour movement to save Germany from death by dismantling. Colleagues like Douglas Jay recall the government generally upholding the notion that, whatever the vagaries of British public opinion, the Germans had to be fed. 'When Frank started to talk of forgiveness though,' Jay says, 'it tended to get people's backs up.'[11] Denis Healey, then Secretary of Labour's International Department, recalls that Longford was 'quite unpopular with a lot of the party' on account of his pro-German stance.

> I was very pro-German in the sense that I had no
> anti-German feeling as such. But I think the basic
> thing with Frank is that he always takes things a bit
> far. Still if you are a minister your job is to promote
> what you see as the interests of the policy you repre-
> sent. And that often makes you unpopular with col-
> leagues. Bevin was a sort of hard-headed, no-
> nonsense trade unionist and Frank was a committed
> but unworldly Christian.[12]

Longford's ultimate avenue of appeal was to Clement Attlee. On numerous occasions he sent impassioned pleas to the Prime Minister to save Germany, adding a threat of resignation. Attlee, according to Elizabeth, 'would send one of his terse replies, which totally ignored Frank's threats and generally ran something like this: "My dear Frank, Thank you for writing. I have noted your points. Yours ever. Clem."'[13] On another occasion, Longford attempted to deliver his resignation to Attlee at his room in the House of Commons only to be interrupted by a carefully stage-managed division bell. When the two men returned after voting, Attlee changed the subject and all talk of resignation 'lapsed through mutual inanition'.[14]

Attlee may have lived to regret the day he appointed Longford to Germany. But the Prime Minister was nothing if not a shrewd manager and he cannot have been surprised at Longford's independent line on Germany. In fact, his passionate commitment may well have been exactly what Attlee intended. As Chancellor of the Duchy of Lancaster, Longford's freedom for manoeuvre was relatively small. He could only influence everyday affairs. The larger decisions were made by Bevin in conjunction with the Russians and the Americans, to whom post-war Britain was deeply in debt. Longford's command of the newspaper headlines gave an exaggerated impression of his powers. After all, he was a new, relatively untried minister, and a member of the House of Lords. He may have had influential sponsors within the party, including Attlee himself, but it is unlikely that the Prime Minister would have entrusted the task of shaping British policy in Germany to one so inexperienced and unpredictable.

However, Longford did not disappoint his Prime Minister in giving a very public impression to the Germans that Britain cared deeply about the post-war chaos, thereby putting a sympathetic human face to a situation that was locked in frigid international dispute. He may have been excessive in speaking of forgiveness, but his essential message tallied with the ideals of any civilised government, particularly those of a recently elected socialist one. And Longford could trumpet these beliefs in a blaze of harmless publicity, his juniority releasing him from any obligation to support his statements with actions that would alienate the Americans and Russians. Indeed one of the reasons Longford had caught the eye of Attlee was his adroit handling of the publicity surrounding the Beveridge Report.

If these were the motives behind Longford's appointment, then Attlee soon began to realise that as a strategy it was suffering from the law of diminishing returns. The British press, initially so enthralled by the irrepressible minister, began to question why the government was not acting to back him up. There was a danger that he might become a hammer to attack the Labour administration.

In Germany too, people began to grow suspicious of Longford. He arranged a representative gathering in the Opera House in Düsseldorf to try to put as good a gloss as possible on the dismantling policy. Sitting on the platform in front of a Union Jack, flanked by two officials, he tried to explain the case for a measure of reparations and restriction of German industry that might be used in warfare. It was not an argument he endorsed in his heart. His audience showed their disaffection by universal rustling and shuffling of their feet. While such displays made little impact on the Cabinet, they did damage Longford's standing in the British zone. 'That afternoon a certain kind of reputation I had acquired in Germany, that of a man about to achieve marvels, disappeared for good.'[15]

Bevin grew more and more exasperated with Longford. After a difference of opinion on currency reform, Bevin sighed, 'You do press me a bit hard, Frank, you really do.' In April of 1948

Longford injured his Achilles tendon and was laid up in Hampstead. Attlee came to call. 'I think it is about time you had a department of your own. I've got civil aviation in mind.'[16]

Bevin had clearly been applying pressure. Longford did not know whether to rejoice or cry. In one sense he felt relieved that a burden was being lifted off his shoulders. The ambitious politician in him could not help but see that his promotion would be judged a mark of his success in Germany. In career terms he was being rewarded.

Yet in another sense, he was being taken off the case, booted upstairs, a blow softened only a little when he was named a Privy Councillor. He felt that he was abandoning the German people and his moral obligations to them. The Catholicism that had been an integral part of his crusade now made him feel guilty. In part he managed to assuage his conscience by continuing to visit Germany regularly – attending for example the re-opening of Cologne cathedral in the summer of 1948 – and by asking awkward questions of his government colleagues about policy there. However, that sense of an incompleted task stayed with him for many years. As he later remarked: 'I hope to be remembered in Germany not for my achievement but for my endeavour.'[17]

Despite his ultimate failure to achieve the goals that he set himself – the political one of an end to dismantling and the moral one of getting the British people to forgive the Germans (still, some would argue, a task waiting to be accomplished) – Longford's record in Germany did include some notable successes.

He oversaw, on behalf of his government, the effective economic and political merger of the British and American zones, a co-operation that was to presage the foundation of the Federal Republic of Germany in the west. The task had already been under way when he took up his responsibilities and continued after he left, but he had played a significant part in it.

Attlee's decision to transfer him came at the outset of the Berlin Air Lift. It proved a turning point in history. The Four Power idea was abandoned and replaced by the concept of America and western Europe aligning in a common front to

Soviet aggression. The Soviets' designs on the whole of Berlin and their suspicions of the economic co-operation between the British and Americans (and ultimately the French) led them to block western supply routes into Berlin. Rather than hand over the people of the city to rule by Soviet puppets, British and American planes kept the 2.25 million people in Berlin's western zones supplied for eleven months. Though Longford was about to leave his post, Bevin sent him out to Berlin at once to reassure German public opinion. 'I like Berlin,' he told his audience with the full backing of the Foreign Secretary, 'and we have no intention of leaving it.'[18] It did not have quite the impact of '*Ich bin ein Berliner*' but expressed the same sentiment.

On 20 June 1948, a couple of months after Longford left his post, the currency reform he had worked on came into effect. The western zones became one economic unit and, with German faith in their currency restored, food began to reappear in markets. When Longford attended the opening of Cologne cathedral in the August, he noticed the difference at once. By that stage, too, western German industry, freed of the Russians' insatiable demands for reparations and bolstered by the Marshall Plan, was beginning its rapid climb to European hegemony.

While Longford played only a supporting role in both the Berlin Air Lift and west German economic revival, his involvement in the political reconstruction of first the British zone, then by association the eventual West Germany, was crucial. The Four Powers had agreed at Potsdam in July 1945 that Germany should be helped along the road to democracy. However, there were different biases involved in seeing the process through. The Russians wanted to encourage Communists and socialists under Walter Ulbricht to form the Socialist Unity Party with Soviet patronage in the east. Longford was quick to see the threat this movement might pose if it gained ground in the western zones. He gave his backing to two parties; the anti-Nazi, anti-Communist Christian Democratic Union, which intended to contest elections all over Germany under the twin banners of religion and democracy; and its secular rival, the Social Democratic Union.

With the Americans, Longford handed over local powers to elected representatives in his zone. Thoughts of a fifty-year occupation were soon forgotten. Aneurin Bevan had argued that Longford's appointment to Germany was a mistake because as a Catholic he would favour the Christian Democrats at the expense of Labour's natural allies, the Social Democrats. However Longford developed a good relationship with Schumacher and Arnold, the SDU leaders, as well as Adenauer. In fact the socialists won three of the four local Länder in the British zone.

Of the German elected representatives, Kurt Schumacher was the least favourably disposed to the British minister. As a fellow socialist, he was disappointed that Longford worked with the Americans – to Schumacher the epitome of capitalism – instead of joining him in precipitating a proletarian revolution. Longford's fear of the Russians made such a course unthinkable. Schumacher's violent anti-Catholicism – he once called the Vatican 'the fifth occupying power' in Germany – gave them little in common.

Carl Arnold was much more in favour of Longford and held a farewell dinner for him in Düsseldorf, attended by leaders of German industry, a mark of their respect for a minister whom they had recognised as on their side. Hans Boeckler, the trade union leader, told Longford, with tears in his eyes, that he would not be forgotten. (One of Longford's lasting achievements in Germany was the encouragement and support he gave to setting up afresh the trade union movement.) Then Arnold stood up to speak and praised Longford as a friend of Germany. Arnold remained bitterly disappointed, though, at the eventual division of Germany into East and West, and recognised that Longford and the British had, by abandoning attempts to placate the Soviets, brought about this partition. Longford was convinced they had had little choice.

Of all the German politicians he dealt with, Longford was closest to Konrad Adenauer. The future Chancellor and founding father of West Germany had been Lord Mayor of Cologne in the pre-war period and an implacable anti-Nazi. When he regained the post in 1945 after the fall of Hitler, the British dismissed him six months later and banned him from politics. His refusal to fall in with the dismantling of his country made him a character they could do without.

Just as he had worked to restore de Valera's reputation from that of dangerous opponent to a statesman with whom the British government could do business, Longford forged a bond with Adenauer after that first meeting in Düsseldorf. He rejected the words of warning from his officials, partly for pragmatic reasons. Adenauer was the elected leader of the CDU and the British therefore had to work with him. Also, Longford and Adenauer shared a belief in the urgent need to rebuild Germany. But the personal sympathy between the two men should not be underestimated. Both were fervent Catholics and that immediately created a bond. Both, while regretting the division of Germany, accepted philosophically that there was little they could do about it.

Moreover Longford admired Adenauer's determination in standing up for his country, at the same time as admitting the consequences of the defeat of a regime he had despised. At a conference of European powers in the Hague in the spring of 1948, attended by Longford, Adenauer led the German delegation.

> [He] told me afterwards that he and his colleagues
> had been deeply touched by the fact that Mr Churchill
> had gone out of his way to receive him personally. 'I
> wanted', he said, 'to tell Mr Churchill that I and all of
> us owed our lives to him – we were Hitler's prisoners,
> and but for Mr Churchill we would not be alive today.
> I wanted to tell him that, and to express our deep
> gratitude.' 'And you did so?' I asked. 'No,' he replied,
> 'I did not. I knew that the Germans are sometimes
> said to grovel in defeat. Mr Churchill has described us
> as always being at your throat or at your feet, and I
> did not feel that I would be serving my country's
> interests if I had appeared fawning or fulsome in the
> moment of national humiliation.'[19]

Besides encouraging the restoration of democracy in western Germany, Longford also placed a heavy emphasis on the need to rebuild its education system. He worked closely with Robert

Birley, the head of Charterhouse, who was educational adviser in the British zone. As a don, Longford knew the value of education. His first, emotional visit to the school in Düsseldorf made sure, within his limited control of the budget, that the provision of books and writing materials had a high priority.

If Longford won plaudits within Germany for his work, then there were those in Britain who considered his spell there the zenith of his political career. It was as minister responsible for the British zone that he made his first significant impact on the political scene. The press, from the moment of the 'Pakenham leap' onwards, were behind him. The *Spectator*'s verdict on his spell in Germany was that he had been 'striving with much gallantry and some success to put some heart into Germany'.

Amongst his peers within and without the Labour Party, Longford's crusade did not go unnoticed or unappreciated. Michael Foot, who worked with Victor Gollancz in the Save Europe Now movement, feels that

> both that campaign and Frank's outspoken stance prepared the way in some measure for the Marshall Plan. I'm not saying that without them there would never have been a Marshall Plan, but that we were doing before what Marshall did later. There was a real danger in 1945 that, thanks to people like Frank, wasn't allowed to turn into deep starvation.[20]

Churchill, too, admired Longford's mettle in standing up for what he believed in. At a Buckingham Palace Garden Party during his period in Germany, Longford was buttonholed by the former Prime Minister. 'I am glad', he said, 'that there is one mind suffering for the miseries of Germany, one English mind suffering for the miseries of Germany.'[21] Lord Carrington, then a young Tory politician, later to face Longford as Leader of the Opposition in the Lords, remembers admiring his courage over Germany.

> It was at a moment when the Germans were not the flavour of the month, so to speak, but Frank showed a

remarkable far-sightedness about Germany and
Germany's position in the future. And he was mag-
nanimous. I think he does have a very great magnan-
imity and understanding.[22]

His work in Germany led Longford into associations with other
groups concerned for the reconstruction of Europe. Among
them was Christian Action, founded in Oxford by Canon John
Collins. Longford was later to become a loyal patron of the
organisation which graduated from preaching reconciliation
with the Germans in the 1940s to opposing nuclear weapons
and apartheid in the 1950s and 1960s. When Christian Action
protested about the treatment of German prisoners-of-war in
Britain and the delay in repatriating them, Collins turned to
Longford for support in lobbying the government and found the
minister sympathetic. Attlee was persuaded to relent and accelerated the process for sending many PoWs home.

'What Frank would dearly have liked to have been', says Jon
Snow, the political journalist, who worked closely with Longford
in the 1970s, 'is a medieval prelate with enormous temporal
powers plus the ability to marry and procreate.'[23]

For a year Longford came close to such a position of supreme
political and moral authority. He was responsible for twenty
million people in the British zone of Germany and oversaw that
duty with a sense of his own Christian crusade to restore the
country to economic and political viability. His tenure was one
of the most intense, rewarding and simultaneously frustrating
periods of his life. Those who worked with him are divided on
the extent of his influence on the emerging West Germany.
Adenauer certainly made clear his belief that Longford had been
one of Germany's principal champions at a time of national
degradation and powerlessness.

Ten

The head of a nationalised industry

'Now Lord Pakenham will be able to have his head always in the clouds'

M. Massigli, French ambassador

Two years before taking up his post at the Ministry of Civil Aviation, Frank Longford had been placed in charge of a ministerial committee looking into the deployment of flying boats. He had written to Elizabeth at the time with some amusement and a mass of exclamation marks at such an unlikely appointment for a self-avowed Philistine in technical and mechanical matters. Attlee had, however, obviously been sufficiently impressed with his work to entrust Longford with unfettered control of Britain's recently nationalised airlines, its airports and state-funded research and development into civilian aircraft.

The Ministry of Civil Aviation had a reputation for being a political graveyard. The previous incumbent, Harry Nathan, had left to return to the business world. In the six and a half years of Labour rule from 1945 onwards, there were five ministers. When he arrived on 2 June 1948, Longford asked his new private secretary to arrange for some family pictures to be put up on the wall of his office and was told by way of a reply that there was not much point since his predecessors had not tended to stick around for very long. Longford's persistence in this matter was rewarded. He stayed put for three years.

His fundamental inspiration for joining the Labour Party had been a desire to right inequalities and injustices in the society around him. To that end, as a politician, he had aspired to a ministerial post in one of the social service ministries. Though in general his interest in foreign affairs took second place to his fascination with the domestic political scene, Germany had had the great merit of providing him with an opportunity to attend to the day-to-day needs of the population of the British zone. Civil Aviation, by contrast, had no human constituency beyond the ministry's 1500 staff at head office and estimated 6000 at various airports and bases around the country. In essence the minister's role was that of technocrat and banker, overseeing operational developments and providing the funding for the state-owned airports and airlines BEA and BOAC.

Appearances suggest that the new job should have been torture for Longford. From his earliest years he had shown no interest in matters technical and little tolerance of those who did. He has never learnt to drive. His failure to master the basic drill of the Army played a part in his military failure. As a man about the house he was a walking disaster. Once, when asked to make a cup of coffee, he was found by one of his daughters putting instant granules into a kettle of water and boiling up the lot. On another occasion, told to turn down the heaters in the dining room, he replied that he would if he could but he did not know how they worked. Even using a razor proved troublesome for him, and frequent were the mornings, before Elizabeth presented him with an electric shaver, that he appeared at breakfast with his face a mass of cuts.

What others might have considered the perks of the job at Civil Aviation, he disliked. The bonhomie of the ex-RAF contingent in the ministry went straight over his head. The growing awareness of technology's potential to transform the world left him admiring but cold. The chance to travel around the British Empire to the opening ceremonies of airports he found tiresome, never having enjoyed overseas journeys. For an aspiring politician and one with a taste for grabbing the headlines, the Ministry of Civil Aviation was a backwater, offering little that was spectacular or indeed even mildly interesting to the general public. From Clement Attlee's point of view, after Longford's regular appearances on the front pages while in Germany, this

227

lack of glamour was a blessing. For the new minister it was frustrating and almost led to his downfall.

However, for all his awkwardness in questioning party policy over Germany, Longford remained a very ambitious man in political terms. He wanted to make it into the Cabinet and believed that his apostasy in Germany had not done him any lasting damage. It is one of the many paradoxes in his personality that at the same time as refusing to play the party political game, he has continued to aspire to high office. Civil Aviation was an interlude where he had to put his head down and tackle an unappealing task in the hope of ultimate salvation in promotion.

His daughter Judith says that her father's eccentricities should not fool one into believing him incapable of pragmatism, indeed that these foibles are often intended to conceal an inherent, if reluctant, adaptability.

> He's a mature personality and he's decided that he's
> not going to do things that bore him. And running a
> home, for example, didn't interest him in the least. So
> he has this tremendous affectation of not being able to
> do things. It's not untypical of men of his age and
> class. But he takes it to ridiculous lengths. Anyone can
> work out how to plug in an electric kettle. But he
> doesn't want to work it out.[1]

Though the idea of Frank Longford running a technical ministry might have caused a wry smile among those of his colleagues who could not see beyond the 'Pakenham leap' and his dishevelled, donnish appearance, he proved to be an excellent administrator, demonstrating that, while details, figures, specifications and careful planning may not have been his natural forte, he was a clever man who could, when necessary, turn his mind to such problems.

Top of his list of priorities at the ministry were the tangled finances of the state-owned airlines. The £11 million annual deficit run up by BEA and BOAC was giving nationalisation a bad name. Committed to the principle of state ownership, Longford did not believe that this excused poor management and necessitated endless subsidies from the tax-payer. He wanted the policy to be shown to work efficiently in the best interests of the nation. His economic training enabled him, in the company of his senior officials, swiftly to identify the causes of the operating losses – outdated equipment, over-manning, poor organisation and a lack of strategic planning.

Longford saw the need to invest in modern aircraft for the two corporations and persuaded a reluctant Cabinet (by that stage applying an increasingly tight rein on public expenditure as the pressure grew to rearm) to equip BOAC with state-of-the-art, efficient Canadair planes. In his struggle to get approval for the necessary funding, he was enthusiastically supported by the Labour leader in the Upper Chamber, Lord Addison, and by Herbert Morrison who had overall responsibility for the nationalised industries at Cabinet level. Morrison and Longford had been in opposite camps in 1945, the former scheming to overthrow and replace Attlee. But they moved closer during the late 1940s through a shared belief in moderation as the party became more polarised between Morrison and his supporters on the right, and Aneurin Bevan and his camp on the left. Hugh Gaitskell wrote in 1950 that

> Frank is now more friendly with Morrison than any of
> the others. He does not like Bevan and was rather
> horrified when I said that I thought Bevan would
> almost certainly be leader of the party and therefore
> Prime Minister sometime.[2]

At Civil Aviation, Longford worked closely with the trade unions to cut staffing levels – never an easy task for a Labour minister – from 24,000 at BOAC in 1947 to 16,000 in 1951 at the same time as increasing productivity. Many of the jobs went with the closing down of a string of air bases under the ministry's control, scattered around the country. He aimed to concentrate resources and was responsible for pushing the development of Heathrow as London's, and indeed Britain's, major airport.

With nationalisation a relatively new phenomenon, the relationship between the management of the state-owned corporations and their political master was, as yet, ill defined. Longford was unusual in allowing those in charge considerable autonomy in day-to-day and technical details – by dint of necessity given his lack of specialist expertise – but at the same time he kept a close watch as the two airlines moved back towards the black. By 1951, their deficit was only £1 million, and that was mainly accounted for by BEA's domestic routes where the need to maintain a public service to outposts like the Scottish Islands outweighed commercial considerations.

'Of course,' he wrote later of this period,

> it is all a question of degree and balance; you don't
> want Parliament, or the Minister for that matter,
> poking his nose into affairs of day-to-day manage-
> ment. You don't want questions in the House when
> the train due at 8.56 arrives at 9.06 on a particular
> Tuesday. But if it does it every day for a year, you
> most certainly do want intervention on behalf of the
> public. A question of only day-to-day significance has
> then passed into a question of general efficiency.[3]

As part of his strategy of exercising this broad, but firm, control, Longford moved to appoint his own men at the head of BEA and BOAC. Both in sacking surplus staff at lower levels and in making changes at the top, he showed that he had sufficient ruthlessness to take tough personnel decisions when necessary. At BOAC he replaced the incumbent chairman with his deputy Miles Thomas and at BEA he brought in Sholto Douglas, erstwhile military governor of the British zone in Germany when Longford first arrived there and a former RAF leader who was also a socialist. Both men went on to make significant contributions to setting their organisations on firm and enduring bases.

In working towards his goal of an efficient, profitable public service, Longford's habitual *modus operandi* was to sketch the broad brush strokes of policy himself and leave the detail to his officials. His gift and the key to his success at Civil Aviation was in surrounding himself with civil servants and with chairmen in whom he had great faith and who felt a strong tie of loyalty to him.

The support that he enjoyed from Herbert Morrison in the matter of the Canadair planes for BOAC was a mark of the recognition from senior Cabinet colleagues that, despite what some of them might have expected, Longford could run an efficient public service and a decidedly technical ministry at that. His star was once more in the ascendant in government circles. However, the showman in him could not resist occasionally playing up to his reputation as an eccentric, scatty don. When inspecting new aircraft, for example, he would walk up and down the aisle and congratulate the engineers and designers on how comfortable the seats were. Once, on an official flight, he spied a man sitting alone away from the main party, seemingly lost in thought. Longford made a special effort by going over to talk to him and offering him a drink. Only later did he learn that the man was one of the senior engineers who was trying to listen to the aircraft engine as part of a safety report.[4] Again when Longford went to greet a visiting Soviet minister at London airport he was accompanied by his son Thomas, by then a teenager and keen on planes. When the younger Pakenham started photographing the Soviet aircraft and various of the surly, affectedly anonymous figures accompanying the minister, he caused a minor diplomatic incident. They suspected the fourteen-year-old of being a cunning British spy, collecting information on Soviet personnel and technical developments.

However, over the crash of a KLM Royal Dutch Airlines plane at Prestwick airport near Glasgow, Longford's fabled eccentricity severely damaged his political career and effectively destroyed any hopes he harboured of entering the Cabinet within the lifetime of Attlee's government. If the Prime Minister had looked on with admiration at Longford's success in operating nationalised industries at Civil Aviation and had calculated that he would not be causing the government any embarrassing headlines there, he was to be disillusioned. Just before midnight on 28 October 1948, a KLM Constellation, with thirty passengers and ten crew on board, crashed five miles short of the runway at Prestwick in thick fog. There were no survivors. Longford was on the scene within hours and moved at once to set up a public inquiry under a Scottish QC, Mr McDonald.

When the report arrived the following August during the Parliamentary recess, both Longford and his officials felt that its conclusion – that the accident was the fault of the air traffic controllers on the ministry's staff at the airport – was not justified by any of the evidence it detailed. The findings of the report appeared to them to point towards pilot error – a verdict later confirmed by Dutch investigators. Longford's first instinct on reading the McDonald report was to defend his own staff against what he considered an unjust accusation. His officials advised him to follow up publication of the report with a statement in the Lords when it reassembled, expressing his own disagreement with its conclusions. Such would have been the pragmatic course for an aspiring politician. A quiet word with more senior colleagues would also have been good tactics, getting them on his side in case the situation became more complicated.

However, Longford did neither. If he was to be confined to a backwater ministry, he felt confident that he could handle the one major incident that was likely to occur during his tenure. To confine his discontent to a statement in the Lords would, he considered, allow the McDonald report too much credence. Just as he had risen to the defence of his constituents in Cowley and of the German people of the British zone, he decided that he must be seen to side with his own officials at Prestwick when they were being falsely accused. A mixture of frustrated ambition, arrogance and his Christian conscience affected his political judgement.

Whatever his feelings for the ministry's staff in the firing line, he does not seem to have pondered the effect his rejection of the report would have on its author. Longford's lack of concern that his decision should be conveyed speedily and sympathetically to the Scottish QC merely compounded the impression of high-handedness. The day before publication of the McDonald report was due, Longford arrived back at his office after lunch to find a hostile letter from the barrister, angry at the minister's betrayal and accusing him of 'making the whole procedure nugatory if not indeed indecently farcical'. Hurrying off to open a House of Lords debate, Longford did not sense any impending danger. Perhaps shouldering the dual responsibilities of a ministry and a central role in guiding Labour's heavy legislative programme through a hostile Lords had also affected his judgement. Whatever his motives, he asked his secretary to call McDonald to placate him and mentioned in passing that he might also inform the Prime Minister and other senior colleagues. He expressed no urgency and none was attached to the task. Regarding the Ministry of Civil Aviation as an area no one took any interest in, he was not prepared for this unfashionable department to be engulfed in controversy.

Later that evening, his speech in the House of Lords having gone down well, Longford returned home with Elizabeth from a dinner to be greeted by a reporter from the *News Chronicle* at his front gate. McDonald was planning, he was informed, to publish his letter of protest at the minister's rejection of his report. Uncharacteristically Longford declined to make any comment. He was convinced that the affair would disappear without trace. He was not unduly alarmed and slept soundly before setting off early the next morning for a two-day visit to a BOAC repair works at Treforest in south Wales and various bases at Filton, Bristol and Bournemouth where large-scale redundancies had been agreed. As he opened the papers, Longford was greeted with headlines such as 'Storm over Air Inquiry. Minister rejects Findings. It's a Farce' in the *Daily Express*. The text of McDonald's letter was included in full.

Still he failed to see the urgency of the situation. On his arrival in Wales, Longford drafted a reply to a Commons question on the subject, including a sentence about his duty to defend civil servants who could not defend themselves, without making it sufficiently clear that he was defending them against what he saw as an injustice, rather than simply backing them up right or wrong. Again he felt that was the end of the matter. He made no attempt to contact any Cabinet member and returned to his tour of inspection.

That afternoon, the Prime Minister was questioned in the Commons by Anthony Eden from the Opposition Front Bench about Longford's actions and the legal precedents for rejecting the findings of a public inquiry. Since he had not been informed by his junior colleague that anything was amiss, Attlee, to his evident discomfiture, could offer no answer. As Longford spent a pleasant evening with his friend Evelyn Waugh at his home at Stinchcombe, discussing everything but civil aviation, a political storm was brewing.

The next morning he was described in the *News Chronicle* as 'a clawing and predatory cat among the legal pigeons'. A message came through from the Prime Minister commanding his presence at the earliest possible opportunity. The Cabinet would be discussing the Prestwick affair that morning.

By the time Longford got back to London after hurrying through the rest of his visit with only half a mind on what was being said to him, the evening papers were baying for his blood. 'Sack for Pakenham' shouted the *Star*. Elizabeth, who had seen the headlines, telephoned to pass on messages of support from Hugh Gaitskell, urging his old friend not to resign. 'He says he knows how quixotic you are but on no account must you.'[5] Longford feared that Attlee might not give him any choice.

At Downing Street, the Prime Minister was waiting in the Cabinet Room with the *Star* and its damning verdict spread out in front of him. Longford got a frosty reception. Attlee's immediate concern was the legality of Longford's decision to reject McDonald's report. 'How can you set up a Court and then refuse to accept its decision when it goes against your own men?' he asked.[6] Not satisfied by Longford's assurance that he had been acting within his constitutional rights and determined to investigate further, Attlee instructed him to draft a Parliamentary statement. Longford had received a severe rap over the knuckles but at least he had not been sacked.

The following afternoon he returned to Downing Street to hear that government lawyers had exonerated him. Since the McDonald report was advisory not mandatory, a Parliamentary apology for his high-handedness would be sufficient. There was still an unpleasant roasting to endure in the House of Lords where he had to cast aside calls for his resignation. The minister emerged from the ordeal to fight another day.

His reputation, however, had suffered. Whatever other good work he did at Civil Aviation, his mishandling of the Prestwick report dominated Longford's tenure of the ministry. In government circles, he was seen as yet again having caused Labour unnecessary embarrassment. His was not a safe pair of hands. At least over Germany and his public stance against the official policy of dismantling, he had been taking a moral position which some of his colleagues could admire if not endorse. Over Prestwick, Longford's protest that he was defending his civil servants cut little ice. Many shared Attlee's belief that a minister should not be seen to be acting only to cover the tracks of his own officials. Whatever his motives, Longford had shown bad political judgement and a lack of concern for his colleagues. One commentator, Alaistair Forbes in the *Sunday Despatch*, even went so far as to suggest that Longford had 'stage-managed mock-martyrdom' in order to remind the public of his existence.

While Attlee would have had little sympathy for such a view, he did feel let down by someone he had singled out for promotion. 'His professional standards were affronted by the clumsiness with which I appeared to him to have handled the situation,' Longford reflected later.[7] By exposing his Prime Minister to humiliation in the Commons, Longford earned a black mark. He was fortunate not to lose his job. Attlee could be ruthless with those whom he judged, as he put it when sacking one junior minister, 'not good enough'. The price of Longford's survival was to be left to languish at Civil Aviation.

The whole episode taught Longford that there were disadvantages as well as benefits to courting the press. He had treated them, as well as McDonald and his colleagues, with arrogance and contempt and had been chastised. If it had been boredom with his job at Civil Aviation that had clouded his judgement and allowed him to sleepwalk into the Prestwick débâcle, then he was going to have to endure a good deal more boredom as a result.

Attlee called a general election in 1950. The Labour government had not lost a by-election in that Parliament. The local elections in 1949 had given grounds for hoping that a Commons majority could be maintained, if not of 1945 proportions. Labour fought on its record – establishing the National Health Service, restoring full employment, creating a balance of trade surplus. The Conservatives, however, pointed to looming economic problems over the cost of rearmament – a result of the deteriorating relationship with the Soviet Union – and to Labour plans for extending nationalisation. On a swing of just over 3 per cent to the Tories, Labour's majority was reduced to a wafer-thin five.

Attlee was clearly in the mood for bringing in new blood and Longford, despite Prestwick, had high hopes of promotion or at least a move. He was disappointed. Hugh Gaitskell was the principal gainer among the younger generation of Labour ministers, promoted to Minister of State for Economic Affairs and, after Cripps' retirement in October, to the Exchequer.

The second term in office was not a happy one for Labour. As well as Cripps, Bevin had to step down from the Foreign Office because of ill-health and died in March 1951. Dalton, so much a force in the early years of the Attlee government, had resigned in 1947 over a Budget leak. Although he later returned to the Cabinet he was by then a spent force. Morrison won few admirers as Bevin's successor, especially as the outbreak of the Korean War in June 1950 heightened world tensions. In April 1950 Aneurin Bevan, Harold Wilson and John Freeman resigned from the government over plans to impose a small range of charges in the NHS – a symptom of the deep economic malaise with which Britain was afflicted.

The sense that an era was coming to an end only deepened Longford's discontent at Civil Aviation. While he continued to work towards running an efficient public service in the hope of winning back Attlee's favour, he began spending more time on other causes close to his heart. Writing of this period later, he commented

> the real strain does not arise from what ministers do
> but from what they feel they ought to be doing. The
> vigilance of the public operates powerfully on the sub-
> conscious. Imagine a devoted GP under constant
> attack for gross negligence in the local press and you

> will get a partial analogy. The occupational disease of
> the good minister is the neurosis, not that he is doing
> anything wrong but that he is not doing anything like
> enough.[8]

From childhood Longford had been a restless sort, unable to be satisfied with anything for very long. Three years at Civil Aviation taxed him almost beyond endurance. Equally his interests had always been in ideas, in doing, in changing things. As a politician he felt he had a duty – a Christian duty – to be acting. At Civil Aviation he had done as much as he could. In the absence of a new challenge from the Prime Minister, he developed his own.

His interest in Germany had never faded and he continued to press his colleagues on their attitude to rebuilding, latterly as one of the founders of the Anglo-German Society. (He failed to persuade Attlee to be president.) In August 1949, when at Civil Aviation, but still watching with a heavy conscience the British government's activities in Germany, he grew alarmed at what turned out to be one of the final acts of dismantling. With Elizabeth's backing, he wrote to Attlee threatening once again to resign but this time adding a time-limit for the government to reconsider its attitude. He was called to Downing Street and was convinced that his time as a minister was about to end in a puff of publicity. Attlee began with questions about Elizabeth and the Longford children. When brought to the point, he replied: 'Oh yes. You mean the matter you wrote to me about. Oh that's quite all right: Ernest Bevin's coming back from Strasbourg tonight, and the whole thing's being looked into afresh.' After another volley of questions about the Longford family, he said goodbye to his junior minister. 'I shambled out of the room,' Longford recalls, 'uncertain then, as I am uncertain now, whether I had achieved something quite substantial or been outwitted once again in the kindliest of all possible ways.'[9]

As the western Allies came increasingly to see Russia and not the Germans as their enemy, Longford's fight for Germany became less of a lonely battle. Within the Labour Party though, many remained suspicious of both his message of Christian forgiveness and his extreme and unguarded antipathy to Communism. His friendship with the emerging West German leader Adenauer and the right of centre Christian Democrats – rather than with Labour's natural allies, the Social Democrats – only further divorced Longford from the mainstream of his own party on the issue of Germany.

When he began once again to turn his attention to Ireland, he was out of step with not just his party but most of the country. In 1948 de Valera and Fianna Fail had fallen out with the Irish electorate to be replaced by the supposedly more moderate John Costello and Fine Gael. Though Fine Gael shared with their rivals a dislike of some of the restrictions placed on Ireland as a member of the Commonwealth – notably the fact that the British Crown retained the right to appoint Ireland's diplomatic and consular representatives – there was widespread shock when Costello broke the existing institutional link with Britain without warning or prior consultation. Had de Valera taken Ireland out of the Commonwealth, the British would have been angry but not altogether surprised.

Longford as much as any other British minister was caught unawares by Costello's action. Yet he and Elizabeth had been dining with the Irish Foreign Minister, Sean MacBride, the night before the Taoiseach made his announcement. A republican whose Clann na Poblachta Party, in coalition with Fine Gael, was opposed to continuing membership of the Commonwealth, MacBride nevertheless discussed with Longford the desirability of Irish attendance at the next Commonwealth summit. During the course of the meal at the Russell Hotel in Dublin, the Foreign Minister had been called away to the telephone. The Longfords did not suspect anything, but the next morning headlines in the Dublin papers revealed that Costello had announced Ireland's withdrawal from the Commonwealth while on a visit to Toronto.

The British response was swift and angry. Attlee resisted pressures to rescind any special status allowed to the Irish living in Britain, but he did endorse popular feeling by passing the Government of Ireland Act of 1949 which stipulated that the existing division of Ireland could not be changed without the consent of the people of the north. In practical terms it only underlined what was already a fact, but it was presented as a necessary reassurance for the people of the north. To Longford, the Act was a calculated snub to the Dublin government, asserting Britain's continuing role in Ireland and seemingly delaying further the day when the partition of 1921, thought then to be a temporary measure, would end.

Longford had little sympathy for Costello and even less for his handling of the situation. Yet the author of *Peace by Ordeal* could not help but regret a government bill that would put back the cause of Irish unity. As early as 1946 David Astor recalls that Longford had been pressing him to put the Northern Ireland question on the political agenda by publishing articles in the *Observer*. And here was his own government, as he saw it, making an already intolerable situation worse in order to pander to xenophobia among the electorate. His conscience told him he should resign. Again his ambition, and his conviction that he was more effective fighting from within as Ireland's only friend in the British government, got the better of him. He satisfied himself with making a personal plea to the Cabinet to change its policy. They took little notice of him. In fact he reported that they were decidedly 'chilly' and he likened his own impact to an explosion that goes off and leaves the house still standing.[10]

Longford's plea merely highlighted his semi-detached status over certain questions and was a measure of the leeway he was granted within Attlee's government. When Frank Beswick, later Longford's number two at Civil Aviation and the ministry's spokesman in the Commons, objected to the 1949 Ireland Act (for quite different reasons), he resigned as a junior minister. Longford, by contrast, was indulged and allowed the luxury of dissent.

The explanation for this special treatment was Longford's seat in the Lords. At a time when they had so few active Labour peers in the Upper Chamber, Labour could ill afford to lose one of its youngest and most able performers. This was especially relevant when the party was engaged in a constitutional struggle between the Commons and Lords. The battle had started when the huge Tory majority in the Upper Chamber made it clear that they were planning to block plans to nationalise the iron and steel industries.

In 1945 Labour found itself in much the same position as the Liberals in 1909 – with a clear Commons majority but facing overwhelming Tory numbers in the Lords. The peers' attempts to block the Liberals had led to the 1911 Parliament Act, which limited the powers of the Upper Chamber. In 1945, the Conservative leaders in the Lords realised their opposition to the elected government's programme might provoke a further reduction of the Second Chamber's role. To avoid such an eventuality, the Tory peers adopted explicit conventions on self-restraint – the Salisbury Rules, named after the Marquis of Salisbury, Conservative leader in the Upper House. These rules set out that the Lords could not vote down any policies that had appeared in the Labour manifesto – as such having been sanctioned by the electorate – though they might suggest constructive amendments. On matters not in the manifesto, the Lords retained a freer hand. The Tories in the Upper House felt that iron and steel nationalisation did not pass the manifesto test and therefore blocked its passage.

Labour responded by publishing a new Parliament Bill in 1947 which reduced the period of the Lords' veto from three parliamentary sessions to two. After unsuccessful attempts to reach agreement on this Bill in the Upper Chamber, it was pushed through and, after the Lords' veto had run its course, was passed in 1949. For a while there was talk of a 'constitutional revolution', and, while a crisis was threatening, Attlee and the Labour leadership needed Frank Longford on the front bench, but the menace petered out.

Attlee finally granted Longford the long-awaited promotion in May 1951. It had been suspected for some time that Lord Addison, the septuagenarian Labour leader in the Upper Chamber, wanted to retire. Attlee himself had hinted that Addison could not go on for ever. Longford harboured hopes of taking over from him in a Cabinet-ranking role when the summons to 10 Downing Street came. However, had Attlee entertained such thoughts, and later events were to show that he did, the shadow of Prestwick decided him against.[11] Instead,

Longford was offered the post of First Lord of the Admiralty, a prestigious and historic office that carried with it a tied cottage in Admiralty House at the other end of the Mall from Buckingham Palace. The First Lord did not sit in the Cabinet, though he was expected to play a substantial role in the Cabinet's Defence Committee.

This role was one of the more appealing aspects of the job for Longford. At least he would have a voice on British policy in Germany and on the broader question of international alliances, where he had clear views about the threat of the Soviet Union. However, Longford was undecided about Attlee's offer and asked for forty-eight hours to think about it. 'Please don't think I don't appreciate the honour,' he told the Prime Minister. 'No one who has read a line of British history or got any feeling for it could fail to be stirred. But the Navy deserves the best. Its traditions are everything to it. I don't think I'm the right sort of person. I mean I am too eccentric.'[12]

Attlee was clearly wise to Longford's habit of exaggerating his own eccentricity. 'I shouldn't worry about that,' he replied. 'The Navy survived Winston [Churchill] and Brendan [Bracken]. It will probably survive you.'[13] What preyed more on Longford's mind was the fact that the day-to-day responsibilities of the First Lord were largely ceremonial. The rearmament programme was well under way and the naval chiefs played the leading role in deciding upon such technical and operational questions. Their political captain was very much an overseer whose interference would be resented. Conscious of tradition and of his own limited knowledge of such matters, not to mention his inglorious war record, he knew that he would be in no position to intervene and make his mark. Wrestling with a newly nationalised airline was one thing, but trying to run the Navy on the basis of little first-hand experience was another for an able man with such reverence for history and who, like his father, held the Forces in such awe. Longford's ancestors had, after all, included the occasional naval figure among the generals it produced. After Longford's father's death, until Edward reached adulthood, the children's trustee had been Cousin Willy, Admiral Sir William Pakenham.

When he heard that Longford was wavering, Hugh Gaitskell, by now Chancellor of the Exchequer, took his old college friend to lunch. He stressed that, whatever he might think, Longford was not out of favour as a result of Prestwick and his pro-German views. Quite the opposite. He was seen, Gaitskell confirmed, as a future Labour leader in the Lords as long as he did not turn down this opportunity.

At this crossroads in Longford's career, normally Evan Durbin, not Gaitskell, would have been guiding Longford in his choice of path. The three New College men had remained close friends since Oxford days. But in the summer of 1948, while on holiday with his family, Durbin had drowned rescuing two young children (one of them his daughter) caught in a dangerous current. Durbin's death affected Longford more than emotionally. Durbin had been destined for high office. Gaitskell and Durbin were Longford's allies. Had Durbin survived, and with Hugh Gaitskell leading a Labour government, there can be little doubt that Longford, as the third part of their triumvirate, would have played an important role. He never found another Durbin to lend him a helping hand.

To succeed in party politics, aspiring Cabinet ministers need to form close alliances with powerful groups and individuals. Denis Healey feels that it was less Longford's eccentricity and commitment to unpopular causes than his failure in the late 1940s and 1950s to fight for his position within the party that was to arrest his progress to high office.

> Frank was odd but then we had many people like that
> in the Labour Party then and now. After all Stafford
> Cripps came of an upper-class family and showed it.
> Beatrice Webb, who was still alive in those days, was
> the daughter of a peer. Attlee himself was a public
> schoolboy. It was Frank's manner that was odd. He
> wasn't a chap who worked with people very much.
> He never in a sense formed alliances, not because he
> didn't get on with people particularly but he just was
> not a political sort of chap.[14]

After Durbin's death, it was Gaitskell who remained as Longford's one main ally, who was steadying Longford's nerves at the time of Prestwick and who now was urging him to take the Admiralty post. Gaitskell had, of course, once proposed to Elizabeth and his diary recorded his feelings for his two old friends after speaking alongside them in February 1950.

> It was strange in a way to be standing in the Oxford
> Union speaking after her [Elizabeth] with Frank there
> as well. I had been a little doubtful as to whether I
> should refer to our long friendship but while waiting
> to speak found out that Elizabeth had already referred
> to it. One could not help feeling what a pleasure it
> was to have such friends in the middle of all this
> political struggle. So far at least there does not seem to
> be any strain in our relationship.[15]

With Gaitskell's encouragement, Longford accepted Attlee's offer. It was a job that emphasised some of his own ambiguities. Taking the salute and being piped on board His Majesty's vessels both thrilled and appalled him. Never one with an eye for minutiae of dress, as he had shown in the Army, he was not natural or indeed comfortable in the role. But the showman in him enjoyed the public spectacle of it, especially when he was at its epicentre.

In August 1951, Gaitskell wrote in his diary: 'Frank and Elizabeth are evidently enormously enjoying his new job, and all the reports I hear about how he conducts himself are excellent.'[16] Another to hear only good words for the new First Lord was his uncle, Arthur Villiers. He sent on to Elizabeth a letter received from one of his 'old boys' at Eton Manor who was now in the Navy.

> I have just returned from the pier where I proudly
> witnessed the arrival of the First Lord. He did very
> well. His bearing and manner is excellent, his keen-
> ness and attention to both officer and rating. His
> saluting (best Naval style which is unusual), every-
> thing very well carried out.[17]

Once again Longford had proved that, if he set his mind to it, he could accomplish a task for which he considered himself congenitally unsuited.

At Admiralty House, Longford found himself back in the world of his childhood: the atmosphere of a stately home, servants on hand to attend to his every whim. In the domestic quarters there were reminders of the great and good at every turn. In the blue Axminster of the master bedroom were the marks left by the feet of Lady Diana Cooper's carved and gilded four poster, designed by Rex Whistler, and installed when her husband Duff was First Lord.

Longford was not so at home with some of the trappings of his position. He always insisted on sitting in the front seat of his government car next to the chauffeur – as indeed he had done when a child, distinguishing himself from the other Pakenham children by addressing the staff as Mr and Mrs rather than by their surnames alone. And he would not abuse the privilege of an official car. One weekend when he invited Evelyn Waugh to Bernhurst, the author was rather disgruntled to find that the black ministerial car that came to collect him from his London home disgorged him soon afterwards at Charing Cross Station to continue the journey by train rather than conveying him all the way to Sussex.

Longford took enormous pleasure in the social round that was part of Admiralty House life. His lifelong love of parties took on an institutional significance and he was able to organise gatherings to honour those he admired – notably the Prime Minister. The only blight was that for much of his tenure at Admiralty House Elizabeth was unwell. On the day he took over he received news that she had been rushed to hospital in Hastings from Bernhurst. She had suffered a miscarriage and, during her convalescence, her eldest daughter Antonia, by now an undergraduate at Oxford, took her mother's place at official functions.

In political terms, Longford did not leave much of a mark on the Navy. His predecessor, Viscount Hall, a veteran of the 1929 Labour government, after five years in office, had left a very tidy, well-run ship. The only matter that detained Longford for any length of time was the need to raise the status of naval aviation within the service and to maintain the pace and flow of finance for rearmament. He was ably assisted in these tasks by James Callaghan as Under-Secretary, though the future Prime Minister records in his autobiography that, having carried the can for Hall in the Commons for eighteen months, he felt he had earned a shot at the top job.[18] Callaghan had reason to feel doubly aggrieved at Longford. In 1946, he had been promised the post of Under-Secretary of State at the War Office by the Labour Chief Whip. He then went on holiday to Czechoslovakia only to find that Longford had got it instead, after his impassioned plea to the Prime Minister to allow him to make good in some small measure his war record.

After just five months in post, Longford left the Admiralty when Labour was defeated in the October 1951 general election. The pressures of rearmament and a spiral of bad economic news – rising prices, growing unemployment and a shortage of houses – combined to usher in a Conservative majority of seventeen, though, because of the vagaries of the British electoral system, Labour actually polled a higher vote than the Tories, 48.8 per cent to their 48 per cent.

However, there were high hopes that Labour would regroup and return to office at the next election. Longford felt confident that, judged on his record under Attlee, and with the outgoing Prime Minister's continuing favour, he could count on being a member of any future Labour Cabinet. He had proved an asset in the House of Lords, been promoted to the Privy Council, had shown that he could run both a technocratic ministry and an historic institution and had, with occasional lapses, carved out something of a reputation for himself in the public eye as a minister, if not of the first rank, then certainly not of grey self-effacement.

Eleven

The criminologist

Lord Pakenham is the ideal schoolmaster, one of
those who would always find something to like
and encourage in the most unattractive of boys

Raymond Mortimer in the Sunday Times *(1953)*

While his colleagues on the Labour front bench in the Commons
buckled down to the collective task of opposing a Conservative
government with an elderly leader in Churchill and a fragile
majority, Frank Longford felt isolated in the Lords, facing the
resident Tory majority. Hitherto as a key member of Labour's
team in the Upper Chamber, he had played a crucial role in
guiding the deluge of landmark Labour legislation that followed
their victory in 1945 through an overwhelmingly Conservative
and hence often hostile house. His success in this task had placed
him at the heart of the government and won him particular
merit in the eyes of the Prime Minister, Clement Attlee.

As part of the opposition, he began to see for the first time the
practical disadvantages of being in the Lords rather than the
Commons. While the party had high hopes of causing the
government difficulties in a finely balanced elected chamber,
there was little prospect of fruitful opposition in the Lords with
just a handful of Labour peers. In effect the Lords became a
backwater, a Conservative rubber stamp, and Longford's role in
the inner counsels of his party was correspondingly reduced.

Loss of ministerial office had other more immediate drawbacks. He had to relinquish his London base at Admiralty House
and his ministerial salary. As a member of the Lords, unlike his
colleagues in the Commons, he could claim no salary. A system

of reimbursing peers' expenses plus an attendance allowance was not introduced until 1957. Psychologically and politically he could not contemplate languishing inactive and out of the mainstream in the Lords for another five years waiting for a Labour victory. In his own estimation, as he confided to his wife in the wake of defeat in 1951, it was more likely to be two terms than one in opposition. Financially, mere procrastination was out of the question.

As a member of the aristocracy, Longford was always considered by his friends in the Commons to have no financial worries. 'Hugh always seemed to think of me as better off than I was, or to underestimate my financial responsibilities,' he wrote of Gaitskell.[1] Yet, as a second son, he had inherited only a tiny part of the family's wealth which his elder brother, Edward, was now pouring into the bottomless pit of the Gate Theatre in Dublin. Both Longford and Elizabeth had small private incomes from their parents and had come into various inheritances from relatives. But these had quickly been spent on the day-to-day costs of bringing up and housing eight children. By 1951 all that was left was Bernhurst and its eighty acres in Sussex.

In short Longford needed to find a job which would provide him with sufficient income to support his family and leave him enough time to continue to play his part, however minor, for Labour in the Lords. He returned to the only profession other than politics that he had enjoyed – academia – and the city that had been as close to a home town as he had ever found – Oxford. Through his old friend Robert Blake, he found a part-time post back at Christ Church teaching politics.[2]

It was not, however, a practical proposition to return the whole Longford family to Oxford. They had only recently been uprooted from Hampstead to Bernhurst. Kevin was born in London in November 1947, the couple's eighth child, when Elizabeth was forty-one. After the 1950 election, she decided that London life as part of the Hampstead set was not her natural habitat and that, more importantly, a move to the country would benefit the children. Bernhurst was the logical choice as the family home and would cut down the expense of running two houses.

Moving away from the capital would mean leaving behind close friends and settling in one of the most Conservative of the shires, away from the centre of Labour life. The activities and influence of the Hampstead set of socialist academics and their families, the Longfords say, were much exaggerated.[3] While the Jays, the Gordon Walkers and rising stars like Roy Jenkins and Tony Crosland would occasionally join the Longfords at the Gaitskells' Hampstead home in Frognal Gardens on a Sunday for a glass of sherry, it was by no means a regular occurrence. The claims made throughout the 1950s by various trade union leaders that party policy was hammered out at such gatherings mistook social occasions for a more sinister conspiracy. It was more often their children that brought the families together.

The scars of its wartime use by Canadians were still all too obvious at Bernhurst. The cement foundations of recently dismantled Nissen huts had replaced the front lawn and barbed wire was tangled around the overgrown flower beds. The sweeping main driveway was a sea of weeds and the 300-year-old oak that dominated the garden had been deformed by having its lower branches chopped away to allow army lorries to pass. Inside, the elegant Georgian house had been well cared for, but had been given a rather incongruous coat of banana yellow paint. With advice from Vita Sackville-West at neighbouring Sissinghurst, Elizabeth began the long process of restoring the garden.

It was an endeavour in which her husband did not share. Despite having spent much of his childhood in the countryside, he found little fascination in nature. With his knack for camouflaging a lack of interest with an insuperable lack of knowledge, he ostentatiously did not know the name of a single flower or plant. He continues to profess to love the country and the view from his study at Bernhurst which stretches over the garden that Elizabeth has so lovingly re-created to the valley beyond. But his interests – politics, academia, meeting people – are best indulged in an urban setting. Even his sporting pursuits were more suburban than rural. He preferred tennis and golf to hunting and shooting. (Though until well into the sixties, he occasionally joined the Westmeath Hunt when at Tully Nally, recalling the earlier exploits of his father.) As his physical vigour faded in his fifties he took up swimming, never previously having learnt – in 1960 Bernhurst acquired a swimming pool. Although he has spent almost every weekend in Sussex since the early 1950s, the house remains very much Elizabeth's home, a reflection of her interests as well as a retreat and a focus for family life rather than a place that reveals a great deal about Longford.

His main contribution there is the small Catholic church built on land donated by the Longfords in 1960. Previously Mass had been in an upper room at the Rose and Crown in Burwash or in the village hall in Hurst Green. Soon after the couple made Bernhurst their family home, the local postmistress, a devout Catholic, made it clear to Longford that as lord of the manor he should do something about a place to worship. After much fund-raising the parish of Hurst Green saw its church opened – a modern, semi-circular chapel with a roof like a fan and crescent-shaped pews from Ireland.

The family left Linnell Drive in July 1950 for Bernhurst. After a visit, Evelyn Waugh described it unkindly as the Longfords' 'new country home in the suburbs'.[4] However, the change from suburban Hampstead to rural Sussex was a dramatic one for the younger children. Rachel and Michael had to leave their convent in Golders Green and start at the village school. Catherine and Kevin would now have the chance to keep animals.

For Longford too it was an upheaval. He no longer had a London base and commuted backwards and forwards to his post at Civil Aviation. His brief spell as First Lord temporarily restored the luxury of a billet in the capital. The family would occasionally take up residence at Admiralty House to enjoy its views of great state occasions like the Trooping of the Colour. But between 1950 and 1952 Bernhurst was their home, with their father often a distant figure rushing back and forth first to London and then, after the fall of the Labour government, to Oxford.

The strain began to tell and in 1952, with their financial situation a little improved by the Christ Church job, Elizabeth decided that the time had come, reluctantly, to return to the city. She found a house in Chelsea's Cheyne Gardens, just behind the more fashionable Cheyne Walk, and a stone's throw away from the Albert Bridge which led on to the road to Sussex for weekends at Bernhurst. It was not just Longford's long commute up to Oxford that persuaded her. Schooling too played its part in the decision to move back – at least for weekdays – to London. While Antonia had been happy at St Mary's Ascot, Judith had disliked her convent boarding school Mayfield and her parents decided that a good Catholic day school would be more appropriate. They chose the newly founded More House, run by the Canonesses of St Augustine, on the Cromwell Road in west London. Rachel and Catherine were to follow Judith through its portals.

Though good socialists in their lifelong commitment to using the NHS and their preference for public transport rather than cars, the Longfords did not even contemplate a state education for their children. They made no efforts to investigate local authority schools in their area. 'You have to do what you think is right for your children,' Longford says. 'You can't let their education be dominated by your politics. At the time people didn't seem to hold it against me as perhaps they would today. Perhaps it was because I was in the Lords. It might have been different in the Commons.'[5]

Except in Antonia's case, the Longfords made a distinction in the education of their sons and daughters. While a small, modestly priced, private day school was considered appropriate for the girls, the Longford boys all attended Ampleforth, run by the Benedictines in north Yorkshire and regarded as Britain's smartest and most expensive Catholic boarding school. It was a differentiation that came about purely by chance, Longford says. After finding a good day school for Judith, it just happened that her younger sisters followed her.

> The boys would have gone to Eton if we hadn't
> become Catholics. It was part of my upbringing but
> also they had grown up among other dons' children
> where it was expected that you went on to a public

school. It would have been seen as very quirky indeed
if I had insisted on them going to state schools.[6]

The couple had high hopes for all their children. Thomas
remembers his father's interest in his education as being broadly
based.

> He's a very ambitious man himself and he's very keen
> on success. So by extension he was very keen on all of
> us succeeding. And that didn't mean in the narrow
> sense of lessons. It would have been in all forms of
> everything. So it would appear to us that he would be
> equally pleased if we were first in the tiddly winks
> competition or in Greek verse. He wouldn't have had
> any kind of snobbery. He wouldn't have discrimi-
> nated. The important thing was to succeed.[7]

The younger children recall a greater emphasis on academic
results, partly as a result of the success of both Thomas and
Antonia. 'Both my parents had very high academic ambitions
for their children and were tremendously pleased by academic
success,' says Rachel.

> There was a competitive atmosphere in that way and I
> wasn't half as academic as most of my brothers and
> sisters. And although I didn't particularly rebel against
> it, looking back I think my interests which were much
> more towards the arts were quite different from the
> others. Nobody said I was inadequate, but I do
> remember feeling it when my younger brother
> Michael used to do his exams at the same time as me
> and get better results.[8]

Such parental expectations were not, however, unusual in the
middle- and upper-middle-class circles in which the Longfords
moved. There were other ways in which the children did feel
set apart from their contemporaries because of their father's
politics and interests. At the private Catholic schools the children

251

attended socialism was seen as at best dangerous and at worst positively harmful. Judith remembers hearing her parents over breakfast condemning the government's policy at the time of the Suez crisis in 1956.

> I went to a very snotty little convent and I mentioned
> what I had heard to my friend. In many ways we
> were two peas in a pod – the same sort of family, the
> same sort of background. And to my utter amazement
> she got very angry and disagreed with me. Her parents
> had been saying at breakfast what a wonderful thing
> for Britain it was.[9]

Likewise when Paddy heard at Ampleforth that his father had been appointed First Lord of the Admiralty, he wrote to his parents that 'the gloomy top-table Tories said they hoped you were resigning . . . Dear bovine Miles said he was glad someone was now able to clear up the mess in Civil Aviation, and it was just bad luck on the British Navy.'[10]

Rachel recalls growing up in a household where the only thing that mattered was politics. 'All their friends were political. It wasn't the slightest bit the "literary Longfords" as people now call us. It was entirely politics.' Specific campaigns of her father had a direct impact.

> I was aware of his feelings for Germany. It was quite
> peculiar because I was watching those war films that
> we were all brought up on, in which the Germans
> were wicked, evil people. And there was my father
> saying that the Germans must be forgiven and
> employing German girls as our nanny.[11]

Throughout their childhood their father's identification with the underdog brought ex-offenders, the homeless, the mentally disturbed to the door asking for Lord Pakenham. 'There was one man who was convinced that he was in fact Lord Pakenham,' says Rachel. 'It was all very puzzling. You'd get this chap ringing up saying, "Hello it's Lord Pakenham", and he wasn't my father.'

On another occasion, she was convinced she was being followed home from school one evening.

> It was in the middle of one of those pea-soupers and I
> kept thinking he was going to murder me. When I
> finally turned into our house, he followed me in and
> rang the doorbell and said he'd come to meet my
> father.[12]

Rachel feels that generally there was a pronounced bias in the Longford household towards the underdog and a reaction against anyone who seemed arrogant, rich or successful. Those who thought that the Longfords themselves fell into the last two categories (and striving after academic success, at least, was a self-confessed vice) had a totally different impression from the children.

> We didn't have any feeling of being born into an
> aristocratic family with a title. When we were in
> Oxford we were an academic family. And then we
> were a political family. I never thought we had any
> money. There were none of those luxuries that chil-
> dren like.[13]

Indeed, beside the financial constraints of bringing up eight children, there was a Puritan streak in the running of the Longford household. Michael used to joke with his brothers and sisters that he would write a book about their childhood called *Look Back in Hunger*. Antonia however, regarded her father

> as a Medici of generosity. If you ever asked him, you
> would get the contents of his pocket which might be
> nothing or might be a crumpled fiver. I think we used
> to think our mother very mean but she was probably
> struggling to keep the home together.[14]

Another element that distinguished the Longford children from their contemporaries, in Rachel's opinion, was their sense of being slightly foreign. Their father came of an Irish family whose seat was in Country Westmeath. From 1954 he worked for an Irish bank. 'We did feel we were Irish – or rather we were keen to feel we were Irish and had this romantic notion about the place.'[15] Such sentiments were, however, not reinforced by any practical experience of Tully Nally. Edward and Christine Longford were not keen on children and the prospect of having eight descend on them was unthinkable. For most of the Longford siblings, their first glance of the ancestral pile came as adults at their uncle's funeral in 1961.

If the Longford children felt set apart from those around them, their parents did their best to insulate them. They grew up in a very protected, inward-looking environment and relied on each other a great deal for company – rather as their father had with his own siblings.

In 1946, Paddy, aged nine, recorded the relative merits of his brothers and sisters:

> Antonia is a girl rather clever when laden with responsibility. Mostly she is very nice.
>
> Thomas is a boy keen on photography and bird-watching. On the whole he is very agreeable, a generous boy.
>
> Judith loves her dolls and treasures them. She adores Antonia immensely because Antonia lets her play with her own very exquisite dolls.
>
> Rachel like Judith likes dolls very much, and often makes them dresses of wool and cotton, being skilled in the art of needlework. She is Thomas's pet and Thomas calls her his 'chubby lassie'.
>
> Catherine a very jolly and stout young baby.
>
> Michael is the one I like best and we are both devoted to each other. We both like playing soldiers. I usually let him win a few battles so he is not discouraged. He likes everybody and everybody likes him but he likes ME best.[16]

'Our parents are such confident people that there was no hand-ringing about how they might be different and therefore we never felt outsiders,' Judith remembers.[17] When it came to launching into a wider world, many of the cherished notions of that protected upbringing were challenged and the contradictions and paradoxes of their parents' beliefs were mirrored in their children's experiences. 'When I went to Oxford I immediately found myself very betwixt and between over things like the Labour Party,' says Judith.

> I was out of the protective family circle that assumed that Labour and socialism were right and this romantic view of the ordinary man and the march of the workers. At the same time we had been living a very upper-middle-class life with two houses. And I really wasn't aware of the schizophrenia of the situation until I went to Oxford and joined the Labour Club where everyone talked with northern accents and about practical, everyday issues. We were different. I was proud of being a socialist but I found I wasn't a real socialist.[18]

Though their father's activities and his growing public reputation affected the Longford children, he remained one step removed from their lives. It was Elizabeth who took responsibility for their upbringing. 'Our mother ran the ship,' says Thomas. 'She was really the skipper. He was a kindly presence in the background. He did have his powers. He was the ultimate authority, the supreme court.'[19]

Whatever his work burdens and other responsibilities, however, Longford was a dutiful father. When his sons were at Ampleforth he would visit once each term. Elizabeth made the trip just once a year. 'It was a kind of pilgrimage for him,' says Thomas.

> We saw him as this kindly figure who came up, we knew, out of duty. But we were grateful because it did mean that we got out to a nice hotel where we could fill ourselves with cream buns and sit on hot pipes without people shouting at us.[20]

Their conversation revolved around sport and studies.

The same sense of duty gave rise to weekly letters from Longford to his sons at boarding school. According to Thomas,

> there was a difference between his letters and our mother's. Our mother wrote in a lovely rounded hand about family news. He wrote in his extraordinary handwriting which nobody has ever been able to read. So what the letter actually had was these hieroglyphs in early Linear B or early Minoan script. And you would read the first two pages in early Minoan and then a desperate passage of capitals which, if you looked very, very carefully, you realised it said in large letters 'do please write to me about this before next Tuesday, Your affectionate Dadda'. And the trouble was you didn't know what 'this' was.[21]

Longford's semi-detached but dutiful approach to fatherhood has left some of his children feeling that there was an emotional void in their upbringing. The lack of warmth that distorted his own childhood, his emotional reserve with all but Elizabeth, affected his relationships with his children. 'I can't praise him for any attention he gave me either as a child or as a teenager,' says Judith. 'I honestly don't think that he noticed if I was there or not.'[22]

His two standard questions to his teenage daughters were 'How's your work?' and 'How's your weight?' Often it was only the latter. For Judith this line of questioning showed his ignorance of 'what hell it is to be a fat teenage girl. He didn't mean to be mean. He felt it was his duty as a father to ask.'[23] Rachel sees it more as reflecting his own fanatical interest in weight and fitness than as his lack of understanding of teenage angst.

> His elder brother was the fattest man in Ireland and I think my father reacted very much against that. He really cared about weight and fitness. He had something called the Alexander Technique which was a

way of breathing and I think it involved all sorts of
things like the height of lavatory seats. I don't think
he ever did anything about it but he was terribly
interested in the theory. I remember this terrible book
with a lot of photographs lying around showing these
men and how they were supposed to sit.[24]

It was an obsession confirmed by Auberon Waugh who, in his
early days as a journalist, was asked by his godfather, Longford,
to write an article in the *Sun* about a book by F. J. Horneybrook
on slimming.[25]

Longford's insensitivity over his daughters' feelings about
being questioned – and, they felt, teased – about their weight
was symptomatic of the fact that they lacked a common
language with which to communicate. With his sons, he could
talk about sport, but while he tried to take an interest in his
daughters' sporting activities, such as they were, he struggled to
forge a bond. Occasionally he would accompany one of them on
an outing. Rachel was a very keen member of the local Pony
Club.

I was terribly self-conscious and was horrified when
he announced that he was going to come riding. The
whole riding school was thrown into chaos to find a
horse big enough for him. He had looked out his old
hunting gear – jodhpurs that went down to the knee
and then he didn't have boots, so it was socks and
shoes. And he'd found a bowler hat. It was absolutely
dreadful, a stream of little children and my father
leaning back at a ridiculous angle on a horse that was
too small for him. Finally I couldn't bear it any longer
and I said, 'Dadda, can't you see that they're all
laughing at you?' He turned to me, completely
unmoved, and said, 'Just remember that if people are
laughing at you, you're giving them pleasure and
that's a good thing.' It was really very good for me
because it is a policy he has carried through himself.
He doesn't mind if people laugh at him. Well, he does
mind, but he doesn't let it change his behaviour.[26]

The younger Longford children were perhaps more aware than their older siblings of their father's shortcomings because throughout the 1950s the head of the household, their mother, became more involved once again in her career. While still living in Hampstead she was approached by the Oxford Labour Party and asked to stand against Quintin Hogg in the 1950 general election. Although Cowley and Headington, strong Labour areas, had now been added to the constituency, Elizabeth did not feel any great optimism about succeeding where her husband had failed five years earlier. The tide was running against Labour. Yet remembering how she had nursed her Birmingham constituency and then reluctantly decided to give it up because of her family responsibilities in 1944, just as victory was in sight, Elizabeth was keen to take on the challenge. 'I had a new feeling in my bones – that I would be defeated if I stood for Oxford in 1950,' she wrote. 'The fight would be a "propaganda" one and none the worse for that. My family would not suffer and I would discharge my political debt.'[27] Harold Wilson and Hugh Gaitskell came to speak for her, as did Longford. Quintin Hogg's verdict was that Elizabeth 'was by far the more formidable antagonist' of the two, but her premonition proved well founded.[28] Hogg increased his 1945 majority.

When the Longfords returned to London in 1952, Elizabeth was working with the Catholic Central Library and with the Paddington and St Pancras Rent Tribunal. She also found herself increasingly in demand as a commentator on family matters – having eight children gave her a halo of wisdom. This in turn led to a series of newspaper columns, starting with the *Daily Express* in 1953. The couple were invited to dinner with Lord Beaverbrook at his home in Surrey with Longford for once playing the consort, a role with which he was later to become well accustomed as his wife's literary career blossomed. In deference to his guests' political sympathies, which differed greatly from his own, Beaverbrook arranged after dinner for a film with a vaguely left-wing moral to be shown in his private cinema.

Prompted by her columns on family issues in the *Express*, and through the good offices of Antonia who was by now working for publisher George Weidenfeld after leaving Oxford, Elizabeth produced a book, *Points for Parents*, in 1954. The previous year she had collected and edited a group of essays entitled *Catholic Approaches*, to which Longford contributed a piece on the Catholic in politics, and Elizabeth a defence – which she now considers unconvincing – of the Catholic ban on birth control. After *Points for Parents*, Elizabeth began to research a full-scale biography of her great-uncle, Joseph Chamberlain. The unavailability of many of the statesman's papers meant that she ended up concentrating on just one episode in which he had been involved as Colonial Secretary, the Jameson Raid, a buccaneering attempt by Cecil Rhodes to seize Johannesburg and thus the whole of South Africa for the British Empire.

Elizabeth's developing literary career was paralleled initially by her husband's renewed interest in writing. He had always been willing to turn his hand to the occasional piece of journalism, usually for his friend David Astor at the *Observer*. But once out of office he was approached by the publishers Chapman and Hall who wanted him to write an account of the past 100 years of British foreign policy. With his recent experience under Bevin at the Foreign Office and his knowledge of the 1921 treaty with Ireland, Longford could claim some expertise in the field. However, international relations had never greatly fascinated him. Domestic policy remained his principal interest. It was not, therefore, a terrible wrench to turn down the Chapman and Hall offer when Jonathan Cape came up with a lucrative alternative – by the standards of the day – of £2000 to write his memoirs.

Born to Believe, published by Cape in 1953, covered Longford's early years, his conversion to socialism and Catholicism, and included an insider's view of the Attlee government. Some reviewers found Longford guilty of rushing to publication and overestimating his own importance and interest to the public. Political memoirs are usually the remit of senior figures in government who have retired from top public office. Longford, by contrast, had not made it into the Cabinet and was still full of ambition to serve in a future Labour administration. Any claim he might have to a higher literary purpose than that of recording events and conveying his personal philosophy was received sceptically by the critics. 'Lord Pakenham, on his own showing, was born to believe a number of things,' said *The Times* review, 'and among them was the fact that it is wise for a public figure to write an autobiography before the age of 50. This, also on his own showing, is a doubtful proposition.'[29] While noting his 'acute ear' for good anecdotes, *The Times* found him prone to praise everyone he came into contact with and lacking sufficient intellectual rigour and political judgement to make his own story interesting. After the unqualified success and continuing reputation of *Peace by Ordeal*, *Born to Believe* had a decidedly mixed reception. While he wrote with an abiding modesty, reviewers felt that to pen an autobiography at all showed a certain arrogance on Longford's part, highlighting his paradoxical combination of humility and showmanship.

His friend Evelyn Waugh had tried hard to convince him to rewrite the book at manuscript, though more on the grounds of the damage its loose and anecdotal style would do to his intellectual reputation than out of concern for Longford's political prospects and profile. Writing in his diary on 28 September 1952 with characteristic venom but an evident affection for his victim, Waugh outlined an argument with Longford over the manuscript of *Born to Believe*.

> I overstated the badness of the writing. I said I wasn't shocked at a politician writing like that but at a don's. It might be worthy of a second year undergraduate at Brasenose. I had in the preceding days taken a physical revulsion to the manuscript and couldn't bring myself to touch it. When challenged to find clichés, failed. Left on bad terms and with the feeling that all Frank's protestations of friendship are blarney and his sense of Catholicism, uplift.[30]

Waugh invited his old friend to come and spend some time at his home in Italy where they could rewrite the manuscript together. Longford declined. His dislike of travel was only part of the reason. Unlike his wife and indeed his two oldest children, Thomas and Antonia, who were to achieve acclaim as historians for their meticulous research, careful attention to detail and elegant prose, Longford tended to rush energetically through his literary efforts, a hobby for weekends and holidays rather than a professional undertaking. Despite his academic background, and his delight in starting new writing projects, Longford lacked the application to see them through over a long period. 'Our mother is the writer,' says their daughter Judith, now herself a poet. 'No one thinks he is the writer. He writes but isn't a writer, more of a publicist and thinker.'[31]

As well as researching and writing her books, Elizabeth kept up her newspaper articles. She moved to the *News of the World* when her contract ran out at the *Express*. She was also, like her husband, trotted out as a 'Catholic expert' on various radio programmes like the 'Brains Trust' and 'Any Questions', though her career at the former, with its decidedly scientific and rational bias, was cut short by her definition of the purpose of life as '*ad majorem Dei gloriam* – to the greater glory of God'.[32]

Through the 1950s the Longfords came to be regarded in the public mind as much for their religion as for their politics. *Born to Believe*, with its heavy emphasis on Catholicism, strengthened this association – as indeed it was meant to. The intertwining of the Catholic and socialist influences in his life continued to affect both his reaction to developments within the Labour Party and his public profile. His Catholicism was as important a feature as his ministerial achievements, and consequently he was in great demand as a high-profile lay champion of the Christian cause. He was invited for example to a Cambridge Union debate with A. L. Rowse on the motion 'God made man in his own image and likeness'. The latter defeated him by four votes.

His essay in *Catholic Approaches*, the Catholic/Christian in politics, became a standard theme in his countless talks to audiences up and down the country. He never felt entirely easy with the topic since it seemed he was – immodestly in his own eyes – claiming the moral high ground. Yet, inevitably, such was the case. 'After all,' he admits,

> when one lectures on 'The Christian in Politics', one is not far from saying: (i) A Christian in politics is a

> better man than other politicians. (ii) I am a Christian
> in politics, therefore I am better than, at any rate,
> most other politicians. (iii) And it may interest you to
> know in what my special virtue consists.[33]

In expanding on that virtue, Longford would draw a distinction between Christian policies and programmes on the one hand and the conduct of the individual Christian in politics on the other. In the latter case, it was a question of a minister or Parliamentarian applying his faith and conscience to his work. He had followed this principle in his approach in Attlee's government – notably over Germany. In so far as specifically Christian policies can exist, Longford saw them in operation mainly in the social field and it was towards this wider, though ill-defined, area that his thoughts were turning in the early 1950s.

> I remain unrepentantly convinced that even though
> the conclusions of the natural law are open to anyone
> with a brain to think with, the average Christian, with
> and without supernatural aid, is much more likely
> than the average non-Christian to try to give effect to
> them. So although in theory I agree that any enlight-
> ened social policy could be hatched by non-Christians,
> in practice it is much more likely to emerge from a
> Christian source, whether or not it can be ascribed to
> it beyond all possibility of argument.[34]

He was searching for a new mission, areas and issues where he could make a distinct contribution, where politics and faith had common ground in their upholding of the equality of all individuals. His quest for a synthesis of the two motivating forces in his life was to dominate Longford's activities for the rest of his political career and beyond. Freed of the constraints of running a department of state, he now had the luxury – from his vantage point in the becalmed House of Lords – of choosing the issues with which to make his mark as a Christian socialist. While his ambition to return to high office remained strong, he began to focus on areas which were not the staples of British political life.

The crusades that had hitherto supplemented Longford's daily parliamentary and ministerial diet were by now waning. Over Ireland, his attempts to get his senior colleagues and newspaper editors like David Astor to take seriously the question of reuniting north and south had failed to arouse interest. His republicanism was scorned by some of his friends. In July 1952, Evelyn Waugh recounted to Nancy Mitford his meeting with 'poor Frankenstein Monster' in London. Longford, Waugh said, 'believes that he is under private instructions from the late King [George VI] to solve the Ulster problem by having Princess Margaret declared Queen of an independent and united Ireland.'[35] It is a story that Longford denies. 'Evelyn put down what amused him or what he thought would amuse his correspondents.'[36]

Over Germany Longford found himself increasingly subsumed in the mainstream of his own party's thinking. The Labour front bench in the Commons took a pro-German line, backing government plans to rearm West Germany and allow it to join the Atlantic Alliance. Though Longford's own theme of Christian forgiveness of the Germans was not widely taken up, the need to build up a bulwark against the expansion of Communism and the significance of Konrad Adenauer as an ally of the West were both recognised. Longford had taken an early lead in questioning the prevailing pro-Soviet, pro-SPD sympathies in his own party. It was over Labour's attitude to German rearmament and the Atlantic Alliance that Hugh Gaitskell and Aneurin Bevan were to clash repeatedly in the early 1950s, with Longford's old room-mate leading the front bench's opposition to Bevan's anti-American stance.

A larger struggle was taking place in the Labour Party in the early 1950s between those who responded to the reverse of 1951 by advocating a period of consolidation on the achievements of 1945–51 and those who wanted to press on with further nationalisation and socialist policies. With Shadow Chancellor Gaitskell and Herbert Morrison leading the consolidators, and Bevan and Harold Wilson at the head of the progressive group, the two camps fought their corners over a number of issues of which German rearmament was just one. They were also battling for the future direction and leadership of the Labour Party with the question of Attlee's successor never far from the surface. Longford had little time for Bevan and sided wholeheartedly with the consolidators, who won out after the 1955 general election defeat. When Attlee subsequently resigned, Gaitskell defeated both Bevan and an out of touch Morrison on the first ballot for the Labour leadership. Yet it was a contest over which Longford could exert little influence.

Compared with the heady days of running the British zone in Germany and battling with the Foreign Secretary, Longford found academia and life at Christ Church rather pale and unchallenging. So much had changed since the frenzied late 1930s and the fight against appeasement. Longford was now a peer and an ex-minister in a government whose politics were inimical to many of the privileges upon which Christ Church rested. He spent from Thursday to Saturday at Oxford and as a part-timer never quite slotted back into college life. Some traditions, he was soon to discover, had remained unchanged since his own Bullingdon days. He was reading in bed one evening when he heard the shouts and approaching footsteps of the Loders Club, part of the smart social whirl. Quickly turning off the light, he lay perfectly still as loud whispering about 'bloody socialists' and drunken laughter filled his study next door. Finally one brave soul was pushed into his bedroom with instructions to capture their prey. The young man lost his nerve and, avoiding turning on the light for fear of being recognised, reported that the room was empty and beat a hasty retreat. Longford survived the assault.[37]

Those of his students who were not involved in such high jinx were undergraduates fresh out of the forces and anxious to complete their degrees as soon as possible and start their careers. A few, however, caught his eye and none more so than a young Australian Rhodes Scholar called Roger Opie who was reading Modern Greats, by now rechristened Politics, Philosophy and Economics. Opie, who went on to teach economics with great distinction for many years at Longford's alma mater, New

College, was sent to Lord Pakenham for political history. 'He took me under his wing. I got the impression that if anyone was prepared to work, he saw it as rather novel.'[38] Opie found that as a tutor Longford was habitually more interested in people and personalities than with issues and concepts.

> If something interested him, he then felt he could
> enthuse you. And he had known so many of the
> people we were studying. And even when he talked
> about Gladstone – whom he obviously hadn't known
> – you felt that he knew that atmosphere. He'd say
> things like 'I don't think you can trust Gladstone an
> inch' or 'Oh, Disraeli was a real charmer'.[39]

While other members of the college, to judge by the Loders incident, felt that Longford was importing his own political prejudices into the tutorial room, Opie found him free from any pronounced bias, though the experience of serving a socialist prime minister was an integral part of his political outlook.

> He would make it clear that he had been a member of
> a Labour government. It was always there, but he
> didn't use it to say 'if only Gladstone had been more
> left-wing . . .' or anything like that.[40]

Opie and Longford, both feeling themselves outsiders in Christ Church, struck up a friendship. They would have lunch with Longford's daughter Antonia – then an undergraduate, following in the footsteps of her mother, at Lady Margaret Hall – in the George, once the den of Acton and the aesthetes. On the last Saturday of summer term in 1953, Longford asked his student, bound for further academic work in the autumn at the London School of Economics, to come and work for him over the long vacation on a study of the causes of crime which he had set up with funding from the Nuffield Foundation.

Here was the new mission he had been seeking since he left the government, an area where his Catholicism and socialism could operate hand in hand. Prisons had been part of his life since the late 1930s when he visited Oxford Jail on behalf of his constituents in Cowley. When he returned to Oxford after his military service and work with Beveridge, he briefly took up prison visiting again but during his period in Attlee's government he had had little time to spare.

Occasionally, however, an old face from the past would crop up to ask for his help. During one particularly heated discussion at the Foreign Office when he was Minister for Germany, Longford was interrupted by his secretary to say that he had a visitor. The man in question, a lay preacher with a long record of custodial sentences for homosexual activity whom Longford had befriended when he was in Oxford Jail, had come to seek his blessing for his forthcoming wedding. When the groom revealed that he had not told his future bride of his past, Longford – 'after some humming and hawing' – advised him not to come clean but, if the truth ever came out, to refer his wife to him. With that he said goodbye and returned to Bevin's office to continue their debate.[41]

Six months later, the lay preacher's wife contacted Longford to say she had discovered the truth about her husband. He entertained the two to lunch at Simpson's and managed to smooth the waters. The episode taught him an important lesson. Spontaneity and warmth are indispensable for winning the regard and confidence of those who turn to you for help, but it requires forethought and follow-through to be effective. The after-care of prisoners should not be left to well-intentioned individuals but to dedicated bodies. The thought echoed in his mind as he began looking into the causes of crime.

The idea for the investigation had come to Longford in a flash one morning as he read *The Times* on 1 December 1952. The article detailed how crime was on the increase. This rise had come at a time of growing prosperity and expanding social services under the Attlee government. Longford had worked with Beveridge in the belief that eliminating want would create a more equal and therefore a better world. Instead higher living standards for those on the lower rungs of society seemed to have accelerated crime. Faced with this conundrum which

gnawed at his most cherished socialist beliefs, Longford decided
that a new Beveridge was needed to examine why crime had
increased as poverty had decreased.

He began by approaching Beveridge himself but his former
boss, now in his seventies, declined to take up the gauntlet.
Through David Astor at the *Observer*, Longford was put in touch
with Leslie Farrer-Brown of the Nuffield Foundation who agreed
to fund a two-year investigation into the causes of crime. Longford would work from Nuffield's headquarters in Regent's Park
when he was not at Christ Church and would be assisted by a
team of secretaries and researchers, in effect his own ministry
team in exile. The aim, announced with some ceremony to the
press, was to publish a report that would both produce an
accurate picture of the extent and nature of crime in Britain and
reveal the motivations of those involved in criminal activity.

Within that framework author and commissioner had differing priorities. Longford's mind was typically racing on to the
conclusions and the practical action that would follow. Nuffield
was keen on a thorough-going assessment and compilation of
existing knowledge and data on the subject. They wanted
Longford to don the mantle of social scientist – rather than
politician – to study crime just as a meteorologist would study
climate. 'They were much less ready than I', he admits, 'to grasp
at limited evidence with a view to immediate action.'[42]

This divergence of purpose was to dog the entire inquiry and
accounts for the schizophrenic way it collected evidence. Psy-
chiatrists, sociologists and various bodies involved in the treatment of offenders would come to Nuffield Lodge to present their
views and undergo cross-examination by Longford and Dr
Grunhut, a reader in criminology at Oxford, Frank Milton, a
north London magistrate, Dr Stafford-Clark of Guy's Hospital
and Dr Trevor Gibbens of the Maudsley Hospital.

In addition to this formal and academic approach, Longford
spent a great deal of time visiting prisons – fifteen are listed in
his final report – borstals, remand homes and approved schools.
On such missions he was usually accompanied by Honor Jones,
who had previously been Secretary to the Howard League for
Penal Reform. As a result of these visits, and through personal

contacts, Longford also talked at great length to offenders and
ex-offenders. As he comments in the foreword to his final
report: 'Those who have worked among ex-prisoners will sympathise with my admission that my scientific interest in individuals yields easily to a sense of human kinship.'[43] While Nuffield
were looking for facts and figures backed up by painstaking
research, Longford, moved by the individuals he met, wanted to
act to change a system which he felt was hopelessly inadequate
– notably in the after-care of offenders once they had left prison.
He quickly became convinced that the search for statistical
evidence was fruitless and instead drew his conclusions from
individual cases.

The disparity between the two approaches left his inquiry
with a confused sense of purpose. From the start some of the
Nuffield staff found Longford's attitude was informal and unbu-
siness-like. Roger Opie remembers that he was just told to turn
up to start work one Monday morning at Nuffield Lodge. He
never had a written contract or terms of reference (though he
was to be eternally grateful to Longford for introducing him to
Norma, his future wife, one of the secretaries on the inquiry
team.)[44]

But it was neither in Longford's nature, nor his intention, to
engage in a long, detailed inquiry. His instincts, fine-tuned at
the Ministry of Civil Aviation, were those of the initiator and
delegator who spots an issue and then sets his team to work. He
regarded it as an advantage as head of the inquiry not to know
anything at the outset about the causes of crime. To be successful, he felt, you needed to think yourself into the role of
someone who is ignorant but who wants to learn, a representative of the public.

Roger Opie recalls his own reaction to this way of working.

> He seemed to think that as a PPE man I could do
> anything. He thought that clever people when asked
> the right questions in the right way at the right time
> would come up with the answers. A subject would
> occur to him and at once he'd be on the phone to
> three or four people whom he just happened to know

who were experts in the field. There was a somewhat
arrogant, upper-class element in thinking that no
problem couldn't be solved. But it was also the academic in him. What he had that many academics lack
though was energy, interest and concern.[45]

While his team were dealing with the central issues in the
inquiry and an ever-lengthening list of submissions, Longford got
more and more embroiled in the cases of individuals prisoners
and in the failings of the prison system as he observed it.

Consequently, the original scientific purpose of the causes of
crime inquiry fell by the wayside. Thanks to Longford's social
connections and his public standing doors were opened wherever he cast his gaze. The Home Office co-operated, though
Roger Opie recalls that their attitude was distant, cool and not
altogether helpful. Yet for all the seriousness that surrounded
the investigation, it was still seen in penal reform circles – and
in the Home Office on Dr Opie's evidence – as essentially a
dilettante effort, an amateur dipping his toe in waters best left
to expert navigators. While no one doubted his sincerity, Longford's manner, his candid assertion that he knew nothing about
the subject before he began, and his penchant for getting
involved in the cases of individuals, only served to further that
shambolic impression among those who were already hostile.

One year into the two years that had been allotted for the
inquiry, Longford was offered a full-time job at the National
Bank and told his backers at Nuffield that, with their leave, he
planned to accept. He felt that his work with them had reached
its limit and was sceptical of the chance of reaching any proven
conclusions about the scale and nature of crime. The foundation
agreed to him cutting short the research, but they were not
happy about his suggestion that his 'findings' should be published under Nuffield's logo. Longford was the first to admit that
measured in strictly scientific terms, the total product of the
inquiry did not amount to much.

If scientific categories were going to be insisted on in
dealing with the questions 'What are the causes of

crime?' and 'Why has crime increased so much in Britain?', the total answer after a year was in one sense a lemon. And it was not likely to look much different a year later.[46]

Longford abandoned the Nuffield inquiry in 1954 and it was not until four years later that his personal account of proceedings appeared as *Causes of Crime* under George Weidenfeld's imprint with Roger Opie receiving a hefty co-writing credit. Sonia Orwell, who had read the manuscript, persuaded Weidenfeld that, whatever Nuffield's reservations, the book should be published.[47] It began by laying great emphasis on the fact that no accurate assessment of the extent of crime was possible because the Home Office did not provide the necessary statistics. Indeed the first chapter concluded that it was impossible to say unequivocally that there had even been an increase in crime since the war. Longford was to take up this matter in various public addresses in the mid-1950s, including a speech to the Magistrates' Association in 1955 where he appealed for a new statistical department to be set up at the Home Office and for a unified set of figures on crime covering all the country's police districts.

Causes of Crime then considered the 'reasons' quoted for the alleged upturn in crime (many of which will be familiar to those who follow contemporary debates on the subject). In addition to events that were specific to the period – the wartime dislocation of social mores, the economic shortages that came with peace and the introduction of the welfare state and its supposed encouragement of a 'something for nothing' mentality – the book mentioned broken homes, the media, police failings, a general decline in morals, the collapse of the family and the weakening of religious belief. Each of these 'reasons' was investigated with detailed summaries of some of the expert witnesses' evidence. The conclusion was in effect that there are as many causes as there are crimes.

Longford's input and opinions shone through the book, which became, after Nuffield's withdrawal, a personal statement. The Christian outlook on crime was discussed at length, reflecting what Roger Opie saw at the time of the inquiry as Longford's personal concern with questions of sin, evil, the devil and redemption. Having noted the lack of accurate statistics that would allow a scientific evaluation of the supposed decline of religion, Longford concluded with his own conviction – without a shred of supporting evidence – that 'there is little crime to be found among active members of the Christian churches'.

In a section advocating 'A New Approach to Crime', based largely on his observations when visiting prisons, Longford touched fleetingly on some of the topics that, in the years to come, were to concern him in his work inside and outside the House of Lords; excessively long sentences that were out of proportion to the crime committed; the need for prison to act not just as punishment but also as a place for rehabilitation; and the relationship between sin and crime.

The book reached few definite conclusions. The answers it sought to the questions addressed by the inquiry could not be backed up by the sort of statistical data that Nuffield had hoped would be forthcoming. In that regard the whole exercise can be said to have lacked any authority and therefore to have failed. Yet it certainly did contribute to growing pressure on the Home Office to put substantially more resources into collecting accurate data, a task which R. A. Butler as Home Secretary was to initiate at about the time *Causes of Crime* was published.

More pertinently though the book signposted a new avenue of activity for Longford. In allowing him to visit prisons, the inquiry drew his attention to a field that hitherto had interested few rising and ambitious politicians, the rehabilitation and after-care of offenders. As in Germany and Ireland, Longford would initially take up the cause of unpopular individuals, then his concern would spread to the wider issues in which they were embroiled. In a sense, the inmates Longford met on his visits to Britain's prisons became a new 'constituency' and, like those over whom he had responsibility as Minister for Germany, this group was neglected and hated by British society. The Establishment's hostility only served to deepen Longford's resolve to help them. Here was a new crusade, an unpopular cause he could champion.

Longford felt drawn to prisoners because they were outcasts, his sympathy with their plight deepened by his own marginalis-ation during his wartime breakdown. Yet now he was part of the Establishment with the influence as a member of the House of Lords to initiate debates and legislation on this overlooked problem. He believed his combination of insight and power would enable him to alter attitudes.

Fear of damaging his political career never once entered Longford's mind as a reason for avoiding the prisons issue. Firstly, he did not see any conflict in his convictions about prison reform as they dovetailed with his political beliefs. Secondly, while he retained his ambitions for high office, his view of party politics was becoming more ambivalent and he was less involved in the daily struggles that were convulsing the party as it came to terms with electoral defeat. Thirdly, he was attaching an increasing importance to his search for a distinct and personal expression of his Christian socialism.

Longford would have the field of crime, in particular the treatment of offenders and ex-offenders, to himself. Penal reform was, indeed largely still is, seen as an issue for individual campaigners rather than as a career boost for politicians anxious to make a name for themselves. It is certainly not a vote winner: the public has only limited sympathy with the notion that prisoners merit its special attention, as Longford repeatedly acknowledged in *Causes of Crime* and in his later book, *The Idea of Punishment*.

However, as a member of an unelected chamber, unconcerned with how electors would respond to his involvement with crimi-nals, as a politician with a record for taking an independent line and as a man who had already experienced the disapproval of those around him, Longford could afford to take up the cause of prisoners. It reflected his fascination with people. Since his earli-est days as a local councillor in Oxford people had been coming to his door asking for his help and a hand-out. Longford had a reputation for offering a warm reception to those down on their luck, a habit only strengthened by his Catholic principles after his conversion. Another aspect of his fascination with people was his attraction to larger-than-life politicians like de Valera and F. E. Smith, both men who were regarded with some suspicion by the Establishment. In the same way Longford was drawn towards criminals who had put themselves on the margins of society, particularly those who had committed notorious crimes.

The concern with sin and redemption that Roger Opie had noted during the causes of crime inquiry was also part of Longford's interest in prisoners. At the most basic level, he was responding to the line in Matthew's gospel 'I was in prison and you came to see me'. He came not to judge or urge prisoners to repent but simply to express his solidarity with them over the period of their ordeal.

> I can't help judging them, disapproving of the crimes
> they have committed. But I constantly remind myself
> and tell them that we are all sinners. I don't get on a
> pedestal. They have failed and I am conscious of
> having failed during the War. My spirit was willing
> but my flesh was weak. That could equally apply to
> them.[48]

Catholicism preaches forgiveness. This, to Longford, is one of the distinguishing Christian virtues and one which he has struggled to act out in his life. He believes that he has to try and forgive even those who have committed terrible crimes. While they may have offended against the laws of the state, he questions whether they have offended against God's law any more than any other member of society. 'As I see it,' he has written, 'we can never be sure that someone who commits a wicked crime is in the sight of God any more wicked than we are.'[49]

In the mid-1950s, Longford's concern for individual prisoners was an instinctive, Christian, humanitarian response to a group of people who had no spokesman. At first he rushed in to seek redress for those who claimed they were unjustly accused. It fulfilled his Catholic sense of duty, or as Evelyn Waugh would cynically put it, 'uplift': the sense of achievement from doing good works and occasionally (though as a result of Longford's public stature rather than conscious exhibitionism), of being seen to do good.

One of the first cases in which Longford became involved was that of Christopher Craig. In 1952 Craig had shot and killed a policeman who had caught him committing an armed robbery. His accomplice, Derek Bentley, already in custody, had shouted to Craig, 'Let him have it, Chris.' At their trial it was accepted that Bentley had in effect been telling Craig to shoot the policeman. As a minor Craig could not receive the death penalty but Bentley, who was mentally retarded, could and did. Bentley's death was to become a *cause célèbre* of the campaign to abolish capital punishment which Longford joined in the mid-1950s. Initially, though, it was the fate of Christopher Craig that attracted him.

Craig was in Wakefield Prison, one of the establishments Longford visited as part of the Nuffield inquiry. The two met and Longford was impressed by the efforts Craig was making at rehabilitation, training as a fitter, improving his education and in general behaving as a model prisoner. After several meetings with Craig's family, Longford began to lobby the Home Office for the young man's release. He pointed to Craig's unhappy family background, the influence of his older brother Niven who was involved in crime from an early age, Christopher's inability to read and write and to his subsequent dramatic change and reform when in prison. To keep Craig locked up for decades would serve no good purpose, Longford was convinced. He had been punished and now there was every chance that he would make a good and honest citizen. Longford was one of a number of prominent people who took up Craig's case and in 1962, after serving ten years of his sentence, he was released.

Another notorious case Longford championed was that of Michael Davies, convicted in 1953 of a brutal murder on Clapham Common in south west London and sentenced to death, later commuted to life imprisonment. The psychiatrist who had examined Davies was one of the experts Longford consulted during his Nuffield inquiry. The connection brought Longford on to the case and he quickly came to share the psychiatrist's conviction of the young man's innocence. Longford commissioned a private detective who compiled a dossier of evidence which appeared to exonerate Davies. This was then passed by Longford to the Home Secretary who was later, having considered it among other submissions, persuaded to release Davies after seven years in prison. Longford was at the gates of Wormwood Scrubs with Elizabeth when Davies was released and took him off to breakfast in Richmond.

While Longford's work with Craig excited few headlines, his connection with Michael Davies was taken up with gusto by the press. In August 1956, the *News of the World* reported that Longford had received a death threat as a result of his campaign on behalf of Davies.[50] He was warned to drop the case or risk being 'done in' with a razor. Relatives of the victim of the Clapham Common stabbing criticised Longford for his interference. Already known to be interested in prisons through his work with Nuffield, Longford was fast establishing a reputation in the press as the prisoners' friend. With his early successes on behalf of Craig and Davies, he soon became a focus for those complaining of the rough justice handed out to them.

Longford wanted to investigate each and every case, to visit anyone who wrote to him. One of the privileges of being a member of the House of Lords was that he could make visits at any of HM prisons without prisoners having to use up one of their precious family visiting slots. After 1957, when peers were allowed some return for their expenses, he was able to get a little financial assistance in his travels. However, the constraints of his other responsibilities – family, the House of Lords and after 1954 the National Bank – prevented Longford from answering every appeal made to him.

Though the showman in him undoubtedly enjoyed the coverage gained by his involvement with high-profile individuals, the bulk of the cases Longford adopted concerned prisoners who were not well known, where his work went unreported. The charge laid against him that he sought out only infamous criminals is unjust. On the whole, he responded to cases brought to him. Inevitably sometimes he was duped. His friend David Astor believes that he has been taken in by some of the prisoners he has befriended. 'He's one of nature's innocents. He's a very clever, very talented, very experienced child. There is nothing worldly about him though he can move in the world.'[51]

Twelve

The City's best-known socialist

I must remind Frank Pakenham that Christ drove
the money-changers from the Temple. He did not
open the doors wide for them to enter. He drove
them away. If we go on to apply the principles of
Christianity to contemporary British society, they
must have been done elsewhere rather better than
they have been done here

Aneurin Bevan(1959)[1]

Though his interest in the cases of individual prisoners and his
growing concern for the after-care of ex-offenders had eclipsed
the original remit of the Nuffield inquiry into the causes of
crime, it was the offer of a job at the National Bank that brought
Frank Longford's work for the foundation to a premature end.
In the autumn of 1954 he became Deputy Chairman and took
over the reins at the start of 1955 at the Bank's headquarters in
Old Broad Street in the City of London.

While there is a long and continuing tradition of Conservative
politicians taking up posts in the City once their careers at
Westminster come to an end, the appointment of a socialist ex-
minister was unusual. That the new chairman retained hopes of
holding high office again, and continued to speak from the
opposition front bench in the House of Lords, was unpre-
cedented. The City was not sure what to make of Longford. As
a descendant of the Jerseys who had owned Child's, an old
Etonian with a first from Oxford in Modern Greats, and now
the head of one of the eleven clearing banks, he could not be
easily dismissed as a light-weight. Yet his politics and his
continuing, albeit minor, role in the leadership of a party that
had a long history of antagonism towards City (Elizabeth had
fought the 1935 general election on a Labour ticket of bank

nationalisation) made him suspect. Even the intervention of his widely respected uncle, Arthur Villiers, nearing the end of his career as a director of Barings, could not prevent Longford from being blackballed by the City Club, one of the Square Mile's more exclusive institutions.[2]

By any standards Longford was an unlikely choice as head of a clearing bank. For all his early interest in economics, his reputation as a minister had been founded more on his Christian response in Germany and his mishandling of the report on the Prestwick disaster than on any financial acumen. Moreover his habit of hitting the headlines and his renown as a colourful eccentric was the very opposite of the grey discretion expected of a City chairman.

However, the National Bank – later taken over in the 1970s by Williams and Glynns Bank and they in turn by the Royal Bank of Scotland – was a unique institution. Its Anglo-Irish roots called for a chairman who had standing on both sides of the Irish Sea. Founded in 1835 by Daniel O'Connell, the 'Great Liberator' and the man who led the campaign that resulted in the Catholic Emancipation Act of 1829, the National Bank had, like the Pakenham family, grown in wealth and influence in an era when the Irish and British economies were as one. In 1859 it had joined the London clearing banks system. There was nothing paradoxical then about a bank whose funds were largely provided in Ireland but whose head office was in London. Branches had been opened all around the British Isles.

By the time that Longford took over as chairman, though, the treaty of 1921 had effectively separated three quarters of Ireland from Britain and the relationship between the National Bank's investors, two thirds of whom were in Ireland, and its investments – mainly in British government securities through the London market – was a delicate one. The National Bank was the only financial institution that attempted to bridge the gap between London and Dublin, with boards of directors in both capitals but London taking precedence. Of the other banks functioning in the Irish Republic at the time, the majority had their headquarters in Dublin and two were based in Belfast. None had a branch network like the National's in Britain.

In London there was a view that the National was an anachronism. The first time Longford attended a meeting of the clearing-bank chairmen one remarked, light-heartedly, 'I always say you oughtn't to be here.'³ However dimly the link with Dublin was regarded by some, the Bank of England had been carefully nurtured by Longford's long-serving predecessor, Michael Cooke, to ensure that the National's dual position was maintained.

Cooke was seventy-three in 1954 and, after twenty-one years as chairman, had been anxious to retire for some years. However, he had failed to find a suitable successor whose credentials would pass muster in London *and* Dublin, who would be able to lunch with other chairmen in the City *and* move easily around the branches in Ireland. The obvious candidate, Antony Acton, a member of the board with ample banking experience, had no Irish links and was not a Catholic. Though religion was kept out of business, the National counted many Irish religious orders among its clients and had to take their preferences and prejudices into account.

Cooke was not looking for a figurehead but for someone who would be prepared to exercise close, day-to-day control. He was a shrewd man who had worked his way to the top from the most junior post. He was able to see through Longford's distracted air to the qualities that brought him success as a manager and financial controller of nationalised industries when he was at Civil Aviation. Longford's training in economics – he had specialised in banking and currency at Oxford – was an added qualification. The approach came through John Dulanty, retired Irish High Commissioner in London and one of those who had dissuaded Longford from resigning in 1949 at the time of the Government of Ireland Act. Longford met Cooke at the Reform Club and listened to the terms and conditions. The job would not be a short-term appointment. While he would be able to continue his work in the Lords, the Bank had to come first.

Longford was in two minds. Cooke was immensely respected and reputedly able to take over every job in the bank at a moment's notice. Longford could not match that sort of expertise and while he had proved himself as a manager, his own approach was more that of an initiator and delegator. There was also the question of becoming less involved in the inner counsels of the Labour Party. Though the Lords was not a significant area for Labour under a Conservative government, Longford still retained an influence on the leadership, especially through his close personal ties with Hugh Gaitskell.

The two lunched at the House of Lords to discuss Cooke's offer. Gaitskell was against Longford accepting. He doubted Longford's contention that an inside view of the City would be valuable to the party. Gaitskell was much more optimistic than his old friend that Labour would win the 1955 general election. In such an event, Longford would be in line for leadership of the House of Lords and a post in Cabinet, Gaitskell pointed out. If he went to the Bank and committed himself to a lengthy stay, he would have to decline such an offer from the Prime Minister. Attlee himself was much more flexible. 'The Tories do it: why shouldn't you?' he told his young colleague.[4]

From a practical point of view, there was a strong financial motivation to accepting the post. As chairman Longford would be able to abandon Christ Church, support his family and pay their school fees. He decided, against Gaitskell's advice, to put the party to one side for the time being at least. It was a choice that shows how far he had travelled since he first joined Labour less than twenty years previously. Then a distraction from politics would have been unthinkable. By 1954, the glitter had tarnished. The same realisation was leading him to branch out into the field of prison reform. He had experienced ministerial office, still nurtured ambitions, but was looking for a new challenge. The Labour Party was no longer his all.

To those on the left of the party Longford's decision to go and work in the City only emphasised their suspicions of his background and Establishment ties. He was also exposing himself to the charge of being a good-time socialist, around and keen when the party was in government and ministerial office was on offer, but looking elsewhere when times were harder.

Such accusations, which significantly reduced Longford's standing in the Labour movement, failed to take into account the isolation and financial constraint he suffered in the Lords, and underestimated the lure of the National's offer to him. To be a socialist in the City, the head of a clearing bank yet still an active politician, was a unique opportunity. To a maverick like Longford, habitually so fascinated by anomalies, by people who could not be pigeonholed, it was irresistible.

Working for the National Bank also appealed to the Irish side of him. Since his first meetings with de Valera and *Peace by Ordeal*, Longford had taken the cause of Ireland to his heart and regarded himself, despite his Ascendancy roots, as an Irishman and a republican. Though he had chosen to make his career in England and had, in effect, turned his back on Ireland, the chance of heading the National Bank, with the largest branch network in the country, gave him an opportunity to play a significant role in Irish economic and political life for the first time. The ambiguities of the National's position, straddling the Irish Sea, reflected Longford's own dual allegiances. Longford's son Thomas, who now divides his time between England and Ireland, sees the concept of being British as the key to his father's dual status.

> It is not a question of him being English or Irish. He comes from an Anglo-Irish family and is, in that sense, both British and Irish. The two are not incompatible. It's not unlike the position of Scottish and Welsh aristocratic families. They would send their children to English public schools just as my father's parents did. And he has retained that dual allegiance, carrying an Irish passport while going on British government business, for example.[5]

As chairman of the National Bank Longford had the role of an executive. To a certain extent, he and his board of mainly distinguished and respected citizens were insulated from the day-to-day business that was handled by the professionals. Technical knowledge and business acumen were the preserve of the general managers, while public contact and overall decision-making remained the responsibility of the board and its chairman.

While Michael Cooke had cast his gaze over the whole organisation, with an eye for even the smallest of matters, Longford quickly moved to delegate lesser details to his general managers. He had neither the expertise nor the interest to keep such a tight rein of control. Over major issues he would consult his directors much more than his predecessor had done and worked to achieve a consensus. In his time at the bank he appointed the entire Irish board and four out of the six English directors. John Leydon, the Irish chairman, played a significant part in the building of Ireland's economy in the inner counsels of Prime Minister Lemass. Longford takes special pride in having promoted David Montagu to the English board. At thirty-three he was one of the youngest men ever to make it on to the board of a major clearing bank, but Longford's concern, besides Montagu's business expertise, was that the commercial banks in Britain in the 1950s were biased against Jews in high positions. At the time of Montagu's appointment, Longford estimates that the only other Jew on the board of any joint-stock bank in the City was the deputy chairman of Lloyd's.

> During my time in the City, I would not describe this
> as deliberate anti-Semitism. In charity one might call
> it an evil legacy, but the result was the same. The
> highest positions in the City were virtually closed to
> Jews.[6]

While at one level being a chairman was akin to running a ministry, at another Longford found that the collective responsibility of two boards of directors was a change of direction, working with a team rather than as a leader.

> The members of the board of a bank share the
> responsibility for policy and for results. The Board of
> the Admiralty presents a superficial analogy, but that
> is recognised fiction. The only ultimate responsibility
> within the department is that of the Minister, i.e. the
> First Lord. In this sense a bank chairman could never
> feel the strain of personal responsibility in any way so
> acutely.[7]

However, as a minister, his ultimate responsibility had been to a Cabinet of which he was not a member and beyond that to the electorate. At the bank there was a greater freedom of manoeuvre. Commercial considerations were the only valid criteria in most decisions. There was little opportunity for publicity or pandering to the electorate. 'In banking,' he wrote of his period as chairman in the 1950s, 'there is an absence of public knowledge and public discussion of the performance of particular institutions. This, while relieving the strain of public scrutiny, restricts, though it does not destroy, the field of public trust.'[8] It is, in short, results rather than intentions and fine words that are the mark of a successful bank chairman. A politician can escape liability for his failings as long as he can talk his way round them. Longford soon recognised that banking was an entirely different affair. He was also quick to realise that in the absence of a minister's constant concern about public opinion, he would be freer to plan and develop the institution he headed.

There were areas where Longford left his imprint. He was very keen that the National should expand its branch network and persuaded his fellow directors to concur. No new English branches had been opened since 1921 and he was determined to build up the British side of operations, especially in the south east.

He took a greater interest in meeting his staff and their welfare than had hitherto been expected of the chairman. He was a passionate advocate of unionisation and was the first bank chairman to address a meeting of the National Union of Bank Employees. To his own staff he pledged that no one at the National should receive less in pay than his or her equivalent colleagues at other clearing banks. In a more relaxed vein he played host once a year at Bernhurst to a cricket match between a bank team and an eleven from Hurst Green. In his dishevelled whites and slightly too short trousers, he joined in with the National's employees before standing them lunch at a local hotel.

Co-ordination of the Irish and British sides of operations involved many journeys across the Irish Sea. Longford made around eighty visits to Ireland in his eight years as chairman. At the outset of his reign, the Irish staff of the National were engaged in a go-slow over conditions. By the end of his period, he had won their affection. They presented Longford with a scroll that paid tribute to him as 'an honoured chairman' but more significantly as 'a great friend'.

> There was a man called Arthur Quirk [recalled Edward Longford's widow Christina] who used to drive him [Frank Longford] all around Ireland to see these sub-offices of the Bank, in quite out of the way places. He was an enormous success. Bank clerks are encouraged to play games and Frank has always been very good on athletics. He would always know the form of practically any footballer in any small town in Ireland. He always talked to bank clerks about that. They'd never had a visiting chairman who could talk to them like that.[9]

Longford's personal attention to detail can also be seen in the case of a young employee who stole £300 from his branch in Ireland and was dismissed. Planning to leave for Canada to avoid the disgrace, the miscreant was contacted by Longford who arranged to see him. The chairman gave the young man a rosary and promised to keep in touch. Within four months he had paid back the money out of his wages in Canada and in later years was to return to Ireland where he and Longford became friends. While Longford's kind gesture was born of philanthropy rather than any attempt to win favour with the staff, the incident was still mentioned years after he had departed.

Having interests in both Ireland and London added impetus to Longford's long-term aim of tackling the problem of the partition in the north. After a debate in the Lords in December 1960 on the future of Ireland in which he spoke, Longford wrote a lengthy piece for the *Observer* advocating what became known as the Cardinal d'Alton solution. The Catholic churchman had given an interview in which he suggested that the two parts of Ireland might unite as one republic but return to the Commonwealth, thereby offering the Loyalists of the North a continuing link with the British Crown and evidence that the Dublin government, in their willingness to rejoin the association of ex-colonies which they had left in 1948, was prepared to make concessions.

It was a novel solution which earned some applause on both sides of the Irish Sea. However, Longford insisted that the initiative must come from the British government. It was quickly made clear that no such gesture was going to be forthcoming. In Ireland, de Valera who had recently assumed the presidency was utterly opposed. Longford found himself once more falling between two stools. 'Some Irishmen thought I had been put up to it in England, some Englishmen that I was an Irish government stooge. In truth, though this seems hard to credit, the initiative was entirely my own.'[10]

On another diplomatic mission between Dublin and London Longford was more successful. Sir Hugh Lane, an Irishman who had made his reputation in England, had been a prolific picture dealer before he was drowned when the *Lusitania* sank in 1915. In a late addition to his will he bequeathed his collection of French Impressionists to Ireland but the codicil was not witnessed. His paintings – including Renoir's *Les Parapluies* – therefore ended up in the National Gallery in London to the intense disappointment of the Irish. The dispute over ownership rumbled on for over forty years and involved such Anglo-Irish figures was W. B. Yeats and Lady Gregory. Longford became involved as a mediator in 1956 at the request of the Irish Prime Minister, Sean Lemass. Under a compromise suggested by the Duke of Wellington, the collection would be shared between Dublin and London, and would spend half the year in each city.

In furtherance of this plan, Longford visited Prime Minister Macmillan at Downing Street in August 1957. The two had met occasionally, when Macmillan spoke for Lindsay in the 1938 Oxford by-election and later at an Anglo-German Association dinner. Macmillan gave his backing to the Duke of Wellington's compromise – as had the Irish government – and eventually the trustees of the National Gallery in London were persuaded to yield. For his part in ending this forty-year battle Longford was awarded an honorary degree by the National University of Ireland.

His success in such delicate negotiations was matched by his achievements at the National Bank, according to several eminent observers. Business in England and Wales increased three times faster than the average of its competitors. The *Daily Telegraph* paid tribute to Longford's business flair and shrewdness. *The Economist* described him as a successful amateur banker. The use of the second adjective is significant. For despite the energy and enthusiasm with which he threw himself into the job, and his wholehearted decision to make the bank his first priority, the world of politics still laid claim to some of Longford's attention. Banking never quite overtook politics in his affections. Rachel recalls that home life continued to be dominated by political discussions. 'He certainly never talked about bank life – except that it was an Irish bank.'[11]

As a socialist in the City, Longford tried to operate as a double agent for his party – and as a rather more successful double agent than he had been in the war on his brief diplomatic mission to see de Valera in Ireland. Although the City had a reputation for being a bastion of Conservatism, among those whom he entertained as chairman Longford found men whose private views he thought would not be antipathetic to some aspects of the Labour Party's commitment to a more equal society. They were a solace to him in the moments when he felt out of place in the banking world. After all it was his uncle, Arthur Villiers, a director of Barings, who had first introduced him to social work at Eton Manor.

Longford embarked on a long campaign to forge if not closer links then at least a cessation of hostility between Labour and the City. He arranged a series of lunches with influential figures in the Square Mile for Hugh Gaitskell, Harold Wilson, Aneurin Bevan, Frank Cousins, the union leader, and James Callaghan, his former number two at the Admiralty and, after Gaitskell's election in late 1955 as Labour leader, a hot tip to be a future Chancellor of the Exchequer. Longford's campaign was similar to John Smith's initiative of the late 1980s and early 1990s to quell City fears in the event of a Labour victory. Both ventures were unsuccessful.

As well as acting in his party's interests, Longford embarked on the 'prawn cocktail initiative' to ease his conscience about working in the City. He believed that many of his staunchest friends in the Labour Party – Gaitskell among them – could not accept that a true socialist would adopt a role in banking. To justify his position, Longford felt he should play the part of Trojan horse in the City. The initiative was spurred on by his discomfort at being both politician and banker during the Commons row over changes in the bank rate in autumn 1957.

Different Chancellors of the Exchequer throughout Longford's spell at the National Bank had varying attitudes to consultation with the clearing-bank chairmen. Peter Thorneycroft, in the midst of a financial crisis in 1957, called them in for a full and open discussion. Great emphasis was placed on secrecy. Longford had already noted how his presence among the clearing banks' delegation as an ex-Labour minister and opposition spokesman in the Lords had embarrassed Thorneycroft's predecessor, Macmillan, and he was scrupulous about leaving politics out of such gatherings.

One item that was not raised at the meeting was that a substantial increase in the bank rate was intended. However, news of the rise leaked out somehow and speculators were able to take advantage. There was an outcry followed by angry scenes in the House of Commons with Harold Wilson leading the Opposition's demands for an enquiry and hinting at collusion between the Conservative Party and the City. Longford found himself with a foot in both camps. He sympathised with Labour's anger and could see the political capital to be made out of Wilson's accusations, but was sure from his inside knowledge of how the City worked that news of the bank rate increase had not come the way his colleague was suggesting. He likened his position at the time to that of Winston Churchill who, when asked which side he was on in the Spanish Civil War, replied 'both'.

The Parker Enquiry was set up to investigate the leak and exonerated all concerned. As it was published Longford, with his dual vantage point, was tempted into print by the *Daily Telegraph*. On 31 January 1958, he defended the standards of professionalism in the City, adding: 'I am not coming forward to say that those I have met in the City are morally better than politicians, but I will certainly swear they are no worse.' He continued with words that were to rebound upon him: 'Some of the most eminent of the leaders in the City have recently vindicated their integrity, never doubted by anyone but a fool or a knave.' Tory MPs seized upon this remark as an indictment of Harold Wilson who had led the Labour assault over the leak. Longford had to write hurriedly to Wilson pointing out that he had not meant to suggest he was a fool or a knave. Wilson accepted his apology and – judging by subsequent events – did not bear a grudge against Longford. But to those who were suspicious of the self-proclaimed socialist in the City, the incident was further evidence that the two interests were incompatible. To others it simply revealed Longford's naivety and his worrying lack of forethought.

However, in the City the article was greeted with great enthusiasm and Longford received a flood of luncheon invitations. He decided to exploit these – and try to undo the damage his article had caused in his party – by inviting along prominent Labour colleagues. In the run-up to the 1959 general election, with the prospect of a Labour victory, both sides expressed an interest in such a *rapprochement*. Longford even managed to persuade other chairmen to consider the appointment of ex-Labour ministers to their boards. However, the sweeping Conservative victory at the polls destroyed the plans' momentum and nothing came of them.

Longford's work on behalf of prisoners took up any spare time he had left over from his City, political and House of Lords duties. While in the Attlee government he had dedicated himself solely to his ministerial responsibilities but from the 1950s onwards he managed to balance professional life between the National Bank and a 'career' in prison reform.

His observations of prison life for the Nuffield report and his friendship with individual prisoners had opened his eyes to the shortcomings of existing provision for the after-care and resettlement of offenders. The various Discharged Prisoners' Aid Societies, set up in Victorian times, were run by good-hearted individuals but were failing to help ex-convicts rehabilitate, often leaving them jobless, homeless and prone to return to crime. Furthermore the societies were regarded by their 'clients' as part of the prison Establishment, a service offered out of duty rather than out of genuine concern. In keeping with his benevolence towards individual prisoners, Longford recognised the need for an organisation that would be sympathetic with those newly released. The New Bridge put that radical idea into practice.

Two ex-prisoners in particular were associated with Longford in the establishment in 1955 of the New Bridge: Lord Edward Montagu and Peter Wildeblood. They had been two of the three men convicted of homosexual offences amid sensational headlines in the early 1950s. Montagu knew Longford's daughter Antonia slightly and the two peers met at Wakefield Prison during the causes of crime inquiry. Though he had no connection with Wildeblood, a *Daily Mail* journalist, Longford sought him out in Wormwood Scrubs. In his account of his prison ordeal, Wildeblood was later to write:

> Two things kept me going. One was the visit every three weeks of Lord Pakenham who was preparing a report for the Nuffield Foundation on the causes of crime. He must have exhausted my views on the subject during the first few visits, but he kept on coming for as long as he was able. Sitting with him there in a room without a warden in the dingy grey suit which I had worn for six months, with my hands scarred by the mail bag needle and my fingernails black with ingrained dirt, I could feel I was still a person. I can never repay him for what he did for me during those months.[12]

Longford could see that Wildeblood was now being treated as a social leper, and that he needed his help more than Montagu. He recognised that the latter, with his Establishment friends, would not go short of visitors or support, while Wildeblood, referred to in court as the peer's 'social inferior', a man with no shame about his homosexuality, and allegedly a thoroughly bad influence on Montagu, would be isolated and abandoned. It is an insight that those who accused Longford of favouring the glamorous criminals often ignore.

Longford's willingness to be associated with both men may seem strange in the light of his own often outspoken homophobic views. His conviction that homosexuality is sinful predates his conversion to Catholicism and is bound up with the Puritanism of his childhood. For a man of his age and background, such a stance is not so unusual. But Catholicism, which sees gay relationships as offending against nature and sex's divine purpose – namely procreation – reinforced his prejudice and made him unashamed to articulate it in public. The combination of Puritanism and Catholicism has made Longford extremely intolerant of homosexuality.

Yet notwithstanding he is tolerant of homosexuals. The paradox is born of the attitude that inspires his work with prisoners. He refuses to judge them – the sinners – but will condemn their crimes – the sin. He makes a clear distinction between the individuals concerned and what he sees as their weakness.

> The fact someone has broken the rules does not upset me. But I can't say that I don't disapprove. I see homosexuality as a handicap.[13]

Such sentiments may sound judgemental to a more tolerant generation that does not distinguish between the person and his or her sexual orientation. For Longford's Augustinian dictum of sins and sinners requires a homosexual to regard his or her sexuality as evil. However, it should be pointed out that, in the days when homosexuality was a criminal offence, Longford opened the first debate in Parliament in favour of the Wolfenden report published in 1956. It recommended that homosexual acts in private between consenting adults over twenty-one should be decriminalised. Longford was in the vanguard of the libertarians. When the Commons avoided discussing the report, Longford used his platform in the Lords to take a forward stand for implementation. He began by outlining his Christian views on homosexuality but, referring obliquely to his friendship with Wildeblood and Montagu, articulated the principle of hating the sin and loving the sinner to advocate reform. During the debate, on 4 December 1957, Lord Boothby referred to him as 'the non-playing captain of the homosexual team'.

After Montagu's release, Longford had dinner with him at the White Tower Restaurant in London. He expressed his keenness that Montagu should take his seat again in the House of Lords and not feel forever stigmatised. The subject naturally led them to discuss after-care facilities for rehabilitation of ex-offenders and Montagu revealed that, since his release, he had been besieged by requests from former inmates who hoped that he, a wealthy man, would understand their plight and lend them a helping hand. He told Longford that he was considering starting the equivalent of Alcoholics Anonymous for ex-offenders. When Longford agreed that the existing after-care organisations were failing, the two decided to pool their efforts and set up a new body which would make good the deficiency. Its aim would be to befriend prisoners and help them find a useful role within society once more.

There followed a dinner where supporters from various areas of Longford's life gathered with Montagu and Wildeblood to endorse the new venture – among them David Astor, Sonia Orwell and Victor Gollancz. The original intention was to call it the Bridge but there was already a left-wing body of the same name. So the word New was added – both Victor Gollancz and Edward Montagu were later to claim the credit for this combination.

The first official meeting of the New Bridge took place in January 1956 at Rubens Hotel in central London. Bill Hewitt, the writer, was elected the first chairman with Norma Opie the secretary and Canon Collins of Christian Action, Longford and his daughter Antonia, who had commissioned Wildeblood to write about his prison experiences for Weidenfeld, as members of the executive.[14] Many were soon to withdraw from an active involvement because of other work. Hewitt stood down as chairman, but Longford, who replaced him, seldom missed a meeting for the next eight years. His clear sense of purpose and his dedication enabled the New Bridge to weather a stormy and often hostile reception in its early years and to mature into a widely respected and pioneering organisation in the area of penal reform.

The first obstacle New Bridge encountered was antipathy from the Home Office and the press who dismissed it as a society organised by homosexuals for homosexuals. The involvement of Montagu and Wildeblood, still remembered after the sensationalism of their trial, and the appointment of a homosexual as secretary to succeed Norma Opie, was much commented on. When one of Longford's friends pointed out to a Home Office official that he had eight children and could scarcely be considered 'suspect', he was allegedly told, 'That's just a cover.' The prejudice took some time to elapse but Longford, with his Gladstonian air of a man beyond reproach as he moved among society's 'sinners', was well-equipped by sheer force of his personality to dispel it.[7]

Whether he showed good judgement in allowing Montagu and Wildeblood to be so publicly associated with the New Bridge is another matter. The whole purpose of the organisation was to provide a bridge between prison and society for ex-offenders. Hence to have discriminated against two founding members would have been to go against the spirit of the organisation and would have pandered to precisely the sort of ill-informed hostility that New Bridge was aiming to make a thing of the past.

Yet Longford might also have reflected that in any attempt to change opinions it helps to begin with the public on one's side. To alienate them at the outset, to allow New Bridge to be dismissed, however unjustly, as something it was not, was to weaken its impact and its campaign. Given public hostility to prisoners in general, he was merely making an already uphill struggle harder.

The second problem facing New Bridge was that, in their enthusiasm to launch the new organisation, its founders did not clarify their purpose nor how they were going to achieve it. Talk

291

of befriending prisoners simply resulted in a constant stream of visitors queuing up at New Bridge's first offices, situated in a church crypt, hoping for a hand-out. When they were offered advice and counselling instead, some were disappointed.

Again, in setting up New Bridge, Longford was the initiator who drew up broad parameters and left the day-to-day running of the charity to its staff. He envisaged an organisation unashamedly siding with the prisoner, working to help individuals rather than lobbying Parliament or ministers over more general issues. He would undertake the latter himself. In effect New Bridge was broadening the scope of his own prison visiting. In its early days, before probation officers routinely went into prisons, New Bridge worked to set up after-care arrangements for those about to be released. In addition, it trained and recruited prison visitors and later ran a specialist employment service.

> What was needed was the acceptance by the com-
> munity for the first time [Longford later wrote] of a
> specific responsibility for providing a minimum stan-
> dard of welfare for the ex-prisoner. That was the
> social principle. What was needed in administrative
> practice was a national network of after-care officers,
> supplemented by voluntary efforts. Some of the vol-
> untary effort should be state-aided, some of it, like
> New Bridge, quite independent. It was not sufficient
> to assume the Welfare State could look after ex-
> prisoners through the same services – the Ministry of
> Labour, the Assistance Board etc – as were adequate
> for other citizens. Prisoners need special help because
> they are specially handicapped.[15]

One of the reasons New Bridge was reluctant to provide direct financial help to prisoners was its shortage of funds. (In more recent times it has received limited and, given Whitehall's initial suspicion, long-awaited help from the Home Office.) Longford threw himself zealously into persuading friends and, through them, institutions to provide financial backing. The minutes of the early meetings abound with reports of fund-raising functions and balls, often organised by Longford. Several of his contacts in the City proved generous, one senior official of another bank making a particular impression on Longford by revealing that he too was a socialist in the sense that he wanted to follow Christ's instruction to the rich man to give up his worldly goods.

Occasionally, in their enthusiasm to help out, Longford's friends could prove an embarrassment. Lord Boothby, a colleague of Elizabeth's on various 'Any Questions' panels and a member of the House of Lords, attended a New Bridge ball and was asked to say a few words. 'With great geniality,' Elizabeth reports, 'he began "There is no audience I like so much as a captive audience. That is why prisoners are the best audience in the world." No laughter. The ex-prisoners present looked as black as thunder.'[16] In spite of such *faux pas*, the charity's bank balances managed to stay in the black while its work and its staff numbers increased.

The largest obstacle to New Bridge, however, were the existing after-care organisations. In the House of Lords in 1961, Longford was to describe the system that greeted him when he undertook his Nuffield inquiry as 'a nonsense, a shambles and a mess'. The Discharged Prisoners' Associations, for their part, regarded New Bridge as interlopers whose very existence amounted to a condemnation of past efforts.

This mutual hostility is evident in the minutes taken by New Bridge of a meeting in October 1957 between Longford and his team and the Royal London Discharged Prisoners' Aid Society. This body had been blocking New Bridge's attempts to get a representative on the discharge board for London's prisons. The only sop they were prepared to offer was a promise to refer ex-prisoners, when appropriate, to New Bridge. Despite Longford's best attempts at reconciliation, the two bodies left the meeting as discordant as they had started and the carefully written minutes cannot disguise a frosty and suspicious atmosphere.[17]

Despite all these obstacles, though, prisoners and well-disposed characters within the system soon realised that New

Bridge was the place to go if you were genuinely seeking to make a fresh start. Longford recalls that one day, a couple of years after the charity had started, he received a visitor at the National Bank's headquarters. The man announced himself as the father of one of the prisoners Longford had been visiting. He had spoken to the prison governor about the support his son would be given after five years inside. 'If you're asking what the state is going to do,' the governor had answered, 'the answer is nothing. You'd better go and see the chairman of the New Bridge.'[18]

Though New Bridge took up much of Longford's 'spare' time outside the bank, it furthered and deepened his knowledge of the penal system and – in the Lords, in Whitehall and on public platforms – intensified his appeals for reform of some of its worst aspects. The brutality of the prison regime, the routine insensitivity with which prisoners were treated, and the appalling conditions in many of Britain's jails shocked Longford. In overcrowded prisons, there was a lack of facilities and of a will to undertake any sort of rehabilitation aimed at sending inmates back into society reformed characters.

From the initial debate he opened in the House of Lords on prisons in 1955 (the first ever debate about prisons in the Chamber), Longford laid great stress on what he called 'the three evil ones' – overcrowding, understaffing and shortage of work for prisoners. Such efforts at bringing the prison service forward in the fight for resources and attention in Whitehall bore fruit in the late 1950s when a reforming Home Secretary, R. A. Butler, decided to make a priority of the Prisons Department, hitherto a neglected domain. In a speech in March 1957, Butler stressed the necessity of more research into the causes of crime, better after-care facilities and a prison building programme through which offenders could be treated according to their needs rather than their deserts.[19] Longford could not help but be delighted that many of the points he had been pressing were part of the Home Secretary's programme. In February 1959 a White Paper, 'Penal Policy in a Changing Society', appeared.

Butler's good intentions were not translated into quite the

revolution for which some had hoped. Prison overcrowding increased rather than diminished over this period. The launch of a £4 million prison-building programme coincided with an upturn in the crime rate and hence a growing prison population. From 2000 sleeping on average three to a cell when Butler became Home Secretary in 1957, the number had risen to over 7000 when he left office in 1962. Longford soon became disappointed with Butler's pledge for reform. His dissatisfaction was not due to political rivalry but to the dismay of an ardent prison reformer at the limitations and pragmatism of a Home Secretary with other concerns to occupy him. Longford's attitude to Butler demonstrates how deeply he had taken the cause of prison reform to heart, to the point of blinding him to political realities such as the public reluctance to spend money on jails. Consideration of public opinion on spending, especially at a time of economic belt-tightening, was an unavoidable part of Butler's job, and played a part in his retreat from the cause of prison reform.

> If he had been entirely engrossed in penal work
> [Longford later wrote of Butler] he would hardly have
> acquiesced so tamely in the frustrating of his high and
> genuine ambitions. He would have tackled the staff
> situation, and the work situation in detail, and called
> the attention of the nation to both.[20]

Such is the verdict of a campaigner not a politician. Others judged Butler the most conscientious Home Secretary about prisons since Churchill, who had stated fifty years earlier 'the mood and temper of the public with regard to the treatment of crime and criminals is one of the unfailing tests of the civilisation of any country'. Butler's wider responsibilities at the Home Office and his designs on the leadership of his party, already once frustrated by Macmillan, did not allow him to push the unpopular prisons issue too far lest it compromise his political career. For Longford, to judge by his verdict on Butler, there would have been no choice. He had never had much taste for party in-fighting and tactical manoeuvring when principles were

295

at stake. His prisons crusade was carrying him ever further away from the Labour mainstream and political preferment.

Longford made several other determined bids to promote greater reflection on the state of Britain's prisons. In 1959, building on his experiences at New Bridge and hoping that Butler's interest in after-care might signal a window of opportunity with Whitehall, he worked with Peter Thompson to produce a report on existing provision for prisoners once they were released.

Thompson, a devout Christian, had made a name for himself in 1958 when he arranged and paid for the defence of a man who had stolen his briefcase. He followed this up by trying in various ways to provide facilities to help ex-offenders, but without much success. He decided to establish a private inquiry into prisoner after-care and attempted to persuade Lord Gardiner, a well-known barrister and later Lord Chancellor in Wilson's government, to chair it. Having failed to secure him, he turned to Longford. Other members included two Catholics, Peter Rawlinson MP, later a Tory Attorney-General and Bob Mellish, a future Labour Chief Whip. A public relations man, Thompson managed to attract a good amount of press publicity for the launch of their investigation.

However, it was not an entirely harmonious collaboration. Despite their shared belief, Longford and Thompson did not work well together from the outset. Thompson was not happy with Longford as chairman, regretting not securing Gerald Gardiner. As the committee embarked on its work, Thompson was also suffering the effects of the psychological stress that was to lead to his mental breakdown in 1964, criminal convictions and ultimately to his being sent to Broadmoor for four years.

Much of the legwork for the eventual report – and the drafting of its recommendations – ended up being carried out by the honorary secretary Jack – later Lord – Donaldson who hitherto had not been much involved in the prison reform field. His work on the Pakenham-Thompson report was followed in 1961 by his appointment as honorary secretary of the National Association of Discharged Prisoners' Societies and later, between 1966 and 1974 as chairman of NACRO, the National Association for the Care and Resettlement of Offenders. He became another outspoken advocate of prison reform from the Labour benches in the House of Lords before he joined the SDP in the 1980s.

In terms of impact the report was one of Longford's more successful attempts at detailed examination of a public issue. Unlike the causes of crime inquiry, it produced specific recommendations about training and work facilities in prisons and how to manage the transition from jail to independent life in the community afterwards. The recommendations were taken up first in a government report and later in legislation that carved out an extended role for a professional probation service. 'I cannot shake off the illusion, if it is one,' Longford later wrote, 'that our Pakenham-Thompson committee had much to do with the establishment of the government's own enquiry into after-care of prisoners.'[21]

Christianity was becoming an increasingly significant factor in Longford's writing and thinking on prisons as he moved beyond practical concerns to examine the philosophy that lay behind Britain's penal system. Building on his personal links with prisoners, he tackled some of the conflicts that his work had raised in his mind. In 1961 he produced an extended and very personal essay, *The Idea of Punishment*, for the Christian publisher, Geoffrey Chapman. Written in academic and occasionally convoluted style, the essay addresses principally the question of whether, as a Christian, Longford believed that prisoners should be punished. Having unashamedly taken their side in the work of New Bridge and in his visiting, he was often accused of advocating that no one should be sent to prison at all. *The Idea of Punishment* attempted to set the record straight.

Essentially it expanded on the idea of loving the sinner and hating the sin, accepting that crime has to be punished but that criminals are sent to prison as a punishment, not in order to receive more punishment when they are there. A prerequisite of the essay was therefore to balance God's law against man's laws, to establish a relationship between crime and sin. Longford quoted St Thomas Aquinas – 'the commands of human law cover only those deeds which concern the public interest, not every deed of every virtue' – to support his own view that the vast majority of our sins must pass unnoticed by the State'. All crimes were sins, but not all sins crimes.

How then should the state punish those sins which contravene its laws? Punishment, Longford suggested, had four aims – retribution, prevention, reform and deterrent. On familiar ground for those aware of his work with New Bridge, he attacked the state's failure to match its commitments over reform of prisoners with actions.

> Reform has established itself in practice as the life's objective of the leaders of the prison service, of all their dedicated members, of the whole probation service, and of many magistrates, doctors, clergy and others concerned with the lives of prisoners . . . Few of us who have had much to do with prisons would deny that a prison sentence is capable on occasion of benefiting a man. We have probably all met with one or two men who were better for a period in gaol. Hardly anyone, however, will seriously argue that in general our prison system as we know it is likely to have this effect. One would need to be far removed from reality to claim that at present we ordinarily send a man to prison to promote his welfare. We ordinarily send him to prison to keep him out of circulation (prevention) and to discourage him and other members of the community from committing a like offence (deterrence).

However, his extended essay was less a political pamphlet, and more a philosophical and theological examination of punishment in general and the notion of retribution in particular. While Longford and other Christian campaigners for penal reform were united with their secular counterparts in condemning the lack of any notion of reform in Britain's prisons, they parted ways significantly over retribution. Many of the latter group hold that criminals are medically unwell, that it is circumstances that led them to break the law, that they therefore carry no moral responsibility for their crime and should not suffer society's retribution but rather its concern and understanding.

Those who claimed that criminals are simply sick were, Longford said, 'abandoning all belief in the freedom of will whether in a Christian or secular sense. In particular one is abandoning the view that we shall one day be judged by God according to the moral or immoral use we make of our freedom of choice in this world.' If crime is dismissed as sickness, there would be no attempt, he continued, to distinguish between good and evil. 'Clearly therefore a Christian can have nothing to do with this doctrine that crime is disease.'

In *The Idea of Punishment*, Longford wanted to distance himself from such a doctrine. Concern and understanding did not preclude retribution, which indeed he saw as an integral part of reform. As a Christian who believed in free will, Longford wrote that those who commit crimes carry a moral responsibility for their actions. It was the acknowledgement of their moral responsibility that started prisoners on the road to reform.

In linking reform to retribution, Longford was anxious to stress that the latter should not be regarded negatively as society extracting its pound of flesh from the criminal. He preferred to use the term 'debt to society' rather than the word retribution. In associating reform with retribution, Longford was placing the responsibility with society as well as with the individual prisoner. Locking people away in prison and imagining the problem was solved was insufficient. Prison was the first stage of their rehabilitation as full members of society and the success of that process depended not just on the criminals but on those charged with their welfare.

> The Christian judge, in the full knowledge that he also
> is a sinner like the man in the dock, judges with love
> and then does all he can to help the prisoner repay.
> And in that duty, the prisoner is seen to be no lonely
> or isolated figure – no second-class human being. For
> repayment is the task of all.

The Idea of Punishment was Longford's attempt to understand his developing apostolate over prisons and its connection with his Christian beliefs. It formed part of a deepening and wide-ranging commitment to all areas of penal reform. He was always ready to make a contribution to any issue that touched on his central concern. Through his old friend Victor Gollancz, for example, he became involved in the campaign for the abolition of capital punishment. Gollancz's pamphlet, written with Arthur Koestler in 1955, *Capital Punishment: The Heart of the Matter*, was part of the mounting pressure for reform. Longford, though in favour of punishment, was a determined opponent of hanging – a view only confirmed by his dealings with Christopher Craig and his co-defendant Derek Bentley. Longford spoke for Gollancz's National Campaign for the Abolition of Capital Punishment and took part – on the losing side – in debates in the House of Lords on the subject in 1956 and 1957 when the peers blocked attempts by the Commons to abolish the death penalty. It was to be under his leadership that the Lords gave its assent to the measure in 1965.

Thirteen

The reluctant earl

We had both looked upon Hugh as our ideal
leader: an orator since his 'Fight, fight and fight
again' speech, every inch a Labour democrat and
known to us through an intimate friendship of
over thirty years

Elizabeth Longford on Hugh Gaitskell[1]

The period between the Labour Party's electoral defeat in 1959
and Hugh Gaitskell's early death in 1963 was one of the most
bitter and stormy in its history. Over unilateral disarmament,
membership of the Common Market and the relationship
between public and private ownership, it was deeply divided.
Hugh Gaitskell was defeated at the annual conference in 1960
over nuclear weapons and soon afterwards faced a leadership
challenge from Harold Wilson, seen by those on the left as
the successor to Aneurin Bevan who had died in July of that
year.

Conflict brought out the best in Gaitskell as he battled to save
his party from collapsing into factions after three successive
defeats at the polls. Hitherto he had failed to convince the
electorate and many of his colleagues that he was at all remarkable. His public oratory had never matched a private eloquence
that had brought tears to the eyes of Marjorie Durbin when
Gaitskell, as a young don, described the sufferings of the working
class during the Industrial Revolution.[2] Aneurin Bevan's famous
jibe about 'the desiccated calculating machine' had stuck.[3] Yet
in these tumultuous years from 1959 to 1963 Gaitskell's passion
and determination, well known to close friends like Longford,
to fight for his beliefs and his party moved even his staunchest

opponents. He successfully reversed the 1960 set-back at the annual conference the following year and put a renewed and united Labour Party, committed to social democracy and a more equal and just society, on course for an eventual victory at the polls in 1964.

Gaitskell was in effect struggling to adapt the Labour Party to the changing economic and social conditions which had transformed post-war Britain, many of them set in motion by the reforms instigated by Attlee's governments. Improvements in the standard of living of the working class had in particular eroded Labour's solid electoral base. People who had moved out of the urban ghettos were no longer so ready to identify themselves as working class. The old rallying cries of nationalisation and full employment had been annexed by the Conservatives during their long spell in office. Tony Crosland, one of Gaitskell's closest supporters, argued for a complete overhaul of the party ideology in his book, *The Future of Socialism*. 'The much-thumbed guide-books of the past must now be thrown away.'[4] Douglas Jay, another prominent Gaitskellite, took matters a stage further in an article in the magazine *Forward* in 1959 where he advocated that Labour should change its name to represent a new image.

Over the issues that split the party in these four years, Longford was a passionate 'Gaitskellite'. After Gaitskell's defeat on the nuclear issue at the 1960 conference Longford was one of the prominent supporters of the Campaign for Democratic Socialism. Set up by the Labour leader's backers, the campaign aimed to rally the party behind his reform programme, especially the urgent task of overturning the unilateral resolution. Longford shared his leader's belief that for Britain to abandon all nuclear capacity, however linked with the Americans, would be to abdicate any role in the post-war settlement of which Bevin had been one of the principal architects. Longford's attachment to the Atlantic Alliance, first forcefully stated during his time in Germany and reinforced by his anti-Communism, was no less passionate that Gaitskell's. His daughter Judith likens her father's relationship with the American president to his devotion to the Pope.

These two seem to be the authority figures in his life.
It is as if he is saying, 'I'll be a maverick, I'll be a rebel,
I'll never tie my shoelaces, but two people I'm always
going to support are the Pope and the President of the
United States who ensures peace in our time.'[5]

Yet, as a Christian, Longford was deeply troubled by the destructive capacity of nuclear weapons. Long-standing colleagues like Canon Collins of Christian Action were in the forefront of CND protests at Aldermaston. Longford attempted to square the circle by advocating, somewhat idealistically, a world government equipped with an international peace force that would eliminate the need for weapons of mass destruction. His argument was then that the nuclear deterrent was a temporary expedient which could be negotiated away. He was immensely impressed by bodies like the United Nations, though he failed to address its inability to break out of the limbo imposed by the Soviet-American rivalry on the Security Council. Habitually the initiator, the academic looking beyond what was politically possible, he was constantly scattering the seeds of reform, some of which were inspired, fired others and became crusades, and some of which were unrealisable pipe dreams.

Over nationalisation and the commitment to public ownership enshrined in Clause Four of the party's constitution, Longford was a firm Gaitskellite, endorsing his old friend's conviction that, after three successive defeats, Labour had to modernise and adapt itself to a mixed economy. The promise of widespread further nationalisation had, many Labour supporters believed, frightened off the electorate as early as 1951. Equally the state control of a range of basic industries between 1945 and 1951 had not subsequently provided the cure for capitalism's cycle of boom and bust that Labour had believed it would when first advocating public ownership. While continuing to acknowledge that there was a role for nationalisation and for its expansion, Gaitskell, aware of the need to convince a sceptical electorate, was attempting to redefine its status in the Labour programme. It would continue to be an important part of Labour's ideology, but not the only, nor indeed the crucial, part.

He stressed instead Labour's commitment to certain moral values to which equality and fraternity were central and public ownership subordinate, an instrument not a goal. Longford, whose socialism sprang out of a belief in the fundamental equality of all men, and whose Catholicism had only served to strengthen his belief in the moral mission of politicians, heartily subscribed to Gaitskell's reforming zeal in this area. It had, after all, been his doubts as to the economic efficacy of Labour's programme that had delayed his joining the party back in the 1930s.

Of the major issues in this period it was only over the Common Market that Longford differed from Gaitskell. Their disagreement came in 1962 after the Labour leader had earned a standing ovation at the annual conference at Brighton by revealing for the first time on a public platform his rejection in principle, if not in practice, of membership of a European Community. Unable to catch the chairman's eye during the conference debate, Longford took issue with the Gaitskell line in a newspaper article the following weekend. 'Never had Hugh Gaitskell risen to such oratorical heights. But for many of us who listened it was a heart-breaking experience,' he wrote in the *Sunday Pictorial*. He was later to record his own preference for George Brown's ardently pro-Europe speech which immediately followed Gaitskell's rousing address.

Longford was enthusiastic about the European vision, inspired by his own experience of the rebuilding of Germany and his friendship with Konrad Adenauer, one of the most fervent backers of closer economic co-operation between the European nations. A united Europe would be the first step on the path to Longford's dream of a world government. The framework of a European Community would provide an excellent structure, Longford felt, within which to resolve the Anglo-Irish impasse over Northern Ireland, an abiding concern. Another element in Longford's pro-Common Market views was his Catholicism. His old Oxford friend Douglas Jay, an ardent opponent of the European Community wrote:

> I felt no disillusion towards Frank Longford as a pro-
> Marketeer. He was a devout Catholic and I noticed

that to many such the Common Market tended to be
equated with Christendom and Eastern Europe with
the anti-Christ.[6]

Their differences over the Common Market did not come
betwen Longford and Gaitskell – or indeed between Longford
and Jay. Longford does not let political matters interfere with
friendship. Yet neither did he allow his friends to think that his
views were passing fancies. They took him seriously.

Longford's friendship with Gaitskell was intensely personal,
dating back to the days when they had shared digs at Oxford
and both fallen for Elizabeth Harman. Gaitskell often referred to
Longford as 'my oldest friend'. Other senior Labour figures –
Jay or Crosland for example – may have been his closest friends
in political terms. But Longford and Gaitskell, along with Evan
Durbin before his death in 1948, had all gone forward from New
College to become young activists in the pre-war Labour movement, and rising stars in Attlee's government.

Once in government Longford initially leapt ahead because of
the dearth of Labour peers in the Lords. Yet when Gaitskell
became Chancellor of the Exchequer in 1950, he eclipsed all the
hopefuls of his generation. That early rivalry at Oxford, both
aiming for a first in Modern Greats, Gaitskell catching their
tutor's eye, but Longford in the end getting the better degree,
never quite evaporated, but by the late 1950s Longford knew
that any hopes he had of holding office in a future Labour
government rested mainly on Gaitskell's esteem.

This realisation did not, however, make him sycophantic.
Longford would occasionally offer Gaitskell amicable advice
when he felt that the latter's tendency to be autocratic was
leaving him exposed. During the battle over Labour's defence
policy, Longford wrote to Gaitskell in June 1960 warning him
of the danger of becoming isolated.

> I am convinced that you are . . . infinitely the best
> leader available . . . But . . . your leadership is in real
> jeopardy . . . I find a widespread conviction that you
> expect loyalty without providing the opportunity of

> consultation which your leading followers might
> reasonably expect . . . particularly some who are
> younger rather than older than you and me and who
> are somewhere near the middle of the road.[7]

Here was the brotherly advice of one whose loyalty to Gaitskell transcended politics.

It was a mark of Gaitskell's respect for Longford's opinions that, on receiving the letter, he rang him at once and arranged a meeting that afternoon. He did not always take Longford's advice to heart. The latter's plea in an *Observer* article prior to the 1961 conference that Gaitskell should pay heed to Frank Cousins, the leader of the Transport and General Workers Union and a convinced unilateralist, was ignored (though later a partial *rapprochement* with Cousins was effected for which Longford received some of the credit).

Lloyd George once said that 'there's no friendship at the top' and Gaitskell's rise to the leadership of the Labour Party inevitably affected his friendship with Longford.

> Complete friendship involves complete equality,
> [Longford was to write after Gaitskell's death] but a
> leader cannot be equal with his followers or 'col-
> leagues', and in one particular way, he is specially cut
> off from them. He more than anyone else alive is in a
> position to influence their fortunes, and they and
> their wives would not be human if those fortunes
> were not their active concern. The friends of the
> leader may be the most altruistic of men, yet it would
> be so much easier to plan their lives effectively, and
> maximise their contribution, if only they knew what
> he thought about them, and intended for them. Yet
> the burning topic cannot be discussed.[8]

That Gaitskell and his wife Dora regarded Frank and Elizabeth Longford as dear friends is in no doubt. The four met regularly. Dora would occasionally consult Longford on prison matters and got involved in the campaign for reform. In later life they would meet at the House of Lords. Gaitskell himself hurried away from a rally at the Royal Albert Hall at the time of the Suez crisis to propose the toast at the Longfords' silver wedding anniversary party on 8 November 1956. But what political plans he had for his old friend were never made clear.

Longford felt that his acceptance of a peerage in 1945 had created a certain distance between them. Gaitskell had no time at all for the House of Lords and while he talked with Longford of the leadership of the Upper Chamber in a future Labour Cabinet, he was adamant that a peer could not hold a major ministry in a socialist government. Indeed, in 1958, when he agreed to Conservative plans to introduce life peerages in the face of vocal opposition from those like Jennie Lee who wanted the Lords abolished at once, he emphasised that election to the Commons was a prerequisite for entry into a Labour Cabinet except in the cases of the Lord Chancellor and Leader of the Upper Chamber.

Gaitskell's dismissal of the Lords occasionally irritated his old friend. In his diary Richard Crossman records a dinner conversation with the Longfords after a World Government rally in Brighton in February 1961.

> As we talked, it became clear that Frank's experience was the same as the rest of us. He just couldn't take Hugh's inability ever to thank him or to show any appreciation for what he has been doing. 'I know that the House of Lords doesn't matter, but it would have been nice if Hugh could, once even, be aware that I have been opening debates there for him for three years.'[9]

After Gaitskell's election in 1955, Longford would now and again touch obliquely on the subject of his own political future. Twice in the early days of ITV, he had been invited to join syndicates that were applying for the various regional franchises. On each occasion he consulted Gaitskell who advised him against accepting on the grounds that a future Labour government might want to reconsider the whole question of commercial television. Longford took his point and declined the invitation.

While he was part of Gaitskell's inner circle of friends, a place where politics was the only topic of conversation, Longford remained outside the heart of the Labour Party organisation throughout the 1950s and early 1960s. He had a full-time job and even attendance at the annual party conference meant rushing to and from the City to balance both his roles, taking part in a debate in the afternoon and dining at the Mansion House in the evening. Chairmanship of the National Bank precluded him from aspiring to the leadership of the Labour peers and the Shadow Cabinet seat that went with it.

Longford was regarded by most colleagues in the Commons as amiable, even colourful, but his past record and his current position in the City left him at best semi-detached. Though it would anyway have been a laborious task to aim for a seat on the National Executive Committee, Longford would not have even contemplated such a move given his antipathy towards fighting his corner within the internal forums of the Labour movement. Never a party politician in the narrow sense, he was reluctant to get involved in the day-to-day battles at Transport House.

Besides occasional contributions to the press on the direction of party policy and speaking in favour of candidates around election time, Longford languished in the Lords, where he lacked any following in the party. The speeches he made were never heard by his fellow party members in the Commons. Though he often spoke for his party on matters of great domestic and international importance, there were often even no Labour peers to back his stance. In 1956, for example, he wound up the Opposition's attack on the Conservative government's handling of the Suez crisis and its disregard of the United Nations, countering Alec Douglas-Home's sterling defence. Longford concluded his speech with great aplomb: 'Everyone on these benches feels as strongly as I do.' When he turned he realised that there was no one on them.[10]

Labour's tenuous numerical position in the Lords began to improve only in 1958 with the introduction of life peerages. In opposition in the 1950s, Longford became increasingly aware of the isolating effect of his decision in 1945 to accept Attlee's offer of a peerage. Regretting that decision was futile. He channelled his surplus energies elsewhere – at the National Bank and over prison reform – convinced that there was no way he could put the clock back.

However, when Anthony Wedgwood-Benn, the son and heir of one of his fellow Labour peers, Viscount Stansgate, began his determined and high-profile campaign to allow members of the Upper Chamber to disclaim their titles and thereby (in his case) hold a seat in the House of Commons, a door was opened for Longford that he had thought closed for ever. Benn won his battle in 1963 when the Peerage Act, shaped by a joint committee of both Houses, was passed.

Benn's campaign offered Longford the chance to contemplate once more a career in the Commons where he hoped his claim to a department of state in any future Labour Cabinet under his friend Gaitskell would be much stronger than it had been from the Lords. His dream was to be Home Secretary and to overhaul the Prisons Department. It was an ambition that caused amusement to some of his friends. Evelyn Waugh, caustic as ever, wrote to Ann Fleming that if Longford ever got the Home Office 'we should all be murdered in our beds by sexual maniacs'.[11]

Elizabeth, who had always had doubts about the wisdom of their joint decision in 1945, was enthusiastic about her husband's suggestion of renouncing his peerage. There were difficulties, though. There was the question of finding a seat. More immediately the National Bank, and the comfort of a chairman's salary, would have to be renounced to permit a return to full-time politics. After seven years Longford had exhausted his interest in the City. No one could claim he had not lived up to his promise to Cooke to leave his mark and he had already identified a worthy successor with the right credentials for the National and its Anglo-Irish ward.

The major obstacle to such a scheme, however, was that the proposals being drawn up as a result of Tony Benn's campaign did not include first creations, only inherited titles. They did not, in short, allow those, like Longford, who had accepted a peerage, then to renounce it within their lifetime. Longford's own situation was complicated by the fact that in February 1961 he had inheritcd a title as well. His elder brother Edward, the sixth Earl of Longford, had died suddenly and unexpectedly. Though it was an Irish earldom, Edward had a seat in the Lords – which he had never occupied – as Baron Silchester, the English title given to the Pakenhams in 1821. The planned legislation would allow Longford to renounce his right to that title but not to his own barony of Cowley, created by Attlee in 1945. If he was to get into the Commons, it would mean fighting for an amendment to the bill and that, Longford calculated, would require the support of Gaitskell.

The Labour leader had written to Longford at the time of Edward's death expressing his sympathy. The loss of his brother had come as a shock to Longford. Edward had made his life in Ireland at Tully Nally, running the Gate Theatre and earning such widespread respect that he was appointed a senator in the upper house of the Irish Parliament. When he died, there was a minute's silence in Dublin's theatres.

However, the two brothers were not close and contact had been sporadic.[12]

The gulf between them did not stop Longford admiring his brother's achievements and being anxious that they should be given due reverence in the English press. Evelyn Waugh describes a meeting with Longford soon after Edward had died. '[Longford] spent the previous evening telephoning everyone he knew seeking publicity for Edward. Pansy, when told he fell dead at the luncheon table, remarked, "Just like Charles Dickens".'[13] John Betjeman, who had remained a close friend of Edward since the summer house party at Tully Nally in 1930, paid tribute to him in a newspaper obituary as 'a man of brilliance, integrity, many interests, a warm heart and great generosity'.[14]

Though Longford had known for many years that he would one day inherit his childless brother's title, he had always assumed that it would be in old age. Edward's death at fifty-eight was unexpected. Though his youthful good looks had

14 Hugh and Dora Gaitskell in 1950. The Labour leader and Longford shared digs in Oxford, when Gaitskell had also proposed to Elizabeth. The two couples went on to become firm friends. Both men were rising stars in the Attlee government. Longford's political ambitions were dashed by the tragic death of Gaitskell in 1963.

15 The Longford children in the garden of their Hampstead home c. 1950. *From left*: Judith, Antonia, Catherine, Rachel, Kevin, Paddy, Michael and Thomas.

16 Longford at Bernhurst on Christmas Day, 1959. His daughter Antonia remarks: 'A typically ambivalent expression to family festivities.'

17 The Leader of the
House of Lords and
his Prime Minister:
Longford and Harold
Wilson at the
wedding of Rachel to
Kevin Billington in
1967.

18 'Lord Porn': the Marc cartoon inspired by Longford's celebrated trip to Copenhagen's red-light district, part of his private commission of inquiry into pornography in 1971.

19 Friend of the friendless: Longford played host in London to the disgraced former American President Richard Nixon in 1978.

20 The Longford family today:
(*standing from the left*) Paddy, who
qualified as a barrister; Michael,
British ambassador to Luxemburg;
Kevin, who works in the City;
Antonia, award-winning historian;
and Thomas, another award-
winning historian (*seated from the
left*) Judith, poet and campaigner;
Elizabeth, Frank and Rachel,
novelist and children's writer.

21 Supporter of good
causes: Longford with
Fr Mark Elvins at a
centre for the
homeless in Brighton.

22 Elizabeth with a
view of Bernhurst.

23 Frank with one of his great-grandchildren.
Philip Howard once wrote in *The Times*: 'Longford
needs an *apologia pro vita sua* less than most . . . His
monuments stand and sit all around him.'

disappeared as he grew fatter and fatter – estimates of his weight vary between 24 and 34 stone – he had appeared to carry it off without any attendant health problems before the stroke that took his life.

> There was never any suggestion that my father
> thought that his brother would die early [says Thomas
> Pakenham]. He had never been ill. It seemed indeed
> that he had the secret of perpetual life and had lived
> for twenty years as this grotesque shape, a human
> sphere. He was so fat that if he leant right over
> backwards, he could roll forwards along the ground.[15]

Thinking that he would not be the seventh earl until he was past caring, and uninterested in any practical sense in Tully Nally, Longford had signed over all of his inheritance, save the title which he could not dispense with so easily, to his eldest son Thomas in 1959. Edward's passion for the Gate Theatre and the endless need to subsidise it had left the family coffers almost empty, but with Thomas the beneficiary Longford was able to tell reporters in 1961, anxious to discover if he was suddenly a wealthy man, 'I haven't got sixpence to my name.'

But he did have the title. His staff at the National Bank report that he found it very hard at first to adjust to being Lord Longford. When people would call asking for him by his new name, he would look puzzled for an instant before realising that they meant him. Elizabeth decided to publish under Longford rather than Pakenham. 'I had by no means made the name so famous that I must cling on to it; besides Longford had fewer letters and was easier to pronounce correctly.'[16] As Longford was now an earl, his daughters received the courtesy title Lady.

Besides the change of name, though, Edward's death had little practical effect on Longford. When he went to talk to Gaitskell in the spring of 1962 about his idea of renouncing his peerage, the Labour leader was at first taken aback at just how lightly he regarded it. 'But do you mean that you wouldn't mind giving up your title?' Gaitskell asked. 'I told him', Longford recalls, 'that I wouldn't mind at all. I honestly think that that surprised

311

and pleased him. He seemed to have thought that it would have seemed a real sacrifice; that that kind of honour mattered to me, perhaps for family reasons.'[17]

While Longford is proud of his Pakenham heritage, and in particular of his Irish roots, he was anxious at that moment to relaunch the political career in the Commons that he had dreamt of throughout the late 1930s and early 1940s. Even though he was in his mid-fifties, it was not too late to build the New Jerusalem and, with Gaitskell at the helm, he felt inspired by the vision of a revitalised Labour Party with a renewed sense of mission. Next to the prospect of claiming a major department of state in a reforming socialist government, there was no sacrifice in renouncing a title that he had inherited by default.

In the face of Longford's determination, Gaitskell was at first evasive. When Longford broached the subject of his being in the Commons, Gaitskell avoided making any commitment. (It may have been that he was aware of Longford's ambitions to be Home Secretary. Gaitskell was a close friend of Ann Fleming to whom Waugh had written ridiculing Longford's aspirations.) The Labour leader needed time to think. He had not been at all enthusiastic about Benn's campaign from the start, seeing it as irrelevant to the electorate. Even when persuaded to join cross-party talks on the issue, he remained suspicious that the Conservatives were trying to use the issue to bolster the powers of the Lords where they had an in-built majority.

Longford and Gaitskell remained amicable. There were various references to the matter when the two met in the ensuing months, but nothing was promised. By December, however, when the Longfords had dinner with the Gaitskells, the Labour leader spoke in enthusiastic terms to his old friend about the chance of adding an amendment to the Peerage Bill then going through Parliament.[18]

Gaitskell had used the intervening period to put Longford to the test on a delicate task. His vote of confidence at the December dinner indicated that he felt the assignment had been successfully carried out. At Gaitskell's request Longford had taken on the chairmanship of an all-party committee looking into London's government. It was set up, under Gaitskell's patronage, at a time when the Conservative administration had announced unpopular plans to reorganise the old Inner London Council. Though Gaitskell had told Longford that the members of the committee had specifically asked for him as chairman (Longford, with his background in local politics in Oxford and in social services via the New Bridge, accepted his words at face value) it was rather that Gaitskell had foisted his old friend on the group. The inquiry itself had failed to deflect the Tories, but the members were won over by their chairman and finally paid handsome tribute to him.

The London government inquiry was just one part of Longford's growing burden of extra-curricular activities as he prepared to return to politics full time. After seven years of trying – though not always succeeding – to avoid the limelight as a bank chairman, he took on a wide range of high-profile appointments. Since July of the previous year he had led, with Douglas Jay, a unit trust which aimed to attract trade union money into industry. Drawing on the knowledge Longford had gained in the City, and designed to promote greater partnership between workers and management, the unit trust invited 180 trade unions to take stakes in industry.

In a similar vein, in June 1962 Longford became deputy chairman of a Wider Share Ownership Council, again trying to break down the barriers between different sectors in industry – though this later venture was a cross-party initiative with Maurice Macmillan, the Prime Minister's son, in the chair. In March 1963 Longford joined his fellow Catholic Leonard Cheshire and the actor Peter Ustinov in sponsoring a call to 5000 young Britons to volunteer to join a world police force, part of a continuing interest in the notion of world government.

Without knowing Gaitskell's final verdict on his hopes of re-entering the Commons, Longford boldly announced his resignation as chairman of the National Bank in July 1962. He would be serving several months' notice and would not be free until the start of 1963. His successor was to be Sir Ivone Kirkpatrick, chairman of the Independent Television Authority. Kirkpatrick, a former permanent under-secretary at the Foreign Office, shared Longford's Anglo-Irish background and had stayed in close contact with home and friends in Ireland while working for the British government.

In the *Evening News* Longford described his return to full-time political life as 'making my small but uninhibited contribution' to the Labour Party.[19] He refused to be drawn on his hopes for high office in a future Labour Cabinet.

He had needed to break his link with the bank before he could start campaigning for the necessary amendment to the Peerage Bill and selling himself to constituency parties as a potential Labour candidate for the House of Commons. While his work at the National had left him space for regular forays into the Lords, to aim for the Commons while still chairman would be to compromise his position, Longford readily recognised. With his political pulse now beating fast, Longford viewed his release from the bank chairmanship with a mixture of regret and relief. Eight years was the longest continuous period he had held one job. Given his tendency towards restlessness, the duration was quite an achievement for Longford as he acknowledged in his remark: 'I had a feeling that if I stayed much longer at the bank I should have shot my bolt.'[20]

He regretted leaving behind employees for whom he felt a genuine affection. They had become like an extended family. As well as the scroll from the Irish staff, he also received as a parting gift a shiny red Mini and a course of driving lessons. His lack of co-ordination and general mechanical ineptitude were to triumph over any will to learn. After two sessions and an unhappy experience around Sloane Square in central London he handed over the rest of his lessons to his daughter Judith and promised to try again later. After another unfortunate attempt on the drive at Bernhurst with his son Kevin, where the Mini ended up embedded in an apple tree, he gave up entirely. Driving remains Elizabeth's preserve in their mutually-agreed division of responsibilities.

With Gaitskell's new-found confidence in Longford, evident in his gift of the chairmanship of the London government inquiry and his positive words at the dinner party of 7 December 1962, Longford had good reason to look forward to 1963. In the course of the evening, Gaitskell had mentioned feeling unwell because of an illness that he had picked up on a trip to Paris. He had been showing signs of strain for some months and in June had blacked out during a television recording. But none of his close circle were unduly alarmed. Indeed Longford's impression was that the Labour leader was on good form that evening.

It proved to be the last dinner party the Gaitskells gave at their home in Hampstead's Frognal Gardens. On 14 December, Gaitskell was admitted to Manor House, the trade union hospital at Golders Green, with 'flu. Tests proved inconclusive and he had discharged himself by Christmas and was talking enthusiastically about his planned trip to Russia in the New Year. However, he was back in hospital in January and died several days later at the age of fifty-six, victim of a rare immunological disease.

> To those who had worked closely with Gaitskell the
> loss went deep [writes his biographer Philip Williams],
> like the unexpected and premature death of a parent.
> For a generation of politically-minded progressive
> people – teachers, journalists, trade unionists, civil
> servants – an inspiration went out of public life.

Even among his opponents there was obvious grief. Harold Macmillan moved the adjournment of the House of Commons on hearing the news – the first and so far only time such a mark of respect has been made for an Opposition leader who had never been Prime Minister.

Both the Longfords were deeply saddened by the loss of one of their oldest, dearest and most loyal friends. The suddenness of his death was a reminder of their own mortality. Later Longford reflected that he missed Gaitskell more, not less, as time went by. Losing Gaitskell was like losing a brother – his death affected Longford more than Edward's had done. Despite having a very large circle of friends, only a handful of people have had an enduring significance in Longford's life. Elizabeth is at its centre, unrivalled. Then there are his children and a small group of intimate friends, like Gaitskell and David Astor, most of whom he has known since his youth, and with whom

he can relax and talk openly. Finally there is his vast array of
social contacts, people for whom the warm-hearted Longford
feels a great affection but from whom he withholds himself to a
certain degree. In front of these he adopts a mask of eccentricity
and distraction, asking questions rather than answering them,
and revelling in amusing and self-deprecating stories that,
according to his children, become more exaggerated with each
retelling.

Longford was full of praise for Gaitskell in the tributes he
wrote. 'He had left the Party more united than at any time since
1945–7, poised and prepared for victory, a Moses on the verge
of the promised land.' In the *Observer*, his article described his
old friend as 'Mr Valiant for Truth'. Gaitskell was, Longford later
wrote, 'the embodiment of principle in politics. Anyone who
sees an old film of him speaking about Suez will feel that
something went out of British politics with his death and never
returned.'[21]

The future for most Gaitskellites without their leader
obviously depended very much on the next leader. For Longford, however, the personal loss of Gaitskell was matched by the
blow that his death dealt in career terms. Of all his closest
friends and confidants in the party from the time of his conversion, Evan Durbin and Hugh Gaitskell were irreplaceable. On
every significant decision in his career, he had turned to them
for advice. Now they had both gone. Longford was without an
influential supporter in Labour circles, though he had many
friends. Just as he had been re-entering the political battle
alongside Gaitskell, his general had been carried off. In political
terms, it was a loss from which he never recovered.

Gaitskell took with him to the grave whatever plans he had
for Longford in a future Labour Cabinet. Those close to the
Labour leader are divided as to what may have been in his mind.

> I think Hugh was very loyal to Frank [says Denis
> Healey] and had he lived I think Frank would have
> had a larger role than he eventually did. Hugh was
> not only loyal to his friends, but he listened to them.[22]

Douglas Jay is less sure.

> Hugh would have admired Frank's qualities but he
> lacked Hugh's political judgement, his knowledge of
> personalities. He had been a part-timer out of office
> and would have been debarred by membership of the
> House of Lords from the highest offices.[23]

Though Jay was one of Gaitskell's inner circle, he does not recall discussing with his leader the subject of Longford disclaiming his peerage, which raises the question of how committed Gaitskell was to the plan in the first place.

As a peer Longford did not have a vote in the ballot to choose Gaitskell's successor. There was no natural heir among his supporters. Tony Crosland and Denis Healey were too young. Douglas Jay and Patrick Gordon Walker had no strong following. George Brown, Gaitskell's deputy, was the obvious candidate. Yet he had never been a Gaitskellite either in spirit (he had, on many occasions, expressed his disdain for socialist intellectuals) or on various policy issues, most notably over Europe. To Crosland Brown was a 'neurotic drunk' and he was one of those who persuaded James Callaghan to stand as an alternative candidate on the right. Of the two Longford preferred George Brown, if only for his ardent Europeanism but was, according to Crossman, 'lukewarm' and would have been happy to see either in charge.[24]

The centre and left – including Elizabeth Longford, habitually more radical than her husband – rallied behind Harold Wilson who, since his 1960 quarrel with Gaitskell, had moderated his own stance while still maintaining a radical veneer. Longford and the Gaitskellites saw Wilson as an opportunist seeking to seize the legacy of a man of principle. Crosland described a Brown-Wilson contest as choosing between a drunk and a crook. Christopher Mayhew, Longford's old student, summed up the distaste of many on the right of the Labour Party for Wilson.

> Politicians tend to be either 'be-ers' or 'do-ers'. That is
> to say, some of them want to *be* something – a

> Minister or a peer, or a Whip, or a social success; and
> some want to *do* something – to abolish nuclear
> weapons, or unify Europe, or reform the electoral
> system . . . Gaitskell was a single-minded 'doer' and
> Wilson a single-minded 'be-er'. Gaitskell was commit-
> ted to social democracy and the Atlantic Alliance.
> Wilson – witness the famous photograph of the short-
> trousered schoolboy in Downing Street – was commit-
> ted to taking up residence at No 10 and staying there
> as long as possible.[25]

Though they had been acquaintances for years and neighbours
in Hampstead where their children used to play together, Wilson
and Longford were not close. Their lives had intersected at
several stages – they were both young dons at Oxford, and
Longford had replaced Wilson as Beveridge's right-hand man.
Yet while Longford was at the heart of the Oxford Labour Party
in the late 1930s, Wilson had scarcely taken part. Though he
lived in Hampstead, Wilson was not a regular visitor at the
Gaitskells' home. Indeed jokes about the Wilsons were part of
the entertainment there. Kenneth Younger, a Wykehamist like
Gaitskell, would perform a satirical song about Wilson. Longford
usually puts Wilson's social isolation in Hampstead down to the
fact that he came from a younger generation than most of the
Gaitskellites, and to his distaste for dinner parties. But he
admitted to Wilson's biographer that 'the Gaitskellites were not
very nice about Wilson. He was felt to be an upstart. Socially he
was from a different class.'[26]

Reporting on Wilson's speech on science and the future of
socialism at the Scarborough conference, Longford emphasised
the social gap between them.

> The faithful son of an industrial chemist from Hudders-
> field, he would feel that kind of future in his bones,
> while some of us Old Etonians and Old Wykehamists
> from the South of England could think it out best with
> our minds.[27]

In political, as well as social, terms Wilson and Longford were poles apart, with Wilson's earlier role as Aneurin Bevan's protégé – Dalton once called him 'Nye's little dog' – enough to make him suspect. Longford's principal reservation over Wilson concerned his vacillation over the Atlantic Alliance. (This particular worry was, however, quickly laid to rest after Wilson's election when he retained Patrick Gordon Walker, a committed Atlanticist, as Shadow Foreign Secretary.)

In the ballot of Labour MPs, the division in the right allowed Wilson to pose as a unity candidate and see off Callaghan in the first round and Brown in the second. Having already publicly announced that he was leaving the bank and re-entering politics full time, Longford had no choice but to attempt to work with the new leader. But the influence he had previously enjoyed was lost. If Wilson was suspicious of the social snobbery of the Gaitskellites, he was hardly likely to go out of his way to help an hereditary peer in their midst. He agreed to back Longford's attempts to amend the Peerage Bill, but with little enthusiasm. Any role he envisaged for him would centre on the Lords. Dingle Foot moved the amendment but, with no signal from the Labour leadership, it was soundly defeated. Frank Pakenham was never to reappear.

Stoically accepting his life sentence in the Lords, Longford was swept up in a flurry of activity in the spring and summer of 1963. From the Opposition front bench he was leading economic and education debates, and tackling issues such as racial discrimination, women in industry and the press. Yet all the shortcomings in terms of influence of being a member of the Upper Chamber remained and with Wilson rather than Gaitskell at the head of the party Longford was even more out on a limb. His mind, restless as ever, turned to other interests to fill the available time and absorb his energy.

He wrote a second volume of autobiography, published in April 1964 by Hutchinson. Originally Harold Harris of Hutchinson had wanted Longford to write on the narrower subject of being a socialist in the City. But Longford ended up expanding the original proposal to take up the story from *Born to Believe* and the fall of the Attlee government in 1951. Its title, *Five Lives*, reflected the many facets of Longford's work. Accounts of his work at the bank, with prisoners, in the Lords, and latterly alongside Hugh Gaitskell, were interspersed with two 'interludes' on Ireland and in praise of Elizabeth's talent, and capped by an epilogue by his daughter Judith on Longford as a father, his fifth life.

The book was hastily assembled, a collection of thoughts without a strong narrative line. His secretary at the time, Angela Lambert, later herself a distinguished journalist, recalled:

> He wrote in his usual terribly undisciplined and
> random fashion, whereby he'd think about it over the
> weekend and occasionally jot down a few notes and
> then dictate quite fast something which really should
> have been just a working basis but which always went
> straight in verbatim.[28]

Roy Jenkins, many years later, was to reflect on Longford's literary style. While praising the energy, gusto and eclecticism of his writing, Jenkins felt that Longford could be criticised both for a lack of meticulous scholarship and for his prose. 'Subjects are often unceremoniously hauled in by the scruff of their necks and the simple device of beginning the sentence "Incidentally" . . .'[29] This tendency to inconsequentiality and lack of stringency in structure was, Jenkins added, offset by a fulsome generosity in Longford's comments about individuals.

> Compliments come naturally to Lord Longford.
> Almost every book cited is 'impressive', 'invaluable',
> 'brilliant' or 'penetrating' and almost every noble
> family justifies its nobility. There is, however, some-
> times a hint of steel beneath the velvet. He can clothe
> a rebuke in a compliment with unique skill.[30]

In the Longford household Elizabeth was the writer. *Five Lives* appeared to mixed reviews in April 1964. Some of the accusations against *Born to Believe* were echoed: that it was somewhat arrogant of Longford to think that a minister who had not been in the Cabinet, was in mid-career and had been out of office for thirteen years, was interesting enough to justify not one but two excursions into autobiogaphy. Six months later Elizabeth's painstakingly researched *Victoria RI* became an over-night bestseller, was heaped with praise by the critics and went on to win the James Tait Black prize for biography. Longford showed not a trace of jealousy, his daughter Judith recalls. 'He has always supported her work and has never been envious of her success. I never felt that he felt put down in any way by it.'[31]

In *Five Lives* Judith's epilogue caught the attention of the popular press rather more than her father's account of his career to date. Near the day of publication the *Sunday Mirror* ran a full-page article entitled 'My Father – writhing in a belly dance while my mother placidly combed her hair'. It was a precis of Judith's account of her father's early morning efforts to keep fit and slim. Longford's public reputation as an eccentric showed no signs of diminishing.

His large number of friends from all areas of life and every shade of political opinion often brought Longford to the fringes of the great public controversies of the day. The summer of 1963 saw Britain obsessed by the Profumo affair. The involvement of the Conservative Secretary of State for War with a call-girl, Christine Keeler, who was also associated with a naval attaché at the Soviet embassy, blew up in the face of a Conservative government, led by an unpopular and ageing Prime Minister unable to lift Britain's economy out of a slump.

Longford knew several of the key players in the drama that unfolded first in court and then in the pages of every news-paper. Profumo had been introduced to Keeler by Stephen Ward, an osteopath fashionable in London society who rented a country cottage on the Cliveden estate of Bill Astor. Astor's name was linked with that of Mandy Rice-Davies, an associate of Keeler's.

Longford had known Bill Astor since student days and the Bullingdon point-to-point. Though his friendship with Astor's younger brother, David, was closer Longford had continued to visit Cliveden and had been there just before the Profumo scandal broke, demonstrating to Astor's wife, Bronwen, his newly acquired ability to swim. Bronwen Astor recalls that as soon as her husband became embroiled in the controversy, Longford was one of the first to offer help and support to the couple at a time when they were shunned by friends in society and virtual prisoners in their home. He continued to stand by them until Astor's death in 1966 and beyond, supporting his widow in the late 1980s when *Scandal*, a film account of the whole affair, reopened old wounds.[32]

It was not a matter of guilt or innocence that prompted Longford but rather loyalty to friends in trouble. At the time of the release of *Scandal* he took Bronwen Astor to lunch at the House of Lords but seemed not to understand her continuing need to vindicate her late husband's name from any suggestion that he was improperly involved with Mandy Rice-Davies.[33]

Longford knew John Profumo slightly before he became a household name, but was to become a good friend afterwards, exposing himself again to the charge that he deliberately seeks out the notorious, finding a certain glamour in their activities. While the Labour front bench in the House of Commons attacked Profumo over a potential breach of national security, Longford's concern was a moral one. Here was a man brought to his knees by the press and public opinion. While he could not condone Profumo's actions, he could sympathise with him as a sinner in his current predicament. There was the element of public failure which Longford could recognise. Again Longford saw someone whom society and his colleagues could not wait to judge, but whom he was not prepared to condemn or shun.

In the debate on public and private morality his innate Puritanism and his Catholicism made him take a hard line. In principle Longford is intolerant. In his view, those who break their marriage vows show a weakness in character that makes them unfit to hold high office.[34] It is a stance he continues to uphold, however unfashionable it has become. Yet his intolerance of breaches of the moral code do not preclude tolerance and forgiveness of the individual perpetrator. Profumo had acknowledged his sin, taken his punishment and should now be left alone.

A few months after Profumo resigned in June 1963, Longford invited him to lunch – without any publicity. Finding his guest conscience-stricken, blaming only himself and determined to rebuild his life with his wife Valerie, Longford recorded that the meeting left him with 'an irresistible conviction – whatever the past and future may hold for him and me, at this moment he is nearer to the Kingdom of God than I am.'[35] Profumo went on to work with the needy and so impressed was Longford by such dedication that he was later to recommend him – and indulge in some lobbying behind the scenes – for a post at Toynbee Hall, a social centre in the East End of London.

A third figure at the centre of the affair, Stephen Ward, had met Longford briefly during one of his visits to Cliveden. He had even offered to use his professional skills to relieve Longford's fibrositis. Longford, knowing about Ward's work with prostitutes, could not bring himself even to contemplate accepting the offer. The puritan in him left little room at that moment for thoughts of the sin and the sinner, while Ward's evident pleasure in his lifestyle repulsed him. The problem with basing one's approach on the idea of forgiving the sinner and hating the sin is that the sinner has to admit that he has committed a sin in the first place. While Profumo's public penance was complete, Ward was unrepentant.

When the osteopath first appeared before a judge charged with living on immoral earnings, Longford admits that he had a

> half-conscious hope that he would be convicted. He
> seemed to me, even in this extremity, to be challeng-
> ing and defying the conventional morals of society.[36]

However, as the court-room proceedings continued, under the ever-watchful gaze of the press, Longford began to realise the shortcomings of his own formula of sins and sinners when dealing with a human being so obviously in distress. Ward was crucified in the court and abandoned by his friends. Society's hand was at his throat.

After he was found guilty, Longford contacted Ward through his barrister and said that he would like to visit him. He felt that Ward had become the focus for a more general unease about moral standards, and, while he could in no way excuse his actions, he did not want to be part of such a scapegoating. The New Bridge was set up to side with those society shunned and vilified. However extreme Ward's case, Longford felt it his duty to try to help him.

His effort came too late. It was guilt (and his inability to say no to a journalist) that led him to accept ITN's invitation after Ward's suicide to appear and speak about their acquaintance. No one else among the osteopath's erstwhile friends and clients would do it. Longford began by stating his own belief that what Ward had done was wrong and could not be tolerated by society. 'But with him lying dead at our feet how can one fail to ask, "Which of us is qualified to cast the first stone?"'[37]

His experience with Ward, and the penance that he undertook so publicly, taught Longford that however heinous a crime, however much it offended his own code of morals, he could not aspire to act as a Christian if he allowed himself to judge. 'When Jesus said "you were in prison and I came to you", He didn't say "you were in prison and I came to you because you were falsely accused."'[38]

Longford's conduct during the Profumo scandal served once again to emphasise the gap between him and the party leadership. While Wilson worked successfully to make political capital by exploiting the affair to discredit Macmillan and his government, Longford was worrying about the moral well-being of the central players. It was not only over Profumo that Longford's Christianity put him out of step with his party in this period.

The early 1960s saw the start of the Second Vatican Council in Rome, summoned by a reforming Pope, John XXIII, who wanted the Catholic Church to get to grips with the modern age. In April 1963, the Pope published *Pacem in Terris* (*Peace on Earth*). For Longford it signalled a change of heart in the Vatican and in his Church towards socialism, hitherto regarded by clerics throughout Europe with suspicion bordering on positive hostility. The Pope even appeared to be taking a softer line on Communism.

> It must be borne in mind that neither can false philo-
> sophical teachings regarding the nature, origin and
> destiny of the universe and of man be identified with
> historical movements that have economic, social, cul-
> tural and political ends, not even when these move-
> ments have originated from those teachings and have
> drawn and still draw inspiration therefrom.

Or, as Longford took it to mean, Marxism as an atheist philosophy could be distinguished from Communism as an historical
movement which has brought some benefits to ordinary men
and women.

The prospect of a Vatican *rapprochement* with eastern Europe
excited Longford and raised the possibility that the godless
Communism he had grown so to despise might be reformed.
Furthermore the general message of *Pacem in Terris* – that all
men were equal, that the advance of the working class and of
women was a positive development, that fundamental human
rights must everywhere be respected – brought mainstream
Catholicism much more in line with Longford's Christian
socialism.

However, the time-honoured Catholic attitudes to divorce,
contraception, homosexuality and assisted fertilisation changed
little in this reforming period – at least on an official level. When
these matters came up in Labour Party debates and in the House
of Lords, Longford felt obliged as a Christian to state his Church's
beliefs, no matter how discordant they were with those of his
colleagues. Other outspoken Catholics in the Lords at the time,
like Lord Iddesleigh, made their contribution from the cross-
benches. But Longford tried to combine the roles of a Catholic –
and one clearly identified as such in the public eye – and a
Labour politician. When inevitable clashes occurred, it was his
party not his Church that saw itself as compromised.

Longford's daughter Antonia, herself by now in demand as a
Catholic commentator on radio and television but taking a softer

line than her father on moral matters, recalls an argument they
had in the early 1960s over Conservative plans, backed wholeheartedly by Labour, to make contraceptive pills freely available
on the NHS.

> He stuck at nothing in his condemnation of that.
> When I tried to talk about the real world, he wouldn't
> have any of it. I think anytime in politics where the
> doctrine of the Catholic Church pointed one way and
> the doctrine of the Labour Party another, he stuck
> with the Church.

Antonia attributes her father's inflexibility over questions like
contraception to more than a blind adherence to the papal line.

> My father, because he had no sexual experience
> before marriage, and I would go to the stake saying
> has had none other than a very happy married life,
> does find it impossible to understand anything extra-
> marital or pre-marital, the guilts, the hopes, the fears,
> the way the world carries on. It isn't that he's
> uncharitable about it. He just cannot understand.[39]

On another occasion, he spoke out in a House of Lords debate
on artificial insemination by donor.

> There are some of us whose main interest in public
> questions derives from a desire to help the weak, the
> afflicted, the poor, the old and the lonely. This senti-
> ment would seem to place us naturally and easily on
> the side of the childless couples, but whatever we like
> to call our ethics, Aristotelian, Kantian, Utilitarian,
> Humanitarian or simply Christian, we must all be
> aware that immediate happiness, while a laudable
> objective to be promoted by all scientific means, is not
> the highest value here. Grapes cannot be grown from
> thorns or figs from thistles. It is literally impossible to
> help anyone, a childless couple or anybody else, how-
> ever humane our purpose, by evil means.[40]

Such uncompromising talk of evil from a front bench Labour spokesman did not pass unnoticed in his party. As Douglas Jay puts it:

> I always felt that Frank answered to a higher set of
> principles than those of party. There was an element
> of the Edwardian politician about him, above party
> concerns, speaking on principle. But on social issues,
> he was right behind the Labour line. It was on moral
> matters that his Christian principles came into conflict
> with party politics and his principles always won
> out.[41]

One area where Longford's principles were in line with those of his party and where his public reputation might be used to enhance Labour's image was that of penal reform. In the middle of 1963, Wilson invited Longford to chair a committee on the prevention and treatment of crime. As a peer, an academic and a man beyond reproach who wore his Christianity on his sleeve, Longford was the natural choice to chair such a high-minded initiative.

The original idea for Labour's report on crime did not come from Harold Wilson. The suggestion was made by Joan Bourne, a member of the party's research department whose brief was minority issues and who had come to know Longford through her interest in penal reform. She approached her head of department, Peter Shore, who in turn took the proposal to Wilson with Longford's name as chairman included in it.

It was Wilson, however, who seized on the scheme both as a way of occupying Longford and also, more importantly, as demonstrating to the electorate, in the run-up to an election, that Labour took the question of crime prevention and penal reform seriously. Other members of the working-party included Gerald Gardiner, later Lord Chancellor, Alice Bacon and Baroness Serota among eight future ministers. Tom Driberg, a left-wing MP and member of the National Executive, was a late recruit. Though Driberg was an Oxford contemporary and interested in penal reform, Longford was initially opposed to his membership. Driberg was gay and made no secret of the fact, delighting in shocking his colleagues in the House of Commons tea-room with news of his latest conquests. Like Stephen Ward before his downfall, Driberg offended Longford's principles by his unashamed behaviour. However, other members of the working party persuaded Longford for once to compromise his personal principles for the good of the cause. Driberg was an influential figure in party circles and would be a useful ally in advocating that the final report should be adopted as official policy.

The impending election gave the exercise a great sense of urgency. If the report was to shape party policy, it had to be completed in record time. With Joan Bourne as secretary giving direction to the group's deliberations, Longford curbed his natural inclinations to be a lone crusader on the issues involved and instead worked hard to achieve a consensus between his colleagues. Other members of the working party like Baroness Serota were later to pay tribute to him for managing both to enthuse them about radical solutions while at the same time keeping the group on common ground and to schedule.

The resulting report *Crime: A Challenge to Us All* was published on 18 June 1964 and in terms of legislation was the most influential in which Longford was ever involved. It had a profound effect between 1964 and 1970 on the Labour government's policy on law and prison reform in general and in particular on the Criminal Justice Act of 1967 which introduced the parole system. Hitherto there had been discretionary release for some 'model' prisoners before they had completed their sentence. Following the recommendations of the Longford committee, the 1967 Act allowed those who satisfied local and national parole boards to be released with as much as two thirds of their sentence still to run. Longford and his working party felt that the prospect of earning remission would encourage prisoners to change their behaviour and smooth their readmission into society. It was the high point of Longford's attempts to bring a more humane approach to punishment and rehabilitation.

Some of the report's proposals concerning young offenders

(for example the idea of Family Courts) were not implemented, but remain the aim of campaigning organisations to this day. Others quickly passed into law. Its recommendations on the setting up of a Family Service to co-ordinate and centralise all other efforts in that area were to inspire the Labour Cabinet to set up the Seebohm Committee, of which Baroness Serota was also a member. As a result it was legislated in the Children and Young Persons' Act of 1969 that all government work concerning family matters should be carried out in a single department within each local authority.

The report also made the abolition of capital punishment a priority. It was generally accepted on the Labour benches that abolition was a good idea. The fact that the future Labour government in 1964 included so many ministers who had been working on the report accelerated the issue through the Commons voting system.

Some time before the 1964 general election, Harold Wilson had visited the retired party leader, Clement Attlee, now an earl and a member of the Lords, to seek his advice on various appointments if, as looked likely from the polls, Labour should win. When it came to the leadership of the House of Lords, Attlee was in no doubt. 'It must be Frank,' he told Wilson. It was a remark Wilson was later to repeat to Longford when offering him the job. Clement Attlee's patronage, so important in starting off Longford's ministerial career and in sustaining it when he made himself unpopular with other colleagues, proved decisive in securing him a place in the Cabinet.[42]

There were those who felt that Longford had disqualified himself by taking too Catholic a line over various moral matters in the previous months. He himself worried that there were others in the Lords who had a stronger claim, most notably the Shadow Leader, Lord Alexander of Hillsborough, and another senior front bench spokesman, Lord Silkin.

Silkin was in his seventies, a former Minister of Town and Country Planning under Attlee, and a man widely regarded for his intellect in the Lords, but not popular. Lord Alexander was in his eighties when Labour scraped home at the polls on 15 October 1964. On the Tory benches he was known rather unflatteringly as 'Dummy Dreadnought' in honour of his time as a minister at the Admiralty. Though Alexander had problems with his leg that limited his mobility, he was keen to carry on as Leader of the Lords. Wilson had, however, made his own youth, and that of the team around him, an election issue. Talk of a white hot age of technology would sound rather strange on the lips of either a septuagenarian or an octogenarian. The latter's leadership of the Protestant Alliance could, on occasion, make him appear every bit as dogmatic as Longford, notably when he was the sole dissenting voice in an Upper Chamber debate on the Archbishop of Canterbury's 1961 meeting with the Pope.

Though Alexander was disappointed to be passed over by Wilson in 1964, he supported Longford's work in the Upper Chamber. For his part, Longford tried to soften the blow by sharing some of the Labour-leader perks – official cars for example – with his predecessor.

From Wilson's point of view, the advantages of appointing Longford outweighed any problems with disgruntled colleagues. For a start the 1964 Cabinet was exceptionally short on experience of government. Only Wilson himself, James Griffiths and Patrick Gordon Walker had been in a Cabinet. (The latter did not last long as Foreign Secretary after his attempts to re-enter the House having lost his Birmingham seat at the general election ended in catastrophe.) Longford, at the Admiralty, had been 'of Cabinet rank' and possessed in the circumstances a relatively lengthy ministerial track record. Equally with a working majority of only five, Wilson's primary aim was party unity. He therefore wanted to give due recognition in Cabinet ranks to the Gaitskellites.

Denis Healey feels that Wilson had no other choice than to appoint Longford in 1964.

> It is a problem finding a leader in the House of Lords. That's the real point. The House of Lords consists of hereditary peers of whom Frank was one. Then there are people who have lost their seats in the House of Commons and taken a life peerage. They are prepared

to continue to do a job of work in the Lords. But
they're usually fairly junior figures. And then there
are people like me who have been senior Cabinet
ministers and are offered a chance to go to the Lords
but who don't want to do a full week's work there. So
finding a leader of the House of Lords who is prepared
to do the work, be there every day and is competent
and of status, all of which you need, is not easy.[43]

Though Denis Healey may be convinced in retrospect, in 1964
Longford did not feel so confident. When news of Labour's
victory came through on the Friday, he was with Elizabeth at
Bernhurst. Longford recalls his dilemma.

If I did not go up to London and sit about in our
Chelsea flat, awaiting the summons from Downing
Street, how would I ever get appointed at all? On the
other hand, to make my way to London quite gratui-
tously on a Saturday morning would be a humiliating
operation and would, in any case, to be effective,
involve a message to Number Ten, to let them know
where I was.[44]

Quite why Wilson or one of his staff could not have found the
telephone numbers – Longford always lists them in *Who's Who*
– is not clear.

He resolved to go the Chelsea flat where his daughter Antonia,
married to the Conservative minister Sir Hugh Fraser and
expecting a baby, sat with him.

It was an agonising time for him. The telephone did
obviously ring finally – though only by tea-time. He
talked a lot while we waited. At first he was very
confident and talked about wanting to be in the
government. But there were doubts, things he didn't
agree with Wilson over.[45]

331

When he went to Downing Street to accept the leadership of the Lords, Longford knew that he had reached his own glass ceiling in the world of politics. With Gaitskell it might have been different. But as a peer, he knew any hopes of a ministry, much less the Home Secretaryship, was pie in the sky.

Fourteen

The Leader of the House of Lords

Certainly we shall not permit effective action to be frustrated by the hereditary and non-elective Conservative majority in the House of Lords

Labour Party manifesto 1964

To be in the Cabinet had been Longford's aim since he joined the Labour Party in 1936. It was not until 1964 that he made it to the top table, the pinnacle of his political career. Now the dream of a New Jerusalem that had inspired him for almost three decades could be put into effect.

Or so he hoped. Yet the lustre of success in achieving a lifetime's ambition could not disguise the fact that Longford's triumph had come too late. He had tried to convince himself that being in the Cabinet as Leader of the Lords would ensure him a substantial role in shaping legislation and a chance to see some of his cherished notions concerning prisons and social services put into practice by his colleagues. He was quickly disabused. From the outset Longford was on the margins of Wilson's Cabinet, at best an irrelevance to many of the members, and occasionally the butt of their jokes. Though he was not slow in realising his fate, and managed on two occasions to persuade the Prime Minister to give him additional responsibilities, Longford found he had neither the strength nor in the end the will to throw off his designation as the jester at Wilson's court.

Longford had left office in 1951 as a rising star, at the heart of an influential, soon to become dominant, grouping in the

Labour Party. He had enjoyed particular favour with his leader, Attlee, and had grown accustomed to running large if not quite first-rank ministries. By contrast, in 1964, at fifty-nine he was regarded by many in the party as already too old to hold high office. Harold Wilson, at forty-eight the youngest Prime Minister in the twentieth century at the time of his election triumph, made it plain that Cabinet ministers should not expect to last much beyond the age of sixty.[1] Moreover, had Gaitskell lived, Longford would have been an influential figure in the Cabinet, with the ear of the Prime Minister. The two had had much common political ground and a passionate commitment to democratic socialism. With Wilson, there was no such bond and Longford soon grew disillusioned at his Prime Minister's lack of principle. In 1964 he was offered not a ministry, with a team of civil servants to support him and the scope for reform and change, but an administrative post, guiding government legislation through the House of Lords.

The Lords was of no interest to the rest of the Cabinet. 'It made me ineffective,' Longford admits. 'The other twenty-two members saw each other every day in the Commons. There was a fraternity. I saw them only at full meetings of the Cabinet.'[2] His speeches there went unnoticed. He recalls that at one crucial juncture of the dispute with Ian Smith in Rhodesia, soon after the Universal Declaration of Independence in November 1965, it fell to him to make a statement for the government in the Lords before it was announced in the Commons. It was vital that the Upper Chamber gave its consent that evening. Wilson was in the gallery and was evidently impressed by Longford's handling of a matter about which several of the peers on the opposition benches harboured strong feelings. Next day Wilson congratulated Longford in front of the Cabinet on his performance. 'I think it came as a real surprise to him,' Longford commented afterwards.[3]

He was, to a large extent, a victim of his own success in handling the Lords. There was enormous potential for a conflict between a Labour majority in the Commons, brimming with ideas and schemes to put into effect after years out of office, and a Conservative majority in the Lords, able to block that legislation. Longford says now:

> I was never sure how Harold Wilson wanted me to
> play it, whether he would have welcomed a clash
> with the Lords or whether he wanted no trouble from
> them. I took his silence as indicating the second but,
> given his subsequent attitude to me, sometimes won-
> dered if I had misunderstood.[4]

A survey of the House of Lords completed in 1968 showed that 116 Labour peers faced 351 Conservatives, with 41 Liberals and 554 peers who sat as independents on the cross-benches.[5] The Labour front bench team in the Upper Chamber was beleaguered. 'As Leader of the Opposition I had an army behind me,' says Lord Carrington. 'As Leader of the House Frank only had a platoon.'[6]

The non-attendance of many of the hereditary element among the Conservative and cross-bench peers evened matters out. In theory, if Longford and his Chief Whip received the support of most of their colleagues and of an above average number of cross-benchers, they could occasionally inflict a defeat on the Conservatives. Harold Wilson made it a point of policy as Prime Minister to refrain from creating sizeable numbers of Conservative life peers – except when it was unavoidable, namely after the dissolution of Parliament in 1964 and 1966. At the same time, he bolstered the ranks of his own party in the Lords with life peers who were prepared to put in a day's work for their title.

However, even such a determined approach could not alter the fact that, as Leader of the Lords, Longford faced defeat on every bill that he tried to put through the House. With Labour's formidable legislative programme Longford opted to employ skill diplomacy, and often good humour, not to mention winning the co-operation of the Leader of the Opposition, to ensure that the Lords did not become a major constitutional stumbling block.

Carrington feels that in such tricky and potentially explosive circumstances Longford was a shrewd appointment by Wilson and that the policy of cohabitation with the Tory majority was the Prime Minister's intention.

> In a House that was still at that point predominantly hereditary, it was one of the sensible things that Wilson did to make a hereditary peer the Labour Leader. The feeling on our benches was that even if, so to speak, 'the fellow's terribly misguided, a socialist, a Bolshevik or whatever, he's still one of us'. That made a difference.[7]

Another factor, according to Carrington, that qualified Longford for the delicate task ahead was his popularity on all sides of the House.

> Frank is extremely adroit. He's an extremely good debater. And he can be extremely sharp. But it is always saved by a wonderful sense of fun and humour. Except on very rare occasions when we got under his skin and prompted him to bite back, he always responded in great good humour with a joke, a laugh or a quip that was never personally wounding. As a result he was enormously popular in the House even among those who did not agree with his politics.[8]

While other members of the Cabinet were engaged in an often bitter party political struggle on the floor of the House of Commons, the composition, history and anomalous constitutional position of the Lords meant that Longford, as Labour Leader, had to proceed along very different lines in order to achieve the same end. 'The Lords isn't like the Commons,' says Lord Carrington. 'Party politics enter into it far less than they do in the Commons and there is a genuine reasonableness on all sides.'[9] In addition to his government and party responsibilities, the Leader has a third role as an avuncular adviser to the House on matters of procedure and orderly behaviour. With no

Speaker, the Leader has an obligation to ensure that all sides are given a fair chance to put their arguments in debate and in committee. Longford's semi-detachment from party politics qualified him for such a task. Lord Carrington is convinced that he is the archetypal Lords man.

> I don't think he would have been very good in the House of Commons. He is essentially a House of Lords figure. I know he's Irish but he's a sort of endearing English eccentric whom their lordships perfectly understand because quite a lot of them are the same.[10]

Yet Longford's eccentricity lay in his manner and appearance. It did not affect his abilities as an organiser. By seeking a consensus and by keeping the House in good spirits, Longford managed to get the business done. As ever, he was the delegator. His deputies – Lord Champion before 1966 and Lord Shackleton afterwards – took care of much of the day-to-day time-tabling, while Longford was involved in Cabinet committees and other such duties. Lord (C.P.) Snow was also in his front bench team. When the government needed to bend procedural rules and hurry legislation through the Lords – as in the case of the Southern Rhodesia Bill of 1965 and the 1966 and 1967 Prices and Incomes Bills – it fell to another of the Labour front bench team, Lord Shepherd, to convince the Opposition to assent grudgingly to what they deemed a 'Shepherd's pie' of emergency business.

While Longford strove to avoid a clash between the Conservative majority in the Lords and the Labour government, he was not blind to the need to reform the Second Chamber. Having sat on the front bench continuously since 1945, he had dwelt on the shortcomings of a largely hereditary institution and its place in the British political system. Labour had fought the 1935 general election on a pledge to abolish the Lords. The fracas of 1948 over iron and steel nationalisation had led Attlee's government to curtail its powers further. Despite modifications with the arrival of life peers in 1958 and Tony Benn's disclaimer in

1963, the Lords in 1964 retained the power to delay government business by two parliamentary sessions. Restrictions on the sort of bills where it would exercise its veto were largely informal.

The Salisbury Rules, drawn up when Labour came to power in 1945 to forbid Tory majorities in the Lords from blocking issues that formed part of the government's election manifesto, had no basis in statute.

Labour was still committed to the idea of further reducing the powers of the Lords in 1964 but had no firm plans as yet to pursue the matter. Longford's skill in working with the Opposition meant that the government's hand was not forced. However, Longford remained totally convinced that the hereditary principle of the House of Lords needed weakening in order to rationalise its position as watchdog of the Commons. Its attempts to influence parliamentary decisions would then no longer be greeted angrily by an electorate unwilling to accept the interference of unelected noblemen. Evelyn Waugh, feeling remorse for the cruel comments he had made about Longford's first volume of autobiography, explained his attitude later: 'I can't see a man painting a gate without wanting to tell him how to paint it better.'[11] Longford shared this zeal. Deprived of any other focus in government for his reforming ardour, he turned his attention to the subject of the House of Lords. It was the aspect of his work in the Second Chamber that most directly impinged on Cabinet meetings.

Reform of the Lords had an obvious personal appeal to Longford. Since his decision to accept a peerage in 1945 had, more or less, consigned his political career to the Upper Chamber, it followed that he should want to make the Lords work as effectively as possible. If its irregular constitutional position could be sorted out, then its politically active members could demand an end to their marginalisation when it came to government jobs.

Since the 1950s when the family had first started going down to Bernhurst, Longford had played a round of golf at the weekend in Rye with Commander Henry Burrows, clerk assistant in the Lords. As they strode along the fairway, the two would discuss how the composition of the Lords could be modified to secure its position in the constitution. Burrows' favoured solution – the two-writ scheme – won Longford's backing. All members of the Lords would continue to have the right to come and speak, but only those who were created peers, either before or after the introduction of the scheme, would be allowed to vote. Hereditary peers would lose the right to vote, though some of their number, like Longford himself, would be given voting peerages to enable them to maintain their active participation in events. The in-built Conservative majority, derived from the hereditary element, would be removed and the main anachronism, from a democratic point of view, would be consigned to history.

It was a pragmatic proposal. The two-writ scheme would not completely disenfranchise the hereditary peers. It would particularly reduce the antagonism that a less gentlemanly solution would have aroused on the Tory benches in the Lords. Evolution rather than revolution was the approach, in keeping with Longford's gentle handling of the Upper Chamber in day-to-day affairs.

As Leader of the Lords he worked with his Cabinet colleague, Lord Gardiner, the Lord Chancellor, to prepare a plan based on the two-writ scheme. He introduced the idea to the Cabinet in June 1966 with high hopes that he would be given at least cautious encouragement to pursue the matter further. The previous item on the agenda had generated much disagreement and Longford's proposal, to his profound dismay, was treated as light relief by his colleagues. Even those who bothered to listen mistook his emphasis. Barbara Castle records in her diary that the plan was 'excellent in tone about the need to reduce their [the Lords'] powers'.[12] Longford's protests that the question was not of a reduction of powers but of a change of composition failed to move her and most of the rest of the Cabinet. Wilson responded: 'Whatever may be said about the last topic, I can imagine nothing quite so divisive as an attempt to reform the House of Lords.'[13]

Longford further undermined his position by angry talk of resignation, a threat he had no intention of carrying out. The Cabinet was not in the mood to be bullied. He backed down but resolved to carry on the fight. The appointment of his old Oxford confrère, Richard Crossman, as Leader of the House of Commons in the autumn of 1966 provided the required opportunity. At the June Cabinet meeting Crossman had provoked much of the laughter that had greeted Longford's proposal with his remark, 'I'm all for a Second Chamber which is indefensible when any alternative must be a check on progress.'[14] Barbara Castle notes that Longford displayed 'shocked pain at such "cynicism"' but that this in turn 'had us almost rolling in the aisles'.[15]

However, only a matter of months later Crossman had revised his opinion and determined on reform both of some of the procedures of the House of Commons and of the Lords at the same time. He lived up to his reputation as 'Double Crossman' by effectively annexing Longford's scheme and then trying to exclude the Leader of the Lords from an active role in its implementation, preferring to work with his close friend and protégé Lord Shackleton, as well as Lord Gardiner and Roy Jenkins as Home Secretary.

After much discussion and debate with his circle of advisers, Crossman came to the Prime Minister and his senior Cabinet colleagues in the autumn of 1967 for advice over how to proceed with Lords reform. George Brown, First Secretary, still felt that it was an unnecessary distraction from the pressing question of unemployment and would be judged as such by the electorate. James Callaghan, Chancellor of the Exchequer, was more in favour but torn between Crossman's two proposals of either a one-tier approach – which eradicated the hereditary element and made working members with inherited titles into life peers – and the two-tier approach, in essence Longford's two-writ scheme. Crossman favoured the second.

In spite of such prevarications Crossman managed to get top-level backing to proceed on the basis of including a general pledge to reform the Lords in the forthcoming Queen's Speech and then negotiating with the Conservatives and Liberals as to the exact details. It was only at this point that Crossman took Longford into his confidence, a remarkable delay given Longford's responsibility at Cabinet level for the Upper Chamber. A working group was established over dinner in Chelsea in October 1967 consisting of Longford, Gardiner, Shackleton, Crossman and Jenkins.

> When all this had been agreed Frank said he thought that I should lead the delegation [Crossman wrote in his diary]. I must say this was very good of him because as Leader of the House, he would naturally like to lead it himself. Considering how passionate he is about this and how much he knows and how little I know, he has shown an astonishing power to put his personal feelings behind him and a real care for the cause we all have at heart.[16]

Longford had decided that the cause was more important than any hurt feelings at his continued relegation to a subordinate role.

Though Crossman led the negotiations and steered them through Cabinet, and Shackleton did much of the detailed drawing up of the reform package with the Tories, Longford remained actively involved until his resignation as Leader of the Lords in January 1968. Understanding the ways of the Lords and its gentlemanly approach rather better than Crossman, he brought the two sides together over dinner at the Café Royal to dispel any antagonism. He also made it his business to keep Carrington and his team fully briefed on Labour's attitudes, a courtesy which could annoy Crossman. In his diary for 24 October 1967, just prior to the announcement of the reform scheme in the Queen's Speech, Crossman complains that the Tory leaders in the Commons knew via Carrington the precise wording of the proposal 'because Frank Longford can't resist talking to them out of office hours'.[17] Despite his gracious acknowledgement weeks earlier that Longford knew more about the subject, Crossman was determined to remain firmly in control and to marginalise the Leader of the Lords.

Though Conservative approval was obtained for a reform package very similar to Longford's preferred two-writ scheme, it was never made into law. Crossman moved in November 1968 to be Secretary of State for Health and Social Security and the measure thereby lost its most eloquent spokesman in the Lower Chamber. The bill was delayed in the Commons by an unlikely combination of resistance from Hugh Fraser and Enoch Powell on the Tory right, and Michael Foot on the Labour left. Foot rallied those of like mind to rebel against the Labour whip with his argument that the Lords should not be reformed but abolished. To tinker with its composition would be to give an unelected chamber an unwarranted place in the system, Foot said. Powell and Fraser, a former Tory minister and husband of Longford's daughter Antonia, were opposed on the basis that any change would alter the constitutional balance. Their long-running battle held up the bill to such an extent that Wilson in 1969 lost patience with a scheme that had never been a top priority anyway and quietly abandoned it.

For Longford the whole episode confirmed the indifference of the Labour Party to the Lords – and hence also to those who worked there.

> Labour politicians [he wrote] unless they were forced
> to think with special clarity by the nature of their
> work, were unable to make up their minds whether
> they wanted the House of Lords to be rational or
> irrational in composition, to be taken seriously or
> laughed at. So long as it remained irrational, it
> remained futile, or at least impotent, and many of
> them preferred it that way. I do not think we would
> have got very far if I, an academic who was quite
> ready to resign on this issue, had not happened to
> coincide with Dick Crossman, also a political theorist,
> who was profoundly committed to a total reform of
> Parliament. It might easily have come off, but it
> didn't.[18]

Such a coincidence of views has not happened since. The scheme that Longford inspired stands as the last attempt made to revamp the Lords. Today, he considers reform of the Upper Chamber so low on the list of political priorities that its realisation seems inconceivable.[19]

In his administrative duties in the Lords, Longford was supported by a small private office. They sifted through his correspondence – he attracted a great deal from prisoners and ex-prisoners – and tried to curb his occasional sartorial excesses, as for example when he was all set to attend the State Opening of Parliament without laces in his shoes.

The majority of his speeches in the Chamber were on routine business, some of them were simply reading out other ministers' statements. As Leader, he was responsible for conveying prepared texts from other ministers in the Commons – a task he found rather tedious. His normal style of speaking in the Lords was informal, some would say almost too casual. But Longford felt that

> reading someone else's statement has a peculiarly
> chilling effect on reader and audience, and I used to
> become more and more frozen as I proceeded. I have
> noticed the same in others, but I suspect I was one of
> the worst offenders, and Wilson's were some of the
> longest statements. The reading finished, one was
> immediately interrogated, frequently with no oppor-
> tunity of providing oneself with supplementary
> replies. The whole thing was apt to be a bit of a
> nightmare.[20]

Occasionally though, a subject would arise about which he felt passionate. The most notable example was the arrival in the Lords of a private member's bill legalising abortion, introduced into the Commons by David Steel and passed by the Lower Chamber. Opposition to abortion is the keystone of orthodoxy in the Catholic Church and Longford was implacably against the measure.

Though Steel had received backing from Roy Jenkins as Home Secretary and the Cabinet was generally in favour of the measure, the issue was left, in theory at least, to the conscience of individual members. However, the government had granted parliamentary time to Steel in the Commons and its tacit approval was no secret. To oppose the measure, Longford would be seen to be going against the spirit of the government and the Cabinet of which he was a member. He would be justifying the criticism in Labour circles that their Leader in the Upper House took an independent Catholic line.

If the bill had been a straight government measure, Longford would have resigned over it. Given its quasi-official status, he decided instead to take temporary leave of absence from his post to speak from the back benches against the measure. As a manoeuvre, it was without precedent constitutionally. As a gesture, it went down very badly with his Cabinet colleagues. As a ploy to sway the House of Lords, it failed miserably. One observer recalls that when Longford spoke, it was the nearest the Lords ever came to booing anyone. He stated clearly that life, in his opinion, began at the moment of conception and that abortion was therefore murder. He developed the 'thin end of the wedge' argument and asked how long it would be before the law allowed elderly members of the House to be bumped off on the grounds of their advanced years. Some responded with cries of shame.

Despite defeat that day and the passage of Steel's bill, as well as the subsequent failure of attempts to reform the substance of the abortion law, Longford remains an unrepentant opponent of abortion. He is president of the Labour Life Group and has defended – not always successfully – its right to be represented at Labour Party conferences in the face of heavy opposition from the pro-choice lobby.

As with the dichotomy in his adamant Catholic stance on other moral matters, Longford's public intolerance of abortion is offset by a private compassion for those who feel driven to terminate their pregnancies. He refuses to condemn them whatever his horror at their actions.

> When I was pregnant with what turned out to be my second child, [his daughter Judith recalls] I went to a Labour Women's conference, representing the Chelsea party. I was about sixteen weeks pregnant and the

subject of abortion came up. I was one of only two
people who voted against supporting the abortion bill.
Afterwards I came back and was having tea with my
mother. She told me that Antonia's daughter, Flora,
then two, had German Measles. I'd been to tea with
Antonia and Flora the week before and had never
been vaccinated. In other words, I feared that my
baby would have all the defects. I immediately
decided I couldn't cope with a defective baby and all
my views changed. There is nothing like a personal
crisis to make you think. When I told my parents
about my fears and what I was going to do, my father
said, 'Whatever you do, I'm going to support you.'
Which is not saying 'I believe in abortion', but that
he'd support me.[21]

In the end it was a false alarm and Judith's daughter Miranda
was born fit and healthy.

Aside from his duties in the Lords, Longford was named by
Wilson in 1964 as Lord Privy Seal. Under Attlee such non-
departmental posts had been filled by men with overall co-
ordinating responsibility for various areas of government policy.
Wilson continued this policy with, for example, Douglas Hough-
ton, the Chancellor of the Duchy of Lancaster, covering the
separate ministries of health and social security in Cabinet. But
as Lord Privy Seal, Longford was given no additional brief. In an
interview in 1977, Wilson attributed his failure to employ
Longford in any broader role than the Lords to the fact that
'senior ministers didn't take him seriously enough'.[22]

Longford was excluded from the chairmanship of any of the
Cabinet committees for the same reason. Again he had hoped –
as the only member of the Cabinet to have headed a clearing
bank and one of the few with previous experience as a senior
minister – to be given a leading role in the smaller groups which
co-ordinate policy between different but overlapping departments. Longford sat on the important economy and defence and
foreign affairs committees. He was kept busy, but it was more a

case of perpetual motion than getting anywhere. Movement should not be mistaken for action. According to Wilson:

> On the financial thing and his [Longford's] expertise in the bank, he always had his chance in committee to make his points, but I don't think the Treasury or the Chancellor would have regarded him as a financial expert just because of the Irish bank. I mean he knew his way round but he wouldn't have been *au fait* with the really hard, tough Treasury and Bank of England decisions.[23]

(The fact that the Chancellor, James Callaghan, was widely regarded as being less than agile in the area of economics apparently did not worry Wilson.)

Longford might have been able to tolerate Wilson's high-handed dismissal of his chairmanship of the National, and indeed of the bank itself and Ireland. He had none the less expected to be treated as a senior counsellor to the Prime Minister, a status akin to that which his predecessor as Labour Leader of the Upper Chamber, Lord Addison, had enjoyed under Attlee. Wilson's reasoning, in the 1977 interview, for quashing such great hopes was

> because he's off-beat. A Cabinet committee chairman ought to be completely neutral, to get a proper discussion and analysis of committee documents, and then sum up. It's not that he'd have wanted to preach but he'd have had preconceived notions about the subject to hand, or at least some of them.[24]

Clearly Longford's outspoken stance on prison reform and associated social matters, not to mention his vocal Christianity, had counted against him in the Prime Minister's eyes. Yet such a verdict overlooked Longford's record of successful chairmanship of various committees, most recently on crime.

Longford did not easily accept his fate as an irrelevance in Cabinet. He lobbied Wilson intensively for greater responsibilities and was successful in winning concessions on two occasions. Yet, both times, he failed to leave any mark on the government.

In December 1965, Wilson reshuffled his Cabinet, moving his close ally Barbara Castle to Transport, replacing her at Overseas Development with Tony Greenwood, until then Colonial Secretary, and awarding Longford Greenwood's old job. According to Wilson, Longford had been 'pressing for an administrative job to combine with his part-time Leadership of the Lords'.[25] (The Prime Minister's description of leading the Upper Chamber as 'part-time' employment is telling.)

Given his choice of any ministry, Longford would have opted for the Home Office where he could have overseen a radical shake-up in the prisons department. But Harold Wilson was not about to entrust one of the three major departments of state to a member of the House of Lords with no support in the party. 'Frank could never have been Home Secretary. You can't afford to have a chap who isn't very strongly clued in to the whole of political life,' says Denis Healey, Secretary of State for Defence from 1964 to 1970. 'For Frank it would have been a question of penal reform but in practice the Home Office is the most disparate collection of responsibilities. You can't afford to have a single issue Home Secretary.'[26]

Such was the number of talented ministers at Wilson's disposal in 1964 that he was forced, initially at least, to leave such rising stars as Roy Jenkins outside the Cabinet. Seen in that light, his offer to Longford of the Colonial Office was not quite as insubstantial as it may seem now. After all, it had been a key ministry when run by Elizabeth's ancestor, Joseph Chamberlain, in the early years of the twentieth century and the appointment did mean that Longford at last had a department behind him.

The major 'colonial' dispute of the day was over Rhodesia and UDI, but Wilson had already made it clear that he was taking personal charge of this area and excluded Longford completely. Furthermore, with the new Commonwealth emerging to replace the old Empire he undisguisedly intended to subsume the Colonial Office into the Foreign Office as soon as possible, and asked Longford to accelerate the winding down process. Essen-

347

tially he was being handed another administrative task, rather than the opportunity to make policy.

Longford's secretary at the time, Angela Lambert, recalled that, despite such drawbacks, he was delighted with the appointment. For the first time in fifteen years he was back in a ministry with all the paraphernalia of civil servants and support that such a post entailed. Longford was stripped of the Colonial Secretaryship just three months later after Labour's victory at the March 1966 general election. Lambert attributed this failure to several factors.

> First of all he was in his sixties then and there were a
> lot of young people around. Secondly he didn't
> change. He didn't become any more organised or
> hard-working. He didn't master his briefs. He never
> got over the conviction that if you carried papers
> around with you for long enough, they would be
> absorbed by a process of osmosis. He didn't read and
> study them and his PPSs used to have to make sum-
> maries of them for him.[27]

While Leadership of the Lords came naturally to Longford, involving thought and diplomacy, not endless hours of reading documents he found tedious, the Colonial Secretaryship exposed his lack of application. As a young ambitious politician in Attlee's government, he had been prepared to buckle down to unpleasant tasks like his post at Civil Aviation, in the hope of future preferment. However, by the time Wilson awarded him a department of his own, he had little incentive to apply himself.

There was no hope of further promotion. As became increasingly obvious to those around him, Longford's mind was turning more and more to matters outside the political mainstream like prison reform – issues that had not impinged significantly on his political career in the late 1940s.

> In Cabinet [says Denis Healey] any minister can play
> as big a role as he wants to and being a peer doesn't
> prevent him at all. Frank is just not very political in an

> odd way. He is not an organisation man. Essentially
> he is one of these chaps who is 150 per cent commit-
> ted on any issue which he feels strongly – like penal
> reform – but on many issues didn't have strong feel-
> ings. He was marginal because of his nature. He didn't
> aspire. He liked to do well and he liked to be well
> regarded but he didn't want to work hard to do well.[28]

In other words through Labour's thirteen years in opposition Longford's growing tendency to become engaged in other issues, to take up a crusading stance, had lowered his tolerance of the everyday issues of government. He was only interested in matters that touched on one of his own personal areas of concern. He was, in effect, a specialist not a generalist. The administrative posts he held, as Leader of the Lords and as Colonial Secretary, demanded managing skills more than reforming zeal. His lack of application to the tasks, uninteresting to him, of Colonial Secretary ruled out any lingering hopes Longford might have held of a more substantial ministry under Wilson.

During his brief tenure of the Colonial Office, there was only one major crisis with which Longford had to deal. When unrest in the British colony of Aden in the autumn and winter of 1965 led to the imposition of a state of emergency, Longford sent out his deputy, Lord Beswick, to investigate rather than go himself. The opportunity to play a constructive role existed, but Longford, fundamentally much more interested in domestic than overseas policy and a lifelong reluctant traveller, passed the buck to Beswick.

However, when his deputy came back and made recommendations against the internment of those fighting for independence, pointing out that they were being made into martyrs, Longford did his best to press the point. Recognising the parallels with the Irish situation after the First World War, he pledged to change the policy. Before he could achieve any results he was sacked.

Even in cases where he had a clear personal interest that might be promoted by his ministerial job, Longford failed to make any great impact. He had long been a vocal supporter of the United Nations and the principle of world government. Harold Wilson appointed Hugh Foot in 1964 as British representative at the UN, raised him to the peerage as Lord Caradon and gave him Cabinet rank as a mark of the importance he placed on the post. Yet beyond that symbolic gesture, Wilson made little progress. As Colonial Secretary, with close links with the Foreign Office, Longford was in an ideal position to add a little impetus. He did not do so.

There were parts of the Colonial Secretary's job that he did enjoy. The ceremonial aspect appealed to him. On one occasion, he lunched alone with the Queen. Her Majesty had just returned from a tour of the West Indies and was eager to discuss some of what she had observed in British colonies there with the relevant minister. As Longford was later to recall with surprising candour for one responsible at that stage for policy in the area:

> We had, in fact, both read the same briefs, supplied by
> the Colonial Office; we were, if I may say so respect-
> fully, in a situation of fellow students. But she was
> well ahead after fieldwork on the ground.[29]

Quite how the Queen reacted to a minister whose knowledge went no further than the briefs they both had studied is not recorded – and given Longford's somewhat casual approach to such a task, Her Majesty may have absorbed some of the detail rather more thoroughly.

There were other social events that went with the job. Elizabeth recollects that

> we had a good time at Lancaster House receiving the
> Commonwealth at the celebration of Parliament's
> Seven Hundred Years. The Prime Minister was down
> on the programme to receive, but Harold Wilson
> happened to be himself receiving an honorary degree
> in Oxford. Several guests asked Frank: 'Have you
> become Prime Minster?'[30]

Despite Wilson's hopes of a swift wind-down of the Colonial Office, Longford was in fact the penultimate Colonial Secretary. The Prime Minister may not have intended it as a verdict on Longford's tenure, but his fulsome praise for his successor, Fred Lee, might be taken as an indication of a certain displeasure at what had gone before. Lee, Wilson wrote in his account of the 1964–70 government, 'took very readily to the job until the position of a separate Secretary of State was abolished the following year'.[31]

If he was disappointed with Longford as Colonial Secretary, Wilson did give him one further chance with a more creative brief than Leadership of the Lords. Mindful that Longford had considerable knowledge of social services and that this was the area where he could potentially make the biggest contribution, Wilson agreed to allow him to undertake an investigation into youth services nationwide. In some respects it was a continuation of the committee on crime that Longford had headed in 1963–4. He had felt then that there was not sufficient attention paid to the needs of young people, and in 1967 he managed to persuade the Prime Minister, himself like Longford a former assistant to Beveridge, that a full report was needed. His brief was to include not only advice and counselling, under the auspices of the Ministry of Education, but also the treatment of young offenders, part of the Home Office's field of responsibility. Both relevant ministers – Tony Crosland and Roy Jenkins – were less than pleased at the Prime Minister's concession to Longford and felt that he was interfering in their domain.

An argument ensued with Jenkins and Crosland successfully combining in Cabinet to limit the scope of Longford's inquiry.

> When it was over, [Jenkins recalls] he upbraided us in the middle of the road outside 10 Downing Street. I think he was quivering with (probably well-justified) rage, but what he actually said was, 'I will still write very favourably about you both in my autobiography but not quite so favourably as I would have done until this morning.'[32]

With Joan Bourne once more as his assistant, Longford set out to do what he liked best – research in the field. He visited various centres for young people around the country looking at issues like health, education, recreation as well as crime and punishment. The deadline for receiving evidence was December 1967. A month later Longford had resigned and without his enthusiasm the whole project collapsed. Though Wilson did at first appoint Michael Stewart and then Richard Crossman to continue the work, there was no momentum and Longford, out of office, did nothing to persuade his former colleagues to continue what he had started. His mind had moved on to new schemes. Joan Bourne was to put together a personal report for the Prime Minister, but, without the backing of a Cabinet minister, it sat on a shelf gathering dust.

The abortive youth inquiry was not Longford's only attempt to bring his expertise as a prison reformer to bear on the policies of the government. As a Cabinet minister, he felt the Home Office should treat him with a little more respect than they had done hitherto when he lobbied them over individual prisoners. Roy Jenkins, appointed Home Secretary in 1965, was not impressed.

> Frank was always on the side of the prisoners. He was considered by the Home Office officials to be very wrong on a lot of things. He's a man of immense charm but there is this flibbertigibbet aspect to Frank. I don't think he would have been a good Home Secretary. I'm afraid that we made jokes about Frank as a prison reformer within the Cabinet and the Home Office. His willingness to pursue something he believes in and his absolute indifference to ridicule or to criticism are absolutely admirable, but they are not balanced, I'm afraid, by a discriminating judgement. Therefore he was just as likely to get involved in a bad case as in a good case.[33]

Jenkins, therefore, listened politely to Longford's various requests on behalf of prisoners, but without any great attention.

Longford's unhappy relationship with the Home Office, already apparent at the time of his Causes of Crime investigation, was not eased by his being a Cabinet minister. Jenkins does qualify his criticisms with praise for Longford's support on one of the major pieces of legislation during his period as Home Secretary: the decriminalisation of homosexuality. And, lest Longford should be dismissed too lightly, several of the other reforms in the criminal justice system that came through in the Wilson years were a direct result of the 1963–4 report on crime.

There were occasions, despite Longford's best intentions, when his involvement with individual prisoners or miscreants clashed with his ministerial responsibilities and landed him in trouble with his colleagues. In May 1965, the papers picked up the case of a cleaner at the Longfords' Chelsea home who appeared in court charged with stealing a pearl and diamond ring worth £105. She was found guilty at Marlborough Street Magistrates' Court and sentenced to two months in prison. Longford paid for a solicitor to defend her.

In December 1967 (when, admittedly, Labour was in a stronger position, with its Commons majority increased from four to ninety-six at the 1966 election, and therefore less sensitive to what the Cabinet saw as Longford's excesses) the *People* did a full-page spread on 'The Moving Story of the Peer and the Prostitute'.[34] It was based on an article Longford had written in the magazine *Christian Action* and reported how the Leader of the House of Lords had befriended an Irish prostitute called Annabel, found her a home in a convent and given her a new life. To Longford, Annabel's story was one of redemption, and he told it in that spirit. To his critics and some of his colleagues, though, it portrayed Longford in a curious light, the politician who cared not only for people's material well-being but also for their souls.

Longford's continuing friendship with Christopher Craig and his brother Niven were to cause Wilson most blushes. Soon after Longford joined the Cabinet, Niven Craig was allowed to work out of prison on a hostel scheme. His fellow inmates, jealous of the privileges he had won and ascribing them to his friendship with Longford, wrote to two Conservative MPs to complain.

353

They accused Longford of having a homosexual relationship with Niven Craig. Even though there was no evidence whatsoever to back the claim, one of the MPs raised the issue of Longford's undue influence in an adjournment debate in the House of Commons.

In the ensuing row, Wilson imposed a rule that ministers would not be allowed to visit prisoners without the Home Secretary or himself being informed. Longford had to curtail his visits, though he did get round the bar by sending his secretary. No sooner had the Niven Craig accusations been forgotten than his younger brother Christopher, released from jail in the early 1960s through the efforts of Longford and others, announced that he was getting married. He invited Longford to the wedding. Given the recent publicity, Longford reluctantly felt he must seek the Prime Minister's advice. Wilson asked him not to attend the ceremony lest it place any more strain on the government's at that stage wafer-thin majority. 'Until 1966,' says Longford, 'when the majority in the Commons increased, there was a siege mentality, a feeling that you should avoid stepping out of line at all costs.'[35] After considerable hesitation, Longford fell in with his wishes, but invited Craig and his fiancée to dinner at the House of Lords on the eve of the wedding. The curtailment of his liberty to follow up his long-standing mission to prisoners and ex-prisoners was the price of holding high office. Yet in view of the limited influence he was gaining as a result, Longford began to wonder whether it was a price worth paying.

Other than establishing a reputation with his Cabinet colleagues as being something of a loose cannon, it is hard to see how Longford affected the course of the Wilson government. No other Cabinet has been so picked over posthumously through the publication of diaries written by some of its principal players. Yet, in the accounts of Richard Crossman, Barbara Castle, Patrick Gordon Walker and Tony Benn, Longford hardly figures. There are occasional cruel asides about his ineffectiveness, but on the major issues that divided this turbulent group of ministers, he rarely played a leading role. Longford himself was later to describe his usual attitude to the regular Thursday morning Cabinet meetings as feeling 'I ought to get my word in in order to show that I was not sulkily aloof.' It was such a dispiriting performance that 'thoughts of lunch alone sustained me'.[36]

On the crucial matter of the government's commitment to maintaining the value of sterling in the face of a balance of payments deficit, Longford, despite being a member of the Cabinet's finance committee, was neither consulted before the decision was taken to defend the pound at all costs, nor was he informed when the policy began to run into serious trouble.

In July 1966, Longford travelled up to London from Bernhurst by train with an old friend from the National Bank. His companion's warning about the impending need to devalue sterling – despite the government's repeated denials that it would happen – prompted Longford to take the unusual step of telephoning the Chancellor when he arrived at his office. When the two met, Longford outlined a package of measures that he felt would ease the run on sterling – including a prices and wages freeze. Callaghan told him that it was too late for such action. The Cabinet was going to have to decide the next day whether or not to devalue. Callaghan was opposed but George Brown, at the Ministry of Economic Affairs, was strongly in favour.

Because the sides in Cabinet were evenly balanced, Callaghan needed Longford's vote and so arranged for him to talk to one of his economic advisers at the Treasury. Still undecided, Longford then went to George Brown and saw one of his officials. Finally he had dinner with Douglas Jay, President of the Board of Trade, and sought his advice. Jay was opposed to devaluation on the grounds that it would damage the government's authority. Longford was convinced and voted accordingly. The Cabinet had expressed a view, on this occasion not to devalue, though they were later to change their minds.

The fact that it took an old colleague from the National Bank to alert Longford to the true seriousness of the matter demonstrates his detachment from the inner workings of the government. The episode shows also how Longford was seen as simply a voting counter to be won over in Cabinet disputes.

The decision to maintain the value of sterling was taken by

Wilson and a small group of ministers – Callaghan, Brown and Jay – immediately after the 1964 election victory. It was a typical example of how the Prime Minister preferred to by-pass the Cabinet and work either with small groups of ministers or with his own team of advisers, the so-called 'kitchen cabinet', which included Wilson's political secretary, Marcia Williams, Gerald Kaufman and Joe Haines, his press officer. Wilson tried, whenever possible, to make the Cabinet a rubber stamp. It meant that Longford was doubly marginalised. Not only did he get pushed to one side in Cabinet discussions, but the Cabinet itself, his only potential forum for influence, was itself being usurped by other bodies. His relationship with individuals close to Wilson was cordial. He remains friendly with Marcia Williams, now Lady Falkender, and was once consulted by her in retirement owing to her interest in Catholicism. However, he was never regarded by the kitchen cabinet as anything but a bit-part player.

His erstwhile Cabinet colleagues today don't remember Longford for any great intellectual or political contribution he made to their many arguments around the table in 10 Downing Street. He himself says that he was 'ineffective'. Only on a personal level did he earn praise. According to Douglas Jay, 'he was always such a personality in his own right, you could never think of him as a straight party member.'[37] Jay valued his long-standing friendship with Longford and having someone he could trust in an invidious atmosphere where intrigue was a way of life. 'You could talk frankly to Frank, knowing that he wasn't a close associate of Wilson's.' On a journey back from Chequers in April 1967 after the Cabinet had discussed the Common Market, Jay revealed his thoughts of resignation to Longford, sure in the knowledge that, although they disagreed on the issue at stake, he would offer honest advice and respect confidentiality. 'Frank was wonderfully friendly and helpful. One could not have wished for a better confidant at such a moment.'[38]

Roy Jenkins, who in 1967 replaced Callaghan as Chancellor after the devaluation crisis, recalls Longford mainly for his good-humoured contributions. 'I remember him making some very good jokes in Cabinet. But to say that he was a weighty member would be an exaggeration.'³⁹ On one occasion, Longford embarrassed his colleagues by attending the fiftieth anniversary celebrations in Dublin of the Easter Rising in 1966. He sat next to President de Valera on a platform at an event commemorating a revolt against British authority in Ireland.

> Wilson attempted in response [Jenkins says] to lay
> down a rule about travelling. It was really a matter of
> rebuking Frank but he tried to couch it in a general
> rule. He always tried to be emollient. 'It would hardly
> be appropriate', he said, 'if members of the Cabinet
> went off for holidays in Vietnam.' And Frank said:
> 'But I think, Prime Minister, very few members of the
> Cabinet have family homes in Vietnam.' It convulsed
> the Cabinet. It was a good example of the way Frank
> dealt with something by being extremely funny but
> self-deprecating at the same time.⁴⁰

As his former New College colleague, Douglas Jay recognised Longford's intellectual pedigree and the strength of his conviction on social issues. He is convinced that by resorting to frivolousness in Cabinet and by succumbing to his self-proclaimed 'fatal desire to amuse' Longford only pushed himself further to the margins, a Cabinet jester whom no one took seriously.⁴¹

His habitual untidiness and carelessness with possessions also heightened his reputation as the joker in the Cabinet pack. In May 1965, after Richard Crossman had left some Cabinet papers behind at a restaurant, Wilson ordered his team to be especially careful. Just weeks later Longford, staying with old friends outside London, left the contents of his despatch boxes all over their study floor. Only a dash up to Whitehall by his hostess saved him from public humiliation.

Some members of Cabinet occasionally regarded his heartfelt contributions as jokes. In July 1967 Barbara Castle noted an exchange that took place over the government's attitude to David Steel's abortion bill. 'A lighter note occurred at the beginning when Longford gave us his usual bleat about our giving time for the abortion bill. I'm afraid he just sounds comical.'[42] It wasn't only his own side that treated Longford with amusement. Edward Heath became involved in a row with Labour back-benchers who sprang, in partisan fashion, to Longford's defence after the Leader of the Opposition allegedly made an unflattering comparison between him and apes. Heath had been at a dinner at the Royal Academy in London in April 1967 and was reputed to have remarked when he saw a portrait of Longford: 'Much as I dislike all that he stands for even I could not have wished this portrait on him. It really does seem to confirm one's inner belief that all socialists are descended from apes.'[43] He later tried to pass the remark off as a political joke but Labour back-benchers, led by Gwyneth Dunwoody, tabled a censure motion in the Commons.

In August 1967, when he was hard at work on the youth report and taking second lead in Crossman's grand design to reform the Lords, Longford was summoned by Wilson and asked to stay on for another year to see the latter project through. Wilson clearly recognised that Longford had particular skills in coaxing their Lordships to accept unpleasant medicine, but he none the less made it plain that he wanted a younger man in charge in the Upper House and had Lord Shackleton in mind for the job.

Longford assented to the arrangement without much of a fight. It would give him time to complete the youth report and he was realistic enough to understand that if he saw the report through and aided the passage of the House of Lords reform, he would have reached the limit of his achievements as a Cabinet minister.

However, events overtook him. By the autumn of 1967 the Wilson government was in the midst of a deepening financial crisis. Sterling had been devalued by 14.3 per cent on 16 November and government expenditure was being cut everywhere. Wilson's phrase 'no sacred cows' set the tone for the exercise. Many suggestions hit at some of the central commitments in Labour's programme. Prescription charges, the issue over which Wilson had resigned from Attlee's government in

1951, were reintroduced in spite of fierce opposition from Jennie Lee, then Arts Minister. National insurance went up. Council house and road building was cut. Free school milk for secondary school pupils was stopped. The F111A bomber order was cancelled – Longford had sided with its backers. British commitments east of Suez were slashed – again against Longford's wishes. In total £716 million was saved.

But the issue that Longford chose to resign over was the deferment until 1973 of the raising of the school-leaving age to sixteen. It was a delay of two additional years. It had long been a central tenet of Labour's manifesto and the postponement caused justified anger, especially among those Cabinet members like James Callaghan, George Brown and Ray Gunter who had enjoyed only the bare minimum of education. They did not resign, however. It was Longford who had benefited from the most privileged of educations, and who had unhesitatingly sent all his children to private schools, who chose to resign over an impediment to the improvement of the state education system.

His vehemence surprised those colleagues like Douglas Jay who recall that he had shown little interest over education policy in general, aside from occasional forays to defend Catholic schools within Whitehall.

The education issue is not as tangential to Longford's main areas of work as might first appear. His inquiry into youth services and his personal contacts with young prisoners had raised his awareness of the role education plays in forming adult characters. He could see that dedicating resources to a good foundation of learning would avert trouble in the future. Longford has loudly opposed the proposal on these grounds from the moment it was mooted in Cabinet. But while other dissidents like George Brown finally acquiesced, Longford stuck to his guns. He must have known that, as a marginal member of Cabinet, he stood little chance of forcing the government to change tack. Furthermore, since Wilson had already indicated that Longford would be dismissed in the autumn, the Prime Minister was hardly going to kowtow to his wishes in order to retain him for a mere eight months longer.

In his letter to the Prime Minister, Longford spoke of the breaking of a promise.

> The step proposed [he wrote on 15 January after his
> final Cabinet meeting] is apparently condemned by
> those whose opinions I value most in the educational
> world. It is sharply opposed, as I see it, to the long-
> term policy and fundamental ideals of our party and
> to the pledge that we gave as recently as last Septem-
> ber. It is inconceivable that I should commend such a
> step to the House of Lords.

The breaking of a pledge was the main contention for Longford and, more particularly, reneging on a neglected and marginalised group of the community, the fifteen-year-old sons and daughters of poor families who could not afford to continue their education. He wrote later:

> I was leaving a Cabinet where the sanctity of promises
> seemed to be on the point of losing its significance.
> This question of whether a government is ever
> entitled to abandon a commitment is full of difficulties
> . . . I should not like to go to the stake, therefore, for
> too rigid an interpretation of the rule that a govern-
> ment's undertakings must be kept in all circumstances
> to the letter. Nevertheless, in the case of raising the
> school-leaving age, the economic advantages of the
> postponement seemed so trivial, the moral commit-
> ment so recent and so glaring, the educational issue so
> obvious, that I have never had any doubts that it was
> a resigning matter as soon as I realised that postpone-
> ment was on the way.[44]

Longford bailed out before he was pushed. As Denis Healey puts it: 'For Frank it wasn't much of a sacrifice but it was a genuinely felt issue.'[45] Resignation was the only course left to him to mark his distaste for the Wilson government's policy-making. He chose to play his hand over an issue where the duplicity and pragmatism of the government was most glaring and at a moment when it would attract most attention. He could not afford to fudge as he had done with Attlee over Germany. While he had known that Attlee was reluctant to lose him, he harboured no illusions as to Wilson's attitude. Longford had to issue his ultimatum and then act upon it.

Harold Wilson was polite, if not devastated, in his response.

> My Dear Frank
> Thank you for your letter of January 15 confirming your decision to resign from the Government because of the reasons stated. I know how strongly you feel about this, though naturally it is a matter of regret to me and my colleagues that you should now be leaving us. As you know from our discussion last August, I was most anxious for you to remain in your position to launch and see through the discussions about the future of the House of Lords, a subject in which you have played such a distinguished part for many months. I am sorry that in these circumstances you will not be able to see the discussion right through to the end, but I should like to thank you for all you have done in that capacity, and more widely as a member of the government.
> Yours, Harold.

Though it was more an appreciation of Longford's usefulness in the Lords than a testament to his enduring contribution to the government, Wilson's letter did at least acknowledge what had been a significant step for a senior colleague. No other member of the Cabinet managed to put pen to paper. Only Lord Gardiner made any attempt – at the last minute – to dissuade Longford. On the eve of the crucial Cabinet meeting, Gardiner called on the Longfords at their Chelsea flat and employed all the skills he had learnt as a barrister to try to convince his colleague to stay on, but to no avail.

Some of the other Cabinet members were scornful. Tony Benn wrote in his diary that Longford's loss 'will not be a serious one'.[46] Crossman noted that 'Cabinet is greatly strengthened by having Frank Pakenham out and Eddie [Shackleton] in'.[47] Patrick Gordon Walker reported that Wilson 'did not seem to mind at all'.[48] The rest were simply so caught up in their other responsibilities that they scarcely noticed his departure. They had grown accustomed to taking little notice of Longford. Years later, facing Roy Jenkins in the House of Lords, Longford recalled his own resignation in 1968. 'There was the compensation', he told the House, 'of many people having been kind and sympathetic.' After a pause for effect, he continued: 'The noble lord, Lord Jenkins of Hillhead, for instance, told me afterwards that he had very nearly written to me.' The Upper Chamber collapsed in laughter. It was a good-humoured revenge.[49]

Central to Longford's failure as a Cabinet minister was his inability to thrive in the poisonous atmosphere of the Wilson government. As Longford had risen to leave the Cabinet Room of 10 Downing Street after being appointed Leader of the House of Lords in 1964, Wilson had promised, 'We'll have a lot of fun together.'[50] The impression given by various accounts of the Labour Cabinets between 1964 and 1970 is that they were anything but fun. The diaries of Richard Crossman, Tony Benn and Barbara Castle, whatever their respective merits as accurate accounts of events, all suggest that the spirit in which proceedings were undertaken was not salubrious.

The Prime Minister himself was largely responsible for the malaise. While other Gaitskellites were slow to come round to Wilson, Longford was willing to work with him. On a personal level, their relationship was cordial. (Yet another instance of Longford never letting political differences get in the way of friendship.) For his part, Wilson showed his esteem for his Leader of the House of Lords by finding time at the height of a Cabinet row over arms sales to South Africa in 1967 to attend and give a speech at the wedding of Longford's daughter, Rachel, to the film and theatre director Kevin Billington. (With Cardinal Heenan, head of the Catholic Church in England and Wales also addressing the guests, Longford had managed to assemble leaders of both Church and state.)

Academic achievement, wit and mental dexterity are all

qualities Longford has admired in his political heroes, and Wilson who had got a First in Modern Greats, conformed to the stereotype. Even after his unhappy period as a Cabinet minister, Longford continues to praise some of Wilson's qualities. Wilson's success in winning four out of five elections, a record rivalled only by that of Gladstone, commends itself to a former teacher of political history.

> He has always possessed an immense power of rapid
> assimilation, a splendid memory (not quite as perfect
> as he supposes), powers of dissection and analysis
> equalled by those of exposition. God has further given
> him a fertile wit and an unforced sense of humour.
> When I add great powers of work, plenty of physical
> and mental stamina and much ambition, we are pre-
> sented with a man who one would think would be
> bound to get to the top.[51]

Both Wilson and Longford perceived themselves as outsiders, but each was in a different kind of exile. Ridiculed by the upper-class Gaitskellites of the Hampstead set, Wilson always felt ostracised according to Douglas Jay. He once described himself as the '14th Mr Wilson' making satirical fun of the Tory leader, the erstwhile 14th Earl of Home. Longford, however, despite being a thorn in the side of the Establishment, notwithstanding his Irish roots and his double conversion to Catholicism and socialism, would always be part of the elite from which Wilson felt excluded.

Politically, Wilson's greatest failing in Longford's eyes was a lack of integrity in his public conduct. From the outset Longford had severe reservations about Wilson's leadership style and the beliefs – or absence of them – that underpinned his government. Wilson's pragmatism was incompatible with Longford's view of politics as a moral crusade. Given such high standards Longford would probably have felt uncomfortable in most Cabinets. But the infighting in Wilson's 1964 team was particularly pronounced and was fuelled by the Prime Minister's paranoia. Longford is full of praise for Wilson's kindness as an individual. Yet in a Prime Minister, Wilson's disloyalty to his colleagues, his manoeuvrings, his easy conscience about changing course, all alienated Longford.

Labour's victory in 1964 had been presented to the electorate as a fresh pursuit of a New Jerusalem in the style of the pioneering Attlee governments of 1945–51. Wilson's talk in the election campaign of 'men with fire in their bellies and humanity in their hearts' appealed to Longford's zeal. There was a virtuous overtone to the manifesto pledge for

> a New Britain – mobilising the resources of tech-
> nology under a national plan; harnessing our national
> wealth in brains, our genius for scientific invention
> and medical discovery, reversing the decline of thir-
> teen wasted years; affording a new opportunity to
> equal, and if possible surpass, the roaring progress of
> other western powers.

Perhaps Longford was naive to believe his own side's propaganda, his party political instincts, as ever, rather blunt. But it was not long before he became dispirited by the constant u-turns over important policy issues. In the wake of talk of economic growth and boom in 1964 came heavy deflation, a statutory wage freeze and defeat of Barbara Castle's attempts (which had had the Prime Minister's backing) to reform the unions. Longford might have forgiven economic woes which are not always entirely in the control of individual governments. However, on ethical matters, like the arbitrary removal of the immigration rights of East African Asians and the response to Ian Smith's break-away in Rhodesia, the government was guilty, in Longford's view, of temporising. The Labour historian David Marquand has written of 'the atmosphere of shabby expediency which hung over the government like a pall'.[53]

The Labour government of 1964–70 lacked the fire and reforming passion that had driven Attlee's administration.

> The spirit [according to Longford] was willing but the
> intellectual guide-lines were lacking. The socialist
> vision had provided not only the moral but the intel-

lectual basis for the great reforms of 1945–51. From
1964–70 we were consulting the sacred books and
finding them more like Delphic oracles.[54]

As one who had shared the sense of purpose of those first-ever
majority Labour governments, Longford found the Wilson years
colourless by comparison.

The conduct of business in Cabinet, the habit of making policy
on the run, aggrieved Longford. In place of Labour's earnest
commitment in 1945 to creating a new Britain under a Prime
Minister Longford held in the highest esteem, in 1964 there
were daily struggles to survive under a Prime Minister whose
primary concern was for himself. In his diary for 28 October
1964, within weeks of the formation of the government, Crossman recorded an acrimonious pre-budget Cabinet meeting
where the level of pensions was debated at length. James
Callaghan, the Chancellor – whom Longford habitually backed
– wanted no more than a ten shilling increase. Others wanted
to make it higher. Wilson swung from one side to the other in
the ensuing argument. Crossman recalls:

> I was absolutely staggered at what happened because I
> am used to the idea that the Cabinet doesn't discuss a
> budget before the budget takes place. Yet here we
> were discussing the budget secrets . . . It was stagger-
> ing, as I said to Frank Longford who was sitting next
> to me; he also, with his experience of the Cabinet [he
> had attended as an observer while at the Admiralty]
> said he had never observed anything so extraordinary
> as this way of conducting business.[55]

Wilson's flexibility in central matters of policy dismayed Longford. Even when he stuck to a principle, Wilson was prepared to
take defeat in his stride and turn it to his advantage in instances
where Longford would have resigned. Over the devaluation of
sterling in 1967, Longford admired Wilson's initial tenacious
defence of the exchange rate.

> But when he was overpowered by circumstances and
> devaluation followed [Longford wrote subsequently]
> he made his famous broadcast in which he reassured
> the public about the £ in their pockets. Whatever the
> precise semantics of the speech and the subsequent
> explanations, this passage did not ring true at the time
> or since. To put matters crudely his instinct to act as a
> public relations officer for his own government has, in
> the long run, cost him dear.[56]

Despite his own appreciation of the benefit of press and public relations, Longford had done his political apprenticeship under the strictly principled Clement Attlee (whom he continued to visit at his central London flat throughout this period) and would have preferred his Prime Minister to have displayed a little more resolution and not to have bowed so readily to expediency.

In a 1984 essay on Harold Wilson, amid a great deal of praise for his former leader's qualities, Longford makes two specific criticisms. Firstly that he was too open with the press and secondly that he talked too freely to everyone, partly out of friendliness, partly out of a desire to impress. There is more than a touch of personal hurt in these comments. Virtually from the instant he joined the Cabinet, Longford was hearing rumours that the Prime Minister wanted to replace him with a younger man.

A schemer by nature, Wilson showed no loyalty to his Leader of the House of Lords in private and at times scant respect in public. He talked openly in 1965 of wanting to replace Longford in the Upper Chamber with an ennobled Frank Cousins, the trade union leader brought in as Minister for Technology in 1964. Patrick Gordon Walker had lunch with Wilson in April of 1966, just a month after the Prime Minister had confirmed Longford in office. But Gordon Walker notes that Wilson 'thought poorly of Frank Pakenham'.[57] At a press conference later that year, Wilson was asked about rumours of a Cabinet reshuffle. He replied that there had been much speculation about the Leadership of the House of Lords and that he didn't want to comment on the matter at that moment. The implication was clearly understood by his audience. While the Prime Minister protested to Longford that he had been quoted out of context, one of the Lobby later showed Longford his notes to confirm Wilson's remarks.

In July 1965, less than ten months after forming his government, Wilson told Cecil King that Longford was 'quite useless – mental age of twelve'.[58] Wilson was later to qualify these remarks, saying that he was referring not to Longford's intellect but to his innocence. Today Longford tries to pass off the indictment with a joke. 'When I was told the remark, I misheard and thought he had said 112. In that context a mental age of twelve doesn't sound so bad.'[59] But to his other colleagues, Wilson's contempt underlined Longford's incompatibility with his Cabinet.

Longford's musings on public platforms and in print about the relationship between faith and political action since his conversion to Catholicism in 1940 would not have been considered eccentric under the Attlee administration. Others there shared his view of politics as a mission, and while they may have held different ideologies, there had been a tangible sense of mission to create a better society. However, as Douglas Jay wrote of the contrast between the 1945 and 1964 governments: 'the moral authority which imbued the first . . . was singularly lacking in the second. Attlee and Gaitskell inspired not merely respect but trust. Wilson did not.'[60] Longford more generously refers to Wilson as 'a beleaguered spirit, a man who rightly or wrongly felt always that he had to get up very early in the morning to survive.'[61] But the latter's paranoid ways imbued the atmosphere of the Wilson Cabinet with a sense of treachery as far as Longford was concerned.

In such an environment talk of Christianity and religion was out of place. 'I expect', Longford later reflected, 'I was something of a nuisance in Cabinet. I was always going on about morality. It was like a gay party of people drinking wine and brandy and I was the only teetotaller. Very tedious.'[62] On one occasion, Longford was challenged by Tony Crosland, the Minister for Education, over a speech he planned to make in the Lords that afternoon which claimed to be speaking for a 'Christian Cabinet'. Longford did a quick head count and replied: 'I make it eleven

Christians and beginning with the top three – Harold Wilson, George Brown and Jim Callaghan – six non- or anti-Christians, and four don't knows. I don't know what they think about religion and I surmise they don't.' Crosland's only response was to ask where he fitted into the picture. Longford had him down as a 'don't know'.[63]

Whatever the religious beliefs of those who sat round the Cabinet table, Longford was one of the few who let his faith affect his work. As Longford would now admit, the ethos was closer to humanism than to Christianity. Barbara Castle recalls another Cabinet meeting in January 1965 when the issue of pensions came up again. George Brown complained that there was 'too much morality and not enough politics' going on around the table. 'Lord Longford nearly swooned at this. He said limply that he hoped he had misheard the First Secretary, but George waved him airily aside.'[64]

Longford's Christianity sometimes publicly conflicted with the Wilson Cabinet's commitment to humanistic concerns of scientific and technological advances. In March 1965, for example, he castigated the BBC for a sketch about birth control in the satirical 'Not So Much a Programme, More a Way of Life'. The government did not appreciate his Catholic objections to artificial contraception. Moreover, his proselytising interest in the fate of his colleagues' eternal souls exposed him to ridicule. In a diary entry recording a visit from Longford, Evelyn Waugh captured this eccentric, evangelising tendency:

> Frank made a splendid entrance to Sunday breakfast,
> his face, neck and shirt covered with blood, brandish-
> ing the Vulgate, crying 'Who will explain to me
> Second Corinthians five, six?' or some text. Of every
> name mentioned Frank asked: 'What chance of their
> coming in?' [to the Church][65]

Given such a context, the most surprising aspect is that Wilson kept Longford in the Cabinet for over three years and that Longford wanted to stay. When he resigned he abandoned party politics altogether. The latter decision was not sudden. It was the result of a change of perspective and priorities in his work. He had always regarded politics as a means to create a New Jerusalem, and not an end in itself. As it became obvious that the desired end could not thus be achieved, he began to withdraw from the battles of Wilson's Cabinet where he was feeling increasingly superfluous. His interest in politics, in political personalities and in the activities and tea-room gossip of Parliament continued, but close scrutiny of the workings of the Cabinet had been a great disappointment.

Though Longford was treated shabbily by the Cabinet at the time of his resignation he did receive a warm farewell from friends and his erstwhile charges in the House of Lords. From the Opposition benches, Viscount Gage wrote to Longford that 'when I looked at you sitting there as Leader of the House, I wondered. You did it very well, of course, but the House of Lords' leadership is such an Establishment thing, that I wondered . . .'[66] Lord Willis underlined the sense of loss.

> I shall miss the sight of that long bean-pole figure
> rising in front of me like a spring slowly uncoiling; I
> shall miss the vision of your lovely blueish-tinged
> pate, catching the amber light from the chamber roof;
> I shall miss those kind thank-you notes you used to
> write at the end of each session, with an absolutely
> unintelligible bit in your own handwriting at the
> bottom: I shall miss you.[67]

Other friends outside Parliament couched their condolences in humour. 'My dear Frank,' wrote Lady Diana Cooper, 'I am so proud of you, in spite of not being your mother. Well, well done. This is not written as a Tory but as an admirer of your character.'[68]

After so many years on the Labour front bench, Longford found the unfamiliar state of no longer having any authority on his side of the House rather unsettling and potentially embarrassing. The Labour peers, however, attempted to reassure Longford of their goodwill by giving him a bust of himself by Judith Bluck (a neighbour from Hurst Green) which won a bronze medal at an international exhibition in Paris. At the presentation, Longford replied to Lord Shackleton's affectionate tribute with one of his favourite quotations from the Scottish novelist Archibald Cronin's *The Stars Look Down*: 'Though he had failed to lead the van in battle, at least he was marching with the men.' It had not been a glorious resignation, he acknowledged, but had been tendered for the right reasons.

At the same occasion Longford pledged his full support to the government and vowed to avoid embarrassing them in any way. Within a couple of weeks, the man who had resigned over a broken promise himself went back on his word. In a debate over the government's plans to limit the number of Kenyan Asians, expelled from their own country but holding British passports, who could enter the United Kingdom, Longford voted against Labour's proposal. It did not deflect the scheme, but was, if confirmation were needed, further evidence of Longford's view that there was a crucial lack of principle at the heart of the Wilson Cabinet. Seeing that he was voting against the government of which he had so recently been a member, Lady Violet Bonham-Carter challenged him. 'Surely you are going to resign over this?' 'Resignation', Longford replied, 'is one thing you can't do twice running.'[69]

PART THREE

The Crusader

Happy are you when people abuse you and
persecute you and speak all kinds of calumny
against you on my account. Rejoice and be glad,
for your reward will be great in heaven; this is
how they persecuted the prophets before you

The Ninth Beatitude

Fifteen

The literary Longfords

It is in fact becoming rather ridiculous that every
time I open a paper I see a member of the family
smiling out of it. Are you all seeing the same press
agent or is there an entire firm under contract?

Michael Pakenham 1969

In his *Who's Who* entry, Frank Longford does not list any
recreations. Until 1968, work had been his life and what little
time it left him was devoted to his family and sport.

Though he had been something of a slow starter when it came
to choosing a career Longford had since the early 1930s been
working extremely hard. Yet in January 1968, all he had striven
for appeared to crumble to dust. His resignation marked the end
of his political ambitions and it had been on the basis of his
position as a prominent politician that everything else had been
built. He could harbour no hopes of a Lazarus-like resurrection
from the grave as the response of his Cabinet colleagues to his
loss made abundantly plain. While they continued with their
internecine struggles and jockeyed for position under their
paranoid leader, Longford retreated to the back benches in the
Lords. They scarcely gave him a second thought.

His political obituaries had been kind. Despite being on the
margins of mainstream Labour life in the Lords, he had cut a
dash as few before him in recent times had managed. He could
now quite gracefully don the mantle of an elder statesman
with a special interest in prisons and a penchant for talking
about morality. He could settle down to a gentle retirement,
devoting himself, like so many a former Cabinet minister who

373

found a niche in later life in the Lords, to his family and his memoirs.

Yet such a lifestyle was never going to satisfy Longford's unassuaged restlessness and residual ambition. He felt he had not made his mark, that there was still much to do and to reform and change. The curtain may have come down on the party political stage before him with only a muffled round of applause, but his outside interests, his social crusades, remained as urgent as ever. As far as writing memoirs was concerned, he had already flooded the market with two volumes. Devoting attention to his family was almost a redundant activity: they were entirely preoccupied with their own literary careers.

As Longford's political star waned, Elizabeth's was blazing bright in the world of books. After the success of *Victoria RI* in 1964 on both sides of the Atlantic, she had embarked on a biography of the Duke of Wellington, an ancestor by marriage of the Pakenhams, her husband's great-great-uncle. As well as being given full access to Wellington's archives at Apsley House in Piccadilly and Stratfield Saye in Hampshire by the current Duke (who referred to his guest as 'Cousin Elizabeth'), the biographer travelled to Waterloo and the Iberian Peninsula to research her subject and his famous battles at first hand. Occasionally she twisted Longford's arm to accompany her but his dislike of travel remained as strong as ever.

> My father has no interest in travel and my mother adores it [says Rachel]. Once she managed to persuade him to go with her to France. On the first day, he took off his shirt and sat on the verandah all the day. He's got very pale skin and he went scarlet. And he turned to my mother and said 'Look what has happened. I knew I shouldn't have come. This is a disaster. I must go at once.' And that was the end of that.[2]

Usually it was one of her children or her widowed sister-in-law Mary Clive who accompanied Elizabeth on her field trips. Longford's support was, as he once put it, 'providing some additional political background and heartfelt encouragement'.[3] Once Elizabeth's literary blood is up, he added, her determination to get the measure of her subject 'is far too strong to depend on external aid'.[4]

Roy Jenkins, himself an acclaimed biographer, praised Elizabeth as having 'a strong narrative gift and an unusual capacity to combine respect for historical fact with what is almost a gossip columnist's instinct for what will interest her readers'.[5] While Longford rejoiced in her success, he could play little part in it.

The first volume of *Wellington* was due to appear in 1969, collecting that year's *Yorkshire Post* literary prize. Elizabeth was hard at work on it when Longford found himself out of a job. Her international reputation as a writer generated enough revenue to compensate for the loss of his Cabinet minister's salary. However, in effect it reversed their roles and, while Longford had decidedly modern views on working women, his wife's preoccupation with her literary career only further underlined the hiatus in his own.

His children too were working on various literary endeavours. Antonia's *Mary Queen of Scots* was to appear in 1969 to transatlantic acclaim and, like *Victoria RI*, was the recipient of the James Tait Black prize. Thomas had begun writing soon after Oxford and his scholarly *Year of Liberty* – on the Irish rebellion of 1798 – came out in the same year as his eldest sister's book. History was not such an obsession with the younger children but they also participated in an impressively productive year during which the phrase the 'literary Longfords' was coined. Rachel's first novel, *All Things Nice*, was published and Judith had completed textbooks on *The Gordon Riots* and *Women in Revolt* before concentrating on poetry. Catherine had not made it into the British Library's catalogue but was a reporter on the *Daily Telegraph*.

The example set by Longford's and Elizabeth's interest in the written word must have had a considerable influence on the intellectual development of this bookish clan. Equally the competitive environment in which the siblings grew up would have played a part in accelerating the progress of their talents. Thomas had various theories on the family's prodigious literary output.

As he once wrote to his father, in the frenzy of 1969 he had attributed it to the fact that

> that cheerful, optimistic temperament we have
> inherited from you must have its darker side: at any
> rate, a taste for melancholy. It is this – a streak of
> melancholy – that must be common to most authors.
> How else to explain the self-exile; the 'long, tranquil,
> lonely days' as Evelyn Waugh called them, facing an
> endless supply of blank paper; the writing and the
> non-writing; the wrestling with the devil for the soul
> of one's narrative.[6]

But, Thomas continued, later, after spending an evening with his brothers and sisters, he thought of another cause of the family's mania for writing:

> We are not writers at all. We are talkers disguised as
> writers. Ten talkers in one family, and no listener: it
> was inevitable that half at least – the weaker half
> perhaps – should be driven to take refuge in author-
> ship in order to try to find an audience.[7]

In addition to the close family circle, Longford's two sisters had become respected authors. Mary Clive produced a life of Edward IV in the early 1970s while Violet Powell wrote on Ivy Compton-Burnett. Violet's husband Anthony had since the mid-1950s been unravelling his 'Dance to the Music of Time' saga. (One of its central characters, the thoroughly unlikeable Widmerpool, is reputed to be based on Longford. Though the image of a lonely, somewhat eccentric figure in his running shoes, obsessed with sport and morality, in the opening volume of the sequence suggests a *prima facie* case, Powell has always dismissed such suggestions. Longford himself, when questioned on the subject on a BBC TV programme, remarked: 'I wouldn't want to be like Widmerpool. He's a repellent character. Last Sunday I was jogging back to our house in the country and it suddenly came on to rain very hard and the rain was splashing off my glasses and I felt very like Widmerpool. He died jogging. I really entered into the spirit of Widmerpool for those few minutes. Please don't think that I insist on being like Widmerpool. It's only that I'm told that I'm like him and I try to see the likeness.')[8]

The Longfords' success was celebrated at a Foyle's literary lunch in 1969. 'One family, seven writers, twenty books' ran the headline after the event at the Dorchester. Their self-image as a political clan was being superseded by their reputation in the publishing world. Longford's political profile was eclipsed by his role as the paterfamilias of a literary brood. Longford was quizzed by reporters at the event as to what it felt like to be the spouse of a famous author. Light-heartedly, he recommended three possible reactions.

> Feigned indifference: Reply, 'I did notice she was scribbling a lot lately'. Therapeutic analysis: Say that writing is a first-rate thing for keeping a woman out of mischief. Self-satisfied: Assume that you did it your-self and say 'We had a bit of trouble with the last chapter but we ironed it out.'

'Pride is a very specific emotion my father does feel towards our writing,' says Judith. 'He'll tell you that he reads my poetry, but I swear he doesn't. It's not his thing at all – imagistic when he is interested in ideas. But he is proud of it.'[9] Longford's evident pride in 1969 in his family's achievements – especially in his wife's success – gave the lie to any suggestion that he resented the loss of the limelight. In any case, his own 'small book' – as he always calls it with apposite modesty – *Humility* was out at the same time, lest anyone in the family should become too big-headed.

Malcolm Muggeridge, a close friend, neighbour and occasional co-worker of the Longfords for many years, was dismissive of all Longford's books save the volume on humility. In an interview he remarked: 'Those autobiographies of his weren't worth writing. They don't tell you anything about the man. But there's more of him in that little book on humility than anywhere else.'[10]

The central dilemma tackled in the book, Longford's first overtly Christian commission, published by Collins, was one that had been omnipresent throughout his political life: how to act as a Christian in public life, whether to take obvious pride in your position and achievements, or whether to recoil from any publicity or recognition? In his opening chapter Longford recalls a remark made about him in the *Sunday Times* by Tom Driberg that his desire to get his own way was at least as strong as his yearning for Christian humility. The same contradiction in Longford's character was much remarked upon when, after publication of the book, he was said to have walked into various shops and demanded to know why it was not on display in the window. (This seems yet again to be an instance of others misconstruing a story Longford has adapted for the purposes of self-mockery. The original story occurs in the introduction of his book on humility and concerns Bishop Ullathorne, one of the Catholic hierarchy, who, when lecturing on humility, is asked by a student which was the best book on the subject. Ullathorne replied: 'There is only one and I wrote it myself.')

The temptations for a senior politician to discard humility were great, Longford admitted in the book.

> When people say or think that politics is a dirty
> business, they have usually in mind the temptations
> against honesty. But I soon realised from my own
> direct experience that the temptations against humil-
> ity were much more insidious. The politician is
> encouraged to think of himself as a very fine fellow.
> His power for good or ill depends upon his popularity.
> It is easy for him to see the achievement and mainten-
> ance of this same popularity as a primary obligation.

How far this was confessional, as Muggeridge suggested, and how far a reflection of his observations of the Wilson Cabinet is hard to establish. Certainly a glance at the Crossman diaries suggests that humility was not the order of the day in ministerial gatherings. Longford stressed in the book that humility, as well as forgiveness, was a key Christian virtue. The question of balancing true Christianity with a career in the public eye had long been troubling the author. His ambition to hold high office, his love of publicity, his ready and potentially cutting wit and a certain in-bred arrogance as the scion of an aristocratic family all contributed to making the struggle to meet the ideal of humility a tough one. Auberon Waugh, his godson, describes this desire to be truly Christian in the eyes of the world as Longford's 'crucifixion complex'.[11] He attempted to tame his natural instincts in order to live up to a lofty ideal.

Where Longford distinguished himself was by being prepared to go on the record as aspiring to be humble, thereby risking the ridicule of those who would chart his every shortcoming in years to come. It was rather like, he says, writing a book about the secret of a successful marriage after being divorced three times. One continues to aspire to the goal but has the sinking feeling one will never quite reach it.

While other members of the Wilson Cabinet worked away on kiss-and-tell diaries, exposing the workings of the administration warts and all, Longford's reaction to resignation was to attempt to reaffirm an ideal for both politicians and others, an aim that he clearly felt he himself had failed to live up to and that others around him had lost sight of. The book does not claim any great success, but in its ambition speaks much of what Longford was trying to achieve in the world of politics. He was later to write in more practical terms about his years in Cabinet, but *Humility* was his immediate response to the ending of his political career, a reflection of what he believed ought to motivate those in public office.

For all its philosophical and theological aspirations, the book was largely a collection of anecdotes, personal reminiscences of the humility of various figures in the public eye. These sketches were reinforced by extracts selected from some of the Christian writers who constituted Longford's regular diet of spiritual reading.

His choice of such an unusual subject was a sign, for those who had not yet realised it, that Lord Longford was no average politician but one for whom moral choices and obligations superseded worldly success. While it may be argued that his thesis had come rather late in the day – since his political career was over and it was easy to preach what he no longer had to practise – Longford's decision to tackle such an elusive subject as hu.nility was indicative both of his indifference to former party colleagues' opinion and of his intention not to disappear from public view altogether. Far from being a backward-looking book in the style of memoirs, *Humility* set an agenda for future endeavours.

His daughter Judith feels that after his resignation in 1968 her father's behaviour towards his family altered. 'Once he got free of having to earn his living and the ambition of trying to get to the top, he relaxed a good deal. He's had a very jolly old age.'[12] Judith considers that it was only when her father's attention was turned away from the world of politics and she had attained adulthood that their relationship developed. Previously he had been too preoccupied to give her much attention.

As a Cabinet minister, Longford had certainly missed out on the joys of being a grandfather according to Antonia.

> In May 1967 my sixth child Orlando was born. I think there had been some complaints in the family that my father never took an interest in his grandchildren and my mother had a word with him. When anybody is in hospital Dadda is determined to visit them. For him it is a corporal work of mercy. I was in Guy's and in bed – you had to be in bed when Dadda visited otherwise it wasn't a visit. Anyway he'd been very busy with various Cabinet matters but he walked in and went straight over to the cot and said: 'Hello, hello, what a sweet fellow' and then gave a very satisfied smile. When he turned to me I couldn't help laughing. The cot was empty. Orlando was in the nursery but my father hadn't noticed.[13]

Though there was much to delight in with his ever-expanding family and their achievements, the everyday role as centre of the family had long ago been filled by Elizabeth. Retirement from politics may have, in theory, given Longford more time to devote to his family, but it was too late to claim back what he had abandoned when they were youngsters. With his eight children now adults and some parents themselves, Longford was to experience some of the griefs of fatherhood – often amid an unpleasant glare of publicity.

His second son Patrick had become a very successful criminal barrister, noted in a family of writers for his verbal prowess when it came to public speaking. Thomas feels that there was a special bond between Longford and Patrick on account of their similar positions among their siblings (each of the Longford children seems to have a different theory on who was their father's favourite – each agrees only that it was not him- or herself).

> It is certainly true that my father identified with Paddy
> because Paddy, like my father, was a second son.
> Paddy was always in trouble and so he identified with
> Paddy to protect Paddy. But to say that Paddy was his
> favourite would be to give a false impression.[14]

In September 1963 tragedy struck Patrick when he was out sailing with two friends and their boat capsized in the English Channel. Patrick's two companions drowned and he spent eighteen hours at sea before being rescued and brought ashore at Hastings, not far from Bernhurst. It was a traumatic experience, but one from which, with the support of those around him, he seemed to have recovered. He returned to work and in 1969 married, and eventually had three children. However, he was to suffer a series of mental breakdowns, accompanied by erratic behaviour. He had to give up his practice at the Bar because of ill-health and his marriage ended. Throughout his periods of sickness Paddy has been able to rely upon the unfailing support of both his parents who have tried, as far as possible, to shelter him from any unwelcome attention from newspapers. They have not always been successful and the exploitation of Paddy's illness by reporters has been one of the most painful ways in which Longford came to realise that being a public figure can have negative as well as positive results.

While the Longfords' marriage is held up as a national

monument to the institution, their children have not been so fortunate. In addition to the ending of Paddy's marriage, their youngest son Kevin, Judith and Antonia have all separated from their partners. As a Catholic Longford is a firm believer in the permanence of marriage and his children's experiences have caused him much pain. As in other matters his ideals have been intruded upon by realities and in this case they were close to home.

Though Longford had acted in 1935 (before he was a Catholic) as election agent in Oxford for A. P. Herbert who later made his mark in Parliament by piloting through a reform of the divorce laws, he later publicly disowned his candidate's crusade. 'I just didn't think very hard about what he was proposing at the time,' he says. 'I expect I may have to do a little extra time in Purgatory for that one.'[15] In 1969, as a member of the House of Lords, he participated in the debate that surrounded the successful Divorce Law Reform of that year. He opposed its introduction of divorce without the consent of both partners after a period of five years' separation.

> I acknowledge that in a few cases these provisions for
> getting rid of an unwanted wife after a few years may,
> on balance, increase rather than diminish the total
> happiness [he told his fellow peers]. But I would say,
> with absolute conviction, that in the vast majority of
> cases these provisions will have a very cruel impact
> and for that reason I am totally against this Bill.

In 1969, he had been speaking from the basis of his own, and his children's, extremely happy marriages. His use of phrases like 'the guilty partner' and 'the innocent partner' demonstrated a somewhat abstract and theological understanding of the issue under discussion. As his daughter Antonia has already pointed out in connection with his views on contraception and sex outside marriage, Longford, lacking the relevant personal experience, seems simply not imaginative enough to understand the reality of others' lives. But even the subsequent practical experience of seeing four of his children split up from their partners has not changed his fundamental belief in the sanctity of marriage as enshrined in Catholic teaching. He has struggled to reconcile his principles with his love of his children.

Judith, when her 1963 marriage to Alec Kazantzis was under strain, simply avoided broaching the subject with her father. 'I never even talked to him about it because I was in such a bad state. I talked to my mother who was very upset and just couldn't believe it. But in the end she had to believe it.'[16]

Longford's sturdy adherence to Catholic principles can, however, open up a gulf between him and his children. Elizabeth, as ever on matters concerning the family, is more pragmatic. Reflecting on her children's marital difficulties, she says:

> If, at the beginning of my married life, when my
> children were being born, some prophet had told me
> that we would be a Catholic family and yet we would
> have these divorces and second marriages, I would
> have felt amazement, disbelief and great unhappiness.
> But for most people life doesn't strike with one great
> hammer blow – it gradually happens, and you get used
> to it, you accept. You know the people involved, you
> admire them and love them whatever has gone wrong,
> and so you're buoyed up. You know it isn't the end.[17]

Although his children may find it hard to talk to their father about their marriages, Judith realises that in times of trouble he is the first person she will turn to.

> He has always been very consoling. I was very ill
> when my marriage ended and my father really put
> himself out to visit me. He's always wonderful when
> you're in real trouble. You can count on him and
> that's very important.[18]

Antonia's experience is similar. 'Even now when I am myself a grandmother, the first person I would go to if I was in trouble would be my father. If something appalling had happened to me, if I murdered someone, I would immediately turn to him.'[19]

383

Yet when her marriage to Hugh Fraser ended in 1977 and she married the playwright Harold Pinter, her relationship with her father suffered because he found it so hard to come to terms with her decision. In the end, though, people are more important to Longford than principles. He may remain implacable in his adherence to the principle that marriage is for life, but he has over a period of time come to accept, if not approve of, his children's choices. Though Harold Pinter tells his father-in-law that as a child he was turned away from Eton Manor because he was Jewish, the two now get on well, with Longford paying tribute to his son-in-law's 'genius' as a writer and both sharing a mutual passion for cricket.

In August 1969, soon after the Foyle's lunch, the Longfords had to shoulder the cruellest blow that can befall a parent. Elizabeth was away in Warsaw with Rachel, visiting her old friend Nicholas Henderson, then the British Ambassador in Poland with Michael Pakenham, a rising young diplomat, as his Second Secretary. Catherine would normally have spent the weekend at Bernhurst with her parents, but with Elizabeth abroad decided to go to East Anglia with a girlfriend. Early on the morning of August 11, as they were returning to work with a photographer friend, a lorry collided with their car. All three were killed instantly.

Longford first heard the news when a journalist from the *Evening Standard* telephoned him to get his reaction. Antonia, who hurried over to be with her father, remembers, even in this moment of desolation, his extraordinary faith. 'He had to go and identify Catherine's body. I was enormously struck by how strong and noble he was. He really did believe she had gone to a better world. His faith was propping him up in a world that otherwise would have been unendurable.'[20] At a moment when darkness might have engulfed even the most convinced believer, Longford was sustained by his belief that Catherine was with her maker. His faith in God now gave him the strength to endure a calamity, a support that had not been evident in his earlier depressive years before he had converted to Catholicism.

Though Catherine had been the most willing of Longford's children to challenge her father on any range of subjects and the two had had a series of heated disagreements, they had developed a closer understanding in the years immediately before her death. He had been particularly proud of her appearance with Malcolm Muggeridge in a television debate where she defended the 1968 papal encyclical *Humanae vitae* which outlawed artificial contraception. Longford's pride was not just because in describing the document as 'very loving', Catherine was echoing his own thoughts, but more because she had briefed herself carefully in advance and performed with such poise and conviction. As he wrote later:

> Her mind was still fresh and eager. In a sense her loss
> was all the greater because her powers were only just
> beginning to blossom. But . . . she had already in the
> deepest sense found herself, and she had nothing to
> fear in this life or the next one.[21]

Many of those who wrote to the family assumed that their Christian faith would prove a consolation. And indeed it did. But for Longford such relief was not automatic. Though he remained true in public to the tenets of his religion, in private there were moments of doubt, as he later admitted. He had to go through a period of agonising as to why God had let such a thing happen to his youngest daughter before his faith reasserted itself.

The loss of his child was also to concentrate his thoughts on a question that had been in the background of his work with prisoners for years – the feelings of the victims.

> I have never been a victim of a serious crime and
> therefore it is hard for me to say how I would feel
> towards the perpetrator. The closest I came was with
> my daughter's death. The lorry driver who caused it
> also died in the crash. But had he lived, I'm not sure
> how I would have felt towards him. I think I would
> have gone to visit him in hospital. I hope I would
> have gone to see him in hospital. I would have seen it
> as a duty.[22]

385

Again the struggle between an instinctive and a Christian response is evident.

For Elizabeth coping with Catherine's death was more of an ordeal. Her children feel that this was the crucial moment in their mother's Catholicism, a make-or-break time. In 1986 she was able to write:

> I think I have got over it. I am sometimes asked whether my faith helped: belief in immortality and a personal resurrection. My answer is that nothing lessens the pain at the time. I remember Frank being sent for by Mrs de Valera, a devout Catholic and wife of the Irish president, soon after Catherine died. 'Tell Elizabeth', she said to him, 'that I cried every day for a year when our youngest son was killed in a riding accident. She will do the same. But now I would not have him back.' Faith saved me from asking the terrible questions, 'Why? Why her? Why me?' I also had a growing conviction that Catherine was all right. It was a comfort to be able to do something for her . . . if only to say a Hail Mary.[23]

Christ's mother, a feature of Catholicism that had given Elizabeth great difficulty when she converted, became a comfort to her in her moment of grief.

A tablet in memory of Catherine was later unveiled in the Hurst Green church and the family decided to establish the Catherine Pakenham Prize in memory of their sister. Since 1971 – in conjunction first with the *Daily Telegraph* and latterly with the *Evening Standard* – it has been awarded to young women journalists, like Catherine, at the outset of their career. Rachel has been one of the stalwarts of the judging panels, taking over in the early 1980s as chairman from her mother. Various friends of the family like the columnist Valerie Grove and the writer Marina Warner, Longford's god-daughter and child of his old Eton friend Esmond Warner, have lent their support. Among rising stars to win the award was Polly Toynbee.

*

Longford slowly managed to pick up some of the threads of his pre-Cabinet minister work when he left office. He was reappointed as a Director of the Alliance Building Society, a lucrative post which he had held while at the National Bank but which he had relinquished on deciding to return full-time to politics in 1963. He also was named a director of the Martin Luther King fund and – by Harold Wilson – Chairman of the Attlee Memorial Fund. The latter had been set up in 1965, when the former Labour leader was still alive, and continued after his death, under Longford's leadership, to raise funds to build Attlee House as part of the facilities at Toynbee Hall in the East End where the ex-Prime Minister had once been Secretary.

These posts did not satisfy Longford's yearning for more demanding employment. At the end of 1968, with the literary Longfords active if not yet celebrated in the publishing world, an offer came from an old friend, the Catholic businessman, Charles Forte. He asked Longford to join the board of the publishing house Sidgwick and Jackson at the start of 1970 with a view to taking on the chairmanship in May of that year.

It would be a part-time post, but very much an active one. Longford was not simply to be a figurehead to create confidence among authors and bankers, but an involved publisher. While as a youngster he had little time for books, he had become increasingly embroiled in the literary world – through his own efforts in print, through those of his family, and by virtue of his daily and incessant reading of spiritual and theological tomes.

It was an imaginative appointment by Forte. Longford was, after all, nearing retirement age, and some questioned whether he would be able to make any sort of impact. A shrewd businessman, Forte was – like Michael Cooke before him – able to see beyond Longford's air of eccentricity and distraction and perceive that he had a sound grasp of the world of books and of what made a good read. While his experience was largely on the authors' side of the publishing equation, Longford was not entirely ignorant of the other end of the business. Two of his daughters, Catherine and Antonia, had worked for George Weidenfeld's publishing house.

Furthermore Longford's commercial experience at the

National Bank had proved his business acumen. His almost unceasing ability to spark off new ideas, to innovate, instigate and then delegate was a formidable tool in the armour of a commissioning editor. He knew how to create public interest. Susan Barnes, in a *Sunday Times* profile in 1971, spoke of his 'disconcerting professionalism towards publicity'.[24] He would, by his very presence, ensure that Sidgwick and Jackson made an impact in its field. Added to all these strengths was his enormous range of social contacts. If anyone was going to be able to bring in eminent authors through personal approaches and without vast expenditure in advances, it would be Longford. In a field that in 1970 was still dominated by maverick gentleman publishers, often of eccentric disposition, Longford would fit like a glove.

Sidgwick and Jackson had been in business since the early part of the twentieth century. Initially it had been in the hands of Frank Sidgwick who had made a reputation through publishing such writers and poets as Rupert Brooke, John Masefield, George Gissing, E. M. Forster and Elizabeth Bowen. He was responsible for starting the career of more than one major author, though many of his writers moved on to bigger firms when their names became better known. Sidgwick is reported to have turned down Forster's *A Passage to India* because it knocked the British Empire and John Betjeman's poems because he thought they were too superficial.

With Sidgwick's death in 1939 the firm had been taken over by an old Etonian, Jimmy Knapp-Fisher, who broadened the range of books it published. In the mid-1960s, however, Knapp-Fisher got into financial difficulties and Charles Forte took over the floundering firm, leaving its previous owner as chairman. When the losses continued, Forte decided to bring in Longford as the man to restore Sidgwick and Jackson's fortunes.

Longford's approach was similar to his attitude at the National Bank. He was happy to delegate most day-to-day decisions to his managing director, William Armstrong, but he insisted on being consulted over which books would be published and over the treatment of staff. He had found himself another mini-constituency. Various employees at Sidgwick and Jackson from his time as chairman until 1980 and later as a director until 1987, remember him welcoming anyone with a problem into his office at the firm's headquarters in Bloomsbury for a glass of sherry and a friendly chat.

His efforts to improve Sidgwick's list soon bore fruit. Among his great triumphs was to persuade the Conservative Prime Minister, Edward Heath, first to write a book about sailing – which leapt to the top of the bestsellers chart and stayed there – and then a follow-up, written after his election defeat, on music which was also a runaway success. Longford once likened the experience of seeing one of his authors in the bestsellers list to being a don at Christ Church. 'I did not personally answer the examination questions, but I gloried sometimes in the published class lists. From my chairman's seat in Sidgwick and Jackson, I gain untold pleasure from the achievements of those I preside over.'[25]

Despite Heath's having apparently compared Longford to an ape, Longford was not sidetracked by such past follies when considering a good commercial prospect. Such clarity of decision was not so prevalent when Sidgwick was offered Cecil King's diaries. The newspaper man had been a confidant of both Wilson and George Brown during the 1964–70 period. Longford found its presentation of the era somewhat distorted. He also could not fail to see Wilson's reference to him as having 'the mental age of a twelve year old'. He was agonising over whether to let his past life affect his present when the burden was lifted from his shoulders. A larger publishing house made an offer to King that Sidgwick and Jackson could not match and the diaries went to the winning bidder.

In general, Longford tried not to let his own concerns influence commercial decisions. He made no attempt, for example, to turn Sidgwick into a religious publisher. Occasionally they would produce a book in which he had a personal interest. John Grigg was commissioned to write a life of Longford's old friend Nancy Astor. Claud Cockburn – originator of the idea of a late 1930s 'Cliveden Set' – was signed up to record his impression of this period in *The Devil's Decade*. Concerning Ireland, another of

Longford's long-term interests, Margery Forrester's bestselling biography of Michael Collins was published by the firm.

Having a husband and father at the head of a publishing house was of only occasional practical benefit to the literary Longfords. It was on Elizabeth's recommendation that Sidgwick took Molly Gillen's *The Prince and His Lady* which had failed to excite other publishers but which received critical acclaim. And when the company decided to move into the field of children's books, Longford published two – *Robin Hood* and *King Arthur* – written by his daughter Antonia several years before, with illustrations by her teenage daughter Rebecca.

Part of Longford's contract at Sidgwick was that he could use his office there as a base for his other works and these sometimes caused a few blushes. There was a steady stream of callers, ex-prisoners, homeless men and women, those down on their luck, asking to see him. On several occasions, he used his office at Sidgwick and Jackson to conduct interviews with pornographers for his inquiry into the subject. Another time he shared a glass of sherry with the mother of one of Myra Hindley's victims.

When he was heavily engaged in the pornography investigation, Sidgwick published *The Professionals* by Ian Scarlet, an account of the world of prostitution. The newspapers responded with headlines of 'Lord Porn to publish a shocker' accusing him of double standards. They drew attention to the mini-skirted legs that adorned the cover (a bad choice of design, Longford later conceded). The book in question, however, was anything but pornographic and, if Longford could be accused of any personal interest in it, it was in the author's presentation of prostitutes as victims and outcasts in society, a group for which the chairman had a long record of sympathy and support.

During Longford's time at Sidgwick and Jackson, they won the Publishers' Publicity Circle silver trophy three years running and in 1977 the Allen Lane award for best publisher of the year. While the achievement was one shared by everyone in the firm, as Longford was the first to point out, the transformation in Sidgwick and Jackson's fortunes was marked under his chairmanship. He had set himself the goal of moving the company up a notch or two on the publishing ladder – from small to medium sized. The number of books was increased and, within four years, Longford was able to report to his board that turnover had quadrupled. In 1978 he was chosen as one of six 'great English publishers' by the *Sunday Times*. With typical self-deprecation, Longford attributes his inclusion to the fact that one fellow publisher had withdrawn from the list when he heard who else was on it.

The aspect of publishing Longford most enjoyed was the opportunity to be creative in a literary sense without having to write a book. His previous efforts in print had not won universal acclaim from the critics for their style and approach and he was generally held to fall short of his wife's, and increasingly his children's, standards and achievements. His joy in writing a book – or for that matter in preparing a speech for the House of Lords – lay in the research. When in his mid-eighties and preparing a book on young offenders, he hurried up to the Blackbird Leys council estate in his old constituency of Oxford to investigate night-time disturbances between joy-riders, local youths and the police. His enthusiasm for fieldwork research was undiluted. But his appetite for the solitary task of writing, never great in the first place, diminished further in his retirement years. Yet as a publisher he was able to bring out the sort of books he felt would interest the public without having to toil over the writing of them himself.

Before he took over the chairman's seat at Sidgwick and Jackson, Longford had completed a biography, for Hutchinson, of his old friend Eamon de Valera. Since the early 1930s when they had first met, the two had been firm – if unlikely – friends, as Thomas Pakenham has pointed out. The years did not diminish Longford's admiration for de Valera. Indeed when he was asked in various interviews to name the figures who had most influenced him, he invariably quoted de Valera alongside Attlee. They did not always see eye to eye. Longford's suggestion of the so-called Cardinal d'Alton solution to the partition of Ireland in the 1950s, with the Dublin government required to request re-admission into the Commonwealth, had prompted de Valera to remark that if it ever came about he would stand down from the largely titular position of Irish President and run once more for Prime Minister on a ticket of opposing any such move. But the close personal bond between the two was not slackened by such differences. When Paddy had his accident in 1963, de Valera rang the Longfords at Bernhurst to offer words of support. At the time of Catherine's death, Mrs de Valera sent a message to Elizabeth.

While in the past the friendship may have raised a few eyebrows in Britain (it caused one of Attlee's doubts as to Longford's suitability for elevation to the House of Lords in 1945, Evan Durbin told him) by the mid-1960s de Valera was no longer seen as a figure to be mistrusted by Whitehall. So when in 1965 Longford was invited to partner Tom O'Neill of the National Library of Ireland in a full-length biography of de Valera, with the subject's co-operation, (as a Cabinet minister) he asked for and obtained the Prime Minister's permission to accept. The completion of the manuscript was delayed by the other commitments of the two authors. Longford was busy with government work until 1968 and O'Neill was appointed to a teaching post at Galway University. With de Valera in Dublin and his two biographers in London and Galway, the project moved at a snail's pace.

The bulk of the research and sifting through de Valera's papers fell to O'Neill and he was responsible for much of the detail concerning Irish politics. But Longford's special knowledge of the events leading up to and following the 1921 treaty – recorded in *Peace by Ordeal* – and his long-standing role as unofficial emissary between the British government and the Irish leader permeate the text. There is an intimacy in some of the accounts of de Valera as a family man that Longford was able to provide as a result of the many occasions on which he had stayed at the president's residence in Dublin's Phoenix Park.

Also evidence of Longford's involvement is the attempt to define de Valera as a man of religion. In de Valera's work Longford found that political achievement and Christian duty were interwoven, a state Longford had sought to attain in his own work. When writing of his other great political hero, Attlee, Longford is hamstrung by the former's attitudes to Christianity – he called it 'mumbo jumbo'. De Valera, however, operating in an overwhelmingly Catholic country where he himself had created a special place for the Church in the constitution, virtually epitomised Longford's aspirations.

The biography was well received on both sides of the Irish Sea and sold well in America. The criticisms directed at Longford's partisan approach in *Peace by Ordeal* to de Valera's role in the 1921 negotiations were reiterated by some reviewers. But the weight of new material in the biography was acknowledged and its enduring status as the standard work on a man who dominated Irish politics for fifty years was assured.

Publication in November 1970 was marred by only one small slip on Longford's part. He travelled to Dublin to give the Irish president a special presentation volume of the book as part of the launch celebrations. Much to his embarrassment, and to the delight of the headline writers who revelled in Longford's eccentricity, he unfortunately misplaced the gift on the eve of handing it over to the eighty-eight-year-old president.

Despite having made his life in Britain, Longford never lost his interest in Ireland and Irish politics. His abiding concern – first expressed in articles in the *Daily Telegraph* in 1938 and 1939 – that the partition of 1921 should be reversed never waned in spite of official indifference. He continued to write in the press at regular intervals on the need to tackle the issue of Northern Ireland. The bitterness of the sectarian divide and the problems that were being stored up for the future was brought home to him forcibly when he was due to speak at Queen's University in Belfast in January 1939 on the subject of an end to partition and was prevented from doing so by Unionist protests.

As a member of Wilson's government, Longford was unable to persuade his colleagues to pay any great attention to Northern Ireland before it was too late. Wilson made several high-profile gestures towards the Irish government as a means of improving relations – notably returning the bones of Sir Roger Casement, the Irish patriot prosecuted in the British courts as a traitor by F. E. Smith and then executed in 1916. But the acknowledged imperfections of the government in Belfast prompted little debate.

However, the growing discontent among the Nationalist population of the north of Ireland was only exacerbated by the seeming indifference of the British government and Cabinet. It was not until Longford had left the government that, in August 1968, the Civil Rights Movement brought matters to a head and forced the British to tackle gerrymandering and anti-Catholic discrimination by the Unionist administration at Stormont. The Loyalist backlash led to violence on the streets and to the arrival of British troops in August 1969.

Earlier that same year, as events in Northern Ireland were moving out of control, Longford was approached, as a man with Anglo-Irish connections with a long-standing interest in the subject, by Robin Denniston, the managing director of Hodder and Stoughton, to write a book about Ulster. He accepted the idea in principle and set about his research, making repeated trips to Belfast to talk to senior politicians and church leaders on both sides of the conflict. Among those he visited was Terence O'Neill, then the Northern Ireland Prime Minister, with whom he had a distant family connection. At the time of their meeting, Longford noted that 'anything, I suppose, might happen this year but, short of civil war which I do not in my heart believe possible, I feel that solid progress has been made . . .'[26]

It was a judgement that was soon to be rendered redundant by events, but Longford was not alone in underestimating the extent of popular anger in the north. With the situation on the ground changing from day to day, he decided that trying to write a book on Ulster on the basis of research trips from London was a hopeless task and he abandoned the project.

He did not, though, stop being interested in the fate of Northern Ireland. In April 1969 he sat spellbound in the House of Commons gallery as twenty-one-year-old Bernadette Devlin, a left-wing Irish republican, made her maiden speech, having sensationally defeated the Unionist candidate in the Mid-Ulster by-election. Though he was to disagree with much of what she said, Longford later wrote:

> I never denied in my heart the truth of her contention
> that the sectarian animosities of Belfast in particular

have owed much to the determination of the Unionist leaders to stay in power at all costs.[27]

As a respected but retired Cabinet minister, with only a seat in the House of Lords as a public platform, Longford had little hope of influencing matters in Northern Ireland. He did try to add what weight he still possessed to the call for the establishment of a coalition government in Belfast made up of Nationalist and Loyalist representatives. Indeed he was one of the first British politicians to back such a proposal. The morning after Ms Devlin's speech, he met with Paddy Devlin, chairman of the Northern Ireland Labour Party and Gerry (later Lord) Fitt, the West Belfast MP, and agreed to send a letter to *The Times* urging Whitehall to force the Unionists' hand on the idea of power-sharing. 'This', he wrote, 'is the only policy that offers a clear possibility of a concerted movement towards peace and progress.'

He was also part of a substantial lobby in September 1971 when, after another visit to Belfast, he wrote in the Catholic weekly *The Tablet* opposing government plans to introduce internment.

> We are given to understand that the British and
> Northern Ireland governments are setting a high
> priority on restoring Catholic confidence and securing
> their increased participation in running the province. I
> cannot myself believe that while internment without
> trial continues, there is the least prospect of anything
> of the sort happening.

In February 1972, Longford returned to his preoccupation with the deteriorating situation in Northern Ireland when he opened a debate on the subject in the House of Lords. Again it was a gesture, unlikely to swing the government one way or another. His Catholicism and his own often stated belief that Ireland was one nation and should, one day, be returned to that state from its current artificial partition only served to weaken his case in the eyes of those who were determined at all costs to maintain the Union. But Longford was equally determined to give the issue an airing in front of the junior ministers on the government benches opposite and their civil servants who passed on reports of what was said in the Upper Chamber to their bosses.

He returned in his opening speech to the subject of power-sharing that he had first raised over two years earlier. This time he was anxious to see Nationalists not just given a role in their own government by the Unionists, but apportioned one in the name of justice. 'It is clearly essential that the minority community should be accorded as of right a participation in the Cabinet [in Belfast],' he told his fellow peers.

The following month Longford was once again in the Commons gallery to see Edward Heath announce the suspension of Stormont. Various attempts were subsequently made at achieving the sort of power-sharing that Longford and many others believe to be the only way out of the Northern Ireland *impasse* but all have floundered. While his attention has moved on to other issues, he remains acutely conscious of the need to promote reconciliation in the north and make known his own special, albeit not unique, Anglo-Irish perspective on the 'Troubles', with a foot on both sides of the Irish Sea. In 1976 he gave his enthusiastic backing to the Northern Ireland Peace People and helped them organise a rally in Trafalgar Square. In May 1988, he was again on his feet in the House of Lords to protest at the 'shockingly high' levels of unemployment in the Nationalist ghetto of west Belfast. After a visit to the city, he urged the government to tackle with 'new vigour' the jobs discrimination that had been one of the key issues in the civil rights campaigns of the late 1960s.

During the 1970s and 1980s, Longford's work with prisoners inevitably brought him into contact with growing numbers of IRA convicts in British jails. His role in visiting some of them caused speculation that he was 'soft' on the terrorists but it is an impression that he has been at pains to dispel. Though he is an unashamed republican in believing in one Ireland, he has repeatedly and unequivocally denounced the IRA campaign of violence from the floor of the House of Lords. One of the bombers' targets had, after all, been his own son-in-law, the Tory minister Hugh Fraser in the 1970s.

However, on the principle of loving the sinner but hating their sin, he was not prepared to ignore the pleas of those IRA prisoners who contacted him. Much attention was focused throughout the 1980s on the campaigns to overturn the convictions of the Guildford Four, the Birmingham Six and the Maguire Seven, all jailed for IRA offences and all subsequently exonerated. Longford visited several of them in prison and supported efforts to establish their innocence wholeheartedly. Once they were released he built friendships with several of the leading protagonists including Anne Maguire.

But Longford's concern in his prison work has never primarily been with innocence or guilt. He does not feel it is his place to judge and condemn and he has never made a distinction in his prison visiting between those who have been justly or unjustly convicted. With so-called Irish or IRA prisoners, his approach has not changed. His role, he believes, is to act as a friend to those with no one else to turn to.

With some, however, he has been gratified to see a change of heart. Shane O'Doherty, convicted of sending parcel bombs on behalf of the IRA, acknowledged his guilt to Longford but while in prison turned back to the Catholic Church and repented of his past crimes. Longford was prepared to accept this as genuine and, when the Parole Board concurred, invited O'Doherty to lunch in the House of Lords. This caused great annoyance among some Tory back-benchers in September 1989. They felt that someone who had done what O'Doherty had should not be accorded such an honour. They did not want him darkening the doorsteps of Parliament. Longford was not deflected, however, and in November 1990 again invited O'Doherty to attend a reception he was organising in the Lords.

Over Ireland, Longford was able to make a good deal of noise, some of it within Westminster itself, without ever being able to claim any great individual success in changing policy. He has the shadow of power without the substance. This was particularly his frustration when in the Wilson government, but has been a feature of sitting in the Lords rather than the Commons almost from the outset. While a maverick MP can make quite a stir if he or she exploits the procedure of the House in the Commons, such impact is mostly denied to those in the Upper Chamber.

This image of Longford with the trappings of power but none of the practical benefits was forcefully emphasised in April 1972 when he was made a Knight of the Garter by the Queen. The Most Noble Order of the Garter was founded in 1348 and membership is in the personal gift of the sovereign. It is an exclusive – some would say the most exclusive – club with just twenty-four members at any one stage. The Prince of Wales, the Duke of Edinburgh and various European sovereigns are additional members.

His elevation was clearly a combination of factors in Her Majesty's estimation, not just his political work. Certainly the announcement caused much comment. News of it came only days after he had revealed his pornography campaign, but the decision had been taken well in advance and the two were unconnected. For Longford it was 'a clear reminder that I was not without recognition'.[28]

Harold Wilson, in a 1977 interview, was challenged to explain why Longford received such a senior honour. Though he was emphatic that he played no role in Her Majesty's decision, he continued: 'I would have thought the answer was rather simple, that she was wanting one or two people on the Labour side and he was a minister of Cabinet rank going back to her father's reign.'[29]

The sight of Longford at Garter ceremonies, processing behind Her Majesty from the chapel at Windsor Castle in his plumed hat and blue velvet mantle gives the impression that he is a man of enormous influence in Britain. He greatly enjoys the Garter ceremony each June. His banner, featuring the crest of the Irish Knights of St Patrick on a red and yellow background, hangs in St George's Chapel between those of Lord Shackleton, his successor as Leader of the Lords, and Edward Heath. Nearby are the banners of Harold Wilson, Quintin Hailsham and James Callaghan, lifelong political friends and foes gathered in retirement in an exclusive conclave.

Sixteen

The leader of the opposition to the permissive society

To every Englishman, Francis Aungier Pakenham,
the Seventh Earl of Longford KG PC, is better
known as 'Lord Porn'

Time Magazine *1972*

At the time of the *Lady Chatterley* trial in 1960, a solicitor for the defence approached Frank Longford and asked him to join the bevy of 'expert witnesses' backing Penguin Books in their attempts to publish D. H. Lawrence's controversial tale of love between the classes. The lawyer obviously assumed that, as a Labour peer and a former academic with well-known liberal sympathies towards prisoners and those on the margins of society, Longford would prove an effective advocate for literary freedom. He was swiftly disillusioned. Longford said that he would happily read the book – then not on open sale – if only to refute his wife's contention that he was far too quick to condemn things he had not studied. But, he added, he was much more likely to feel inclined to speak for the prosecution than for the defence. When the solicitor expressed surprise, Longford proclaimed himself a Puritan. 'But D. H. Lawrence was a Puritan,' the solicitor replied. 'Not my kind of Puritan,' Longford said firmly.[1]

As one who refers openly and often to his Catholicism, Longford has never been shy about moralising in public, even when it was becoming increasingly unfashionable in the 1960s. His form of Puritanism is to speak out unambiguously for the moral code and ideals of both his Edwardian childhood and of his Church. When his daughter Rachel was an undergraduate at St Clare's College in 1961, she went with her sister Judith to hear their father speak in an Oxford Union debate on the proposition 'Is chastity an outmoded concept?'

> My father was needless to say defending the motion, and he did a perfectly fine speech. Judith and I were in the gallery and he must have looked up halfway through his peroration to see his daughters sitting there. 'And how can you say that chastity is an outmoded concept,' he went on, 'when you look up there and see in the gallery two beautiful examples of perfect chastity?' And he pointed to us. I've never quite got over the horror as everyone turned to look at us. I fled and never appeared at the supper afterwards as arranged. The weight of this perfect chastity was too much.[2]

On questions of sexual morality, Longford has never budged from a black-and-white Catholic viewpoint in principle (though in individual cases he is much more tolerant and became more so as his own children grew up). Sex outside marriage is wrong and any exploitation of sexuality degrades a precious gift from God. Though he was willing in the 1960s to express such views in public, they were never a particular theme of his. Given *carte blanche* he would always return to subjects like crime, prisons, young people or Ireland before he would hold forth on sex. Certainly pornography had not figured at all in his public pronouncements – or indeed his private thoughts. When Jon Snow was working with Longford at the New Horizon Youth Centre, they would occasionally go into Soho for lunch. 'We would pass enormous lurid breasts hanging out of doorways and he wouldn't even notice. I felt we could probably have run into a naked woman in the street and he wouldn't have noticed.'[3]

Until he began preparing for a debate on pornography which he initiated in the House of Lords on 21 April 1971, Longford had scarcely given the subject more than fleeting attention. The changing sexual climate in the 1960s had provoked an ambiguous reaction in him. While his Catholicism and his innate Puritanism made him an implacable opponent of liberalising measures over abortion and divorce, he had spoken in favour of the decriminalisation of homosexuality. The earliest advocate, in 1957, of the Wolfenden report in Parliament, he broadly subscribed to its principle that 'it is not the function of the law to intervene in the private lives of citizens'. While he personally viewed much of the sexual liberalism of the sixties with distaste and, as a Christian, as sinful, he did not see it as his public role to sit in judgement or condemn.

In an interview in *The Times* in August 1966 he spoke with a detached interest of the 'swinging sixties'.[4] His own moral code remained rooted in an earlier age but Longford has always had a knack for drawing out the views of others, especially the children and grandchildren of friends and family, hence managing to stay abreast of what was going on around him in society. He told journalist Stella King that he had just bought Elizabeth a handbag from Mary Quant's 'just so that I could see what it was like in there'. (His lack of interest in his own appearance has never prevented him, on birthdays or anniversaries, from having a sharp eye for the sort of clothes that will appeal to his elegant wife.) The Longfords' flat in Chelsea is just off the King's Road, epicentre of the sixties 'revolution'.

> I was fascinated [Longford went on] to read that a Chelsea restaurant I visit frequently was the nub of swinging London. Apparently it was happening around me and I never noticed.
> I am sure that this new atmosphere and the freedom with which men and women can associate is a tremendous asset, even though it may possibly cause an increase in pre-marital relations. I am convinced, in spite of what everybody says, that homosexuality is much less prevalent now.

He may not quite have had his finger on the pulse, but Longford was more fascinated than condemnatory.

However, with the abolition of the Lord Chamberlain's role as theatre censor in 1968, various plays and revues began to attract a great deal of popular interest and comment. Longford, though no avid theatre-goer, was intrigued by what interested the public and made it his business to see what all the fuss was about. He walked out of a play called *America, hurrah!*, mounted at the Royal Court in London soon after censorship was lifted, when a huge four-letter word was displayed on stage. But the real starting point for his anti-pornography crusade came in the summer of 1970 when he left *Oh! Calcutta!* at the interval in disgust.

He had been prompted to go to see *Oh! Calcutta!* by an article in *The Times* on 26 August 1970 by Sir Alan Herbert, president of the Society of Authors, and one of the prime movers in the relaxation of the law on obscenity in 1959.[5] Herbert argued that the production showed that the new liberalism in the theatre had gone too far. 'My colleagues and I, in 1954, began a worthy struggle for reasonable liberty for honest writers,' he wrote. 'I am sorry to think that our efforts seem to have ended in a right to represent copulation, veraciously, on the public stage.' Just as Herbert had changed sides, Longford, thus far convinced that the criminal law had no business prescribing individuals' choices, began to question if some form of censorship was not needed.

Oh! Calcutta!, which its producer Kenneth Tynan described as 'elegant erotica', set out to offend from the start – the safety curtain was decorated with a large pair of buttocks, with the word 'bum' added in case anyone should miss the point. It followed this up with scenes of attempted rape, flagellation and a liberal sprinkling of obscenities. Longford went to the revue with his son-in-law, Hugh Fraser. When Elizabeth and Antonia had expressed an interest in accompanying their spouses, they had been told that 'it isn't the sort of thing one goes to with ladies'. Not to be put off by such Edwardian stereotyping, they got two tickets and sat in a separate part of the theatre, joining their spouses later for dinner.[6]

In accord with Herbert having seen half the show, Longford began to consider raising the question of pornography in the House of Lords. Yet he felt no real sense of mission as yet. When, however, he began taking soundings on the matter, almost at once he was handed explicit magazines and booklets which, he was informed, were circulating among schoolchildren. These so shocked him that he felt he had to act. The crusading spirit within him had been awakened. One of Longford's abiding concerns during the entire pornography inquiry was the potential damage that pornography could do to the young. Through New Horizon and in a variety of other ways, he had tried, sometimes falteringly, to keep the needs of young people in the forefront of his public activities. 'I don't think that he was ever interested in the use of pornography as pornography, old men in raincoats hanging round Soho and that kind of thing,' says Marigold Johnson who worked as his assistant in the later stages of the report. 'It was principally his teaching thing, an old-fashioned idea that society must protect the young. It was the effect pornography might have on children and young people that worried him.'[7] In that regard the pornography report can be seen as a natural progression from other aspects of Longford's work.

Elizabeth is adamant that from the outset her husband tackled the subject out of a sense of public duty.

> Far from being a cover for his own smutty-minded-
> ness, as some critics suggested – just as our eight
> children were once said to be a cover for his own
> homosexuality – porn was distasteful, utterly boring
> to him. Neither of us had read a word of it until the
> campaign opened, and Frank was profoundly thankful
> not to have to read another line after it closed. Though
> an exceptionally amusing after-dinner speaker, his wit
> depended not at all on dirty stories.[8]

With assistance from the Home Office Longford began by looking into the prevailing legal position over obscenity. He soon became convinced that the law was not strong enough to counter the menace posed by pornography. 'I think he had made up his mind long before the committee ever met,' says Marigold Johnson. 'They were the umbrella under which he was able to put together something which he had already decided needed to be written.'⁹

Longford also prepared for the Lords debate by reading the handful of other reports undertaken on the subject. There was an American Presidential Commission inquiry which had tentatively established links between sexual violence and pornography. By contrast, in Britain, the Arts Council – of which his daughter Antonia was then a member – had commissioned a working party under the chairmanship of John Montgomerie which reported in 1969. This had come down in favour of a *laissez-faire* approach, concluding that there was no evidence to suggest that obscene publications did any harm and that restrictions should therefore be lifted because they interfered with freedom of expression.

The government itself had no official position on the subject. In March 1970, the Labour Home Secretary, James Callaghan, had backed the police in their attempts to clamp down on pornography. In November of the same year, his Conservative successor declined a request in Parliament for an inquiry into the workings of the obscenity laws.

Longford quickly became aware, however, that there were others, especially in church circles, just as concerned as he was about what they perceived as the growth in pornography. In the autumn of 1970 a group of Christians protested outside another London play, *Council of Love*, and one of their number, Lady Birdwood, attempted unsuccessfully to mount a private prosecution against it. In east London Christians demonstrated outside cinemas showing what they considered to be pornographic films. In the November of the same year, the Church of England's Board of Social Responsibility produced a report, *Obscene Publications: Law and Practice*, which contained a strongly worded attack on the growth of pornography. Two months earlier, the Archbishop of Canterbury had called on Christians everywhere to protest at blasphemy and obscenity. And in March 1971, the Bishop of Blackburn led a protest march to demand higher moral standards in society.

It was not only in church circles that there was a growing concern over pornography. In December 1970, for example, the actors' union Equity came to an agreement with employers over a new performers' contract which would allow its members to opt out of unacceptable scenes. Christianity provided a vital common ingredient for the majority of campaigners. Because of his own faith, Longford was naturally sympathetic with these groups and was soon working closely with them. As part of his research in preparation for his House of Lords speech, Longford came into contact with people like the future Cabinet minister and member of the Church of England General Synod, John Gummer MP, who in 1971 published a book entitled *The Permissive Society*. It argued that the new emancipation had brought negative rather than positive benefits and highlighted what the author saw as the failure of experiments with permissiveness in Denmark. Longford was also working alongside figures like the headteacher Elizabeth Manners who had made national headlines in 1970 with a speech attacking the damaging effects of the commercialisation of sex on her pupils; the organisers of the primarily Christian Festival of Light events around the country, which strove to reinforce family values; and the members of the self-styled Responsible Society, set up to counter permissiveness through medical and educational research.

Most significantly he also came into contact with Mary Whitehouse, a devout Christian and a teacher from Shropshire who in 1964 had founded the Clean Up TV campaign, becoming in 1965 Honorary General Secretary of the National Viewers and Listeners Association. Ridiculed in the press and the butt of every satirist, Whitehouse had displayed great courage in refusing to be silenced by such a wave of criticism. Throughout his life, Longford has always admired physical and moral courage. It was something he aspired to, and he was immediately drawn to Whitehouse.

When Longford stood up in the House of Lords in April 1971, he had already attracted enough media attention to make him feel that he could not leave the matter to rest after addressing the Upper Chamber. There had been newspaper articles, radio debates and the first flood of correspondence from the public. He had clearly touched a nerve. Therefore in advance of his speech he had discussed with prominent Christians in the anti-permissiveness movement the idea of establishing a committee to investigate pornography. Yet he maintains to this day that he had no idea that his remarks in the Lords that day would release the tide of national interest that was to follow over the next eighteen months, eclipsing his previous reputation as a distinguished prison reformer and a somewhat eccentric but well-liked Cabinet minister, and labelling him in the minds of a generation as 'Lord Porn'.

In the Upper Chamber, Longford quoted various examples of materials he had seen – including, just a few days before the debate, a school sex education film, *Growing Up*, which included graphic sections on masturbation – to demonstrate his contention that the young and impressionable were at risk. There was a free trade in what he could only describe as obscene and evil materials, he continued. Nobody liked censorship, Longford acknowledged, least of all himself, but what was being produced in the name of freedom was depraving and damaging its audience. He suggested that the government should as a matter of urgency set up a commission to look into agreeing a form of control that would answer public concern. Failing that, he continued, he and a group of individuals would prepare a privately funded report.

From the government benches, Lord Eccles, as Longford had expected, declined to assent to an official inquiry. He did wish the proposed private initiative well. Lord Beswick, speaking for Labour, responded in similarly general terms. Other old friends of Longford on the Labour benches were, however, vehement in their opposition to his suggestion of limitations on freedom of expression. Dora Gaitskell, ennobled by Harold Wilson as a mark of respect to her late husband, joined with Jennie Lee and Lord Willis to denounce Longford's proposal. Even Elizabeth was initially opposed to her husband's crusade on anti-censorship grounds, 'until I read some of the hard porn that was circulating in comprehensive schools among girls of twelve. If one is against racism, sadism and sexist exploitation, one must be in favour of banning these cesspits that degrade the name of "book".'[10] Their daughter, Antonia, was never reconciled to her father's campaign, though she avoided criticising it in public at the time. 'I just couldn't get interested in pornography and I feel that self-constituted investigations can be very ugly, trailing around and announcing how things should be.'[11]

However, Longford's outspoken attack in the Upper Chamber was widely reported the next day in the press. Few other speeches in the comparative backwater of the House of Lords can have made such an impact in recent times. Letters poured in by the sack-load, the vast majority echoing his concerns. He was so overwhelmed by correspondence that a batch of tickets for his family and friends to the ceremony where he was to be made a Knight of the Garter by the Queen was buried until after the event. Among the many offers of support was one from the Dulverton Trust, a grant-giving body, set up in 1949 out of the proceeds of a tobacco fortune. It included an interest in religion and education among its remits. Longford had announced his plans to set up an inquiry before having any financial backing at all. The trust made good the shortfall. (Some critics leapt on this to ask, if Longford was concerned with damage to the young, why was he taking money from the tobacco industry.)

Whatever the ridicule that was later heaped on the pornography commission, it is undeniable that there was a genuine and broadly based public interest in Longford's speech in the House of Lords on 21 April. There were many – not all of them Christians – who shared his concern at changing standards as epitomised by such shows as *Oh! Calcutta!* and the musical *Hair* where the cast took their clothes off on stage. (Longford was not to see *Hair* until 1972 when he told waiting journalists that he had found some of the language offensive and declined an invitation from the cast to join them in a dance on stage.)

There was clearly an appetite for a national debate on the subject. The anti-censorship lobby lined up against Longford and his backers. How that debate might best be carried out should have been Longford's next question. Instead, egged on by his supporters in Christian circles, and knowing Whitehall well enough to realise that the government was not about to instigate its own investigation, he had already committed himself to a private commission of inquiry that was attacked from the outset as being partial.

Friends and admirers maintain that to a large degree Longford was hijacked by those around him over pornography. As a widely respected, socially active, former Cabinet minister with a reputation for holding radical views over matters like prison reform, he was quite a catch to some of the fringe campaigners, who until then had been struggling to find mainstream respectability, an Establishment convert to their cause. To Christians who felt that their Church had been too defensive in response to the dawn of the permissive society, he was a man from another age who was unafraid to speak up for moral values and go on the attack. 'I felt that the porn thing was an interesting example of how Frank can be manipulated,' says Jon Snow. 'There were other people in that campaign who clearly did have a very organised axe to grind and they used Frank. Some fairly unattractive forces managed to muscle in on his innocence.'[12]

Marigold Johnson disagrees.

> I don't think it is fair to say that Mary Whitehouse
> hijacked him. He was very much on the same wave
> length as her. What did go wrong with the pornogra
> phy report was to do with the number of people who
> were on his commission for the wrong reasons. It was
> absurdly large to start with. For some it was a social
> thing. Many of them just put their names to it and
> never turned up.[13]

Whatever the different motives of those embarking on the pornography inquiry and Longford's personal lack of interest in the subject *per se*, he relished the prospect of compiling the report. He takes particular pleasure in such exercises in research – travelling the country investigating issues at first hand and then making recommendations for change. It is, perhaps, the type of work he most enjoys and he had a distinguished record of successfully conducting such studies in the past.

Despite Longford's previous experience with similar private reports, the pornography inquiry was different in several respects from his previous excursions. Most significantly there was no restraining factor. Nuffield had struggled, unsuccessfully on the whole, to make Longford begin by proving his hypothesis in 1954 that crime was on the increase, before going on to theorise as to the cause. With his crime working party for the Labour Party and his group on London government, there was some higher authority to answer to, someone to monitor progress and give a gentle nudge on the tiller. Even with the Pakenham-Thompson report, he had been restrained by the presence of a co-chairman. But over pornography, the whole inquiry was very much Longford's charge, a self-constituted watchdog serving a public that certainly existed but which was ill-defined. The Dulverton Trust gave him a free hand.

The only restraint on Longford was exerted by the other members of the committee. When he announced the composition of his inquiry team on 21 May, Longford was attacked in the press for packing the committee with friends, fellow Christians and those who shared his opinions. The *New Statesman* denounced the whole venture as 'full frontal hypocrisy' and the *Guardian* accused his colleagues of being 'stooges'.

Longford had certainly gathered the committee with the same speed and reliance on instinct that he had employed in appointing previous helpers like Roger Opie. Some of the team had already been advising him in the run-up to his House of Lords speech. Through Mary Whitehouse he met Professor Norman Anderson, chairman of the House of Laity in the Church of England and vice-chairman of the pornography committee. Given his own beliefs and the prominence of the churches in highlighting the menace of pornography, it seemed natural to Longford to include their representatives. Other clerics who took part were the Archbishop of York, Dr Donald Coggan, Bishop Christopher Butler, one of the auxiliaries to the Catholic Cardinal Heenan, Dr Ronald Williams, Anglican Bishop of Leicester, Bishop Trevor Huddleston, the anti-apartheid campaigner, then Bishop of Stepney, Lord Soper, the Methodist leader, the Jesuit Father Thomas Corbishley, who had written the foreword to Longford's book *Humility*, Canon Sydney Hall, dean of King's

College, London, the Revd Joseph McCulloch, rector of St Mary-le-Bow in the City of London, and the Revd Keith Steven of the Church of Scotland committee on moral welfare. Among prominent Christian laity who were members of the commission were the broadcaster Jimmy Savile, Lady Masham, and the journalist Peregrine Worsthorne. Longford recruited several of his old friends including Dr Agnes Headlam-Morley, an academic who had advised him when he was working in Germany and who had become a family friend, Lord Shawcross, Attorney-General in Attlee's government and later chairman of the Royal Commission on the Press, and Malcolm Muggeridge who, after years of rejecting Christianity, published in 1971 *Something Beautiful for God*, his tribute to Mother Teresa of Calcutta, and later joined the Catholic Church with Longford as his sponsor. All had some form of expertise to offer, but he had not been careful enough to avoid giving the impression, unjustified by subsequent disagreements over the drafting of the final report, that he was packing the committee.

In his introduction to the report, Longford claimed to have attempted to construct a committee made up of representatives of the Church, the Law, medicine, the teaching profession, the arts, industry, and social services. True to his word there were members from most of these areas, some of them distinguished in their fields. Over half of the eventual members were not known to Longford before the committee began its work.

However, the over-representation of the Church and the corresponding shortage of figures from the world of the arts gave the inquiry more the semblance of a crusade than an investigation. Longford was particularly disappointed that the novelists Kingsley Amis and Elizabeth Jane Howard, then husband and wife, refused to sign the final report. They would have given the committee's findings more standing in literary circles. Amis and Howard did contribute an essay on freedom of expression in literature which was included in the final document.

In its brief, the committee pledged 'to see what means of tackling the problem of pornography would commend general support'. The fact that pornography was from the start regarded as a 'problem' again contributed to the impression that the inquiry was coming down heavily on one side of the debate. Longford himself comments in his introduction to the final report:

> It would not be true to assume that all those who took
> part in our inquiry agreed with my House of Lords
> proposition that pornography was a manifest evil,
> though anyone who thought that I was completely on
> the wrong tack would hardly have agreed to serve
> under my chairmanship.

In the immediate aftermath of his House of Lords speech and the fuss surrounding the assembling of the committee, Longford's spirits were high. It was, after all, the first time one of his pronouncements in the Upper Chamber had solicited such a postbag. His appeals for better conditions in prisons habitually fell on deaf ears. The setting up of the committee also gave him a new focus. Though he was enjoying his work at Sidgwick and Jackson it was not fully occupying his attention. Past retirement age when the pornography committee began its work, Longford was none the less still full of restless energy. He was still driven by a yearning to be useful, by his own unquiet conscience. Now he had a new channel.

He realised, in the wake of the response to his speech, that leading a national debate about pornography would propel him into the headlines. He had always found publicity attractive and believed that, by and large, it could be manipulated to good advantage. In the left-wing Labour circles of the 1930s in which Longford had done his political apprenticeship, there was a genuine belief that if one could get important issues into print, one could change hearts and minds. For that reason Longford had bought the *Town Crier* in the late 1930s. He thought that newspapers could play a role in educating people.

Yet by the early 1970s the *Sun*, recently acquired by Rupert Murdoch and developing its own style of tabloid journalism, had turned such notions on their head. Any residual faith

411

Longford had in the value of the press as a megaphone was dashed by his treatment during the pornography inquiry.

There was another, more personal, appeal to the publicity potential of the pornography inquiry. 'What he loved about doing it was that he was the centre of attention. He was no longer a back number. Wherever he would go, people would be saying to each other, "Isn't that Lord Porn?"' recalls Marigold Johnson.[14] Having slipped into relative obscurity after his resignation from the Cabinet in 1968, Longford found in the pornography inquiry a public role once more. Longford himself is not unaware of his own liking for publicity. In a diary he was commissioned by George Weidenfeld to keep for 1981 – his only attempt at the genre – Longford noted some comments from a book he had been reading which suggested that those who have never felt loved can be unduly egotistic.

> Without, I hope, undue self-pity, I think of myself as someone who needs a full measure of encouragement in just the sense described, whether or not because of my experiences in boyhood. My alleged craving for publicity originates, it may be, here. Without Elizabeth, I would never have overcome my temperamental weakness to a point where any kind of achievement was possible.[15]

It was a rare reference to childhood and his mother's lack of affection for him, a deficiency which he felt had been more than compensated for by his wife's devotion.

In his organisation of the inquiry, Longford adopted much the same pattern as he had with previous ventures. He employed a small office team to take care of administrative and secretarial matters, and he invited interested groups and individuals to present oral and written evidence for inclusion in the final report. Because of the scope of the subject under review, and Longford's conviction that reports should be completed in no more than a year, lest the momentum and public interest be lost, different areas were dealt out to sub-committees. Professor Anderson chaired the group looking at the effect and control of pornography, Malcolm Muggeridge those who investigated broadcasting, Father Corbishley sex education, James Sharkey cinema and theatre, Ronald Kirkwood advertising and so on. Longford was a member of the cinema and theatre sub-group, but had a free hand in participating in the work of other committees. He undertook some of the detailed questioning of individuals involved in the pornography trade and it was to Longford that all the correspondence from concerned members of the public was directed. He held the reins of control tightly.

It was he, for example, who set up meetings with newspaper editors and proprietors. Marigold Johnson who accompanied him witnessed his technique of investigation.

> He didn't behave in the way an official commission of inquiry would. He, in effect, tried to persuade news- paper editors to be caricatures of themselves. We went round and had endless cups of coffee with the likes of Larry Lamb and David Astor. And Frank would ask whatever question he thought would get the right answer. 'But surely you would draw the line at naked women on page three?' to David Astor. And David would say 'Of course I would, Frank' because that wasn't what the *Observer* wanted.[16]

Longford also spent much time trying to find sociological and statistical information on the damaging effects of pornography. Though he worked with several academics who believed there was a link, the final report could not prove cause and effect conclusively, just as his Nuffield inquiry had not been able to provide prerequisite statistics for the increase in crime rate. Neither report was scientific in its presentation of the evidence but rather a collection of views from expert witnesses. To Longford this was not a drawback. He had never hoped for absolute proof and believed that, however extensive the inquiry, it would have been impossible to reach a completely unequivocal conclusion.

> A fair-minded person reading our report must con- cede that pornography *sometimes* does harm. How *often*

413

it does harm and how *much* harm it does, and what
kind of harm is done by particular kinds of pornography remain questions which are never likely to be
finally disposed of [he wrote later]. From the angle of
practical policy they have, I believe, been much clari-
fied by our exertions.[17]

There were moments, however, when he found the lack of
scientific back-up frustrating and disheartening. He commissioned Maurice Yaffe, a research psychologist at the Institute
of Psychiatry in London, to conduct a survey into the harmful
effects of pornography, hopeful that it would prove that there
was at least a strong case to answer. To Longford's deep
disappointment, the resulting paper came back with no conclusions. It was the one moment during the inquiry, his close
colleagues say, when Longford thought of giving up. In the end,
Dr Yaffe's survey was tucked away as an appendix to the report,
with a note added by a child psychiatrist and an educationalist
who were members of the main committee describing it as 'not
helpful'.

There were also moments when he was tempted to readjust
the focus of the inquiry and direct it more towards the damaging
effects of the portrayal of violence in the media. Several of the
academics he consulted – and a large number of his correspondents – identified the graphic depiction of violence as a more
easily quantifiable danger to impressionable minds. Longford
began to follow up this avenue – going to watch Stanley
Kubrick's film, *A Clockwork Orange* – but such efforts were not
sustained.

Though there were some who felt uneasy about the pornography committee from the start, there were few who mocked
it mercilessly in the late spring of 1971. The satirical magazine
Private Eye, which managed to get one of the committee to leak
reports of proceedings, did its best to turn the whole venture
into a joke, but nationwide notoriety did not descend upon
Longford until he decided to visit Denmark at the end of August
1971. The Arts Council working party had concluded in 1969
that the free availability of hardcore pornography in Denmark

had reduced sexual crime by as much as a quarter. John Gummer, in his book *The Permissive Society*, rejected this proposition. In view of the disparity of opinions, Longford decided that his own inquiry would not be complete without a first-hand investigation of the 'Danish experiment'.

He ignored all advice to the contrary. Malcolm Muggeridge recalled:

> When the Danish expedition was on, he wanted me to go. I said, 'Absolutely out of the question because you'll be made a monkey of by the press.' I knew because I'd been a journalist and I know what I would have felt if someone had said 'Go and cover Lord Longford in Denmark.' I'd have jumped at it. I told him I didn't think it was wise either from his point of view or from the point of view of the credibility of the report we were supposed to be producing. But he couldn't see it. He's got a strange feeling that to be in the public eye is *per se* good.[18]

Not only did Longford ignore Muggeridge's advice – prophetic as it transpired – and go to Denmark. He also agreed to being accompanied by a group of journalists, or rather he stated beforehand that it was not for him to stop anybody coming. 'This was treated as a warm invitation. If I had known how much excitement our trip would arouse, I might have been less cordial,' he later wrote.[19] It is no excuse. Muggeridge had already made the situation clear to him.

Much of the two-day visit was spent meeting Danish officials and Church leaders, seeking their opinions about the effects of Denmark's liberal laws. The claims of those who argued that sex crimes had gone down in Denmark since reform of the obscenity laws were debunked. No such evidence existed, Longford and his team heard from Danish officials.

From the moment they had seen Longford reading the Bible on the plane over, the press sensed that there would be more column inches in the unofficial aspects of the Copenhagen trip. After a full day of meetings, Longford and his five companions

415

split into three teams and set out to experience something of Copenhagen's notorious night life. Accompanied by Dr Christine Saville, a psychiatrist with much experience of drug addiction whom he had met through New Horizon, Longford paid £7 a head to witness a live sex show. It did not take him long to see enough to know he had to leave.

> In a sense the audience were almost more horrifying than the performers [he recalled]. To join in 'the fun' even by remaining there at all seemed to be sharing the humiliation to which the girl was subjected. The fact that she appeared not to realise her own degradation increased rather than diminished one's sense of revulsion from those who had brought her to this.[20]

Yet, despite his horror at what he had seen, and the baying of the press, Longford and his companion proceeded to another club. 'Peer defies the Whip' cried the *Guardian* headline the next morning. 'A beautiful young woman pressed a whip into Lord Longford's hand and invited him to beat her. His Lordship declined,' ran the report.[21] Confronted by the model – who turned out to be a man in drag – Longford walked out of the club.

In one evening, Longford destroyed the credibility of the pornography inquiry. To the journalists who accompanied him, it was a dream of a story – the serious-minded, if eccentric, inquirer who was so shocked by his subject that he had to run from the room, Longford, with his noble cranium and mad scientist's tonsure, rejecting the charms of Denmark's very own Miss Whiplash.

Though he had earlier told the *Guardian*'s correspondent that he would not be corrupted by seeing Copenhagen's seedy clubs, Longford had underestimated how alienating he would find the whole experience. Had he listened to the advice of his friends and colleagues, a little more worldly wise, Longford would never have found himself in such a situation in the glare of media attention. Though he had seen a seedy side of life in prisons, he remained a sheltered and idealistic Puritan in sexual matters.

However, his blind faith in publicity, his previous enjoyment of research and his obstinate refusal to heed wiser counsels, combined, in a few short minutes, to turn his inquiry into a laughing stock. Even the *Observer* in a generally favourable profile – written, many assumed at the time, by Longford's old student Philip Toynbee with help from his editor, David Astor – asked: 'How can one deny that to walk indignantly out of such a performance, which he was supposed to be watching in a data-collecting mood of appraisal, showed some confusion in his approach?'[22] Far from coming to investigate, Longford appeared, on the evidence of his swift exit, to have made up his mind already.

He had placed himself in a no-win situation. To have stayed at the first show would have been to confirm all the suspicions, thinly veiled by some journalists, that he was nothing but a dirty old man disguising his own lascivious lusts with a high-minded inquiry. To walk out and then to go to a second show to repeat the experience simply made him look foolish. As he himself described the experience: 'I was sitting there like a stage professor in a house of ill-fame.'[23]

Though Longford was later to regret his actions, his response was not so out of character. He had found himself in an impossible situation through a combination of innocence and lack of foresight. Once there he had reacted instinctively, the Puritan in him overriding any pragmatic thoughts about how to extricate himself with the minimum of embarrassment. 'I think he embarked on the inquiry as a very naive man who genuinely believed that anybody who was not married should not have sex,' says Marigold Johnson. 'And here he was confronted with somewhere where you paid £7 to see sex. He was very shocked.'[24]

On his return from Copenhagen, Lord Longford could at least take comfort in the fact that his inquiry was headline news. It was also being ridiculed in every quarter. Some writers were dismissive in an affectionate way. *Daily Express* columnist Jean Rook labelled Longford 'a strayed and silly old goat'. Others were more cruel. A *Daily Mirror* leader described the whole Danish episode as 'sensationally foolish'. Robert Robinson dismissed the inquiry as 'the lost cause of 1971'. Mark Boxer produced a cartoon, exploiting Longford's height and bald pate to turn him into a walking phallus.

Stories began to proliferate in the tabloids about 'Lord Porn'. One told of how he was stopped at an airport customs desk and asked to explain why he had a suitcase full of pornographic magazines. In another he had been invited to become a playmate at the Playboy Club. Even his supporters began to join in the general air of merriment. Gyles Brandreth, now a Tory MP, was a recent Oxford graduate when he was invited to join the inquiry team. He had met Longford during a debate on prison reform at the Oxford Union where he had been president and had later written a light-hearted article in the *Manchester Evening News* which attracted Mary Whitehouse's admiration, advocating the showing of old Hollywood romances instead of sex education films in schools.

Brandreth travelled to Copenhagen but was not as convinced as his chairman as to the failure of the 'Danish experiment'. He and other members of the team managed to sit through the performances that so shocked Longford. Brandreth told reporters accompanying the party that 'when the commission was set up there was a theory that we were all Lord Longford's stooges. Our differences of opinion show that this is not the case.'[25] He was at once dubbed a 'Porno Rebel' by the *Sun* and stories about a split in the inquiry team abounded. Longford dismissed them saying that there was simply a healthy divergence of opinion as to where to draw the line on pornography. Brandreth, however, wrote a tongue-in-cheek piece for the *Spectator* and then a diary of the Copenhagen visit for *Nova* magazine. Longford saw this as a betrayal and asked him to leave the inquiry amid more headlines.

Yet, despite all the media attention, Longford continued to court publicity, justifying it as contributing to the wider dissemination of the inquiry's work, the old idea of a mission to educate. Talking to Terry Coleman in a *Guardian* series of interviews entitled 'The New Taboos', he highlighted the link between his ridiculed work on pornography and his widely admired interest in social services.

> It fits in all right, but it isn't something new. It isn't as if I've discovered some new philosophy of life. And, up to now, I've been a bit, probably, reluctant to denounce evil. As soon as one begins denouncing evil, I think one does get into difficulties. . . . The temptation now comes to be very self-righteous.[26]

Such was certainly the impression Coleman sought to convey: a self-righteous and zealous Christian attempting to pull society back from the precipice of hell. It was an image that echoed through the work of other journalists who covered the inquiry. Where previously Longford's vocal Christianity had been regarded as on the whole admirable or at least harmless and a feature to distinguish him from other politicians, in the context of a pornography campaign that was aiming at censorship it became another stone to throw at him.

> There was genuine public concern about pornography [says John Cunningham who covered the Copenhagen trip]. It was a subject already very much in the media before Longford began his inquiry. So his work was like giving sweets to a child. And then Longford was just so eccentric, so much a good man walking among the wicked rather as Gladstone had once gone out rescuing prostitutes. The subject was all theoretical for Longford, something he talked about rather than did. In that sense he was well protected, a man beyond reproach, happily married with a large family. There was nothing there for journalists to expose, so we could either take him seriously, or after Copenhagen we could laugh.[27]

The sort of personal mockery that was made of Longford cannot only be explained by his subject, his approach or the offence it caused in the liberal arts and media Establishments. Among the tabloids in particular, there was a palpable sense of vying to make him look more ridiculous. His every move prompted a 'Lord Porn' headline. If he was seen lunching in Soho, it would make a story. When Rachel published a novel with a bedroom scene, the papers cried out 'Lord Porn's daughter shocks father'.

Longford became one of the first in a long time of tabloid anti-heroes, public figures who, because they have caused offence to the prevailing attitude of the papers, have therefore to be destroyed by ridicule, often with their own unwitting assistance – witness Copenhagen. In the early 1970s, the *Sun* was just getting into its stride of personality assassination and page-three pin-ups. By his anti-pornography crusade, Longford was seen to be attempting to stop the great British public getting its daily diet of busty beauties. He was so easy to lampoon. When he was not busy posing with Bunny Girls at charity football matches for New Horizon, his Professor Brainstorm appearance was a gift to the picture desk. Here was an aristocrat who was trying to preach morality to the masses in the manner of a character out of P. G. Wodehouse. Furthermore he had a group of famous children. And because of his wife's work as a biographer and his own award of the Garter, he was linked with the Royal Family. 'It was an age when the tabloids couldn't get away with "doing" the royals, but Frank was as near as they could go, and get away with it,' says Jon Snow.[28]

Longford managed to give the appearance of laughing off most of the hostile publicity. He had long been indifferent to what people said if he thought he was doing the right thing. But during the pornography inquiry, the barrage of criticism did begin to get to him. 'He really does care what people say,' according to his daughter Antonia. 'He gets quite angry sometimes. And good for him. He minds being a figure of fun.'[29]

In his introduction to the committee's final report, Longford was philosophical that his work

> has brought me an extraordinary amount of personal
> notoriety . . . There will be those who feel that this
> personal publicity could have been handled more
> prudently. They may be right. I would not be the one

> to judge. From the beginning it was obvious that all of
> us, and I particularly, were bound to encounter vehe-
> ment opposition — some of it frankly based on vested
> interest but some of it deriving from libertarian con-
> victions. One would expect that we would be either
> ignored or denounced or ridiculed. In the event we
> have certainly not been ignored. For a time we cer-
> tainly were denounced but rather half-heartedly. In a
> country as proud, on the whole rightly, as Britain of
> its rational discussions, it is hard to go on denouncing
> an inquiry as such. So ridicule it had to be.

His close friends, not all of whom agreed with his stance on pornography, admired his resilience in the face of attack. 'Frank really is a person of great moral strength,' says David Astor. 'His capacity to follow his own line, regardless of what any and everyone may say, is, I think, a very great achievement.'[30]

However much the press might laugh at Longford, they could not force him to retire hurt. Neither could they ignore him. On the day the pornography report appeared, 21 September 1972, he starred on nine radio and television programmes. Those who expected him to be a push-over were surprised by his vigorous and feisty defence of his report. Only on BBC Radio's 'Midweek' did he lose his rag and accuse the presenter of being partisan — an error for which Elizabeth, listening down at Bernhurst, was later gently to rebuke him. By contrast, when Diana Dors took the chair in a debate on Southern Television on the pornography report, she made plain her agreement with its author and the two became friends.

There were many others who did not subscribe to the view of Longford as a joke. A couple of weeks before publication he had been one of two speakers at a Savoy luncheon to honour 'Men of the Year' on the grounds of courage and achievement. At the time of publication, Longford was the subject of a BBC Tele-vision 'Panorama' programme and numerous newspaper pro-files. He came fifth in a BBC Radio poll of 'Men of the Year' for 1972, behind Enoch Powell and Edward Heath but ahead of Harold Wilson. The public were not as hostile as the press.

421

While Longford was soaking up the media's hostility, the work of the committee continued apace, collecting evidence and testimonies, circulating a questionnaire to the public to find out their attitude. Though Longford attracted most of the attention, the range of the final report was truly a collective effort.

One of the hardest issues for the committee to agree on was a final definition of pornography. Their chosen form emerged after heated discussions: it is 'that which exploits and which dehumanises sex, so that human beings are treated as things and women in particular as sex objects'. The bulk of the report detailed the information that had been submitted to the committee. Marigold Johnson did most of the drafting.

> It was a patchwork job. Clearly there was no chance
> of putting in everything we had received and it was a
> case of picking out the best. I knew perfectly well that
> it would be read for its entertainment value more
> than anything else. So we were quite unscrupulous in
> choosing things that were more interesting than
> worthy.[31]

Regarding the establishment of institutions, the report came down in favour of a body, akin to the National Council for Civil Liberties or the Press Council, to uphold public decency in various areas – broadcasting, cinema, the theatre. On the question of sex education, it advocated a shift in responsibility from teachers to parents.

The report also included a draft bill to amend the Obscene Publications Acts of 1959 and 1964 and the liberalising Theatres Act of 1968 'to make further provision for prohibiting the public exploitation of indecent matter; to penalise the exploitation of actors and models for purposes of obscene or indecent shows and pictures'. The bill would make it illegal both to display in a street or other public place any written, pictorial or other material which was held to be indecent and to produce or sell any article which 'outraged contemporary standards of decency or humanity which were accepted by the public at large'.

Though the report was completed and signed in July, it did

not appear until September when it was published in paperback by Hodder and Stoughton in its Coronet imprint where it went on to be a bestseller.

On the eve of publication, the *Daily Mail* offered Longford £10,000 for serialisation rights. He was inclined to accept.

> I tried to explain to him that if he did that [Malcolm Muggeridge recalled later] he would get absolutely no serious press attention at all. It meant cutting himself off from any possibility of being taken seriously. And it was only with some difficulty that I persuaded him to see that. In other words, on this question of publicity and the media, he is in a way a tremendous innocent.[32]

Though Muggeridge was right to criticise in this case, it was only because Longford had kept the inquiry in the public eye – by his own efforts, not all of them conscious – that such an offer could be made. As in other areas of his life, Longford's innocence was imbued with shrewdness.

Despite its lack of scientific back-up, some critics felt that, in the mass of detail it crammed into just under 500 pages, the Longford report did demonstrate that there was a case to be answered against pornography.

> It may well prove [the *Daily Telegraph* wrote in a leading article the morning after publication] that the research by the Longford committee investigating pornography is of more value than the actual recommendations which it makes. Few people will have any doubts, after reading the report, about accepting two things as established fact – one is that the commercial exploitation of pornography has extended and is expanding vastly. The other is that in many cases pornography does lead to sexual attitudes which cause unhappiness and social malaise.

Other papers were not quite so welcoming but they certainly did not ignore the publication. The *Sun* headed its front page with 'Lord Porn's gospel: Send these filth pedlars to jail' but opposed the recommendations in its leading article. *The Times*, *Express* and *Mail* took the report seriously but remained to be convinced. Only the *Guardian* more or less ignored the event.

Individuals who reviewed the report were again mixed in their opinions. Bernard Levin in the *Observer* denounced the committee for insisting that sex and love must always go together – a clear legacy of Longford's own view. 'The fact that the claim is not only untrue but manifestly ridiculous does not seem to have occurred to Lord Longford and his colleagues,' Levin wrote. In the *Listener* Professor Dworkin suggested that the draft bill had been the work of a group of 'ignorant schoolboys' (despite the fact that Lord Justice Edmund Davies had been among the authors). Cyril Connolly in the *Sunday Times*, however, felt that the report was 'perfectly respectworthy; it is reasonable, well documented, cool, unbiased and in no sense an inquisition'.

Among other friends and former colleagues in government, the Longford report did not solicit any great enthusiasm. Roy Jenkins was not impressed. 'I felt he made an absolute ass of himself on pornography.'[33] Tony Benn took the trouble to buy a copy but recorded his reaction in his diary: 'very poor stuff'.[34]

Longford's political career was already over when he embarked on the pornography inquiry. But his work with prisoners and over penal reform was still continuing. He was a leading and respected spokesman for that cause in April 1971. By damaging his public reputation in Copenhagen, by allowing the press to make him a laughing stock, Longford diminished his own ability to further the campaign that had long been the closest to his heart. Among those who felt most aggrieved at his conduct of the inquiry and the fall-out that came in its wake were his friends in the penal reform movement. His dabbling in other areas lessened his effect as their spokesman. His judgement would forever now be suspect.

On an official level, the report had little effect on government policy. Robert Carr, the Home Secretary, spoke of the menace of pornography at the Conservative Party conference shortly afterwards, but he rejected changing the obscenity laws. Attempts by back-benchers to raise the subject in Parliament quickly subsided. In November, eighteen months after Longford had first mentioned pornography in the Upper Chamber, the Bishop of Leicester opened a debate in the Lords on the report he had put his name to. It was a gentlemanly affair. Publication did not seem to have swayed many of the members from the position they had taken in April of the previous year. To that extent, the report must be judged a failure. It neither prompted legislation nor did it fuel a continuing campaign.

In fact the contents of the pornography report were quickly forgotten. No commission was set up to pursue the subject. Some of the members of the committee – notably Mary Whitehouse – pressed on. Longford remains friendly with many of them. But after publication, he left the subject alone. He rarely mentioned it again in public, though he vehemently denies that he changed his mind. He probably simply lost interest. 'He is like quite a lot of men of action,' says Marigold Johnson. 'They move on to the next thing. They don't waste time wondering if they did the right thing. They don't brood.'[35]

If Longford decided to put the inquiry behind him, the press were not about to let him forget so easily. Throughout the autumn and winter of 1972 they ran story after story about 'Lord Porn' – from tales about him being offended by the saucy calendar in his local café (unlikely since his lack of interest in his surroundings is legendary) to reports that he and his wife occasionally swam naked in their pool at Bernhurst. In March 1973 his visit to the cinema to see *Last Tango in Paris* made headline news: 'It's Lord Tango'. Whatever the other failures of the pornography report, it succeeded in making Longford a national celebrity, at best eccentric and misguided, at worst a figure of fun.

There was little that Longford could do to reverse the trend. Memories of Copenhagen were long. In July 1973, Mary Whitehouse, always more prone to litigation than Longford, did try to stop the worst of the jokes. She successfully objected to the use of a picture of the two of them embracing in the street after lunch that appeared under the satirical caption 'Dream the Impossible Dream'. Left to his own devices, Longford, like the royal family, never rose to the bait of the press and satirists,

425

even when they wounded him. He realised that no court verdict could dispel the reputation of Lord Porn.

Two decades after the publication of the report that has so much shaped his public image, Longford might take a little comfort from the fact that subsequent developments have shown that he was not quite so wrong or out of touch as was suggested at the time. Indeed some might even suggest that rather than being the product of a mind stuck in a by-gone era of morality, there was just a hint of prophetic vision in the report.

The first direct result of the inquiry came quite soon after publication. Part of the investigation had focused on the organisation of the trade in pornography which was carried out, Longford began to suspect, with the connivance of senior figures in the police. At about the same time as he was going to Copenhagen, Longford employed the same private investigator, Major Matt Oliver, who had helped him with gathering information to clear Michael Davies of the Clapham Common murder back in the 1950s.

Oliver compiled a dossier, revealing malpractice by the police. Longford was unsure about how to proceed. When he consulted his committee they made it plain that it was not within the remit of the inquiry to tackle police corruption. Longford could not let the matter rest and he decided, in a private capacity, to hand over the information to Sir John Waldron, Metropolitan Police Commissioner, who promised to investigate.

Longford also encouraged Oliver to take his dossier to the *Sunday People* which put a team of undercover reporters on the case. In February of the following year the paper ran an exposé on police corruption and the pornography trade which in the summer of 1973 resulted in eighteen senior officers being tried and sentenced to a total of 116 years in jail. Although the history of the pornography inquiry is largely one of journalists working against Longford, in this instance a successful partnership was forged.

A year after publication the *Daily Telegraph* reported from Copenhagen: 'Danes curb sex clubs after Longford's visit'. While the British press had laughed at Longford's antics, the Danish media had presented the very fact that their capital was inspected as the centre of Europe's porn industry as a national disgrace. Moves were made to tighten up the prevailing libertarian laws and clubs were closed. Amsterdam took over Copenhagen's role as the mecca for pornographers.

In the 1980s, Margaret Thatcher's Conservative government introduced a series of measures that were very much in the spirit of revoking the unfettered freedoms of the 1960s and 1970s. The Broadcasting Standards Authority is just the sort of watchdog that the Longford committee suggested, though its brief is broader than obscenity. Legislation was also enacted giving parents a greater say over matters like sex education in schools – another recommendation of the report. An Indecent Displays Act in 1981 tackled the type of pornography that could be put on open shelves. Longford broke his silence on the subject to speak in favour of this measure in the Lords.

In the age of Thatcher, the national climate changed and, while there was much in the ideology of the period that Longford found unattractive and damaging, the public emphasis on family and time-honoured values created an atmosphere where, perhaps, an initiative like the pornography report might have been more favourably received. A walk round Soho today reveals that it is a very different place from the maze of sleazy clubs and brothels that existed in 1971. Westminster City Council responded to public concern and attempted to 'clean up' the centre of the porn trade. The peep shows and strip clubs were mostly superseded by literary clubs, fashionable restaurants and designer shops.

In recent debates about the depiction of sex and of violence in the media and the damaging effects that they might have on impressionable minds, the mere suggestion that limits should be imposed no longer provokes the immediate howl of opposition that once it did.

> I suppose I was easily swayed by fashion [says Marigold Johnson], but I have come round to thinking that Frank was much more right in the line that he took than we thought at the time. In the 1970s it

seemed too restrictive. People had an entirely different view. When the porn report came out in 1972 it was impossible to imagine *Guardian* readers approving of what anybody who disliked pornography said.[36]

Yet in the same paper that led the attack on the Longford report, today writers like Geoffrey Wheatcroft contribute double-page spreads suggesting that something has gone wrong since the introduction of a more liberal obscenity law in 1959 and the *Lady Chatterley* trial – memorably held to be the dawn of the swinging sixties by Philip Larkin. 'The ultimate beneficiaries of the act and the trial', Wheatcroft wrote in June 1993, 'have been Page Three and Rupert Murdoch, the girlie mags and the sex-and-shopping novels on sale in every bookshop and airport.'[37]

When Longford tried to stand against the tide in 1971, he offended the literary world, the anti-censorship and newspaper philosophers. Today they might be more prepared to listen. Certainly when respected figures on the Left like Clare Short have tackled the whole issue of censorship and obscenity, they have not been marginalised in the same way that Longford was. The Labour MP's campaign against page three pin-ups may have brought down on her head much the same sort of tabloid ridicule that Longford once faced, but she has continued to hold the respect of her colleagues and to be a part of Labour's front bench team. Many would say that she is an asset, that her outspokenness on this issue has contributed to her political career.

Longford had abandoned all hopes of further political significance before he embarked on the pornography report. But he had not given up his ambition to shape a more humane prison system and it was to that subject that he redirected his attention once the findings of the inquiry had been compiled.

Seventeen

The only friend
of Myra Hindley

*My father's natural habitat is hanging around on
railway stations or waiting for the Isle of Wight
ferry when he goes to visit prisoners*

Rachel Billington[1]

In September 1972 the hysteria surrounding the pornography
inquiry was at its height. The final report was due out any day.
Lord Longford was already a name to command headlines in
every national newspaper. Since Copenhagen his work had
been the butt of every budding satirist. But the smiles and
bemusement turned to anger when it was revealed that he had
visited Myra Hindley in prison and had been doing so regularly
since May 1969. To those who knew little about Longford's long
record as a friend of prisoners and who thought of him only as
'Lord Porn', it was a horrifying revelation which at once altered
his status from misguided eccentric to potential danger to
society. Even to those who admired Longford's commitment to
marginalised causes, the news came as a shock.

Few murders have so shaken and repulsed the public as the
crimes committed by Hindley and her lover, Ian Brady. They
were arrested on 7 October 1965 after Hindley's brother-in-law,
Dave Smith, confessed to the police that he had witnessed the
brutal bludgeoning to death of seventeen-year-old Edward
Evans by Brady with Hindley's assistance the previous evening.
When detectives began investigating that crime, the trail led
them to Saddleworth Moor above Manchester and ultimately to
the graves of ten-year-old Lesley Anne Downey who had

disappeared on Boxing Day 1964 and John Kilbride, twelve, who had vanished on the night after John F. Kennedy was assassinated. In the neat, unremarkable council house Brady shared with Hindley and her grandmother in the Manchester suburb of Hattersley, police found a tape recording of Lesley Anne Downey's tormented last hours and photographs which Brady had taken of her.

The trial at Chester Crown Court of the Moors murderers, as they became known, dominated the news in April and May 1966 and left an indelible mark on the public consciousness. In court, as Brady's admiration of Adolf Hitler and the Marquis de Sade was detailed, the gruesome tape recording played and the crimes against defenceless children recounted, Hindley sat impassive, betraying no emotion and showing no remorse. They were both convicted and sentenced to life imprisonment.

So high was the level of public anger and disgust that a petition of 30,000 names was collected demanding the return of capital punishment for the couple. A relative of Lesley Anne Downey stood and was defeated in the 1966 general election against Sidney Silverman whose private members' bill had led in 1965 to the abolition of hanging. In his bestselling book about the case, *Beyond Belief*, Emlyn Williams summed up the popular wish for revenge at the time of the trial.

> Their continued existence is indeed hard to tolerate.
> Public feeling being what it is – and about these two
> the public will have a long memory – it is unlikely
> they will ever be released, and it is natural for tax-
> payers to be incensed at the thought of their being
> maintained, for life, by the State.[2]

John Stalker, later Deputy Chief Constable of Greater Manchester but then a humble detective sergeant on the case, recalls: 'Nothing in criminal behaviour, before or since, has penetrated my heart with quite the same paralysing intensity as those emerging details of the Moors murders.'[3]

Much of the horror at the crimes focused on Hindley though from the start it was clear to police that she had been Brady's accomplice, a willing helper in his evil schemes but not the instigator. The idea that a woman, whose body is designed to bring children into the world and whose traditional role has been as a nurturer and protector of the young, could take part in such atrocities engulfed Hindley in a storm of national hatred which continues to this day. The photograph of her used at the trial, and ever after, as a Medusa-like blonde with a stern, unyielding expression and a blank stare, has become an icon of crime and evil-doings in the twentieth century.

At the trial Hindley never once tried to distance herself from Brady or anything he had done. At one stage she described him as her 'god' and she remained fanatically loyal to him. She made plain that what he had done, she had done. It was her over-whelming desire to see Brady again, once she had been begun her sentence, that prompted her to write to Longford. She maintains to this day that she knew nothing of his reputation as a campaigner for penal reform. She did not approach him as a soft touch but rather through the good offices of Lady Anne Tree who was visiting her in prison and who knew of Hindley's fervent desire to have face-to-face meetings with Brady rather than just a correspondence.

Longford's approach to prisoners has always been based on a refusal to sit in judgement and an unconditional offer of forgiveness and friendship whatever their crime. It is his unshakeable belief that no prisoner is beyond redemption. While the public put Hindley in a special category, beyond the pale, he refused to do so. To him she was neither a monster nor evil.

Yet after Lady Anne Tree's approach, Longford was cautious about leaping to Hindley's rescue. The enormity of her crime – like that of the former concentration camp guards he had met when he was a minister in Germany – made even him pause to draw breath for a moment. Before agreeing to get involved in lobbying the Home Office, he arranged to visit her at Holloway Prison. After talking to Hindley, he still was not convinced that greater contact with Brady would be of any benefit to her.

However, after listening to others who had been visiting Hindley, he was brought round to the view that the prospect of seeing Brady again was important to Hindley's emotional equilibrium and he agreed to make representations of her behalf. Though he failed to make much headway with the Home Office, Longford gradually became more involved in her case. He began visiting Hindley every three months.

Elizabeth, who had always supported her husband in his mission to prisoners in the past, was opposed at the outset. 'I didn't want Frank to have anything to do with these people. I wanted him to keep his hands clean of these monsters.'[4] For once he did not listen to his wife's counsel. It is significant that over both pornography and Myra Hindley, the two crusades that have done so much to damage Longford's public image and eclipse his record as a politician and reformer, Elizabeth began by advising him against taking them up (though she was later converted to both).

Longford was determined to press on but accepted at first the wisdom of doing so without attracting any publicity. Through his contact with Hindley, he began corresponding with Brady. His relationship with Brady, which continued for many years, was principally conducted at an intellectual level. Longford would send him books to read (including his own volume *Humility*, Elizabeth's life of Wellington and Antonia's *Mary, Queen of Scots*) and then discuss them with him by letter and on regular visits. After a fourteen-year struggle he influenced the Home Office to send Brady to a special hospital for the treatment hitherto denied him by officials.

However, it has been Longford's friendship with Hindley – a very different relationship from that with Brady – that has won him notoriety and dwarfed in the public mind his wider campaign for prisoners. In the early 1970s he saw the Moors murderers gradually drift apart, Brady in no fit mental state to contemplate release, but Hindley hoping that one day, in the distant future, she might be set free.

Hindley feels that Longford played an important part in her decision to return to the Catholic faith of her teenage years. Other prison officers who befriended her were just as important, but Longford gave her the courage to start attending the sacraments again in spite of the adverse reaction she feared from both fellow worshippers and clergy.

Hindley's renewed faith completed her break from Brady who despised religion. At the same time it cemented her bond with Longford. Though many, including not a few senior Church figures, have subsequently doubted the sincerity of her conversion, seeing it as a ploy to dupe Longford and those dealing with her case, his belief in her genuine return to religion has been echoed by the chaplains and Christians who have either visited or written to Hindley in the subsequent years.

Their shared Catholicism has been a central topic of conversation during Longford's visits – first at Holloway, then in the grim, high-security environment of Durham and finally in the more relaxed atmosphere of Cookham Wood in Chatham. (Longford was instrumental in getting Hindley transferred to the Kent prison, fearing for her mental well-being in the high-security confines of Durham.) Both feel no inhibition in talking openly about God and faith and how it has affected their lives. Both share a devotion to St Francis. Longford joined the Catholic Church in a Franciscan parish while Hindley's most loyal friends among the clergy have been Franciscan priests and brothers. Both read extensively on religious topics – Longford with his daily diet of spiritual books and Hindley the Divine Office and a wide range of other texts by Christian figures.

But the friendship that has developed between them is not just to do with religion. Hindley puts Longford's devotion to the cause of her release down to a kind of Sir Galahad complex, wanting to ride in on his charger and save her. Through that devotion, she has become an honorary member of his family. They discuss his children and grandchildren, exchange birthday cards. Once converted to Hindley's case, Elizabeth Longford occasionally joined her husband on visits to Cookham Wood. His and Hindley's relationship is not like that of solicitor and client. Longford and Hindley are like two old friends who know each other's weaknesses and strengths inside out. She is like another daughter to him.

At their meetings, once the topics of religion, family and politics had been exhausted, the talk inevitably would come round to the campaign for Hindley's release. Every three months Longford would report on the ups and downs of the Home

Office's attitudes and his attempts to lobby support on her behalf. With a paternal understanding he has followed her mood swings, between hope that the Parole Board was about to yield to pressure and deep despair with each setback. He has introduced her to other friends who have become regular visitors and correspondents, who can inform her of life in the outside world. Together they have contributed to stimulating Hindley's mind, engaging her curiosity in events beyond the prison gates, developing in her a lively and articulate interest in politics. Longford has encouraged her to follow Open University studies and urged her on in her long-running attempt to set down her thoughts in book form.

Once Longford takes on a cause, he can be extremely difficult to sidetrack. 'He's a bit like a battle-cruiser, steaming ahead, not looking what is to his left or right, utterly convinced that he is on the right course and that everyone else will eventually fall into line,' says Sheila Childs who has worked with him for prisoners through New Bridge for many years.[5] He began to speak to friends and colleagues of his conviction that Myra Hindley was a reformed character, that, finally freed of the malign influence of Ian Brady, she was a decent human being, and that one day she might be released. He embarked on what has become his best-known campaign, the long and continuing battle to persuade a reluctant Home Office and an implacably opposed public to free Hindley on parole.

It is often said that Longford is obsessed with Hindley. Some of his critics have even gone so far as to suggest that he is in love with her. As with all his relationships with women, there is an element of flirtation in his approach. One of his standard ploys, many of his women friends recount, is to insist that they wear their glasses, telling them not to be shy of the signs of ageing and reassuring them that they look more attractive. Hindley is no exception.

However, such friendly banter can be misinterpreted and, often, details of their private meetings would be leaked to an eager press by sources within the prisons. In the end their visits were conducted in private rooms, either alone or in the presence of the governor or assistant governor.

From the start even those with great sympathy for Longford's work with prisoners wondered why he was concentrating so much effort on this one case. There were, by conventional standards, many more deserving cases than Myra Hindley, many more friendless victims of injustice, of over-long sentences, whose crimes were as nothing beside hers. But to be thus bewildered is to misunderstand why Longford gets involved with prisoners. He is not a campaigner for those who have been wrongly convicted. He leaves that largely to others, though he has on occasion undertaken such appeals. The cases with which Longford is primarily concerned involve prisoners who are being punished to no purpose, or cast out of society when they have tried to repay their debt to it. As a general rule – as he explained to the House of Lords in a speech in March 1980 – he is in favour of all prisoners being eligible to apply for parole after ten years. Sentences of twenty or thirty years 'cast a spell of peculiar horror because the life prisoner has no definite assurance that he or she will ever come out before being hopelessly enfeebled'.

One of the distinguishing features of Hindley's case is that she is among the very few prisoners serving life sentences in British jails who have never been allotted a 'tariff date', an indication from the Home Secretary, on the basis of the trial judge's recommendations, as to when they will be considered for parole. As far as officialdom is concerned, Hindley has been locked up and the key thrown away. To Longford this is a gross injustice which he has fought to overturn by lobbying the prison department, various Home Secretaries and ultimately the European Courts. A ruling in the House of Lords in 1993 has, it is thought, increased the pressure on the Home Secretary to reveal such a tariff date to Hindley and – inevitably – to the public.

In the mid-1970s, Longford managed to persuade Harold Evans, then editor of the *Sunday Times*, to publish some of Hindley's letters which set out her profound remorse at her crimes. But the public has never been convinced of her sincerity. In 1987 she broke her silence about Brady's role in the deaths of Pauline Reade and Keith Bennett, always thought by police to be victims of the Moors murderers but never proved to be such, and agreed to assist in a new searching on the Moors for the children's bodies. To Longford it was an act of compassion towards their parents made at the cost of damaging her own chances of parole. To the press, it served only to reinforce their image of a calculating woman who had hidden the evidence of the killings for years.

He has also tried to persuade Hindley to express her remorse in a letter to Ann West, the mother of Lesley Anne Downey and a vocal campaigner against parole. In his diary entry for 15 January 1981, considering the apology sent by another of 'his prisoners', Shane O'Doherty, to the victims of his IRA parcel bomb, Longford wrote: 'It would indeed be helpful if Myra could send a similar apology to Mrs West. But Myra clings to her own sincerity which makes it harder.'[6]

Longford has never wavered from his belief that Hindley should be judged by the authorities on the basis of her efforts at reform rather than the popular prejudice against her which shows few signs of abating. But the extent to which her cause became a personal crusade for him throughout the 1970s and 1980s, overshadowing his concern for other prisoners similarly afflicted, can only be explained by a certain allure she held for him − as indeed she has a certain fascination for the general public. It was not the love that some critics hinted at. Rather Longford has always been interested in interesting people, those who have done something out of the ordinary, who do not fit into standard moulds. That interest covers both those who have done good deeds and those who have done evil. Hence he was drawn in his political career to larger-than-life figures like F. E. Smith and de Valera. And hence, also, in his work with prisoners of every description, he is drawn especially to the infamous. Men like the mass murderer Dennis Nilsen, whom Longford visits regularly at Albany Prison, are 'very interesting by any standards', he says.[7]

With inmates such as Nilsen and particularly with Hindley, Longford is putting his Christianity to the test. He is challenging himself to practise what he preaches − that he should forgive unconditionally even people whose crimes he accepts are horrific. For most people it would be one thing to offer unconditional forgiveness to a prisoner who has defrauded the tax authorities, but quite another to forgive a woman who participated in the sadistic killing of children. Longford's Christian conviction that no sin is any more or less forgivable than another makes him aspire to treat them both in the same way, evincing what Auberon Waugh has already dubbed a 'crucifixion complex'.

Longford takes this message a stage further. Not content with accepting the challenge for himself in regard to Hindley, he tries to evangelise society and persuade others to forgive. It was, as Jon Snow has described it, part of Longford's attempt 'to stake out a moral and spiritual position that no politician ever even begins to think about'.[8]

As a public figure and one with an abiding, though strained, belief in the efficacy of publicity, Longford has not limited himself to lobbying Whitehall over Hindley. He has attempted, in a principled but naive fashion, to win over public opinion, calculating quite correctly that without it she will never be released.

However, he has placed too much faith both in the public's capacity to follow his example of forgiveness, and in the media's willingness to promote such a message. Hindley's name on the front page of newspapers sells extra copies. The press has no interest in presenting her as a reformed character. Their stake is in maintaining the spectre of an evil monster who might one day be let loose on society. Longford simply has become part of their strategy, paraded by the press as the 'loony' peer who has been duped by a scheming murderess and who would let her free to prey on children again. Longford, never camera shy, plays into their hands.

The first of many of Longford's skirmishes with the press over Myra Hindley occurred just a week before the pornography report was due to be published. The *Daily Express* had learnt that the governor of Holloway, Mrs D. M. Wing, had taken Hindley for a brief walk outside the prison walls. It was not an unusual privilege to grant model prisoners. But the *Express* was intent on exploiting the anger that the public would feel at such a special concession to a hated prisoner. Longford, when telephoned by a reporter, said that he knew nothing of Mrs Wing's initiative but that it sounded to him like an excellent idea. The Home

Secretary, Robert Carr, thought otherwise and rebuked Mrs Wing.

The Home Secretary had a surer grasp of what his electorate wanted to hear. Longford's response, typically, was not shaped by a politician's pragmatism, but by his knowledge of the prisoner and his conviction that she was a reformed character. The public has not witnessed that transformation. Nor do they want to. Longford's attempts to convince them have betrayed a lack of appreciation for how strongly people felt about the Moors murders, a lack of sensitivity to the horror that many had experienced at the crimes and their desire for vengeance. There is just a hint of arrogance in Longford when he miscalculates such revulsion. As over pornography, he is sure he is right and is convinced that if he states his views often and clearly enough, he will win others round.

When he was proved wrong and his statements about Hindley began to attract a negative response, Longford's natural impatience came to the surface. Malcolm Muggeridge once remarked charitably of this side of Longford's character that 'he has the gift of clowns. He can make all worldliness seem farce.'[9] He would speak testily and provocatively to those who challenged him, for example, when he appeared on the BBC TV discussion programme 'Kilroy' and said that anyone who did not believe Hindley should be released was essentially stupid. 'He has a brilliant mind and complete commitment to the cause,' says Hindley's solicitor Andrew McCooey who appeared on the same programme, 'but there's not a standing back to consider the views of the man in the street, to ask, "Am I being perceived as being obsessed, as having an axe to grind?" Objectivity and understanding of others' feelings is very important in dealing with this case.'[10]

The connection between Lord Porn and the Moors murderess makes an irresistible tabloid cocktail. Each time the papers report attacks in prison on Hindley or the continuing distress of the parents of her victims, they can add a sting in the tail of their stories by quoting Lord Longford as saying she should be released. Where they overstate their case, he responds in kind. With Hindley out of reach behind bars, Longford has become a scapegoat for her crimes. His status as a tabloid anti-hero has been confirmed. His attempts at educating and enlightening the public, convincing them that Hindley is not a monster but a human being, have come to naught.

Having set Longford up as Hindley's only friend, the press then exploited the traumatised mother of Lesley Anne Downey, Ann West, as his antithesis. Several confrontations were stage-managed between the two and Longford was attacked for lacking sympathy for the relatives of those Hindley killed. He could quite legitimately point to efforts in the early 1960s as chairman of a committee for the charity Justice, which investigated compensating the victims of crime. Throughout the late 1970s he was part of a committee on victims which reported in 1978 and whose recommendations formed the basis for a private members bill that Longford introduced in the House of Lords in July 1979.

Though such efforts were seldom reported, Longford refused to let the danger of being misrepresented distract him from the main purpose of his campaign. Therefore he agreed to appear on several television programmes with a distressed Mrs West who, understandably, has little sympathy for his opinions. She has made her personal lack of regard for Longford plain on many occasions. In her autobiography she writes:

> I find him a most dangerous and woolly-minded buf-
> foon whose views are taken seriously because of his
> accidental social status rather than because of the
> validity of his ideas.[11]

In July 1977 the two were together on a BBC TV 'Brass Tacks' programme on the subject of Hindley's parole which included a phone-in. Again Longford was judged to have exhibited impatience with those who disagreed with him. His remarks led to an interview the following week with Jean Rook in the *Daily Express* where the popular columnist summed up a widespread reaction to his crusade:

> That this campaign to free Hindley is obscene. That
> Longford's obsession with shining like a crusader
> among the sordid and squalid is offensive. That his
> grasping for publicity is unnaturally avid and as great
> as his talent for obtaining it.[12]

Longford refused to rise to the bait of personal insult. His experience as chairman of the pornography committee had taught him to ignore such taunts. If anything they merely convinced him that he had hit a nerve. He did however defend Hindley and spoke of her as reborn. 'She's completely changed. Before the murders and the corruption she was an innocent, eighteen-year-old Lancashire girl. Now she is back to herself again.' He went on to refer to her as 'rather beautiful in a sad sort of way'.[13] If such comments were designed to win converts, they failed. Far from advancing Hindley's cause, Longford appeared only to be pouring petrol on a fire and inflaming public opinion.

He could point out with some justification that journalists approached such interviews with a set agenda and a closed mind and that, whatever he said, they would present his comments in the worst possible light. The logical follow-up of such a complaint might have been to decline requests for interviews. But, in view of his decision to soldier on against steadily increasing odds, Longford's failure to convey the essence of his case and his tendency to be lured into making personal comments about Hindley must be counted against him. While his hopes of educating the public were naive from the start, his suggestion, for example, that her degree of culpability in the crimes was less than that of Brady advanced her cause not one inch. (Hindley herself seeks to make no such excuses and has acknowledged that she knew what Brady was doing and did nothing to stop him, and that without her Brady would not have been able to lure his victims.)

Faced by a sympathetic journalist, or in private conversation, Longford makes a strong argument for releasing Hindley that rests not on her personal attributes but on the workings of the parole system. In an interview with the *Catholic Herald* in June

1985 after the National Parole Board had just rejected Hindley's application, he made such a telling case that the paper backed his campaign in a leading article. The local review board, Longford said, had recommended Hindley's release on licence. They had based such a conclusion on the Home Secretary's instructions that prisoners should be judged primarily on the basis of whether they were still a danger to society. Hindley posed no danger at all, had been punished enough and should be freed, they concluded.

In the vast majority of parole cases the judgement of the local experts is endorsed by the National Parole Board and sent forward to the Home Secretary for approval. In Hindley's case, however, the local board's ruling was summarily dismissed at a higher level. Longford believed that this move was due to the weight of public opinion and the then Home Secretary Leon Brittan's unwillingness to handle such a political hot potato. Yet, according to Longford, the Parole Board has no mandate to consider such factors. Parole should not be judged on what is acceptable to public opinion – and particularly a public opinion manipulated by tabloid journals which carry labels on files about Hindley instructing that her name must always be prefixed by the adjective 'evil'. Parole should be determined by the standards the Home Secretary himself had set out – was the prisoner still a danger to society? – and by the regulations laid out in the law that Longford himself had played a substantial part in introducing after his 1963 report on crime was taken up by the Labour government.

Such an argument steered clear of the emotional minefield that surrounded any suggestion that Hindley was reformed, but its effectiveness still rested on a Home Secretary having the political courage to release her. As a politician of many years' standing, Longford should have known that, with public opinion rightly or wrongly still so vigorously opposed, no ambitious minister would take that risk. 'Myra Hindley will always be one of the symbols of crime and to be seen to go soft on her will be to be seen to go soft on crime,' says her solicitor Andrew McCooey. 'No Home Secretary is going to take the decision.'[14]

If public opinion is what prevents Hindley being released,

rather than any belief in the Home Office that she is a danger to society, then Longford must be seen as having played a part in stirring rather than soothing popular fears. By linking himself with her, in effect mortgaging his own good name and reputation in pursuit of her cause, Longford has made a great sacrifice. But equally the interest of 'Lord Porn' in Hindley's case has meant that many more stories have been written about her than would have been otherwise. He has contributed to keeping her name in the news.

Hindley was aware almost from the outset that Longford's campaign could backfire on her. Unable to speak out for herself, she was a silent and increasingly disturbed onlooker as Longford tried to put her case. Time after time, he would conclude his visit to her by promising that he would answer any journalist's question about her with a simple 'no comment'. Then days later she would read his comments with what she describes as a mixture of anger and frustration. When he engaged in a war of words over her case with Robert Maxwell in the *Daily Mirror* in the mid-1980s, she pleaded with him to keep quiet. But he was unable to and when challenged on subsequent visits he would respond that he could not face St Peter at the end of his life with a clear conscience if he thought he had turned down an opportunity to do her good. Longford's sense of mission was so strong that he stubbornly continued on a course that even the woman he was supposed to be helping considered damaging. The crusade had almost grown more important than the person. Hindley's conviction that his public campaign was doing her harm made no impression on him.

Hindley was not the only one who grew increasingly alarmed at the negative effects of the campaign. David Astor felt moved to raise the question of its efficacy with Longford in the late 1970s.

> He was absolutely right to defend her as a human
> being when no one else would [says Astor], but
> accidentally he did her harm by exciting the press,
> encouraging them to treat him as a 'loony lord' and
> therefore make her position worse. Frank was very

reluctant to see this when we talked about it. He
thought that to go quiet about Myra's case would be
seen as abandoning her. He was horrified at the idea
that he might have been counter-productive to her –
and to himself. It was to help both of them that I got
involved. I agreed that if Frank would lay off, the *quid
pro quo* would be that I would visit Myra along with
Peter Timms, a former prison governor. Frank bought
this compromise only with a great deal of difficulty.[15]

Though they are close in age, have been friends since they were
young men and share a liberal, left-leaning outlook, Longford
and Astor could not be more different in their approach to
publicity and in particular over how to handle Hindley's case.
While Longford enjoys the spotlight and believes that minds can
be changed through the media, Astor shuns any personal
attention and, as a former newspaper editor, is aware that
courting the press can have adverse effects. Though he was
convinced on meeting Hindley that she should be paroled, Astor
and her other close advisers believe that a low profile is in her
best interests, that no publicity can be good publicity and that
any future hopes of release lie in the hands of her lawyers.
Occasionally Astor will be tempted to write a reasoned, clearly
argued, unsensational article in a quality broadsheet outlining
the case for Hindley being paroled. His January 1990 piece in
the *Guardian* contained many of the arguments that Longford
had used in Hindley's defence. But Astor's presentation was not
confrontational or provocative.

In recent years it has been Astor and a small circle of advisers
who have handled Hindley's affairs. Longford has effectively
been supplanted and has agreed to confine his comments about
Hindley to the House of Lords. He still continues to lobby
privately – out of the media's eye – for her eventual release and
to recruit prominent figures to her cause, but their close friendship has now cooled.

Though the two correspond and Hindley speaks of Longford
in the warmest terms, she has asked him to stop visiting her for
the time being. His trips to Cookham Wood inevitably attract

443

publicity. As he was leaving after his final visit, he was stopped by a *Sun* reporter in the car park outside and a story appeared the next day in the paper. Anxious to keep a low profile, Hindley has tried, gently but firmly, to change the basis of their friendship. He is kept informed of the latest moves by her advisers, who include his grandson-in-law, the barrister Edward Fitzgerald, husband of Antonia's daughter Rebecca.

In the end Longford's conviction that Hindley should be released has, by its longevity and its robustness in the face of perpetual onslaught, impressed many close to him. At the outset some of his former political colleagues thought Longford was utterly mistaken. Some hold to that position. Lord Carrington, his opposite number when he was Leader of the House of Lords, says: 'I think he shot himself in the foot over Myra Hindley. I think that the ordinary, average citizen does not think that redemption goes as far as Frank does and, by going over the top, he has damaged his credibility.'[16] Lord Hailsham, who as Quintin Hogg stood against Longford (and later Elizabeth) in Oxford, questioned his old adversary's judgement, saying he has 'the knack of giving equal, ludicrous weight to both the trivial and the substantial'.

Others, however, have come eventually to reconsider in the light of Longford's dedication and unflinching position. Roy Jenkins, as Home Secretary in the mid-1970s, was approached by Longford over Hindley but gave no ground. However, now he says:

> I take his interest in Myra Hindley rather more
> seriously than pornography. I rather respect him for
> it. He has no doubt damaged his public reputation
> with many people, but not with me. His willingness to
> stick to a difficult issue like that increased my respect
> for him.[17]

Though it has attracted most publicity and taken a disproportionate share of his effort and time, Longford's campaign for Hindley has been only a part of his broader work with prisoners. He continues to be involved with New Bridge, witnessing its growth into a respected organisation in the penal reform world, offering a specialised employment service to ex-prisoners and *Inside Time*, the only national newspaper for those in jail. He has taken considerable pleasure in the growing involvement in New Bridge of his daughter Rachel. Her 1992 novel, *Bodily Harm*, is set in a prison and, as part of her research, she talked to former inmates and heard of conditions behind bars. This led to a position as editorial adviser to *Inside Time* and, after the publication of the novel, to regular visits to prisons. Though she points out that since she did not start getting involved until she was fifty she can scarcely be described as inheriting her father's sense of mission, she concedes that having prisons and prisoners so much a part of her family life for so long must have had an effect. 'What I do think I have got from my father', says Rachel, 'is his reluctance to condemn people and especially those who have committed crimes. I think there are times when it is necessary to condemn people, but I find it very hard to do.'[18]

Longford became a trustee of New Bridge in 1987 when he stood down as president but he continues to advise the director, Eric McGrath. As the organisation has developed and expanded, Longford has taken a back seat. It is not just a question of his advancing years, but of his natural tendency to instigate a project and then hand over the running of it to others.

> Frank has been enormously important in pushing forward the whole question of prison reform [says McGrath]. There is a tendency now to remember organisations like the Howard League and NACRO and major reports like Wolfenden rather than individuals like Frank Longford who were the initiators. He was talking about the issues a long time before most people were. It has reached a stage now where the organisations have taken over from the early pioneers and it is sometimes easy to forget them.[19]

When Longford became involved in prison reform in the 1950s, there were no ex-prisoners organisations like New Bridge or NACRO. Now, largely through his efforts, that gap has been filled. Equally when he first initiated debates in the Lords on conditions in Britain's jails, he was a lone voice, calling attention to an issue that had not previously been discussed. Today, he is a member of a Parliamentary all-party penal reform group and is one among many campaigners.

Some, however, take the view that, because of his association with Myra Hindley and his notoriety in the press, Longford is less than an asset to groups set up to lobby on prison policy. When the Prison Reform Trust was set up in September 1981 by David Astor among others with the aim of informing public opinion on the topic, Longford was treated with deference but – much to his chagrin – excluded from any active participation. He was judged to be a barrier to communicating a new message on prisons.

> The idea [he wrote rather crossly after attending the launch] is that fresh faces and fresh voices should be introduced into the penal scene. The trouble about that is that these novices, however distinguished elsewhere, may take years to learn about prisons and the Trust initially intends to operate for only three years.[20]

Longford's main work in recent years has been prison visiting, the mission he first took up in Oxford in the late 1930s. Even in his late eighties, he still travels at least once a week to see someone behind bars. Some of those he seeks out are infamous. Longford visits those that no one else would contemplate seeing, such as Dennis Nilsen, whose developing interest in art and music he has encouraged, and Peter Sutcliffe, the 'Yorkshire Ripper' in Broadmoor. Longford has in the past seen the Kray brothers – persuaded to do so by their formidable mother Violet. As boys they frequented Eton Manor.

> Looking at the twins now, [he wrote] one would not connect them instinctively with atrocities and gang horrors. They still, however, retain the look of very tough customers – good friends but, one would imagine, bad enemies.[21]

Yet, without attracting any attention at all, Longford also visits prisoners whose cases will never hit the headlines, but who are lonely and desperate. The charge often levelled against him that he visits only those with well-known names is nonsense. Through Andrew McCooey, Myra Hindley's solicitor, he has been put into contact with and helped several inmates who otherwise would be completely alone in their ordeal.

> I was representing a young man who had brought
> drugs into the country. He was arrested, charged,
> sentenced and sent to Albany. He was from a wealthy
> family in Holland but his parents disowned him. He
> was HIV positive. Frank was prepared to travel to the
> Isle of Wight just to say he cared. That's the sort of
> thing the *Sun* doesn't publish. And the young man
> was very pleased that someone of such high standing
> would go all that way to, if nothing else, hold his
> hand, notwithstanding that he was a criminal, that he
> had AIDS. In those situations Frank is someone you
> can always turn to. It was a noble thing to do.[22]

Longford has a routine before setting off on a prison visit. 'I pray beforehand that I might be of some use and I pray for the person,' he says. 'I sometimes suppose that he's paying me and then I try to make sure that our half hour talk isn't dull.' With someone like Nilsen, he explains, 'my approach is just to listen. If he wants to talk about his crime, I let him. If he doesn't, I don't press him. He said to me recently, "If I knew why I did it, I wouldn't be here now."'[23] Longford's gift for listening, for forgetting himself and concentrating on others, has proved an invaluable asset in his prison visiting.

Just as the public can be suspicious of his motives, he sometimes gets a cool reception from the prison authorities – and occasionally from the prisoners he is visiting.

> Others tell them that being connected with me will do
> them no good at all. The officers can be hostile. I
> suppose they treat me like any member of the public.

447

> They sometimes make it as difficult as possible even
> though I have arranged my visit with the governor's
> secretary.[24]

On one visit to Albany in the Isle of Wight to see Nilsen, Longford took him some laxative pills. The prison officers made a great fuss about them and kept him waiting for twenty minutes. 'At the end there was no apology. I try to be tolerant. Their life makes them like that.'[25] On another occasion prison officers at Brixton tried to cut short, after fifteen minutes, his visit to a young man who had been accused of an armed robbery. Angered at such rough treatment, Longford demanded to see the governor and insisted that as a Member of Parliament he had always been allowed at least half an hour with prisoners. The governor backed down. The police, too, have shown their hostility to Longford's interest in prisoners. In February 1985, the *Police Review* described him as 'giving do-gooding a bad name'.

Seen from the other side of the visiting room, Longford's visits can be a life-saver in the dreary routine of prison. Rosie Johnston, convicted in December 1986 of drug-related offences after the death of her friend Olivia Channon, was the daughter of a friend of Longford.

> When I was first in prison he rang my mother and
> said he could come and visit me as a peer without
> depriving me of other family visits and asked if I
> would like to see him. The week that he was due to
> visit the snows fell. The prison was completely cut off.
> We couldn't get letters, food, anything, but he got
> there. He got a train and then a taxi and bullied them
> to battle through the snow and there he was, I
> couldn't believe it. Nothing else had got in through
> the prison gates for weeks. He was wearing a big grey
> coat but he didn't have any hat. There were snow-
> flakes in his hair and his pate was practically blue.
>   I had no preconceptions. I knew that he visited
> Myra Hindley but that didn't bother me. In fact I was

448

fascinated. When you're in that situation, you've been in prison for two months, any visit is completely welcome. We completely and totally hit it off. He's the biggest flirt. That was what I couldn't believe. He just flirted – he'd say, my dear you are charming, you've got such a charming face. When you look like shit and you've been eating white bread for months, it was wonderful. He gave me a copy of the *Spectator* and we sat down and talked a lot about lesbians. It was so funny. He said, 'Well, tell me are there lots of lesbians here?' And I said, 'Yes, of course.' And then we had a good giggle about that. We just giggled really.[26]

She recalls that his connection with Hindley meant that many of the women she was imprisoned with treated him with suspicion, bordering on disdain.

They couldn't understand why I wanted to see him. 'What do you want to go and be visited by that loony who visits Myra Hindley for – daft bugger.' I'd say, 'I don't think he's daft.' They were very suspicious of him. Because he was championing Myra Hindley they thought he must be either under her influence or mad.[27]

Though it is his Christian beliefs that inspire his prison visiting, Longford does not try to push his faith on those he meets, according to Johnston.

He did talk about Christianity – in a didactic way, that what he felt with Myra Hindley was that Christians should forgive each other, and I can't disagree with that. But I made it clear that I was never ripe for conversion. But I don't think he does it with a view to convert. He just talks about it because it is his thing – like I talk about my work. I think he has a terribly strong sense of suffering and people who are in a position where they cannot get help. He does have a crusade. The penal system is not a vote winner, an

electoral issue. It appeals to his sense of injustice. He
wants to make it better. He takes on his own
shoulders the injustice of a group of people who have
no rights and cannot speak for themselves and who
have no one to represent them.[28]

After her release, Longford invited Johnston to lunch in the
House of Lords. It is a gesture he makes to most of the prisoners
he has been visiting when they are set free, an attempt to ease
their reintegration back into society by bringing them to the seat
of the Establishment. Occasionally it can land him in trouble –
as when he invited Shane O'Doherty – but most of the time the
gesture of friendship passes unnoticed, save by those to whom
it is extended.

His interest in a prisoner does not end on the day of his or her
release. To some ex-prisoners, he offers hospitality in his own
home. Others he directs to New Bridge for help in rebuilding
their lives and finding a job. The ex-Labour MP, John Stonehouse, who was sent to prison after faking his own disappear-
ance, was visited by Longford in jail when all his other
colleagues deserted him. When Stonehouse married his secretary, Sheila Buckley, on his release in 1979, Longford was
there among the guests – to the delight of the *Daily Mail* reporter.

His efforts on behalf of prisoners have also stretched to
standing up for them when they are in court. However, his open
bias towards prisoners has damaged the credibility a retired
Cabinet minister would normally carry as a character witness. It
is not only on account of his support for Myra Hindley. Longford's trust has, on occasion, been betrayed when people he has
vouched for have gone on to commit more offences. He lent his
support, for example, to Niven Craig, brother of Christopher.
But he then continued to break the law.

Judges have come to doubt his judgement. In August 1982
Judge Cooke, sitting in the Inner London Crown Court, listened
respectfully as Longford spoke up for thirty-nine-year-old John
Masterson, an associate of the Krays and a habitual offender
whom he had met while in prison. Longford asked the judge to
favour a suspended sentence on Masterson who was convicted

of an assault charge, but a prison term was awarded. Choosing between a long list of previous offences and Longford's sincere belief that the person in question should be given another chance, the judge stuck to the form book. Solicitor Andrew McCooey says that Longford's effectiveness as a character witness with judges is now much diminished and that he would avoid calling him. 'You sense that the judge is thinking, "Well, Frank, would say that wouldn't he".'[29]

The judge hearing the case of Eddie Richardson at Winchester Crown Court in October 1990 was clearly of that opinion. Richardson, with a long record of violent crimes and extortion going back to the 1960s when he had received a fifteen-year sentence, was on trial for his part in a drug-smuggling plot. He was found guilty and sent down for twenty-five years, but not before Longford had stood up with a plea for clemency. Richardson obviously did not bear a grudge and, as he developed his talent as an artist, was later to paint a portrait of Longford.

While the judge paid little attention to Longford's plea, it caught the attention of Bernard Levin, writing in *The Times*. Levin had been one of the fiercest critics of the pornography report, but was apparently converted by Longford's long campaign for prisoners. 'Everybody asks the wrong question about Lord Longford, viz., is he barmy? The question is not worth asking: of *course* he is barmy. What we should be discussing is something quite different: is he right?' Levin wrote that he was quite prepared to take Longford's word that there was 'another side' to Richardson and that Myra Hindley was a reformed character. He expressed his admiration for Longford's indifference to those who ridiculed him and asked why the churches had not joined him in his crusade. 'If there is one dominant theme in Christian scripture, it is surely that no one, no one at all, is past hope of redemption and forgiveness.'[30] In speaking of the possibility of redemption – however idealistically – Longford was, Levin said, acting as Christ would and pointing to a central dilemma that society and the Home Office preferred to ignore. Whatever prisoners have done, are they beyond salvation? In refusing to accept that they are, Longford had Levin's support and his unqualified esteem. To have won such a distinguished –

and previously hostile – convert delighted Longford. The fact that Levin recorded his conversion in a lengthy and prominent article in *The Times* only added to the pleasure.

Raising the much neglected question about what Christ would have done is important in evaluating this area of Longford's work. His work with prisoners is directly inspired by his Christianity, by his daily reading of the Bible. In the gospels, Christ did not judge. He did not take the moral high ground but offered unconditional forgiveness. When He was among the sinners and the prostitutes like Mary Magdalen, they recognised in Him, unlike the scribes and pharisees, that lack of judgement and they were drawn to Him. He did not want to put them in their place.

> In his own very small way, Frank tries to imitate
> Christ [says Andrew McCooey]. A lot of Christians can
> make you feel uncomfortable because they are right-
> eous and judgemental. But Frank is not like that. And
> prisoners sense that in him, his concern and forgive-
> ness. It endears him to them. He touches the values
> that in your heart of hearts you know are right. He
> cares for people, for the underdog and he's always got
> time for you. It's the closest you can come to what a
> Christian can be.[31]

Roy Jenkins, like Bernard Levin, has been convinced by Longford's long campaign for a changed attitude to prisoners.

> I think Frank has shown dedication to the issue and
> even though he has been a nuisance to successive
> Home Secretaries, he has done a lot of good. I deeply
> respect him for his dedication on the issue and his
> absolute indifference to being put down or made to
> appear ridiculous by the press. Running through my
> slight impatience with what I regard as his occasional
> misjudgements, there is an underlying streak of
> admiration and a feeling that on balance, though an
> irritant, he has done good.[32]

Denis Healey is another who, while feeling that Longford has perhaps overstated the case for Hindley, considers that his record on prisons is second to none. 'The area where Frank has made a major personal imprint is in penal reform. It is usually an area where the individual rather than the party does it.'[33] Without political ambition since leaving Wilson's Cabinet, Longford has been able to put any party considerations behind him in his campaign for prisoners. Where previously he had felt a certain restraint, a wish to avoid embarrassing his party and his leader, in retirement he has been able to practise what he believes. He has become to prison visiting what Lord Soper is to Christian evangelism, a tireless, fearless campaigner who has faced down those who ridicule him and in recent times has begun to win their grudging respect by dint of sheer persistence.

It was from his work with prisoners – and in particular with young offenders – that the New Horizon Youth Centre grew. Longford's involvement with disadvantaged youngsters dates back to his childhood links with the Eton Manor Boys Club. He had been engaged on an inquiry into youth services when he left the Wilson Cabinet in 1968 and later that year spent a brief spell in charge of the National Youth Employment Council.

As early as 1960, however, Longford spoke to the executive committee of the New Bridge about the need for what he called a 'junior New Bridge', geared specifically to young offenders.[34] At the end of his government career, he was finally able to realise this dream. The New Horizon Youth Centre was launched in November of 1968 from the crypt of St Botolph's Church in Aldgate in the City of London, offering help and advice to youngsters. It was a pioneering venture, stresses Jon Snow, who was later to work at the centre before going on to become a familiar face on the television news.

> New Horizon was the first of its kind. Before then
> there had been no provision for young people in need
> in the capital. Frank had no idea what he was doing,
> but he could see youngsters on the streets and he
> knew he had to help them.[35]

New Horizon was not, however, an instant success. *The Times* criticised its brief as 'unclear' and the involvement of John Profumo attracted some adverse comment. Young people did not flock to its doors at first. Longford sat waiting with one assistant in St Botolph's for callers and there was scarcely a knock at the door.

He attributed this failure to location and, through a contact at New Bridge, was able to find a new headquarters in St Anne's Church in Soho. He also recruited some young blood in the shape of Martin Walker who had caught Longford's eye during student protests at the Hornsey College of Art the previous year. Longford had been called in as a mediator and had befriended Walker.

As the client base began to grow, Longford took more of a back seat. It was Walker that the youngsters wanted to talk to, not an elderly peer. Longford took care of fund-raising. There were fundamental differences between the two men which were to take New Horizon away from the original course that Longford had envisaged. Walker had no time at all for Christianity and rejected the notion of, as he later described it, 'handing out soup and sacraments'.[36] He felt uncomfortable with New Horizon's location within a church building, and, despite a rapid increase in the numbers of those using the centre, felt that the link with organised religion – however tenuous – might put off potential visitors.

Yet for Longford the Christian element was the key to his vision of New Horizon. The very name has biblical overtones. His aim was not to force his own personal beliefs on those who came to ask for help, but, just as he does in prisons, to offer support unconditionally. He is not an evangelist in the narrow sense, but neither is he afraid to talk of his Christian convictions when challenged.

Walker left after a year and a half, and was replaced by Jon Snow. Snow recalls that the most difficult task for Longford at New Horizon was bridging the age gap with the young visitors.

> He was extremely uncomfortable in conversation. Part
> of his Catholicism is, I suspect, about being

uncomfortable with sinners. And gauche. And yet he
sticks at it. The youngsters started on the basis of
laughing at him and on occasions even abusing him.
Then, because he sits and takes it and even asks
sensitive questions, they have to think again. That is
how I think he breaks through in prisons too. Of
course, it can work both ways. Because he is open, he
can end up by being duped.[37]

While Walker found the Christian ethos to be a barrier between
him and Longford, Snow praises the founder's tolerance. Writing of the initial period when he was around in the office,
Longford noted: 'It was, however, of immense value to have the
place run actively day by day . . . for a short time, and to have
to answer telephone enquiries of all kinds, including requests
for abortion to which I was chilly.'[38]

Yet a year and a half later, Snow found Longford more
tolerant.

He gave us complete freedom to do whatever we felt
was right. For example, he felt very strongly about
abortion, but if he'd walked in and heard us advising
somebody on how to get to the Brook Advisory Clinic,
there's no way he would have interfered. For one
who is so often portrayed as intolerant, he is
immensely tolerant.[39]

New Horizon continued to grow, moving to new premises in
Drury Lane and in 1972, by a vote of the staff, changing its role
to that of a seven-days-a-week walk-in centre, open until late at
night and offering hostel accommodation. Longford regularly
dropped in to see how things were going – as indeed he still
does – but his role became increasingly that of fund-raiser. Jon
Snow recalls that, even in the mid-1970s, Longford's name still
attracted funds.

He could tap ILEA for one. I remember ringing someone at County Hall and asking for an appointment

about New Horizon. When I mentioned Lord Longford was coming too, there was a marked change.
Suddenly it was, 'yes sir, no sir, three bags full sir'.[40]

As with his work with prisoners, Longford cannot sustain a
profound commitment to an organisation. He is too much the
individualist, his mission too much a personal one aimed at
individuals. At both New Bridge and New Horizon he remains a
respected father figure, distant but not indifferent.

Eighteen

The elder statesman

The newspapers, the telly and indeed the subject
himself, have seen to it that we are all fully aware
of Lord Longford. The snaps can be unfortunate.
The wild chevelure that frames the bald dome, the
unusual eyes and the glinting gig-lamps make him
seem like a mad professor in juvenile fiction, often
called something jovial such as Dr Oddsbodski

Arthur Marshall[1]

President Truman was once asked, during his twenty years in
retirement after leaving the White House, to define an elder
statesman. 'Someone who has been dead for fifteen years,' he
replied. Though he is very much alive and active, Frank Longford has a strong though neglected claim to be among the elder
statesmen of the Labour Party.

He is, after all, a former Cabinet minister, one of a handful of
survivors of the Attlee government. He spent twenty-two years
continuously on the Labour front bench in the Lords, a record
which no other member of the Upper Chamber can match. And
he remains active in Parliament, attending most weekdays, a
familiar figure in the corridors and tea-rooms of Westminster and
still a potent debater in exchanges across the floor of the House.

Yet to the public he is no longer known as a politician at all.
It is his crusade against pornography and his work for prisoners,
and in particular his friendship with Myra Hindley, that have
shaped his image, divorcing the present from the past, politics
from social concerns. And in Labour Party circles too, those
recent campaigns dominate any discussion about Frank Longford. Even among those old enough to know better, his reputation as a political maverick counterbalances any claim he has to
sit as a Labour elder statesman alongside other survivors of the

Attlee era, like James Callaghan and Douglas Jay and the senior citizens who once battled in Wilson's Cabinets.

Despite his preoccupation with non-party political matters in recent years, Longford's allegiance to Labour has remained unshakeable during the wilderness years of four election defeats since 1979. He continues to attend meetings of the Parliamentary Labour Party, to involve himself in its bruising internal battles and to attend the annual conference. It is all a far cry from the heady days of Scarborough and Brighton in the late 1950s and early 1960s when he was in the thick of things as his old friend Hugh Gaitskell fought with the unilateralists. Today Longford goes more in the spirit of an interested observer, occasionally offering an historical perspective to younger colleagues and enjoying the chance to meet a dwindling bunch of old friends and adversaries.

> I feel more ambiguous now about socialism [he says].
> If I'm asked, 'Are you in favour of socialism?', I would
> always say, yes. It's rather like being asked if you're
> against sin. There is only one answer. Equality
> remains the most important thing. As a moral ideal, as
> the goal of socialism, it has not changed. But the
> superficial things have changed. Socialism used, for
> example, to mean nationalisation, but now all that
> has changed.[2]

Longford remains one of a shrinking number of avowedly Christian Socialists in the Labour Party. Once a significant grouping, headed by party leaders like Lansbury and senior figures in the Cabinet such as Cripps, they are today on the margins of the party, with only the odd MP like Frank Field still carrying the torch in the Commons.

If there was a moment when Longford might have turned his back on Labour it was in 1981 with the founding of the SDP. Labour's drift to the left under Michael Foot (with whom Longford shares a lack of attention to dress and for whom he was once mistaken in a hospital waiting room) had seen it embrace unilaterialism and question the Atlantic Alliance, to

Longford the keystone of any British foreign policy. Those on the right of the party departed in substantial numbers. Longford's daughter Rachel and son Kevin became members of the SDP. But the Longfords remained dedicated to fighting from within to save the party they had joined almost fifty years previously. 'At my age,' Longford told his friends, 'the question of leaving the Labour Party does not arise.'[3] In an article in *The Times* on the day of the special Labour conference at Wembley in January 1981 to agree on how the leader should be chosen, Longford gave a fuller account of his reasons for not following Shirley Williams, David Owen, Bill Rodgers and Roy Jenkins.

Under the banner 'Why I must stay', Longford noted that there was nothing new in the charges of extremist infiltration of local Labour groups. It was a question of having the courage to stand up and fight.

> When I was elected to the Oxford City Council for the Cowley and Iffley ward in the late 1930s, my colleague on the ticket was a communist organiser who was narrowly defeated. 'Crypto-coms' were not unknown in our party, but complacency, or alternatively impotent rage, are no substitute for dealing firmly with anti-democratic forces. I must hope and pray that democratic socialists will bestir themselves more actively than in the past.

Moving on to the argument about the future direction of the party, Longford defended his continuing allegiance in personal terms:

> The Labour Party with all its faults stands, as it has always stood, for an idea, for a belief that all men and women are of equal significance in the sight of God and should be treated accordingly in human arrangements. Or to make use of a Christian text: 'When thou givest a feast, thou shalt call the poor, the maimed, the lame and the blind and thou shalt be blessed.' Black, white, yellow and brown, all are

459

> included. No one questions the motives or for that
> matter the Christianity of those who adhere to other
> parties. But no other party proclaims as lofty an
> aspiration as does the Labour Party. As long as I can
> continue to work within the party, for the causes and
> ideals I believe in, I cannot see myself leaving it.[4]

Elizabeth had supplied the last line, and it was, in effect, a statement from both of them. When they took their seats at the Wembley conference, Roy Hattersley was among those who came to congratulate Longford. Despite Michael Foot's defeat at the end of the gathering, Elizabeth told her husband on the journey home that 'they' – the left – 'have over-reached themselves'.[5] Her political instinct was characteristically acute.

Only a couple of weeks before the Wembley conference Longford made probably his final appearance as a party spokesman in Parliament. After a thirteen-year gap since his resignation from the Cabinet, he was drafted in by the Chief Whip, Lady Llewelyn-Davies, to wind up a debate on the disabled for the Opposition.[6] It was a subject that he had held dear since 1970 when he piloted Labour MP Alf Morris's Chronically Sick and Disabled Persons Bill through the Lords. He sat on the front bench again, albeit briefly, doomed at the end of the debate like Cinderella to return to the shadows from whence he came. Longford's swansong left him feeling exhilarated.

At least when Michael Foot, Tony Benn and Denis Healey were battling it out in the early 1980s for the soul of the party, Longford knew the principal players well. They had grown up together in the party. The age of Neil Kinnock – whose forthright repudiation of belief in God Longford found alienating – and John Smith has left him out on a limb, a relic of a previous generation.

The Longfords had a personal link with Margaret Thatcher. They had lived in adjoining streets in Chelsea and, in the late 1970s, the Thatchers, who had a house at Lamberhurst, came to dinner with the Longfords at Bernhurst. Longford gets on well with Denis Thatcher, the two sharing a love of rugby and the same experience of being the butt of cartoonists and satirists.

Though Longford admired Mrs Thatcher as 'a sincere but unintellectual Christian', he found her policies and, in particular, the social inequality that they promoted, antithetical to what he regards as the essence of Christianity.

As a former right-hand man to Beveridge, Longford might have been expected to play a leading role in the attack on Conservative reforms of the system whose birth he attended. Yet Longford believes that the best way to remain effective is to focus attention on a narrow range of issues and speak with authority. He takes an active part in every debate about prisons, youth policy and the treatment of the mentally ill. He initiates at least two debates a year around these central issues.

One undeniable privilege of the House of Lords is that you never have to retire. Longford has retired twice from politics – compulsorily in 1951 and voluntarily in 1968. He also retired from the National Bank in 1963 and from the chairmanship of Sidgwick and Jackson in 1980. But in the Upper Chamber the concept has no meaning. It is a place where sixty-fifth birthdays excite little comment. Indeed a good number of its members join only when they have passed that landmark in the Commons. 'The wonderful thing about this geriatric place is that you can strut about here and no one knows if you've retired or not,' says Longford.[7]

As a long-serving member of the Upper House, he has watched as his former Cabinet and government colleagues have come to the end of their Commons careers and filled the benches around him. It is like a club for all his old friends and foes. He has enjoyed what he sees as the privilege of introducing several newly ennobled former government colleagues to the House. It was Longford, for example, who acted as sponsor to Harold Wilson when he joined the Lords. He believes that many senior statesmen have become more effective performers in the less confrontational environment of the Upper Chamber. 'Old people tend, in my experience, to speak better. Macmillan, for example, was a much better speaker in the Lords than he ever was in the Commons.'[8]

Aside from his regular attendance in the House of Lords and his work with prisoners, Longford's other main activity of recent years has been to write. He remained a director of Sidgwick and Jackson after he resigned as chairman and worked with the editorial team there to woo such old friends as Diana Mosley and Jon Snow to sign up to produce books. He kept his office and part-time secretarial help at Sidgwick and Jackson's Bloomsbury offices until 1987.

In the wake of the pornography enquiry and with his involvement with Myra Hindley much debated, he produced another volume of autobiography in 1974. *The Grain of Wheat* was published by Collins and covered his activities in the decade since he had joined Wilson's Cabinet. The *Sunday Times* thought it an important enough book to run a large extract at the time of publication, featuring Longford's own account of his visit to Copenhagen.

Some reviewers, however, were not convinced of its merits. Richard Ingrams, who as editor of *Private Eye* had been responsible for some of the most damning satire about the pornography inquiry, dismissed *The Grain of Wheat* in 'Books and Bookmen'. He wrote of Longford: 'His political achievements are minimal, his writings are piffle and his pronouncements on religion and pornography are entirely worthless.' Ingrams found Longford's account in the book of visiting the Krays in prison 'nauseating' and accused him of being blind to the nature of evil. Longford was hurt by the criticism, especially since he regarded Ingrams as a friend and shared a link with him through Arthur Villiers who was Ingrams' godfather.

Freed of the workload of the pornography inquiry, Longford turned to writing with enthusiasm. Roy Jenkins, casting an eye over the long list of titles Longford has produced in the past twenty years, is full of admiration. 'His eclecticism has been almost limitless . . . The full variety is an almost breath-taking tribute to sustained energy and dauntless self-confidence.' Longford's delight in researching books has always been greater than his enjoyment of the process of writing. However, with time on his hands at weekends and holidays as his political activities wound down, he turned his mind to profiling some of the people he most admired. In 1974, the same year that *The Grain of Wheat* appeared, Longford also produced a biography of

Abraham Lincoln and a very personal portrait of Jesus Christ. Both subjects were hardly original, but the attractions of Lincoln are obvious to someone like Longford who has attempted to take a moral rather than a pragmatic line in politics. In 1976, Longford published a brief life of John F. Kennedy which was rather overtaken by events. Longford tried to present his subject as a Catholic statesman answering to a higher moral code. But news of Kennedy's insatiable womanising had begun to be made public, leaving the Longford thesis looking rather redundant. The omission did not, however, affect sales in Ireland where the book became a bestseller.

After a life of St Francis of Assisi, who – like Longford – had befriended the marginalised, Longford reverted in 1980 to contemporary biography with Richard Nixon. His fall from grace in the Watergate scandal had been a public humiliation which had left Nixon an outcast. Longford was anxious to welcome him back into the fold, forgive him as he forgave prisoners. In December 1978, Longford had given a lunch for the ex-president at the Hyde Park Hotel and persuaded senior British politicians, including Reginald Maudling and James Prior, to attend.

After finally completing his long-promised book on Ulster in 1981, he was drafted in at the eleventh hour to produce an official portrait of Pope John Paul II to coincide with the Polish Pontiff's visit to Britain. Elizabeth had been the first choice of the publishers, but she was tied up with her research for *The Queen as Monarch* and suggested her husband. He took to the task with alacrity and managed to secure a private interview with the Pope in the Vatican. In 1975 Longford had been accorded the rare honour of the Grand Cross of the Papal Knights of St Gregory. He joined a club almost as exclusive – in Catholic terms – as that of the Garter Knights. There were only two other recipients of the medal in Britain.

In 1982 as well Longford produced *Diary of a Year*, detailing his activities throughout 1981. It was a more successful book than many of those that had gone before, carrying the reader along with witty asides and a procession of well-known names and revealing in the process something about its author. Auberon Waugh, Longford's godson and a critic with a reputation for being just as cutting as Richard Ingrams, wrote a glowing review in the *Sunday Telegraph*.

> For the first time in his life, he [Longford] has written a vastly entertaining book which reflects that goodness, that intelligence and that genuine, usually lovable, eccentricity. I hope it is permitted reading in all the monasteries and that Catholic schoolboys will be allowed to read it in retreat.[9]

Heartened by such praise, Longford's literary output increased as his other work dwindled. *Eleven at No 10* in 1984 told of the prime ministers he had known, while *One Man's Faith*, published the same year, was another exercise in autobiography. *The Search for Peace*, which appeared in 1985, pondered again the Irish problem among others, while *The Bishops* in 1986 and *Saints* in 1987 were both collections of essays about some of the Christian figures Longford revered.

A History of the House of Lords appeared in 1988, with an introduction by Elizabeth, once a fervent opponent of the Upper Chamber. *Forgiveness*, published by a small independent printing press in 1989, was intended as a companion volume to *Humility* and depicted another of the central Christian virtues and a recurrent theme in his own life. In 1991, he began a trilogy of books on prisons policy with *Punishment and the Punished*, followed in 1992 by *Prisoner or Patient*, and in 1993 by *Young Offenders*.

Some of the books in this extensive bibliography betray the signs of having been hastily written. The trilogy, for example, is a collection of transcripts of interviews carried out by Lord Longford and typed up by his devoted secretary, Gwen Keeble. Having identified an interesting area and carried out his research, Longford let himself down at the last hurdle and assembled rather than wrote the book.

There is also a good deal of overlap in many of the volumes. Marigold Johnson, who continued to work part-time with Longford once the pornography report was over, recalls that his approach to meeting a publisher's deadline was unusual.

> He would sit in his office with all the various talks,
> notes and bits of books that he had already written on
> any related subject, and he would then say, 'I'm going
> to work now' and we would all disappear. And then
> he would come out and get his secretary, Gwen, to
> retype it. Occasionally I caught a glimpse of these
> manuscripts. He would just recycle paragraphs, chap-
> ters, pages quite ruthlessly. And he would cross things
> out and say, 'That will do.' That's how he has man-
> aged to turn out so many books in such a short
> period.[10]

Longford himself would not lay claim to any great literary talent. That area is the prerogative of his wife and children. But his books have at least raised prompted coverage for some of the subjects that interest him. His name is usually enough, if not to draw a large publisher's advance, then to attract a healthy crop of generally respectful reviews.

If Longford's literary activities are more of a hobby – his alternative to the more standard pastimes of old age, gardening and travel, neither of which interest him – it is Elizabeth's carefully crafted, thoroughly researched biographies and inves-tigations into the state of the monarchy that keep the family finances afloat. Rather like the royal family, Longford, betraying his aristocratic upbringing, never carries any cash with him. He tends to invite people to lunch with him either in the Lords or at restaurants where he is known. Marigold Johnson recalls that when she was hard at work on the pornography report, Long-ford would take her to lunch at the Gay Hussar in Soho.

> He had a regular table there and I never saw him
> produce a coin. He would just sign the bill. It's not
> that he's mean. He just doesn't carry money. He once
> took me to the theatre. When we arrived, he said,
> 'Would you mind buying me a programme? I'm afraid
> I haven't got any money.'[11]

Longford is still the party-goer of his younger days; social life and evenings out with friends continue to fill his diary. Weekends at Bernhurst are sacred. He once turned down an invitation to a ball on a Saturday evening, saying, 'If I came back to London at the weekend, my wife would divorce me.' Even in the country the couple have a stream of visitors, children, grandchildren (of whom they have twenty-seven) and even great-grandchildren. Until his death, Malcolm Muggeridge and his wife Kitty used to get together with the Longfords each weekend. Muggeridge's combination of spiritual reflections, news and gossip about mutual friends and acquaintances appealed to both the weighty and the frivolous sides of Longford's character.

When they are at their flat in Chelsea during the week, the Longfords are hard to reach, Frank at the Lords and Elizabeth off researching or writing her latest book. They remain close, both emotionally and physically, to their children. Antonia, Rachel, Judith and Thomas – when he's not in Ireland – all live nearby with their families. 'My mother still thinks she has to take care of us,' says Rachel. 'If we've been out shopping, she will insist on calling me a taxi to see me safely home.'[12]

The Longfords seem always to be celebrating some achievement by their children, their children's partners and their grandchildren: Thomas's *The Struggle for Africa* winning the W. H. Smith award; Antonia's *The Six Wives of Henry VIII* topping the bestsellers chart; Michael appointed ambassador to Luxembourg; Rachel's latest novel; her husband Kevin's latest play or film. Though no one has followed their father into politics, his interests are reflected in the activities of his clan. Rachel works with prisoners. Kevin is in the City. Judith, as well as publishing poetry, is a political lobbyist on various third world issues. The Pakenhams are forever in the news.

Elizabeth does not quite have her husband's appetite for parties. He has no patience with television, is not a keen theatre or cinema goer, but delights in meeting people. His wit and continuing fame make him a desirable guest at most parties. So he fills his evenings with book launches, exhibition openings, anniversary celebrations, regularly cropping up in social diaries in the press as 'deep in conversation with . . .' or sharing a thought about such and such a prisoner that he visits.

Longford's speciality when it comes to entertaining is lunch

or dinner at the House of Lords. His guests come from all walks
of life. As well as newly released prisoners, there are old friends
with whom he still keeps in touch. He lunches or dines with Jon
Snow every month. Others are figures in the public eye to
whom he feels attracted or who he thinks have been having a
tough time. On one occasion when Princess Michael of Kent
had been given an especially rough ride by the press, the
Longfords asked her to be their guest as an act of solidarity. On
another he invited Kelvin MacKenzie, then editor of the *Sun*, to
join him.

Though the meal is a social occasion, he sometimes has an
agenda – wanting MacKenzie, for example, to relax his paper's
campaign against Myra Hindley. More often, though, it is simply
that he is interested in hearing what others are thinking and
doing. One of the ways he has kept young and interesting is his
contact with those in the thick of things. 'Most elderly politicians
are about as newsworthy as last year's beauty queen, but Frank
always somehow manages to keep in the swim,' says one of his
old Cabinet colleagues.

Elizabeth sometimes joins her husband in the Lords dining
room. In her absence Antonia or Rachel, with or without their
partners, will make up the party. Occasionally Longford invites
fellow peers to join the group. Marigold Johnson and her
husband, the newspaper columnist Paul Johnson, have often
attended such events.

> They are always very funny, very lively lunches. You
> talk about everything under the sun. Frank has
> always done his homework to such an extent that not
> a single moment passes when he isn't introducing a
> topic that is of interest to one of us. No politician,
> active or not, could handle the groups of disparate
> people he gathers better. It's like a star performance
> and he keeps all the information in his head.[13]

Both the Longfords have been blessed with remarkable health.
Mentally and physically they have remained fit and active into
their late eighties. Longford continues to jog – at a sedate pace –

several miles each weekend when he is at Bernhurst. Until Malcolm Muggeridge's death Longford was almost a tourist attraction, jogging along the main road from Hurst Green to the Muggeridges' cottage at Robertsbridge, highly visible in the yellow reflectors provided by Thomas. Weekend visitors to Bernhurst will often find Longford in his running shoes ensconced in his chaotic study amid a mass of books, putting together a manuscript, preparing for a Lords debate, or replying to a correspondent, all under the watchful gaze of Lady Mary Villiers whose portrait hangs above the fireplace. Across the corridor, Elizabeth, elegant and welcoming, is making the final corrections to her latest book in the drawing room, with its panoramic views over the Bernhurst garden and the six-sided greenhouse where she does much of her writing.

Longford disclaims any secret recipe for longevity and continuing vigour but he has never smoked, exercises regularly and has always been careful about his diet. His one weakness is alcohol. Many has been the Lent when he tries to give up drink, but his addiction is a moderate one.

In 1992, he slipped and fell down the stairs at Bernhurst, colliding with the grandfather clock, breaking a couple of ribs and rupturing his spleen. Given that their father was eighty-six, his children hurried to his bedside at Hastings Hospital fearing the worst. Rachel was with Longford when the consultant told him that he would have to remove his spleen.

> His only reply was, 'But I've got my secretary coming tomorrow and then I've got to be in the House of Lords for a debate.' The consultant said that they would have to see how it went. It was a major operation for someone of his age. At which point my father said, 'Well, let's get on with it.' I was sitting with my mother waiting for him to come back from surgery. We were there for about an hour and a half on this long ward full of men who were all twenty years younger than Dadda and looked twenty years older. And then I heard the rattle of the trolley and I looked up to the end of the ward and I saw this man

in a paper cowl with his bare arms above his head in a
victory salute. It was my father.[14]

Though he recovered and was out and about in London only a
couple of weeks later, Longford will admit that he has begun to
pace himself more. 'There is a great loss of vigour in old age. I
find myself getting very tired and have to rest. The days are
therefore shorter.'

Inevitably his thoughts and his daily dose of Christian reading
have strayed into contemplating death and an after-life. He is
sure that there is a heaven. 'But only after a long spell in
Purgatory. I see Purgatory as a purification period. I can't picture
it, but I can't believe that you go straight to heaven.' There are
no specific preparations you can make for death, he believes.
You will be judged on what you have done on earth.

> I have talked about preparing for death with Douglas
> Houghton [an active nonagenarian member of the
> Lords who sat with Longford in the Wilson Cabinet]
> and he says he lives each day as if it's his last. He
> never post-dates cheques. But I do try to prepare a
> little for the future, to look ahead a year or two, live
> life as if I'm going to live for ever.[15]

Ageing and coping with the prospect of death were subjects that
the Longfords would occasionally discuss with the Muggeridges
at their weekend gatherings in Sussex. Longford was in awe of
Kitty Muggeridge's ability to detach herself from the world and
focus her attention on the spiritual.

> As the years pass [he noted], she thinks less and less
> of this world and more and more of the world to
> come . . . The supernatural world seems to her more
> and more the real one. She points to the chairs and
> sofas in her drawing room and says 'They are losing
> their texture, they are beginning to become pale
> reflections of the spiritual reality.'[16]

The conversation made Longford pause to consider whether as a committed Christian, he should not wind down his worldly affairs, his work in the Lords, his prison visiting, and emulate his old friend in 'making her soul'. But even in his late eighties, such a passive role would be unbearable to Longford. His preparation for life after death has been life itself. As Philip Howard was to write in *The Times*, at the time of the Longfords' golden wedding celebrations, under a Lichfield photograph of their family:

> He [Longford] needs an *apologia pro vita sua* less than most of our generation, though he will keep on writing them. His monuments stand and sit all around him.[17]

Notes

Introduction

1 *The Times*, 19 Oct 1978
2 Author interview with Lord Healey
3 *The Times*, 15 Oct 1990

1 The second son

1 Stephen Gwynn, *Exploits of a Literary Man* (1926)
2 Graham Myers was the architect who worked on Tully Nally in the 1770s.
3 Lady Mary Clive, *Brought Up and Brought Out* (1938)
4 Longford signed over his rights to his inheritance, including Tully Nally, to his eldest son Thomas in 1959.
5 The Duke of Wellington married Lady Katharine Pakenham in 1806.
6 Elizabeth Longford, *The Pebbled Shore* (1986)
7 Frank Longford, *Peace by Ordeal* (1935)
8 Diana Norman, *Terrible Beauty* (1987)
9 Author interview with Thomas Pakenham
10 Pakenham family records kept at Tully Nally
11 Lady Mary Clive, op. cit.
12 Frank Longford, *Born to Believe* (1953)
13 Ibid.
14 Author interview with Maureen, Marchioness of Dufferin and Ava
15 Lady Mary Clive, op. cit.
16 Lady Violet Powell, *Five Out of Six* (1960)
17 Lady Mary Clive, op. cit.
18 Ibid.
19 Elizabeth Longford, *The Pebbled Shore*
20 See Jonathan Gaythorn-Hardy's *The English Nanny*
21 Author interview with Lord Longford
22 Ibid.
23 Frank Longford, *Born to Believe* (1953)

24 Author interview with Thomas Pakenham
25 Author interview with Lord Longford
26 *Financial Times*, 28 Apr 1990
27 Michael Davie (ed), *Evelyn Waugh's Diaries* (1976)
28 Lady Mary Clive, op. cit.
29 Ibid.
30 Author interview with Thomas Pakenham
31 Lady Mary Clive, op. cit.
32 Ibid.
33 Ibid.
34 Ibid.
35 Ibid.
36 Ibid.
37 Ibid.
38 Padraic Pearse (1879–1916)
39 Lady Mary Clive, op. cit.
40 Ibid.

2 The distracted scholar

1 Author interview with Lord Longford
2 Frank Longford, *Born to Believe*
3 Elizabeth Longford, *The Pebbled Shore*
4 Christie was to inherit a fortune at thirty on condition that he earned his living first. Thus he took up the teaching profession but with a distracted air.
5 Frank Longford, *Born to Believe*
6 Ibid.
7 Author interview with Lord Longford
8 Elizabeth Longford, *The Pebbled Shore*
9 Frank Longford, *Born to Believe*
10 Author interview with Valerie Pakenham
11 Interview with Mary Craig (1977)
12 Ibid.
13 Quoted in Philip Williams, *Hugh Gaitskell* (1979)
14 Douglas Jay, *Change and Fortune* (1980)
15 Interview with Mary Craig
16 John Betjeman in *My Oxford* (1977)
17 Francis Wheen, *Tom Driberg* (1990)
18 Harold Acton, *Memoirs of an Aesthete* (1948)
19 Evelyn Waugh, *Decline and Fall* (1928)
20 Author interview with Lord Jay
21 Alan Palmer, *The East End* (1989)
22 Frank Longford, *Born to Believe*

23 Ibid.
24 Ibid.
25 Ibid.
26 Keynes's *The General Theory of Employment, Interest and Money* was not published until 1936 and was widely taken up after the Second World War.
27 Frank Longford, *Born to Believe*
28 Quoted in Philip Williams, *Hugh Gaitskell*
29 Elizabeth Longford, *The Pebbled Shore*

3 The party-goer

1 Evelyn Waugh, *Vile Bodies* (1930)
2 Author interview with Lord Longford
3 Caroline Blackwood, *Great Granny Webster* (1977). The eccentric central character, Lady Dunmartin, is reputedly based on Basil Dufferin's mother, Lady Brenda.
4 Quoted in Bevis Hillier, *Young Betjeman* (1988)
5 Elizabeth Longford, *The Pebbled Shore*
6 Author interview with Maureen, Marchioness of Dufferin and Ava
7 Frank Longford, *Born to Believe*
8 Author interview with Lord Longford
9 Frank Longford, *Born to Believe*
10 Ibid.
11 Author interview with Lord Longford
12 Ibid.
13 Ibid.
14 Frank Longford, *Born to Believe*
15 Author interview with Bronwen Astor
16 Author interview with David Astor
17 Author interview with Lord Longford
18 Frank Longford, *Born to Believe*
19 Author interview with David Astor
20 Lucy Kavaler, *The Astors* (1966)
21 Ibid.
22 Frank Longford, *Diary of a Year* (1982)
23 Author interview with David Astor
24 Ibid.
25 Author interview with Lord Longford
26 Frank Longford, *Diary of a Year*
27 Frank Longford, *Born to Believe*
28 Philip Williams, *Hugh Gaitskell*
29 Elizabeth Longford, *The Pebbled Shore*
30 Frank Longford, *Born to Believe*

31 Elizabeth Longford, *The Pebbled Shore*
32 Author interview with Maureen, Marchioness of Dufferin and Ava
33 Author interview with Lord Longford
34 House of Lords debate on the economic and social consequences of government policy, 23 Feb 1993
35 Author interview with Lord Longford
36 Elizabeth Longford, *The Pebbled Shore*
37 Ibid.
38 In his obituary for Edward Longford (1961)
39 Elizabeth Longford, *The Pebbled Shore*
40 Ibid.
41 Ibid.
42 Ibid.
43 Ibid.
44 Ibid.
45 Ibid.

4 The Irish socialist

1 Quentin Bell
2 Elizabeth Longford, *The Pebbled Shore*
3 Ibid.
4 Oliver St John Gogarty (1878–1957) was an Irish senator from 1922 to 1936 and is best remembered for his book of literary reminiscences *As I was Going Down Sackville Street* (1937).
5 Lord Dunsany had married Mary Longford's sister, Beatrice.
6 Frank Longford, *Born to Believe*
7 Author interview with Lord Longford
8 Elizabeth Longford, *The Pebbled Shore*
9 Ibid. and Frank Longford, *Born to Believe* though Maureen Dufferin now has no recollection of the incident.
10 Author interview with Lord Longford
11 Author interview with Thomas Pakenham
12 Frank Longford, *Born to Believe*
13 Ibid.
14 Ibid.
15 Author interview with Michael Foot
16 Ibid.
17 Quoted by Lord Longford in his foreword to the 1992 edition of *Peace by Ordeal*
18 Frank Longford, *Born to Believe*
19 A reference to Birkenhead's earlier championing of the Unionist cause and alliance with its leader, Lord Carson.
20 Author interview with Lord Longford

21 Ibid.
22 Frank Longford, *Born to Believe*
23 Ibid.
24 Elizabeth Longford, *The Pebbled Shore*
25 Author interview with David Astor
26 Author interview with Lady Longford
27 Interview in 1977 with Mary Craig
28 Ibid.
29 Ibid.
30 Ibid.
31 Philip Williams, *Hugh Gaitskell*
32 Frank Longford, *Born to Believe*
33 Author interview with Frank Longford
34 Frank Longford, *Born to Believe*
35 Author interview with Frank Longford
36 Author interview with Lord Jenkins of Hillhead
37 Author interview with David Astor
38 Interview in 1977 with Mary Craig

5   The radical don

1 David Marquand, *The Progressive Dilemma*, Heinemann (1991)
2 Author interview with Lady Longford
3 Elizabeth Longford, *The Pebbled Shore*
4 In an article in *The Times*, 24 Jan 1981
5 At the 1939 Labour conference
6 Robert Pearce (ed), *Patrick Gordon Walker – Political Diaries 1932–1971* (1980)
7 Author interview with Lady Longford
8 Ian Mikado, *Backbencher* (1988)
9 Frank Longford, *Born to Believe*
10 Quintin Hailsham, *A Sparrow's Flight* (1990)
11 Author interview with Lord Longford
12 Chris Cook and John Ramsden (eds), *By-Elections in British Politics* (1973)
13 Elizabeth Longford, *The Pebbled Shore*
14 Ibid.
15 Ibid.
16 Ibid.
17 *Daily Express*, 23 Aug 1990
18 Author interview with Lady Longford
19 Ibid.
20 Elizabeth Longford, *The Pebbled Shore*
21 Author interview with Maureen, Marchioness of Dufferin and Ava

22 Lucy Kavaler, *The Astors*
23 Quoted by Longford in his essay on Churchill in *Eleven at No 10* (1984)
24 Elizabeth Longford, *The Pebbled Shore*
25 Ibid.
26 Author interview with Lady Longford
27 Quintin Hailsham, *A Sparrow's Flight*
28 Ibid.
29 Elizabeth Longford, *The Pebbled Shore*
30 Interview in 1977 with Mary Craig
31 Quintin Hailsham, *A Sparrow's Flight*
32 Author interview with Lady Antonia Fraser
33 Patrick O'Donovan: *A Journalist's Odyssey* (1985)
34 Elizabeth Longford, *The Pebbled Shore*
35 Chris Cook and John Ramsden (eds), *By-Elections in British Politics*
36 Ibid.
37 Quintin Hailsham, *A Sparrow's Flight*
38 Ibid.

6   The outcast

1 Michael Davie (ed), *Evelyn Waugh's Diaries*
2 Author interview with Lord Healey
3 Frank Longford, *Born to Believe*
4 Ibid.
5 Ibid.
6 Author interview with Lord Healey
7 Elizabeth Longford, *The Pebbled Shore*
8 Author interview with Lady Antonia Fraser
9 Elizabeth Longford, *The Pebbled Shore*
10 Author interview with Lord Longford
11 Elizabeth Longford, *The Pebbled Shore*
12 Frank Longford, *Born to Believe*
13 Author interview with Lord Longford
14 Author interview with Auberon Waugh
15 Frank Longford, *Born to Believe*
16 Evelyn Waugh, *Brideshead Revisited* (1945)
17 Author interview with Lord Longford
18 Author interview with Lady Longford
19 Ibid.
20 Author interview with David Astor
21 Author interview with Lady Antonia Fraser
22 Michael Davie (ed), *Evelyn Waugh's Diaries*
23 Elizabeth Longford, *The Pebbled Shore*
24 Author interview with Lord Longford

25 Elizabeth Longford, *The Pebbled Shore*
26 Author interview with David Astor

7   The post-war planner

1 Frank Longford, *Born to Believe*
2 Ibid.
3 Author interview with Lady Longford
4 Elizabeth Longford (ed), *Catholic Approaches* (1953)
5 Janet Beveridge, *Beveridge and His Plan* (1954)
6 Author interview with Lord Longford
7 Author interview with David Astor
8 Author interview with Lord Longford
9 Elizabeth Longford, *The Pebbled Shore*
10 Janet Beveridge, *Beveridge and His Plan*
11 Author interview with Lady Antonia Fraser
12 Elizabeth Longford, *The Pebbled Shore*
13 Janet Beveridge, *Beveridge and His Plan*
14 Ibid.
15 Frank Longford, *Born To Believe*
16 Ibid.
17 Interview in 1977 with Mary Craig
18 Janet Beveridge, *Beveridge and His Plan*
19 Frank Longford, *Born to Believe*
20 Quoted by Longford in his essay on Attlee in *Eleven at No 10*
21 Frank Longford, *Born to Believe*
22 Author interview with David Astor
23 Janet Beveridge, *Beveridge and His Plan*
24 Author interview with David Astor
25 Frank Longford, *Born to Believe*
26 Author interview with Lady Antonia Fraser

8   The Lord-in-Waiting

1 *Daily Express*, 26 May 1953
2 Quintin Hailsham, *A Sparrow's Flight*
3 Michael Davie (ed), *Evelyn Waugh's Diaries*
4 Mark Amory (ed), *Letters of Evelyn Waugh* (1980)
5 Quintin Hailsham, *A Sparrow's Flight*
6 Author interview with Lady Antonia Fraser
7 Ben Pimlott, *Hugh Dalton* (1985)
8 Elizabeth Longford, *The Pebbled Shore*
9 Frank Longford, *Born to Believe*
10 Elizabeth Longford, *The Pebbled Shore*

11 Author interview with Lord Longford
12 Author interview with Lady Longford
13 Frank Longford, *Born to Believe*
14 Author interview with Lord Longford
15 Michael Davie (ed), *Evelyn Waugh's Diaries*
16 Author interview with Lady Antonia Fraser
17 Author interview with Lord Longford
18 Interview in 1977 with Mary Craig
19 Frank Longford, *Born to Believe*
20 Ibid.
21 Elizabeth Longford, *The Pebbled Shore*
22 Ibid.
23 Author interview with Lady Antonia Fraser
24 Author interview with Thomas Pakenham
25 Elizabeth Longford, *The Pebbled Shore*
26 Author interview with Lord Longford
27 Quoted in Longford's essay on Attlee in *Eleven at No 10*
28 Author interview with Lord Longford
29 Kenneth Harris, *Attlee* (1976)
30 Ruth Dudley Edwards, *Victor Gollancz* (1987)

9   The minister for Germany

1 Author interview with Lady Antonia Fraser
2 Ruth Dudley Edwards, *Victor Gollancz*
3 Frank Longford, *Born to Believe*
4 Interview in 1977 with Mary Craig
5 Frank Longford, *Born to Believe*
6 Author interview with David Astor
7 Frank Longford, *Born to Believe*
8 Frank Roberts, *Dealing with Dictators* (1991)
9 Michael Davie (ed), *Evelyn Waugh's Diaries*
10 Frank Longford, *Born to Believe*
11 Author interview with Lord Jay
12 Author interview with Lord Healey
13 Elizabeth Longford, *The Pebbled Shore*
14 Frank Longford, *Born to Believe*
15 Ibid.
16 Ibid.
17 Author interview with Lord Longford
18 Frank Longford, *Born to Believe*
19 Ibid.
20 Author interview with Michael Foot
21 Quoted in Longford's essay on Churchill in *Eleven at No 10*

22 Author interview with Lord Carrington
23 Author interview with Jon Snow

10   The head of a nationalised industry

1 Author interview with Judith Kazantzis
2 Philip Williams (ed), *The Diary of Hugh Gaitskell (1945–1956)* (1983)
3 Frank Longford, *Born to Believe*
4 Author interview with Maureen, Marchioness of Dufferin and Ava
5 Elizabeth Longford, *The Pebbled Shore*
6 Frank Longford, *Born to Believe*
7 Ibid.
8 Ibid.
9 Ibid.
10 Frank Longford, *The Grain of Wheat* (1974)
11 It was Attlee, in retirement, who persuaded Wilson to appoint Longford to the Cabinet in 1964.
12 Frank Longford, *Born to Believe*
13 Ibid.
14 Author interview with Lord Healey
15 Philip Williams (ed), *The Diary of Hugh Gaitskell (1945–1956)*
16 Ibid.
17 Elizabeth Longford, *The Pebbled Shore*
18 Lord Callaghan, *Time and Change* (1987)

11   The criminologist

1 Frank Longford, *Five Lives* (1964)
2 Then a fellow at Christ Church teaching politics, later Lord Blake and Pro-Vice Chancellor of Oxford (1971–87)
3 Author interview with Lord Longford
4 Mark Amory (ed), *Letters of Evelyn Waugh*
5 Author interview with Lord Longford
6 Ibid.
7 Author interview with Thomas Pakenham
8 Author interview with Rachel Billington
9 Author interview with Judith Kazantzis
10 Elizabeth Longford, *The Pebbled Shore*
11 Author interview with Rachel Billington
12 Ibid.
13 Ibid.
14 Author interview with Lady Antonia Fraser
15 Author interview with Rachel Billington
16 Elizabeth Longford, *The Pebbled Shore*
17 Author interview with Judith Kazantzis

18 Ibid.
19 Author interview with Thomas Pakenham
20 Ibid.
21 Ibid.
22 Author interview with Judith Kazantzis
23 Ibid.
24 Author interview with Rachel Billington
25 Author interview with Auberon Waugh
26 Author interview with Rachel Billington
27 Elizabeth Longford, *The Pebbled Shore*
28 Quintin Hailsham, *A Sparrow's Flight*
29 *The Times*, 30 May 1953
30 Michael Davie (ed), *Evelyn Waugh's Diaries*
31 Author interview with Judith Kazantzis
32 Elizabeth Longford, *The Pebbled Shore*
33 Frank Longford, *Five Lives*
34 Ibid.
35 Mark Amory (ed), *Letters of Evelyn Waugh*
36 Frank Longford, *Diary of a Year*
37 Elizabeth Longford, *The Pebbled Shore*
38 Author interview with Roger Opie
39 Ibid.
40 Ibid.
41 Frank Longford, *Five Lives*
42 Ibid.
43 Frank Longford with Roger Opie, *Causes of Crime* (1958)
44 Author interview with Roger Opie
45 Ibid.
46 Frank Longford, *Five Lives*
47 Widow of George Orwell
48 Author interview with Lord Longford
49 Frank Longford, *The Idea of Punishment* (1961)
50 *News of the World*, 12 Aug 1956
51 Author interview with David Astor

12   The City's best-known socialist

1 Michael Foot, *Aneurin Bevan* (1973)
2 Author interview with Lord Longford
3 Frank Longford, *Five Lives*
4 Ibid.
5 Author interview with Thomas Pakenham
6 Frank Longford, *Five Lives*
7 Ibid.

8 Ibid.
9 Interview in 1977 with Mary Craig
10 Frank Longford, *Five Lives*
11 Author interview with Rachel Billington
12 Peter Wildeblood, *Against the Law* (1955)
13 Author interview with Lord Longford
14 New Bridge archives
15 Frank Longford, *Five Lives*
16 Elizabeth Longford, *The Pebbled Shore*
17 New Bridge archives
18 Frank Longford, *Five Lives*
19 Anthony Howard, *RAB: The Life of R. A. Butler* (1987)
20 Frank Longford, *Five Lives*
21 Ibid.

13   The reluctant earl

1 Elizabeth Longford, *The Pebbled Shore*
2 Philip Williams, *Hugh Gaitskell*
3 Though Bevan never specifically attached the label to Gaitskell
4 Antony Crosland, *The Future of Socialism* (1956)
5 Author interview with Judith Kazantzis
6 Douglas Jay, *Change of Fortune* (1980)
7 Frank Longford, *Five Lives*
8 Ibid.
9 Richard Crossman, *Diaries*
10 Frank Longford, *A History of the House of Lords* (1986)
11 Mark Amory (ed), *Letters of Evelyn Waugh*
12 Author interview with Rachel Billington
13 Michael Davie (ed), *Evelyn Waugh's Diaries*
14 *Daily Telegraph*, 6 Feb 1961
15 Author interview with Thomas Pakenham
16 Elizabeth Longford, *The Pebbled Shore*
17 Frank Longford *Five Lives*
18 Ibid.
19 *Evening News*, 25 Jul 1962
20 Frank Longford *Five Lives*
21 Ibid.
22 Author interview with Lord Healey
23 Author inteview with Lord Jay
24 Richard Crossman, *Diaries*
25 Christopher Mayhew, *Time to Explain* (1987)
26 Ben Pimlott, *Harold Wilson* (1993)
27 Frank Longford *Five Lives*

28 Interview in 1977 with Mary Craig
29 Essay on the Longfords by Lord Jenkins given by him to the author
30 Ibid.
31 Author interview with Judith Kazantzis
32 Author interview with Bronwen Astor
33 Ibid.
34 Author interview with Lord Longford
35 Frank Longford, *Five Lives*
36 Ibid.
37 Ibid.
38 Author interview with Lord Longford
39 Author interview with Lady Antonia Fraser
40 Frank Longford, *Five Lives*
41 Author interview with Lord Jay
42 Frank Longford, *The Grain of Wheat*
43 Author interview with Lord Healey
44 Frank Longford, *The Grain of Wheat*
45 Author interview with Lady Antonia Fraser

14   The Leader of the House of Lords

1 Wilson himself was to do as he preached when he resigned at the age
  of sixty in 1976.
2 Author interview with Lord Longford
3 Ibid.
4 Ibid.
5 Janet Morgan, *The House of Lords and the Labour Government
  (1964–1970)* (1975)
6 Author interview with Lord Carrington
7 Ibid.
8 Ibid.
9 Ibid.
10 Ibid.
11 Frank Longford, *The Grain of Wheat*
12 Barbara Castle, *Diaries* (1974)
13 Frank Longford, *The Grain of Wheat*
14 Barbara Castle, *Diaries*
15 Ibid.
16 Richard Crossman, *Diaries*
17 Ibid.
18 Frank Longford, *The Grain of Wheat*
19 Author interview with Lord Longford
20 Frank Longford, *The Grain of Wheat*
21 Author interview with Judith Kazantzis

22 Interview in 1977 with Mary Craig
23 Ibid.
24 Ibid.
25 Harold Wilson, *The Labour Government 1964–1970* (1971)
26 Author interview with Lord Healey
27 Interview in 1977 with Mary Craig
28 Author interview with Lord Healey
29 Frank Longford, *The Grain of Wheat*
30 Elizabeth Longford, *The Pebbled Shore*
31 Harold Wilson, *The Labour Government 1964–1970*
32 Author interview with Lord Jenkins of Hillhead
33 Ibid.
34 *The People*, 7 Dec 1967
35 Author interview with Lord Longford
36 Frank Longford, *Diary of a Year*
37 Author interview with Lord Jay
38 Ibid.
39 Author interview with Lord Jenkins of Hillhead
40 Ibid.
41 Author interview with Lord Jay
42 Barbara Castle, *Diaries*
43 *Daily Mail* 22 Apr 1967
44 Frank Longford, *The Grain of Wheat*
45 Author interview with Lord Healey
46 Tony Benn, *Office Without Power* (1988)
47 Richard Crossman, *Diaries*
48 Robert Pearce (ed), *Patrick Gordon Walker – Political Diaries (1932–1971)*
49 Author interview with Lord Jenkins of Hillhead
50 Frank Longford, *The Grain of Wheat*
51 Quoted in an essay on Wilson in Frank Longford, *Eleven at No 10*
52 Author interview with Lord Jay
53 David Marquand, *The Progressive Dilemma*
54 Frank Longford, *The Grain of Wheat*
55 Richard Crossman, *Diaries*
56 Frank Longford, *The Grain of Wheat*
57 Robert Pearce (ed), *Patrick Gordon-Walker – Political Diaries (1932–1971)*
58 Cecil King: *Diaries* (1972)
59 Author interview with Lord Longford
60 Author interview with Lord Jay
61 Quoted in an essay on Wilson in Frank Longford, *Eleven at No 10*
62 *Sunday Times*, 21 Mar 1971
63 Frank Longford, *The Grain of Wheat*

64 Barbara Castle, *Diaries*
65 Michael Davie (ed), *Evelyn Waugh's Diaries*
66 Frank Longford, *The Grain of Wheat*
67 Elizabeth Longford, *The Pebbled Shore*
68 Ibid.
69 Frank Longford, *The Grain of Wheat*

15   The literary Longfords

1 Elizabeth Longford, *The Pebbled Shore*
2 Author interview with Rachel Billington
3 Frank Longford, *The Grain of Wheat*
4 Ibid.
5 From an essay on the Longfords by Lord Jenkins given by him to the author
6 Frank Longford, *The Grain of Wheat*
7 Ibid.
8 'Arena', BBC TV, 26 Mar 1993
9 Author interview with Judith Kazantzis
10 Interview in 1977 with Mary Craig
11 Author interview with Auberon Waugh
12 Author interview with Judith Kazantzis
13 Author interview with Lady Antonia Fraser
14 Author interview with Thomas Pakenham
15 Author interview with Lord Longford
16 Author interview with Judith Kazantzis
17 Interview in *The Oldie* (June 1993)
18 Author interview with Judith Kazantzis
19 Author interview with Lady Antonia Fraser
20 Ibid.
21 Frank Longford, *The Grain of Wheat*
22 Author interview with Lord Longford
23 Elizabeth Longford, *The Pebbled Shore*
24 *Sunday Times*, 21 Mar 1971
25 Frank Longford, *The Grain of Wheat*
26 Ibid.
27 Ibid.
28 Ibid.
29 Interview in 1977 with Mary Craig

16   The leader of the opposition to the permissive society

1 Frank Longford, *The Grain of Wheat*
2 Author interview with Rachel Billington

3 Author interview with Jon Snow
4 *The Times*, 18 Aug 1966
5 The same A. P. Herbert for whom Longford had acted as election agent in1935
6 Author interview with Lady Antonia Fraser
7 Author interview with Marigold Johnson
8 Elizabeth Longford, *The Pebbled Shore*
9 Author interview with Marigold Johnson
10 Elizabeth Longford, *The Pebbled Shore*
11 Author interview with Lady Antonia Fraser
12 Author interview with Jon Snow
13 Author interview with Marigold Johnson
14 Ibid.
15 Frank Longford, *Diary of a Year*
16 Author interview with Marigold Johnson
17 Frank Longford, *The Grain of Wheat*
18 Interview in 1977 with Mary Craig
19 Frank Longford, *The Grain of Wheat*
20 Ibid.
21 *Guardian*, 25 Aug 1971
22 *Observer*, 17 Sep 1972
23 Frank Longford, *The Grain of Wheat*
24 Author interview with Marigold Johnson
25 *Guardian*, 26 Aug 1971
26 *Guardian*, 28 Sep 1971
27 Author interview with John Cunningham
28 Author interview with Jon Snow
29 Author interview with Lady Antonia Fraser
30 Author interview with David Astor
31 Author interview with Marigold Johnson
32 Interview in 1977 with Mary Craig
33 Author interview with Lord Jenkins of Hillhead
34 Tony Benn, *Office Without Power*
35 Author interview with Marigold Johnson
36 Ibid.
37 *Guardian*, 29 Jun 1993

17   The only friend of Myra Hindley

1 Author interview with Rachel Billington
2 Emlyn Williams, *Beyond Belief* (1967)
3 In foreword to Ann West, *For the Love of Lesley* (1989)
4 Interviewed by Jean Rook, 1 Jan 1978
5 Author interview with Sheila Childs

6 Frank Longford, *Diary of a Year*
7 Author interview with Lord Longford
8 Author interview with Jon Snow
9 Interviewed in 1977 by Mary Craig
10 Author interview with Andrew McCooey
11 In foreword to Ann West, *For the Love of Lesley*
12 *Daily Express*, 22 Jul 1977
13 Ibid.
14 Author interview with Andrew McCooey
15 Author interview with David Astor
16 Author interview with Lord Carrington
17 Author interview with Lord Jenkins of Hillhead
18 Author interview with Rachel Billington
19 Author interview with Eric McGrath
20 Frank Longford, *Diary of a Year*
21 Frank Longford, *The Grain of Wheat*
22 Author interview with Andrew McCooey
23 Author interview with Lord Longford
24 Ibid.
25 Ibid.
26 Author interview with Rosie Johnston
27 Ibid.
28 Ibid.
29 Author interview with Andrew McCooey
30 *The Times*, 15 Oct 1990
31 Author interview with Andrew McCooey
32 Author interview with Lord Jenkins of Hillhead
33 Author interview with Lord Healey
34 New Bridge archives
35 Author interview with Jon Snow
36 Frank Longford, *The Grain of Wheat*
37 Author interview with Jon Snow
38 Frank Longford, *Diary of a Year*
39 Author interview with Jon Snow
40 Ibid.

18   The elder statesman

1 *Sunday Telegraph*, 24 Sep 1978
2 Author interview with Lord Longford
3 Frank Longford, *Diary of a Year*
4 *The Times*, 24 Jan 1981
5 Frank Longford, *Diary of a Year*
6 House of Lords, 14 Jan 1981

7 Author interview with Lord Longford
8 Ibid.
9 *Sunday Telegraph*, 8 Aug 1982
10 Author interview with Marigold Johnson
11 Ibid.
12 Author interview with Rachel Billington
13 Author interview with Marigold Johnson
14 Author interview with Rachel Billington
15 Author interview with Lord Longford
16 Frank Longford, *Diary of a Year*
17 *The Times*, 3 Nov 1981

Bibliography

Childhood and Youth

Acton, Harold, *Memoirs of an Aesthete* (Hamish Hamilton, 1948)
Becket, J. C. , *The Anglo-Irish Tradition* (Faber, 1976)
Betjeman, John, essay in *My Oxford* (Robson Books, 1977)
Blackwood, Caroline, *Great Granny Webster* (Picador, 1977)
Hillier, Bevis, *Young Betjeman* (John Murray, 1988)
Norman, Diana, *Terrible Beauty* (Hodder and Stoughton, 1987)
Palmer, Alan, *The East End* (John Murray, 1989)
Waugh, Evelyn, *Decline and Fall* (Chapman and Hall, 1928)
Waugh, Evelyn, *Vile Bodies* (Chapman and Hall, 1930)
Wheen, Francis, *Tom Driberg* (Chatto and Windus, 1990)

Political Life

Benn, Tony, *Office Without Power* (Hutchinson, 1988)
Birkenhead, Lord, *Frederick Edwin, Earl of Birkenhead* (Butterworth, 1935)
Callaghan, James, *Time and Change* (Collins, 1987)
Castle, Barbara, *The Castle Diaries* (Weidenfeld, 1974)
Cook, Chris and Ramsden, John (eds), *By-Elections in British Politics* (Macmillan, 1973)
Foot, Michael, *Aneurin Bevan*, vols I and II, (Davis Poynter, 1973)
Grigg, Jon, *Nancy Astor* (Sidgwick, 1980)
Hailsham, Lord, *A Sparrow's Flight: The Memoirs of Lord Hailsham* (Collins, 1990)
Harris, Kenneth, *Attlee* (Weidenfeld, 1976)
Healey, Denis, *The Time of My Life* (Michael Joseph, 1989)
Howard, Anthony (ed), *The Crossman Diaries* (Hamish Hamilton, 1975)
Howard, Anthony, *RAB: The Life of R. A. Butler* (Jonathan Cape, 1987)
Jay, Douglas, *Change and Fortune* (Heinemann, 1980)
Kavaler, Lucy, *The Astors* (Harrap, 1966)
King, Cecil, *The Cecil King Diaries 1965–1970* (Jonathan Cape, 1975)
Marqu·and, David, *The Progressive Dilemma* (Heinemann, 1991)

488

Mayhew, Christopher, *A Time to Explain* (Hutchinson, 1987)
Mikado, Ian, *Back-bencher* (Weidenfeld, 1988)
Morgan, Janet, *The House of Lords and the Labour Government 1964–1970* (Oxford, 1975)
Pearce, Robert (ed), *Patrick Gordon Walker: Political Diaries 1932–1971* (The Historian's Press, 1991)
Pimlott, Ben, *Hugh Dalton*, (Jonathan Cape, 1985)
Pimlott, Ben, *Harold Wilson* (HarperCollins, 1993)
Williams, Philip (ed), *The Diary of Hugh Gaitskell* (Jonathan Cape, 1983)
Williams, Philip, *Hugh Gaitskell* (Jonathan Cape, 1979)
Wilson, Harold, *The Labour Government 1964–1970* (Weidenfeld, 1971)

Germany

Balfour, Michael, *West Germany: A Contemporary History*, (Croom Helm, 1982)
Cairncross, Sir Alec, *The Price of War* (Blackwell, 1986)
Collins, Canon John, *Faith under Fire* (Leslie Frewin, 1966)
Dudley Edwards, Ruth, *Victor Gollancz* (Gollancz, 1987)
Roberts, Frank, *Dealing with Dictators* (Weidenfeld, 1991)

Social Concerns

Beveridge, Janet, *Beveridge and His Plan* (Hodder, 1954)
West, Ann, *For the Love of Lesley* (W. H. Allen, 1989)
Williams, Emlyn, *Beyond Belief: The Moors Murders* (Hamish Hamilton, 1967)

By the Longfords

Clive, Lady Mary, *Brought Up and Brought Out* (Cobden-Sanderson, 1938)
Longford, Elizabeth, *The Pebbled Shore* (Weidenfeld, 1986)
Longford, Frank, *A History of the House of Lords* (Collins, 1988)
Longford, Frank, *Abraham Lincoln* (Weidenfeld, 1974)
Longford, Frank, *Diary of a Year* (Weidenfeld, 1982)
Longford, Frank and O'Neill, Tim, *Eamon de Valera* (Hutchinson, 1970)
Longford, Frank, *Eleven at Number 10* (Harrap, 1984)
Longford, Frank, *Five Lives* (Hutchinson, 1964)
Longford, Frank, *Forgiveness of Man by Man* (Buchebroc, 1989)
Longford, Frank, *Francis of Assisi* (Weidenfeld, 1978)
Longford, Frank, *Humility* (Collins, 1969)
Longford, Frank, *Kennedy* (Weidenfeld, 1976)
Longford, Frank, *Nixon: A Study of Extremes of Fortune* (Weidenfeld, 1980)
Longford, Frank, *One Man's Faith* (Hodder, 1984)

Longford, Frank, *Pope John Paul II* (Collins, 1982)
Longford,Frank, *Pornography: The Longford Report* (Coronet, 1972)
Longford, Frank, *Prisoner or Patient* (Chapmans, 1992)
Longford, Frank, *Punishment and the Punished* (Chapmans, 1991)
Longford, Frank, *Saints* (Hutchinson, 1987)
Longford, Frank, *The Bishops* (Sidgwick, 1986)
Longford, Frank, *The Grain of Wheat* (Collins, 1974)
Longford, Frank, *The Life of Jesus Christ* (Weidenfeld, 1974)
Longford, Frank and McHardy, Anne, *Ulster* (Weidenfeld, 1981)
Longford, Frank, *Young Offenders* (Chapmans, 1993)
Pakenham, Elizabeth (ed), *Catholic Approaches* (Weidenfeld, 1953)
Pakenham, Frank with Opie, Roger, *Causes of Crime* (Weidenfeld, 1958)
Pakenham, Frank, *Born to Believe* (Jonathan Cape, 1953)
Pakenham, Frank, *Peace by Ordeal* (Jonathan Cape, 1935)
Pakenham, Frank, *The Idea of Punishment* (Geoffrey Chapman, 1961)
Powell, Lady Violet, *Five Out of Six* (Heinemann, 1960)
Powell, Lady Violet, *Within the Family Circle* (Heinemann, 1976)

Friends and foes

Amory, Mark (ed), *Letters of Evelyn Waugh* (Weidenfeld, 1980)
Craig, Mary, *Longford: A Biographical Portrait* (Hodder, 1978)
Davie, Michael (ed), *Evelyn Waugh's Diaries* (Weidenfeld 1976)
O'Donovan, Patrick, *A Journalist's Odyssey* (Esmonde, 1985)
Wildeblood, Peter, *Against the Law* (Weidenfeld, 1955)

Index